GIFT of the COTTON MAIDEN

TEXTILES OF FLORES AND THE SOLOR ISLANDS

Gift of the Cotton Maiden

TEXTILES OF FLORES AND THE SOLOR ISLANDS

ROY W. HAMILTON, EDITOR

WITH CONTRIBUTIONS BY

RUTH BARNES
MARIBETH ERB
PENELOPE GRAHAM
ROY W. HAMILTON
WILLEMIJN DE JONG
E. D. LEWIS
MICHAEL P. VISCHER

FOWLER MUSEUM OF CULTURAL HISTORY
UNIVERSITY OF CALIFORNIA, LOS ANGELES

Funding for this catalogue and its associated exhibition provided by

The National Endowment for the Arts,
The National Endowment for the Humanities,
The Ahmanson Foundation,
The Times-Mirror Foundation,
The Ethnic Arts Council of Los Angeles,
The Gerard Hendrik Kluck Memorial Fund,
and Manus, the Support Group of the Fowler Museum.
Catalogue published with the assistance of the Getty Grant Program.

FOWLER MUSEUM OF CULTURAL HISTORY
UNIVERSITY OF CALIFORNIA, LOS ANGELES
405 HILGARD AVENUE
LOS ANGELES, CALIFORNIA, USA 90024-1549

PRINTED ON ACID-FREE PAPER AND BOUND IN HONG KONG
BY PEARL RIVER PRINTING COMPANY, LTD.

LIBRARY OF CONGRESS CATALOG CARD NUMBER: 94-71658

ISBN 0-930741-37-4 (HARDBOUND)
ISBN 0-930741-38-2 (SOFTBOUND)

Contents

Foreword

THE FOWLER MUSEUM OF CULTURAL HISTORY'S INTEREST IN INDONESIAN TEXTILES dates from its founding in 1963 when the Kathryn Mershon collection became part of the core holdings of the fledgling museum then called the Museum and Laboratories of Ethnic Arts and Technology. These textiles were the subject of a few modest exhibitions in the museum's early years. During the 1970s George R. Ellis, then Associate Director of the museum, dramatically increased the quality and scale of the UCLA Indonesian textile collections. This was accomplished with the enthusiastic support and financial assistance of Elizabeth and Richard Rogers, William Lloyd Davis, and Mrs. W. Thomas Davis.

A key point in the history of Indonesian textile studies at UCLA occurred with the arrival at the museum of Roy Hamilton, who systematically catalogued the collections during the 1986/87 academic year. Shortly after this the museum published what was seen as the first in a series of volumes on Indonesian textiles and dress, *To Speak with Cloth: Studies in Indonesian Textiles* edited by Dr. Mattiebelle Gittinger in 1989. Roy Hamilton returned to the Fowler Museum of Cultural History in 1992 as curator of Southeast Asian and Oceanic collections, after completing a Museum Studies degree in the Anthropology Department at the University of Washington and a two year stint as a researcher in the Asian Cultural History Program at the National Museum of Natural History. We are extremely grateful to Roy for his considerable efforts in bringing this present volume and its associated exhibition to fruition. With characteristic hard work, meticulous scholarship and enlightened attention to detail, he has assembled an impressive body of research on a relatively ignored area of Indonesian studies. We are also very appreciative of the insights provided by our outside contributors to this publication. Their varied and thoughtful perspectives demonstrate the complexity of function, history, and meaning in the textile traditions from Flores and the Solor Islands. We join Roy in thanking the staff at the Fowler Museum of Cultural History for another superlative effort. Funding for the project came from a variety of sources. We would like to thank the National Endowment for the Arts for a presentation of collections grant and the National Endowment of the Humanities for a challenge grant that helped subsidize our publication and exhibition programs. The J. Paul Getty Trust also provided substantial support; we are especially grateful to Jack Meyer and Charlene Miller for their assistance with the Getty Grant Program. Contributions from the Ahmanson Foundation and the Times-Mirror Foundation have ensured the continuing success of our school tour program. As with many of our museum's major projects, the Ethnic Arts Council of Los Angeles also provided important assistance. Finally we would like to thank the collective membership of Manus, the support group of the UCLA Fowler Museum of Cultural History, for their ongoing and crucial support of our programs.

CHRISTOPHER B. DONNAN, *Director*
DORAN H. ROSS, *Deputy Director*
DONALD McCLELLAND, *Assistant Director*

Preface

NTEREST IN INDONESIAN TEXTILES GAINED MOMENTUM IN THE UNITED STATES in the late 1970s through a number of exhibitions and accompanying publications (Kahlenberg 1977, Gittinger 1979, Fischer 1979). In the years since then, this field of scholarship has become very active, with many exhibitions and publications, including several volumes of research papers (Gittinger 1980 and 1989; Völger & Welck 1991; Nabholz-Kartaschoff, Barnes & Stuart-Fox 1993). Most of the publications have fallen into two categories: on one hand are the general works that attempt to cover all of Indonesia and on the other the research papers and a smaller number of monographs that focus on single traditions in greater depth. Although a tremendous amount of new scholarship has been made available to the public, a persistent shortcoming is that the general works can devote only a few pages to any single tradition, while the coverage of the more specific studies is still very spotty.

The textiles of the island of Flores and the smaller, neighboring Solor Islands, which are closely akin to Flores culturally and politically, offer a case in point. The anthropologist Raymond Kennedy dismissed the textiles he found in this region, saying "...the colors are always dull [and the] designs are small and indecisive" (1955:26). Although this prejudice has often been repeated, spectacular cloths from Flores appeared in small numbers in the various exhibitions and publications. Their patterns and colors varied dramatically from one ethnic group to another and, as everywhere in Indonesia, they occupied central roles in the cultures of the people who produced them. Yet no general work presented more than a tantalizing sample and there were no detailed accounts of specific textile traditions in the region, with the exception of a single monograph (Ruth Barnes 1989a) and a few obscure articles in European journals.

The goals that motivated the development of this book, then, were to offer a far broader and more systematic sampling of the textile art of Flores and to present it in as full a cultural context as possible. I hope that someday this effort will take its place beside other publications, including the recent *Textiles in Bali* (Hauser-Schäublin, Nabholz-Kartaschoff & Ramseyer 1991), to form a new generation of regional studies of Indonesian textiles. The regional approach will allow for more detailed investigation, while at the same time, especially in ethnically diverse areas such as Flores, promoting productive comparisons among the textiles of neighboring ethnic groups.

The increased attention brought to Indonesian textiles by the rapidly growing body of scholarship is in some ways a mixed blessing. Indonesian weavers, even in remote regions like Flores, have long made textiles for barter or sale as well as for their own use, but the phenomenal growth of the international art trade, in which publications such as this are inextricably involved, raises ethical issues on a new scale. Surely, on the whole, the promulgation of knowledge is a good thing. The textile traditions of places like Flores can be lifted from obscurity and made part of a broader human heritage of cultural and artistic achievement. Weavers can gain new options about how to pursue their art and their livelihood. Large numbers of textiles can enter museum collections, where they will be studied, preserved, and used as vehicles of public education. But there is undeniably a darker side to this process as well. Weavers may remain anonymous and often desperately poor, while large profits are made bringing their work to the outside world. The pressure to produce quickly for cash income may force compromises in quality. In extreme cases communities can be stripped of their own artistic heritage, interfering with their ability to carry on cherished cultural institutions (Ruth Barnes 1991b, Taylor 1994).

With these moral dilemmas in mind, it is hoped that this publication will do more to illuminate, preserve, and inspire than to remove and destroy. Many elders on Flores have approached me to say how much they appreciate an outsider expressing an interest in their culture, and sometimes even that my interest has sparked a new awareness on their part about the significance and value of their traditions. When weavers on Flores are asked whether they would like their art to be better known in the outside world, their response is universally enthusiastic. Wherever possible the personal names of outstanding textile artists have been included in this publication. This is intended to bring well-deserved recognition and also to counter the outmoded notion that "crafts" of the developing world are anonymous while "art" from the West is not. As a matter of policy, names have been published only with the expressed permission of the artist. Most women were proud to have their names go on record in this way, but a few declined out of modesty and one agreed only on the condition that her name appear together with that of her husband.

Because it is impossible for a single author to know all parts of Flores in detail, this book was from the beginning conceived as an anthology. Other scholars who have conducted research in various parts of Flores were invited to contribute essays. The results have been arranged in three parts, with each part successively narrowing the focus of investigation. **Part One, Introduction**, deals with general themes of culture and textiles throughout Flores and the Solor Islands. In **Part Two, Regional Surveys**, separate chapters are devoted to each of the islands' five political divisions (regencies or *kabupaten*). Taken together, these five chapters present a systematic survey of the peoples of Flores and their textiles. **Part Three, Case Studies**, consists of four detailed reports, each the result of the author's prolonged research in a single community.

ROY W. HAMILTON

Acknowledgments

M Y PRIMARY DEBT OF GRATITUDE IS TO MY SIX COLLEAGUES, who graciously agreed to participate as contributing authors and gave freely of their time and knowledge. I thank them in particular for their close cooperation throughout the editing process, which was essential for bringing the book to completion. Each of them also generously shared photographs from their field research and textiles from their personal collections.

By the close of the exhibition that this publication accompanies, every staff member at the Fowler Museum will have been involved in one way or another. Among the many, I wish especially to thank Doran H. Ross, without whose consistent support and encouragement neither the book nor the exhibition could have come into being; Henrietta Cosentino, whose editing improved the manuscript immeasurably; and Anthony Kluck, who conceived the design that gave form to what was once only two bursting loose-leaf binders. Denis Nervig took the studio photographs and Jill Ball made the drawings. David Mayo and Jo A. Hill were instrumental in designing and mounting the exhibition.

This book also owes a great deal to three individuals who provided much of the underlying inspiration. Dr. Mattiebelle Gittinger, of The Textile Museum in Washington, has given encouragement and established a standard of excellence for all who work in the field of Indonesian textile studies. Prof. James Fox, Chairman of Anthropology at the Research School for Pacific and Asian Studies of the Australian National University, has provided leadership for a new generation of anthropological research in eastern Indonesia. Robyn Maxwell, Associate Curator of Asian Art at the National Gallery of Australia, compiled a preliminary but systematic survey of the textiles of Flores (Maxwell 1980) that served as a guide throughout my work.

Staff members at a number of international institutions have been helpful in assisting with research. Among them I would like in particular to thank Achim Sibeth at the Museum für Völkerkunde in Frankfurt am Main, Peter ter Keurs at the Rijksmuseum voor Volkenkunde in Leiden, J. H. van Brakel and H. W. van Rinsum at the Tropenmuseum in Amsterdam, Father Henk de Beer of the Society of the Divine Word in Teteringen (Netherlands), Dr. Marie-Louise Nabholz-Kartaschoff at the Museum für Völkerkunde in Basel, and Dr. Heide Leigh-Theisen at the Museum für Völkerkunde in Vienna. Similar roles were fulfilled at the National Gallery of Australia by Robyn Maxwell and in North America by Lynne Milgram at the Museum for Textiles in Toronto, Carol Robbins at the Dallas Museum of Art, and Pamela McClusky at Seattle Art Musuem.

Private collectors who kindly made material available for research or for the exhibition include August Flick, Frank R. Wiggers, Mary Jane Leland, Drs. John and Anne Summerfield, and Kent Watters.

In Indonesia, the research of each of the contributing authors was sponsored by Nusa Cendana University in Kupang, where Dr. Munanjar Widiyatmika has consistently been helpful in making arrangements. All research was conducted under the auspices of the Indonesia Institute of Sciences. Indonesian government officials too numerous to name, from Jakarta to the smallest villages, very often gave assistance beyond the call of duty.

On Flores, my warmest thanks go to Bapak Josef Ghani Api and Mama Martina Minu of Onelako, who cared and watched over me; to Drs. Muhamad Fatta of Ende and Bapak Emiel Waso Ea of Boawae, who housed and encouraged me; and to Marthin Kally of Ende and Kletus Dhena of Boawae, who provided friendship and assisted me in countless ways. As for the weavers and dyers of Flores, who welcomed a stranger's questions and shared their life's work, I am deeply honored to have met them.

ROY W. HAMILTON, *Curator*

INTRODUCTION

Myanmar
China
Taiwan
Laos
Thailand
Vietnam
Cambodia
Philippine Islands
PACIFIC OCEAN
MINDANAO
MALAY PENINSULA
Brunei Darussalam
MALAYSIA
SABAH
Malacca
SARAWAK
Singapore
Borneo
KALIMANTAN
Sulawesi
MOLUCCA ISLANDS
IRIAN JAYA
PAPUA NEW GUINEA
New Guinea
INDONESIA
Jakarta
Java
LESSER SUNDA ISLANDS
INDIAN OCEAN
Flores
Australia
Sumatra

F L O R E S
PALU'É
Reo
Manggarai Regency
Labuhanbajo
MANGGARAI
Ngada Regency
Ende Reg
MANDUWOSO
RANAKAH
KELIMUTU
KELIMARA
ENDENESE
Ruteng
NAGÉ
ENDE BAY
LIO
MULES ISLAND
NGADHA
EBULOBO
Bajawa
KÉO
INERIE
ENDE ISLAND
TYA
Ende
S A V U

Borneo
KALIMANTAN
Sulawesi
Buru
MAKASSARESE
BUGIS
Ujung Pandang
(Makassar)
Goa
Buton
Selayar
Wetar
Majapahit
FLORES SEA
Alor
Java
LESSER SUNDA ISLANDS
Bali
Lombok
Sumbawa
Bima
FLORES
Solor
Adonara
Lembata
Timor
Sumba
SAVU SEA
Savu
Kupang
Roti

SEA
Larantuka
KÉDANG
Sikka Regency
ILI MANDIRI
Adonara
ILI API
ILI BOLENG
LAMAHOLOT
Solor Strait
Lembata
PULAU
BESAR
Solor
KIMANG
Maumere
LOBE TOBI
LABALEKANG
SIKKANESE
EGON
East Flores Regency
SEA

KEY
Ruin
VOLCANO
ETHNIC GROUP

Behind the Cloth

The History and Culture of Flores

ROY W. HAMILTON

FLORES IS THE SECOND LARGEST OF THE LESSER SUNDA ISLANDS, an 800-mile long volcanic chain that stretches eastward from Java toward New Guinea (see MAP, pp. 18-19). The best known of these islands is Bali, but the larger islands farther east are more isolated and their people have little in common culturally with the Balinese. The 1.4 million people of Flores belong to several distinct ethnic groups, each with its own language and customs. In all of these societies, handwoven textiles play a central role, serving not only as clothing, but also as key ingredients in a web of social and economic transactions and as a leading focus of artistic expression. The remarkable wealth of ethnic variety is clearly expressed in the island's cloth, both in its colorful patterning, and in the myriad details of its manufacture and use (FIGURES 1-2, 1-3, 1-4).

The diversity of Flores' people is the product of a number of geographical, cultural, and historical factors. Foremost among them is the island's rugged topography, which presents formidable barriers to communication and transportation. Hostility among neighboring villages, which prevailed until Dutch colonial authority brought an end to inter-village warfare in the early decades of the twentieth century, further encouraged cultural fragmentation. From the fourteenth century onward, a quickening influx of outsiders brought additional sources of cultural differentiation. Although some aspects of today's textile traditions, including certain patterns and techniques, can be traced to specific historical sources, many basic questions remain unanswered due to the difficulties of documenting change in past centuries.

Anthropologists classify Flores' ethnic groups primarily on the basis of language. The five major groups recognized by linguists are Manggarai, Ngadha, Ende-Lio, Sikka, and Lamaholot (Wurm & Hattori 1981).[1] While these divisions provide a key to understanding the island's ethnic diversity, they do not necessarily signify entities that have been either culturally homogeneous or politically united. Customs, including the names and motifs of textiles, frequently vary from one village to another, even within the same linguistic area. Political organization beyond the village level generally occurred only after it was imposed by outsiders in recent centuries. Even now, an individual's identity is likely to be more closely tied to family and village than to linguistic groups or modern political structures.

FIGURE 1-1 (OPPOSITE). Characteristic textiles distinguish the ceremonial dress of each ethnic group. This man wears the Lio ikat shoulder cloth (*sémba*). His gold breast plate (*gebé*) is a clan heirloom. The smaller gold ornaments (*omé mbulu*) strung around his neck are a component of bridewealth in the Lio region. Technically they are ear ornaments, intended to be worn through pierced ears, but quantities of them may be accumulated for use in bridewealth exchanges. Photographed prior to 1953. Koninklijk Instituut voor de Tropen, Amsterdam.

FIGURES 1-2, 1-3, 1-4.
The range of dress among the diverse ethnic groups of Flores can be seen in the costumes of these three women. LEFT: Siti Hawa Saira, from Mbay, wears a sarong and shoulder cloth decorated with the colorful supplementary-weft technique. CENTER: Siti Habibah Haji Abu Bekar, a Lio woman from Wolojita, wears an ikat sarong dyed with indigo and morinda. RIGHT: Clan headwoman Du'a Harut Iri dances at a ceremony in Tana 'Ai, Sikka Regency, wearing a striped sarong, with a trade textile fragment from India draped around her shoulders. In all cases the sarongs were woven locally but the blouses were made from imported fabrics.

Today Flores forms part of the Indonesian province of Nusa Tenggara Timur (East Lesser Sundas). The provincial capital is at Kupang, on the island of Timor. Five of the province's twelve administrative divisions, called regencies (*kabupaten*), are located on Flores. Although the regency boundaries are an artifice of colonial administration, they roughly correspond with the island's major ethnic divisions. The capitals of the five regencies are the main towns. They are connected by public bus service, but the going is often difficult on the twisting, partly unpaved highway. The trip along the 225-mile length of the island requires three days or more. Most of the population lives in rural areas. Some villages are connected to the highway by unpaved spur roads, but others are accessible only on foot or by boat. It is village women who are the producers of the island's textiles. Although some cloth eventually enters international markets, production takes place within the context of the village economy in this relatively poor and isolated region of a developing nation.

WEAVING ON FLORES: UNCERTAIN ORIGINS

Little archaeological work has been conducted on Flores and only the very general outlines of its prehistory are known. The island's people are at least in part descended from populations of seafaring agriculturalists who advanced gradually southward from Taiwan, reaching the Lesser Sundas by about 2500 B.C. (Bellwood 1985:233).[2] These groups of people spoke languages belonging to the Austronesian language phylum and are thought to have been familiar with weaving technology, which they presumably would have brought with them as they expanded southward.[3] That woven textiles are so deeply imbedded in the social and religious life of most Indonesian ethnic groups is another basic argument for their antiquity (Gittinger 1979:17). The occurrence of body-tension looms in many places settled by Austronesian-speaking peoples – from Taiwan, through the Philippines, across almost all of Indonesia, and in Madagascar – further suggests that weaving was an element of a common cultural heritage carried from place to place by Austronesian expansion. Nevertheless, weaving cannot be assumed to have followed Austronesian expansion everywhere. Particularly down the Philippine-Sulawesi-Lesser Sunda axis, it appears to have declined in importance (Bellwood 1985:232). For the Lesser Sundas, there is no archaeological evidence to prove that weaving was present in the prehistoric period.[4] Therefore, it is impossible to say whether weaving was brought to Flores by the earliest Austronesian settlers or was introduced only more recently.

If woven cloth was present from the earliest Austronesian times, it may have had little in common with today's textiles. Cotton cultivation originated in India and did not spread to Southeast Asia until the mid first millennium A.D. (Watson 1977:357), so only bast fibers would have been available initially. There may have been a long period during which only plain or simple warp-striped fabrics were made. The origin of ikat, the most important decorative technique, is far from certain.[5] The complex mordant dye procedures used to create red-brown tones on cotton were perfected in India and, unless they were independently discovered in the archipelago, would not have been available in the Lesser Sundas until recent centuries.[6] The introduction of the supplementary-weft technique is unquestionably tied to relatively recent historical events (see CHAPTER 5). Photographs from the early decades of the twentieth century reveal that much of the cloth woven at that time was plain, either the natural color of cotton or colored with various plant or mud dyes (FIGURES 1-5, 1-6).

FIGURE 1-5 (BELOW, LEFT). Clad in a plain sarong of heavy, handspun cotton, a man makes his rounds to tap flower stalks of the lontar palm (*Borassus flabellifer*). The sap he obtains can be fermented into a beer-like brew or distilled to produce more potent spirits. Rian Kamie, East Flores, 1920s. Koninklijk Instituut voor de Tropen, Amsterdam.

FIGURE 1-6 (BELOW, RIGHT). Two Manggarai women carry water, one in a plain sarong and the other in an indigo-dyed sarong decorated with simple supplementary-weft motifs. The difference in their dress may simply reflect individual preference or circumstances, but older women often prefer dark colors and may have better access to indigo. 1920s. Koninklijk Instituut voor de Tropen, Amsterdam.

The history of woven cloth in the archipelago is entwined with that of its counterpart, beaten bark-cloth. Stone beaters found in archaeological sites on Taiwan indicate that the making of bark-cloth was present from the earliest days of Austronesian expansion. Made with resources readily gathered in the forest, it required less labor to produce than woven cloth. Until recent times, people who did not weave had access to woven cloth only through costly trade. Particularly in the interior of many of Indonesia's larger islands, they were heavily dependent on bark-cloth. A nineteenth-century European observer remarked that both men and women in mountain areas of Flores wore only "a cincture of beaten tree-bark" (Riedel 1886:68). Bark-cloth is no longer made on the island, but elderly people still recall its use with derision.

On the nearby islands of Alor and Sumba, the making of bark-cloth continues on a small scale today. Descriptions of village life on Alor in the 1930s serve to illustrate the relationship between bark-cloth use and textile trade. When children in interior villages matured, their parents gave them loincloths as symbols of their increasing status. Boys, accorded more privileged status than girls, were given expensive woven cloth traded from the coast. Girls received only locally made bark-cloth (DuBois 1944:64). A similar balancing between the desire for woven cloth and the economy of bark-cloth must also have prevailed in many parts of Flores.

EARLY ETHNOGRAPHIC REPORTS OF SOCIETIES ON FLORES

The first comprehensive picture of the various societies of Flores comes from ethnographic reports written in the first half of the twentieth century, many of them by missionaries and colonial administrators.[7] Although Europeans had been in contact with the island since the sixteenth century, it was not until 1907 that the Dutch colonial government acted to establish a direct presence throughout Flores. The early ethnographers were able to gather information in many places from a generation of elders who had come to maturity in the period before intensive European intervention began to bring about rapid social change. Some made no more than passing note of the island's textiles, but others (especially Arndt, Suchtelen, Tietze, and Vatter) recorded details that can no longer be observed today. More generally, the accounts of the early ethnographers describe the social context within which textiles were made and used.

Although the amount of ethnic diversity on Flores makes it difficult to generalize, colonial era ethnographers recorded a number of traits that were common to many communities on the island. In the discussion that follows, the use of the past tense is intended to reflect conditions at the dawn of direct colonial administration in the first decade of the twentieth century. Many of the features described remain influential today, but others have disappeared, most notably the hierarchical social structure that included a slave class.

The people lived in settled villages (or sometimes in clusters of smaller hamlets) that formed independent units. Sometimes villages were grouped together into ceremonial "domains," but centralized political authority under a local ruler or *raja* appears to have been a non-indigenous institution imposed from outside only in recent centuries. Villages were composed of a number of clans or lineages, but the most important social units were named "houses" that made up the clans.[8] Some of the more highly structured communities had several different titled offices distributed among the leading clans. Often there was

FIGURE 1-7.
These two men are members of the clan Sa'o Ria (Great House), historically the leading clan in the Lio village of Wolotopo. As hereditary head of the clan (*mosa laki*), Pius Pangge (LEFT) wears the aristocratic shoulder cloth *sémba*. Gregorius Ele (RIGHT), the clan's appointee to the traditional village council (*ata laki*), wears a woman's red blouse as part of his dress of office. The wearing of the blouse is said to symbolize bravery and is a prerogative traced to Da Seko, the heroic founding ancestor of Sa'o Ria clan (see also FIGURES 1-9, 1-11). Such cross-gender dressing in Indonesia often marks extraordinary individuals or events. Both men wear the Lio men's sarong (*luka*), plus gold ornaments from the clan treasury. 1988.

a dualistic separation of power, with authority over internal affairs (and especially land use rights) vested in the leader of one clan or lineage, while external affairs (i.e., speaking for the community) were handled by the leader of another.[9] The distinctions drawn among officials were at times reflected in styles of dress, as can still be seen today in the ceremonial dress of clan officers in certain Lio villages (FIGURE 1-7). The leading clans cooperated in the management of the village, in some cases through a formalized village council consisting of all the titled leaders. Subsidiary clans could be integrated into the

village by being recognized as clients of the leading clans, but often newcomers were merely regarded as outsiders with few rights.

The most important lineages maintained special dwellings that served as ceremonial headquarters, and among some ethnic groups as the principle residence of all lineage members. In the most massive houses, as many as two hundred individuals lived together under the leadership of the head of the lineage (FIGURE 1-8). Inside, the house was divided into a number of hearths maintained by separate branches of the lineage. Lineage houses were arranged around a plaza containing the tombs of prominent ancestors and other special ceremonial structures, which varied in form from one ethnic group to another (FIGURES 1-9, 1-10, 1-11). The plaza was used for rituals and dances that were part of the annual cycle of religious ceremonies. The ceremonial cycle was timed in accordance with the agricultural seasons and the various seasonal rites were held to promote the regeneration of both crops and human society. At much greater intervals, larger cycles of rites were held for a variety of purposes. These included dedication ceremonies for reconstructed lineage houses or ceremonial structures that had fallen into disrepair; rites of this kind are still major community events today (FIGURE 1-12). Religious rites were conducted by clan leaders skilled in oratory, who wore special items of ceremonial dress.[10]

The degree to which class concepts shaped daily life varied from place to place, with some communities hierarchical and others more egalitarian. In the most highly stratified communities, the titled heads of the village's leading lineages formed an aristocracy. The bulk of the population consisted of commoners, who were relatively free to organize their own economic activities and enjoy the fruits of their labor. A slave class worked entirely under

FIGURE I-9 (LEFT).
Ceremonial structures stand on the raised stone plaza (*kanga*) in the Lio village of Wolotopo. The larger, thatched structure is the *keda*, "temple" or "spirit house." The smaller structure to the right, the *Balé Da,* shelters a coffin containing the remains of Wolotopo's revered ancestor, Da Seko. Pelzer Collection, National Anthropological Archives, Smithsonian Institution, Washington.

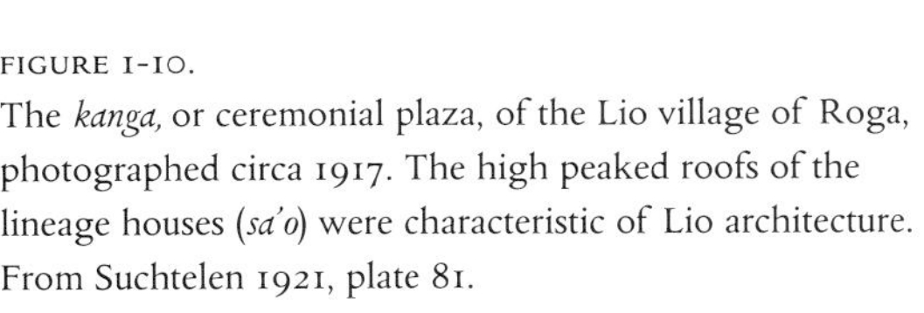

FIGURE I-10.
The *kanga,* or ceremonial plaza, of the Lio village of Roga, photographed circa 1917. The high peaked roofs of the lineage houses (*sa'o*) were characteristic of Lio architecture. From Suchtelen 1921, plate 81.

FIGURE I-11.
In the interior of the Wolotopo *keda,* a wooden figure (*ana déo*) representing the village ancestors is dressed with a woman's red blouse, recalling the ceremonial garb of officers of the village council (FIGURE I-7). 1988.

FIGURE 1-12 (LEFT). Clan leaders in ceremonial dress prepare to sacrifice four water buffalo at a 1991 dedication of reconstructed ceremonial structures in a village in the Kéo region. The thatched structure under which the buffalo are tied is the *basa damba*, which holds the village's war drum (*damba*). This and two other ceremonial structures were painstakingly reconstructed over the preceding two years.

FIGURE 1-13 (RIGHT). A group of kinswomen in the Lio village of Onelako deliver rice and other gifts to their in-laws, making good on an obligation stemming from a marriage that had taken place a year earlier. 1988.

the control of the aristocracy.[11] In such communities, it was aristocratic women who were in the best position to develop the time-consuming skills needed to produce the finest textiles. This hierarchical class structure, however, may have developed only in recent centuries as a result of exposure to imported forms of political organization. More typically, there were only modest distinctions drawn between the heads of lineages who had authority over land use rights and the bulk of the population. Lineage heads, commoners, and slaves all coexisted within the clan framework, bound together by mutual obligation. In the least stratified communities, the economic realities of a life of subsistence agriculture, shared by all alike, meant that such distinctions were of little significance.

In addition to class hierarchy, marriage alliance was an important structural principle. Marriages were arranged asymmetrically, meaning that brothers married women from one set of lineages, while their sisters could marry men only from a different set of lineages. This marriage pattern created relationships among groups that anthropologists have called "wife-givers" and "wife-takers."[12] Groups allied in this manner were committed to meet reciprocal obligations. At marriage rites and funerals, they exchanged food, textiles, and other valuable goods, a practice that is still of great importance today (FIGURE 1-13). The social ideal was to perpetuate these relationships generation after generation through first-cousin marriage.

Despite the long coastline, only a minority of communities on Flores were oriented toward fishing and the sea. More typically, life was strongly centered in agriculture and the land (FIGURE 1-14). An indication of this landward orientation can be found in the mythology of many groups, in which the origin of human society is attributed to an ancestor couple who resided on a prominent mountain top located in the interior of the group's territory.[13] The

FIGURE 1-14.
Houses and granaries cluster together in a Lio mountain hamlet in Detusoko District, photographed in 1965. The surrounding hillside gardens are nourished by the moist mountain climate. Pelzer Collection, National Anthropological Archives, Smithsonian Institution, Washington.

major crops included cotton and indigo in addition to the staple foods, rice and corn (maize), grown by shifting cultivation in dry, hillside fields. Rainfall on Flores is irregular and unevenly distributed, making agriculture unpredictable despite its centrality. Under such conditions agriculture was a primary focus of political and ritual efforts, some of which continue today (FIGURES 1-15, 1-16).

Very generally, these were some of the common themes documented by the early ethnographers. It is tempting to think of them as expressions of the indigenous culture of the island, established many centuries before European contact and changing only very slowly. Unfortunately, such generalizations mask a great deal of variation among the diverse ethnic groups. In reality, little is known about how the different groups evolved and came to be distributed as the early ethnographers found them.[14] Some coastal communities surely developed in recent centuries through the mixing of seafaring groups from other parts of Indonesia with the pre-existing population, but the origins of the major indigenous ethnic groups are as shrouded as the misty peaks from whose summits their ancestors are said to have descended.

THE HISTORICAL PERIOD

The Indic influences that produced Hindu and Buddhist kingdoms in Java during the first millennium A.D. appear not to have extended in any major way to Flores. Only in the fourteenth century did the islands in the eastern Lesser Sundas begin to enter the historical record directly. Their belated appearance suggests that the region had remained relatively isolated until that time.[15] A Chinese "Description of the Barbarians of the Isles," dated 1349, mentions ports on the coast of Timor where silver, iron, porcelain, and cloth were traded for sandalwood (Rockhill 1915:257-258).[16] An expeditionary force from the Hindu-Javanese kingdom of Majapahit reached Flores in 1357 and the *Nagarakertagama*, a Majapahit chronicle, includes a list of dependencies thought to have been founded at that time in the vicinity of the Solor Islands.[17] Unfortunately, the extent and impact of the Majapahit presence on Flores remain unknown (Dietrich 1984:320).

The waning of Majapahit's strength in the fifteenth century was in part the result of expanding Islamic trade in the Java Sea and throughout the archipelago. From approximately 1400 until 1511, the predominant entrepôt in Southeast Asia was the Islamic sultanate of Malacca on the Malay Peninsula. The vast, rich trading system based at Malacca encompassed Sumba and Timor, where sandalwood was exchanged primarily for textiles of Indian and Javanese manufacture. Flores was never a major source of sandalwood and appears to have remained peripheral to the Malacca trade, being known best as a source of sulfur.[18]

What can be concluded about the impact of these early contacts with regard to local textile production? As we have seen, it is not certain that the early Austronesian-derived populations of Flores were familiar with weaving. Prior to the first consistent contacts with the technologically more advanced societies of Java and the Asian mainland, it is possible that bark-cloth was the only available option for clothing. If the body-tension loom was present, it was probably used to make plain or warp-striped cloth from bast fibers. Cotton cultivation, the ikat technique, and mordant-dyeing procedures may not have been available until the fourteenth century or possibly even later. In Bellwood's words (1985:141), "virtually the whole archipelago became connected to the greater Asian world between the tenth and fifteenth centuries to an extent far greater than in the earlier Indianizing period." Perhaps this is the most likely time frame for the introduction of materials and technologies that were not part of the original Austronesian repertoire. Unfortunately, without a better archaeological record, these ideas remain speculative.

FIGURE I-15.
During the ceremonial opening of the planting season, women of Léwotala, East Flores, distributing seed rice into holes made by men using dibble sticks in conscious imitation of ancestral farming methods. The field has been cleared by cutting and burning the secondary forest. 1986.

More definite conclusions can be drawn only with regard to some of the motifs and design formats that eventually came to predominate on Flores, for many of them are indisputably derived from the patterning of Indian trade textiles and could not have been present in the Lesser Sundas before the era of increasing trade. Foremost among the trade cloths were the prestigious double-ikat silks from Gujerat known as *patola*. The patola trade is believed to have predated the arrival of Europeans in the archipelago (Bühler & Fischer 1979:278) and the pervasive influence these cloths came to exert over Indonesian textile design has long been recognized (FIGURES 1-17, 1-18). Although Indian textiles were involved in the Timor sandalwood trade, it is uncertain when the first patola arrived on Flores or, more importantly, when local weavers first began to produce patola-inspired patterns.[19]

In 1511 Malacca fell to the Portuguese, who thereafter made annual trading voyages to the Moluccas and Lesser Sundas (FIGURE 1-19). In 1566 they constructed a fort and mission on Solor, where the protected waters of Solor Strait provided a haven (FIGURE 1-20). A second fort was built circa 1570 on Ende Island, off the south coast of Flores in Ende Bay.[20] Dominican priests baptized large numbers of the native people and by 1600 the Portuguese controlled a total of twenty-seven communities located on Solor Strait, in the Sikka region, and around the shores of Ende Bay (Visser 1925, Boxer 1968:175). Portuguese soldiers, sailors, and traders intermarried with local women, producing a community of mixed-blood Catholics who came to be known as the Black Portuguese. In 1613 the Solor fort was seized by the Dutch United East India Company (*Vereenigde Oost-Indische Compagnie*) and the Black Portuguese established their headquarters at Larantuka. There they developed a fractious state under local rulers selected from their own

FIGURE 1-16.
At a harvest festival in Léwotala, a woman's tubular cloth and a blouse laid over the stone seat at the ritual center of the field represent the place of the "rice maiden," who is credited with the original introduction of rice. Conducting the proper rituals is considered a prerequisite for the continuing regeneration of the rice. 1988.

FIGURE I-17.
Of the many Indian-made patola designs found on Flores, this eight-pointed floral motif is the most common. Here it adorns a cloth belonging to a family in Ende. It has been widely imitated in locally produced textiles and the interplay between the floral roundels and the interspersed diamond forms has been a fertile source of design inspiration.

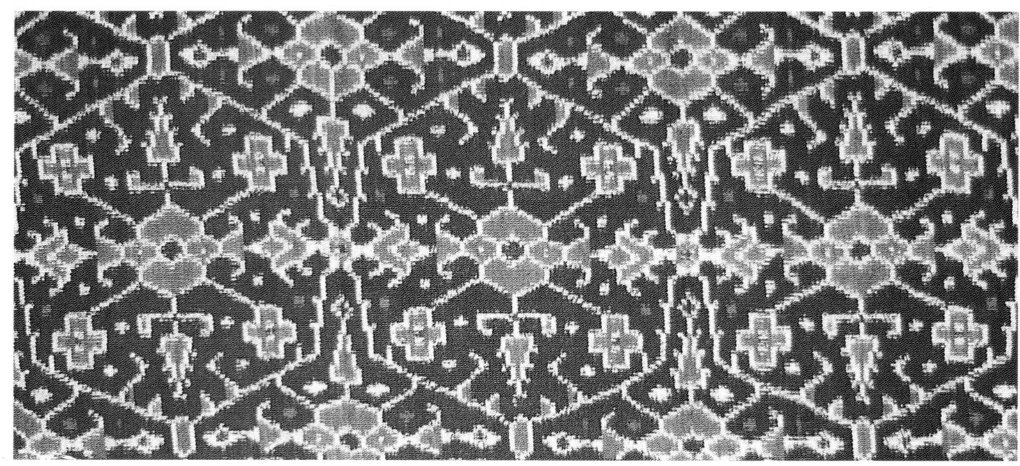

FIGURE I-18.
The same design can be seen in this detail of a chemically dyed woman's sarong made in the 1980s by a Lio weaver living in Ende. Weavers on Flores use only the warp-ikat technique rather than the double-ikat technique of the Gujerati cloths, a more complex process that requires ikat dyeing of both the warp and weft.

FIGURE I-19 (OPPOSITE, TOP).
This early drawing, believed to represent the village of Mausambi on the north coast of Flores, appeared in a nautical manual compiled prior to 1515 by the Portuguese pilot Francisco Rodrigues. From Cortesão 1944, plate X, with permission of the Bibliothèque de l'Assemblée Nationale, Paris.

FIGURE I-20 (OPPOSITE, BOTTOM).
A rendition of the Solor Fort, as it appeared in approximately 1633, from a 1646 manuscript. British Museum, London.

community and only nominally under the authority of the Lisbon government and its official representatives on Timor (Boxer 1968:181). The Black Portuguese over the centuries become fully integrated into the population as a whole, but some elements of Portuguese culture are still identifiable, particularly in the Sikka and Larantuka areas (FIGURE I-21).

In 1641 the Dutch East India Company captured Malacca. The Dutch found the pre-existing trade in Indian textiles so well established and so specialized that they were forced to accommodate to it by purchasing huge quantities of textiles in India and carrying them to the Indies (Gittinger 1982:137). The Company attempted to control the luxury patola trade, which accounts in part for the high status of these cloths and their influence as sources of inspiration for locally produced cloths. The following passage, regarding the islands of Roti and Savu, is probably equally valid for Flores:

> Trade was conducted at an elite level. Each ruler or 'regent' would provide tribute — in slaves, wax, foodstuffs — from his domain in return for muskets, gin, and royal regalia, which consisted mainly of silk *patola* cloth.... The Dutch awarded *patola* cloth only to the highest rulers with whom they traded, and the right to wear this cloth became the exclusive prerogative of the top nobility of each island.
>
> (Fox 1977:948)

Camadinga
SOLOR.

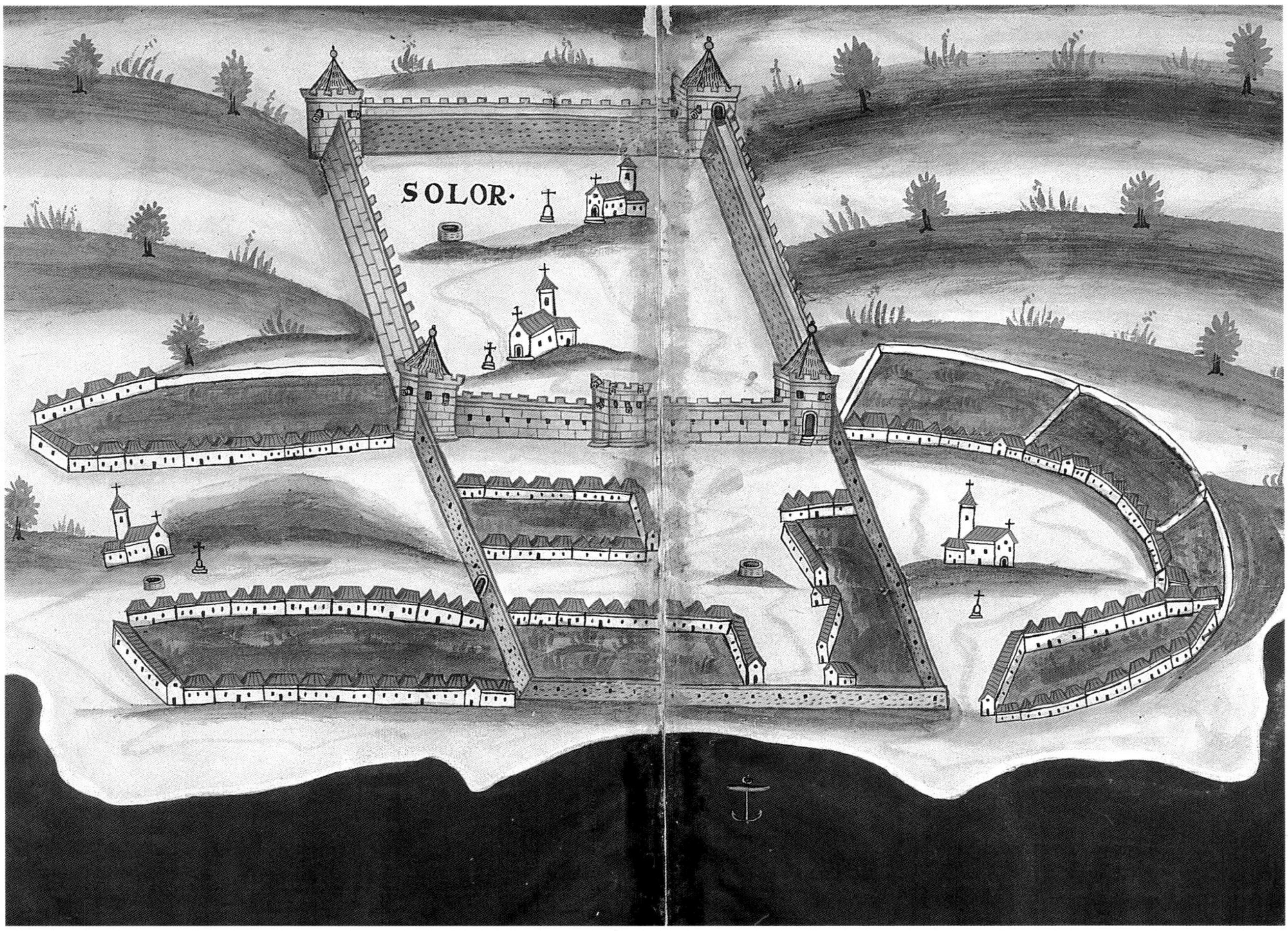

Islamic expansion into the Lesser Sundas in the sixteenth and seventeenth centuries was no less dramatic than that of the Europeans. To understand why, it is necessary to look to the island of Sulawesi and the rivalry there between the Makassarese and Bugis people, both of whom became famous throughout Indonesia as seafarers and traders. In the first decade of the seventeenth century, the Makassarese kingdom of Goa subdued its Bugis enemies and emerged as the major sea power in the region. Goa exacted tribute from the surrounding islands, including the Manggarai region of Flores.[21] To counter Makassarese power, the Dutch allied themselves with the Bugis and in 1669 succeeded in crushing Goa. The result was a diaspora of Makassarese refugees across the archipelago: "The groups migrating overseas were so vast that the fleets were likened to floating cities…. The sudden appearance of these fleets of armed men aroused terror in the local populations, which were incapable of repelling the newcomers" (Andaya 1981:210).

Undoubtedly many coastal Islamic communities on Flores and neighboring islands owe their existence to Makassarese expansion subsequent to these events. The influence of the Makassarese was especially strong along the north coast of Manggarai and Ngada regencies. Prominent weaving communities along this coast, such as Mbay, trace their ancestry to immigrants from Sulawesi. The textiles of this region remain distinctive today, relying primarily on supplementary-weft decoration rather than the ikat technique that prevails over much of the rest of Flores (see CHAPTERS 4 & 5). The Makassarese were also active around the shores of Ende Bay, where they mixed with the local populations and produced vigorous trading communities. In Ende this culminated in the formation of an Islamic state under the control of its own raja (Andaya 1981:63, Needham 1983:17).

The Islamic sultanate of Bima, located in eastern Sumbawa, was another contender for regional power. Bima was overcome by Goa in 1633 and thereafter became a vassal state, the royal families of the two sultanates intermarrying (Andaya 1981:280). With the defeat of Goa in 1669 the situation became more complex. Bima had to contend both with the new rulers in Sulawesi and with the exiled Makassarese. A major prize at stake was the control of Manggarai. The Sultan of Bima eventually prevailed and Manggarai remained at least nominally under Bimanese control, administered via the port of Reo, into the twentieth century. The enduring influence of Bima is clearly evident today in Manggarai's textiles (FIGURE 1-22).

The conflicting interests established by European and Islamic expansion persisted through the eighteenth and nineteenth centuries. Islamic traders from Sulawesi and Bima continued to settle on Flores. Ende, Bima, and the United East India Company were all deeply involved in the trading of slaves.[22] A report that the Endenese traded Sumbanese slaves in return for rice from Bali (Alderwerelt 1906) suggests that slave trading became a fundamental economic strategy for some non-agricultural coastal communities. Aside from slaves, exports from Flores included wild cinnamon, beeswax, edible bird's nest, dried shark fin and sea cucumber, coconut oil, sappan and other dye woods, sugar palm fiber, and cotton. The main imports were gold, porcelain, ivory tusks, and iron-bladed tools (Metzner 1982:70).

Cloth was both imported and exported. The imports were primarily textiles from Java and India. The patola trade peaked in the 1700s and then began to decline after the Dutch government dismantled the insolvent United East India Company at the close of the century. This decline may have been a crucial factor in stimulating the local production of patola-inspired designs in the Lesser Sundas (Fox 1977:98). Nevertheless, smaller quantities of patola and other types of Indian cloth, including mordant-printed textiles with similar patterns, continued to be traded to the Lesser Sundas into the early twentieth century. Today such cloths can still be found in some villages, where they have been preserved as clan heirlooms.

Less is known about the textiles that were exported, but Endenese cloths are reported to have been used for purchasing slaves on Sumba, at the rate of five or six decorated cloths per child slave (Roos 1872:10). Cloths from the Lesser Sundas, including Flores, were traded as far east as New Guinea, where they eventually became the focus of a unique exchange system (Elmberg 1968, Maxwell 1990:397).

Upon the demise of the United East India Company, the Dutch government assumed responsibility over the Company's holdings. Flores was considered an unprofitable island and at first the official policy was to govern indirectly, without interfering in the internal affairs of the existing rajas. Each of these "rajadoms" (including Larantuka, Sikka, Ende, and Reo) had as its nucleus a port town that was more the product of outside forces than a natural outgrowth of indigenous political institutions. Real Dutch control over the population of Flores was limited and the Lesser Sundas gained a reputation as a neglected area plagued by piracy.

Despite the official hands-off policy, the Dutch found themselves increasingly drawn into conflicts.[23] A critical policy shift took place in the first decade of the twentieth century, in the form of the so-called Ethical Policy. Under pressure for reform from the home country, the colonial government determined to exert direct administrative control over all its holdings. Throughout the archipelago, this brought the Dutch into interior areas with which they had had little previous contact. In 1907-08, military patrols were sent throughout Flores, an action the government justified in the name of pacification (FIGURE 1-23). Despite minor resistance that continued sporadically for several years, Dutch control over the island was quickly and thoroughly established.

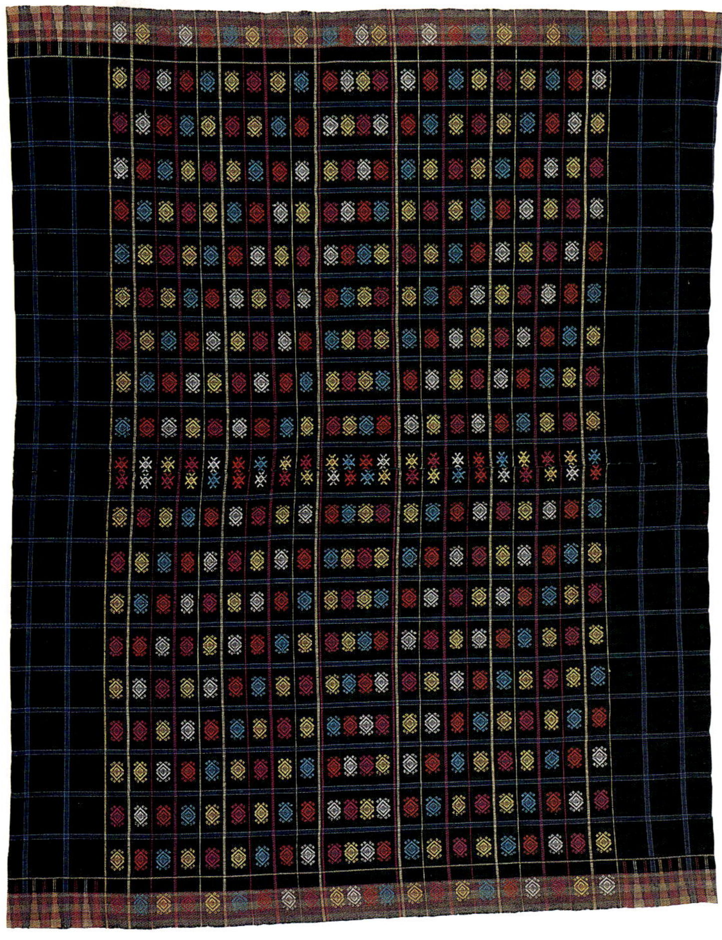

FIGURE 1-22. This sarong from the Rembong region of Manggarai is a close replica of sarongs known as *weri* in Bima (see Hitchcock 1983: fig. 36a). The design was probably introduced to Rembong by Bimanese weavers settled in coastal towns such as Pota (see FIGURE 4-18). In Rembong, such sarongs are called *lipa pungsa ula zua* (sarong with stripes in two shades of blue) or *lipa talaq* (sarong with star motifs). Made in Golo Lijun, circa 1990, 143 x 109 cm. FMCH X91.1618.

In the wake of Dutch civil authority, Catholic missions and schools were established in many parts of the island. By the 1920s, church and state had become powerful vectors of social change. In particular, the suppression of inter-village hostility, the abolition of aristocratic control over a slave class, and Catholic opposition to many traditional religious practices brought about a changed environment. With impressed labor, the Dutch began building the first roads on the island. Favored local leaders were appointed as rajas over areas that had not previously been united politically. Western styles of dress became more common, particularly among those who desired to emulate the Dutch (FIGURE 1-24). At the same time, social change began to undermine traditional society, in which textiles had figured so prominently.

CONTINUITY AND TRANSFORMATION

It is against this background of change that the early ethnographic reports must be viewed. Four hundred years of contact and trade had significantly altered some coastal communities by creating new populations, importing new religions, and imposing alien forms of social and political organization. Prior to 1907, interior communities were much less altered by these processes, but the dynamics between coastal rajadoms and interior villages remain poorly understood. Due to the landward orientation of many of the island's ethnic groups, interior areas formed what might be viewed as conservative cultural heartlands. Attitudes of mutual hostility and suspicion had been severely exacerbated by slave raiding. Yet despite the obstacles, at least some degree of contact and trade prevailed, allowing vital links to be forged through the barter of basic commodities, especially textiles and food. Perhaps the most succinct statement of the relationship between the coast and the interior is provided by a folksong once sung in the mountains above Ende:

> *Father, we are guilty most certainly;*
> *But think as well,*
> *The gunpowder did not come from the mountains,*
> *The powder came from the coast.*[24]

The tendency for change to proceed at different rates in different communities continues today, but is shaped by new factors. Generally, villages located near towns or on the main highway are likely to have experienced the most change. Certain aspects of traditional social structure and religion are still maintained in some villages (FIGURE 1-25), while in others young people have little knowledge of practices abandoned in their grandparents' time. Increased levels of education and the promulgation of an egalitarian ideology, considered to be two of the most important accomplishments of Indonesian independence since 1945, have rendered unacceptable the class divisions that were once at the core of traditional social organization. Former clan leaders, or their descendants, are still regarded as respected elders, but their real authority in most places is now limited to immediate family matters. Some communities find themselves torn between a diminished traditional authority structure and a modern bureaucratic administration that is viewed with suspicion as an imposed institution.

Lineage houses can still be found in many villages, but today they rarely serve as the residence for large groups of kin. Communal housing was discouraged by the Catholic

FIGURE 1-23.
A patrol of Dutch and native soldiers at Bajawa, 1909. Koninklijk Instituut voor Taal-, Land- en Volkenkunde, Leiden.

FIGURE 1-24.
Mbaki Mbani (CENTER) was proclaimed Raja of Ndona in 1909 after helping the Dutch defend Ende from rebel attack. Here his costume clearly emulates European dress. Nevertheless Dutch displeasure with his conversion to Islam in 1918 contributed to the decision in 1920 to abolish his office and place Ndona under the authority of the distant Raja of Wolowaru. From Suchtelen 1921, plate 61.

church and prohibited by local governments, both before and after independence. These actions were promoted in the name of sanitation, but the suppression of communal housing was in reality a veiled attack on traditional social organization, of which the housing pattern was but an obvious manifestation. Today most villagers live in nuclear-family dwellings. The cycles of ceremonies that once centered on the lineage houses have been reduced in scope or abandoned altogether. Nearly all the people of Flores now profess adherence to either Roman Catholicism (85%) or Islam.

Other aspects of traditional society have proved more tenacious. The kinship framework of birth family and in-laws still provides the major source of reference for individuals. Due to Catholic opposition to arranged first-cousin marriages, and to the

increasing exercise of choice on the part of young people, more marriages are now concluded between parties not previously involved with each other in marriage alliances, but such new alliances are still routinely formalized through bridewealth exchanges.

Agriculture continues to be the predominant means of livelihood for most villagers, but there have been important crop changes. In many areas, cassava and irrigated rice have replaced corn and dry field rice as the main staples. These new crops are more suitable to permanent cultivation, which is replacing shifting cultivation.[25] As transportation and marketing systems have improved, cash crops such as copra, coffee, cloves, and market fruits and vegetables have become increasingly important. In many places, cotton cultivation has been abandoned because imported yarn is now readily available. Unfortunately, population growth and the natural limits of agriculture in dry and mountainous terrain leave many village families in precarious positions today. Parents strive especially hard to educate their children because they do not expect them to be able to make a living from the land. At the same time, employment in the government bureaucracy, the traditional path for advancement among the educated elite, can no longer keep pace with the rising numbers of graduating students.

It is within this difficult economic environment that the women of Flores must now find a place for weaving. Few can afford the luxury of producing the most labor-intensive types of textiles for their own use without regard to the value of their effort. Time-consuming procedures and low profit margins mitigate against continued production of handwoven cloth. At the same time, the lack of alternative cash-producing occupations in many cases continues to stimulate production. Economics aside, cultural considerations still play a critical role in underpinning the island's textile traditions. ❖ NOTES, page 268.

The film *Ria Rago*

A surprising glimpse of Lio costume in the early 20th century comes from the silent feature film *Ria Rago*, made in Ndona in 1929 by Fathers P. Beltjens and S. Buis, missionaries of the Society of the Divine Word. A film review appearing in a 1931 Catholic magazine reveals the attitudes of the era:

❦ *Ria Rago, the heroine, is a Christian maiden, baptized and educated in the mission. She is a charming girl, beautiful and attractive, as the natives rate these qualities. Dapu, a heathen, a divorced man, sues for her hand in marriage. He brings his wares, as is the native custom, to the father and mother to barter for the girl. She, well educated in the law of God, steadfastly refuses his advances. She is vilely persecuted, beaten, and made to suffer by her cruel parents. She makes her escape from the paternal roof and betakes herself to the Sisters. There she is tenderly cared for, her wounds washed and bound up. Fury seizes upon the father when he discovers she has escaped. Hostile forces are summoned, and on Sunday afternoon while the Sisters and children are at devotion, Ria Rago is captured and carried off. Here in captivity she is subjected to most inhuman treatment. She is steadfast and will not yield. God's law cannot be violated. In a nocturnal orgy, held by the seemingly triumphant forces of evil, she again makes her escape. She swoons from sheer exhaustion on the doorsteps of the catechist's home.... The doctor is summoned. Her case is serious. The last sacraments are dispensed. Her parents arrive and beg her pardon. Ria Rago forgives them. What a triumph of Christian fortitude over pagan cruelty.*

(Dooley 1931:184)

The missionaries used local actors. Ria's father was played by a real-life clan headman named Ragho Dao (whose name was mispelled in the film). Ragho was among the most prominent men in his community to have been baptized in the early days of the Catholic mission. There were many ironies in a Catholic clan leader agreeing to play a distorted version of his former pagan self for a Western audience, presumably because he believed it would benefit his community.

The film successfully toured England, Belgium, France, and the American Midwest in the 1930s. Admission was free, but contributions for the missionary effort were solicited at the conclusion of the showing. The last known copies were printed in 1949. The film was never shown in Ndona, reportedly for fear of angering local Muslims, who comprise one-third of the community. A surviving copy was discovered in 1990 in the attic of an abandoned garage in Belgium (pers. com., Father Henk de Beer) and the film has now been preserved by the Nederlands Filmmuseum, Amsterdam.

TOP: In the film, Ragho Dao appears to wear a sarong tucked up on both sides, a style that is today only found on the remote, offshore island of Palu'é (FIGURE 12-12). Courtesy of the Society of the Divine Word and the Nederlands Filmmuseum.

CENTER: Beltjens and Buis with Ragho Dao and his wife, who also played a role in the film. Courtesy of the Society of the Divine Word, Teteringen (Netherlands).

BOTTOM: Beltjens and Buis at their film drying rack. From Dooley 1931, p. 184.

LEFT: Buis, who was a trained photographer, took this portrait of Dhapo Ndoki, another man who appeared in the film. He wears a *sémba* shoulder cloth and carries a plaited bag made from pandanus leaves. From Heerkens 1943.

2

The Many Roles of Weaving and Textiles

ROY W. HAMILTON

A TUBULAR GARMENT KNOWN AS A SARONG IS NOW CONSIDERED THE BASIC ITEM of traditional costume for both men and women on Flores.[1] In earlier times men in some areas wore loincloths made of beaten bark-cloth or woven cotton (FIGURE 2-2). Women may once have worn similar loincloths or aprons, but there is no remaining evidence or memory of this. Today among most ethnic groups, men's sarongs are distinguished from women's on the basis of the patterns and decorative techniques used. They also tend to be wider and shorter than women's. Small sarongs are sometimes made for children, but formerly children went naked until ceremonially presented with their first garments as part of a series of maturation rites. Today most children wear Western-style clothes, including school uniforms.

Sarongs are most often used as lower-body garments, simply secured at the waist by rolling the top edge of the cloth. They are extremely versatile, however, and extensive vocabularies in the local languages describe various alternative ways of wearing them (FIGURES 2-3, 2-4, 2-5). Both men and women commonly readjust their sarongs to suit the particular needs of the moment.[2] For example, a sarong may be brought up over a shoulder, or even over the back of the head, to provide warmth or a greater sense of privacy in public. In some cases, there are special regional practices. Ngadha women, for example, attach tie strings to hold the garment closed at the shoulders, while Lamaholot women sometimes use wooden pins for this purpose.

FIGURE 2-1 (OPPOSITE). Full ceremonial attire appears at major community rituals, such as this dedication of rebuilt ceremonial structures in a Kéo village in 1991. The weapons, gold head ornaments, and cowrie shell necklaces are clan treasures.

FIGURE 2-2 (LEFT). The loincloth is an archaic form of dress remembered today primarily for its use by mountain villagers in non-weaving areas. This Lio man was photographed in the 1920s. His loincloth is made of woven cotton obtained from weaving villages, but bark-cloth was also used in a similar manner. Koninklijk Instituut voor de Tropen, Amsterdam.

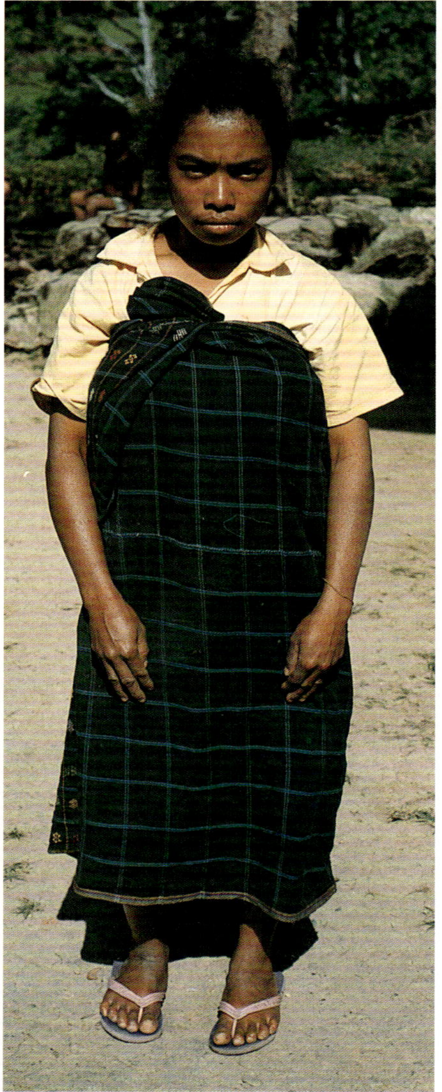

FIGURES 2-3, 2-4, 2-5. As elsewhere on Flores, the people of Rembong wear sarongs in many different ways, each with its own name. LEFT: This woman has rolled hers under the arms, a style called *ambos* in the Rembong language. CENTER: The sarong is supported over one shoulder (known as *lempas*, "free" or "unattached"). RIGHT: Men often set out from home with a sarong slung across the torso, called *kélé*. These sarongs also illustrate a range of the supplementary-weft pattern combinations found in northeastern Manggarai. Lempang-Paji, 1992.

In addition to tubular sarongs, weavers of most ethnic groups also make flat rectangular cloths, which are usually fringed at the ends. These cloths are now regarded primarily as men's shoulder cloths, although in the past they were sometime worn as lower-body garments and even today they are put to many other uses (FIGURES 2-6, 2-7). Before the availability of foreign styles of shirts or jackets, shoulder cloths were the only upper-body garments available for men, but they were not necessarily used unless needed to ward off the mountain chill or to complete the more formal dress required for ceremonial occasions.[3] Today men often wear shirts of various Western styles with their sarongs; shoulder cloths appear almost exclusively at special occasions.

Square or rectangular headcloths for men were also once woven by women of most ethnic groups. These have now been replaced in all but a few areas with batik headcloths imported from Java, and even these are normally seen only on special occasions. Additional accessories, such as belts, vests, weapons, and woven or plaited bags completed men's ceremonial costume.

Women throughout Flores now almost always wear blouses with their sarongs, but these are not indigenous garments. In some areas, elderly people recall a time when women wore no upper-body garment, while in other areas there is no such memory because blouses were adopted in the more distant past. The standards of propriety of both of the major imported religions, Roman Catholicism and Islam, have played the decisive role. Local informants report that in the 1950s in the Islamic port of Ende, women did not appear in public without being well covered, including their heads. In Catholic areas, it was the influence of the missionaries that provided the major impetus for the adoption of blouses.

The most common type of blouse is patterned after the Javanese *kebaya*, a long-sleeved style now widespread in Indonesia. Women of some ethnic groups in Ngada Regency wear sleeveless blouses of very simple construction. The blouse worn by Ende and Lio women is of particular interest because it is similar in cut to the South Sulawesi blouse known as *baju bodo*. This is just one of many instances of Sulawesi influence in the textile traditions of Flores related to the historical expansion of the Makassarese into the Lesser Sundas. Blouses were once made of plain handwoven cloth, often dyed black, but currently they are nearly always made from commercial cloth imported to the island. Today most women prefer synthetic fabrics printed with floral patterns.

TEXTILES IN SOCIAL AND CEREMONIAL LIFE

Although traditional garments are similar in form from one region to another, they vary tremendously in decorative technique, design format, and motif. This variation conveys information about the wearer. Most obviously, items of dress provide an immediate clue to the individual's ethnic identity. In former times class status was also communicated through clothing. Elaborate versions of traditional costume, complete with jewelry and other accessories, were worn primarily by individuals of the highest social standing. People of ordinary means imitated this style of dress as best they could, particularly for ceremonial occasions, but everyday dress normally consisted of only one or two simple garments.

In some cases, more specific information regarding the identity or achievements of an individual are encoded in the designs that appear on clothing. In the traditional system of status ranking in the Ngadha region, for example, only when a man and his wife had successfully organized certain feasts did they earn the right to wear sarongs decorated with motifs appropriate to their new status. In the Lamaholot areas, certain patterns are associated

FIGURE 2-6 (LEFT). Shoulder cloths are often used in the context of social dancing, as at weddings or other celebrations. After taking a turn, the dancer passes the cloth to another person, who is then obligated to dance. Wolotopo, 1988.

FIGURE 2-7 (RIGHT). Ikat shoulder cloths are used in Lio villages to drape coffins that contain the remains of particularly revered ancestors, maintained in special ceremonial structures (*balé*). A similar shoulder cloth, and an antique sword as well, serve as part of the ceremonial garb of one of today's elders. Roworeke, 1988.

FIGURE 2-8 (LEFT). Women in Tana 'Ai construct a model loom over the grave of a kinswoman. Over men's graves, mourners place hunting implements such as bows, arrows, and spears, reflecting notions of the division of labor between the sexes.

FIGURE 2-9 (RIGHT). A Lio elder makes an offering wearing a simple shoulder cloth and headcloth over his everyday clothing. The thin, flat stone is all that remains of an abandoned village site, where it once served as the ritual seat of a specific titled clan leader. Such stones are still revered due to their association with important ancestors and ancestral village sites. Puutuga, 1988.

with particular clans. In the Sikka region, married women weave sarongs with motifs learned from their mothers, but arrange those motifs within a design format associated with the household of their husbands. The finished sarong thus carries a visible expression of the relationship between the two kin groups (see CHAPTER 7).

In addition to providing information about individuals, textiles also serve as markers of special events or objects. Even weaving tools can serve this function (FIGURE 2-8). Religious rites held for any of a wide variety of purposes require ceremonial dress on the part of the leading participants (FIGURES 2-9 through 2-11). For a major ceremonial event, leaders wear their finest garments, plus valuable ornaments that constitute the heirloom property of the clan (FIGURE 2-1). These traditions have been adapted to Roman Catholic ceremony, and events such as the investiture of a new priest are now significant occasions for the wearing of traditional garments.

Throughout Indonesia great emphasis is put on wedding costume and bridal couples dress in the finest garments the families can muster. Traditional forms of dress tend to be maintained for weddings even where they are no longer worn on a daily basis. Today on Flores wedding costume usually consists of high-quality sarongs and other traditional garments, but weddings are as varied as the individuals who organize them and some couples currently favor imported styles of dress (FIGURE 2-12).

No matter what is worn at the wedding ceremony, it is in the context of bridewealth exchange that textiles offer their richest realm of meaning on Flores. Marriage practices differ according to ethnic group and religion, but the concept of bridewealth is found in one form or another throughout Flores.[4] Before a wedding can take place, an agreement must be negotiated regarding the bridewealth goods that will be given by the groom's kin to the bride's (FIGURE 2-13).[5] The total bridewealth actually consists of a complex series of separate gifts to specific relatives of the bride.[6] Each of these installments must be reciprocated by the bride's kin with return gifts, especially of rice and textiles (FIGURE 2-14).

FIGURES 2-10 (TOP), 2-11 (BOTTOM).
After a tragic accident, mourners
gather in front of a truck that
overturned on the highway, killing
a child. In the village they perform a
ritual called *kéo rado,* held for *ata golo,*
those who die a "bad death" such as
by accident or murder. In addition
to traditional textiles, the main
participants have donned a number
of special items, including the plaited
hat (*kibi*) worn by a woman and the
cowry shell necklace (*wuli*) worn by
one of the men. Another man wears
a substitute necklace made of the
fruit of a plant (*wuli bara*). The
individuals designated to wear these
items and lead the ritual are selected
by divination from among the
relatives of the proper category in
relation to the deceased (pers. com.,
Andrea Molnar). Sara Sedu region,
Ngada Regency, 1992.

In Sikka and East Flores, the bridewealth good par excellence is ivory (FIGURE 2-15).[7] Whole tusks are now scarce, but still change hands in some weddings. Elsewhere the main components of bridewealth are gold and livestock (usually horses, cattle, or pigs).[8] Gold is given in the form of heirloom jewelry, particularly ear ornaments that appear in related forms throughout the Lesser Sundas (FIGURE 1-1). Specific names are used for the various shapes and weights of these ornaments and providing the proper type is an important issue during bridewealth negotiations.

Despite the hard bargaining that may occur over the value of goods involved, bridewealth is not viewed as a payment required to obtain a wife.[9] Nor are the rice and textiles given in return thought of in purely economic terms. Rather, these interactions constitute an ongoing series of gift exchanges between the kin groups involved. The bridewealth negotiations and the wedding rites form a sequence of events, occupying a period of several weeks or more. Subsequent rites, which mark advancing stages in the couple's relationship, may occur throughout their lifetime. Each step of the process concludes with some exchange of goods, for which each set of kin must provide the appropriate objects. Rarely is the entire sum of the bridewealth surrendered at one time. Typically only a small installment is presented at the time of the wedding; the rest is deferred indefinitely. This creates a continuing bond of obligations between the two kin groups, which can be drawn upon as need arises.

In the past, the groom was sometimes required to live with the bride's family until the entire bridewealth was surrendered. Only then did the couple move to live with the groom's kin. Children did not assume their place in their patrilineage until the bridewealth was presented in full. This practice reveals one of the prime preoccupations of marriage alliance ideology: the securing of the reproductive capabilities of the bride for the groom's lineage. Actual practice was more flexible than this ideology would suggest, however. A number of alternative types of marriage arrangements, including elopement, were available depending on the circumstances of the families involved. Today if couples

are unable to settle in a home of their own, they live with whichever family is best able to accommodate them.

The principle of asymmetry in marriage alliance is most clearly demonstrated by the flow of goods in bridewealth exchanges. To his wife-giving in-laws, a man provides the "masculine" goods: ivory, gold, and livestock. In return he receives the "feminine" goods: textiles and rice. From his wife-takers, on the other hand, he receives ivory, gold, and livestock, giving textiles and rice in return. Thus the two categories of goods circulate in opposite directions in a never-ending flow through the kin groups that make up society.[10] For help in assembling the required goods when a marriage is being negotiated, families can call upon their in-laws. However, this must be done only within the proper direction of the flow of goods. If gold is needed for bridewealth, a man must go to his wife-takers, where a claim can usually be made on the basis of outstanding obligations stemming from previous marriages. If rice or textiles are needed for a counter-prestation, it must be sought from wife-givers.

Most weddings are conducted following the gathering of the harvest, when food for feasts is plentiful and there is a lull in the cycle of agricultural labor. A single individual may be involved in a number of marriage negotiations simultaneously, in some as a member of the bride's kin and in others as a member of the groom's. He will strive to take in more exchange goods than he gives out, or failing that, at least to maintain a balanced flow. Although at the end of the wedding season he may have roughly the equivalent of what he started out with, the actual objects involved will have changed hands, publicly dramatizing the social relationships that bind kin groups together in mutual obligation.

The relationships between allied kin groups encompass the individual from cradle to grave. When a death occurs, messengers are sent to inform those who are related to the deceased through marriage. It is the duty of those called upon to provide the necessary goods for the funeral, especially cloth to cover the body, plus rice, meat, and distilled palm spirits for the funeral guests. These items must be provided in accord with the proper direction of

FIGURE 2-14 (LEFT).
The Wolotopo bridewealth negotiations shown in FIGURE 2-13 concluded with the acceptance of the first installment of the bridewealth goods, followed by a feast. Afterward, the kinswomen of the future bride assembled textiles destined as gifts for their counterparts among the groom's kin. Seen here are a number of women's sarongs, folded in stacks.

FIGURE 2-15 (RIGHT).
Four tusks of ivory received as bridewealth goods in the Ili Mandiri region of East Flores, photographed in 1929. From Vatter 1932, plate 14, fig. 1.

FIGURE 2-16.
This clan heirloom, decorated with shell beads and bands of red trade cloth, is said to have been the loincloth of an heroic ancestor in the Soa region of Ngada Regency (see also FIGURE 4-4). A backing of modern cloth has been added to strengthen the decaying fabric. Heirloom cloths often have special ceremonial functions; this cloth was recently used to cover the log for the making of a new *péo*, or forked ceremonial pole, when it was brought from the forest into the village. According to local belief, a man who has not yet sponsored a feast will become infertile if he handles the cloth.

flow of goods – the textiles and rice being offered by the wife-givers of the deceased, and the livestock (for meat) by the wife-takers.[11]

Large numbers of textiles serve in bridewealth exchanges, but only a few become imbued with the status of heirlooms. These are cloths maintained on behalf of the clan or lineage by its leader. Frequently they are associated with legends about the exploits of an important ancestor who used them. Sometimes heirlooms are rare imported cloths, such as silk patola, but often they are ordinary cloths of local manufacture. Even when in tatters due to the ravages of the tropical climate, they serve as revered symbols (FIGURES 2-16, 2-17).

TEXTILES AS ECONOMIC GOODS

The territories of many of the major ethnic groups on Flores are divided into weaving and non-weaving areas. The bartering of cloth for goods produced in non-weaving areas was a basic component of pre-colonial economic organization. This division of labor was based in part on ecological factors. In the precipitous terrain of Flores, parched, rocky coastal slopes may be only a few hours walk from broad upland valleys with deeper soils and more adequate rainfall (FIGURE 2-18). The production of rice and corn was more dependable in the interior, whereas cotton ripened best in the pronounced dry season of the hot coastal areas. Bartering allowed the fullest exploitation of this environmental diversity. Women's labor in coastal villages was most productively invested in the making of textiles, which could be bartered in times of need for surplus food produced in the interior. In non-weaving interior areas, women's labor was devoted primarily to agricultural production.

This type of barter system has been documented in a number of areas. Barter was ideally based on fixed rates of exchange. In Ndona District, near Ende, a woman's ikat sarong could be traded in the 1920s for ten sacks of unhusked rice, five sacks of husked rice, or 1,500 ears of corn. Many who are middle-aged today can still recall accompanying

FIGURE 2-17 (ABOVE).
A patola cloth, preserved as an heirloom, is draped over a stone clan seat during a festival for an ancestral temple (*koko*). Léwotala, 1987.

FIGURE 2-18 (LEFT).
The rugged topography of Flores produces microclimates that shape patterns of agriculture and trade. For example, the sugar palm (*Arenga pinnata*) growing on this cool, moist ridge in Ndona District could not survive on the hot coastal plain below. Mountain villagers trade *moké,* the spirits distilled from the fermented sap of its flower stalks, to their lowland neighbors.

their parents on treks into the mountains, returning with heavy sacks of grain. Direct bartering of textiles for food in Ndona District came to an end by the 1960s with the development of cash-based marketing and improvements in transportation, but on Lembata the bartering system is still in operation. Women carrying textiles leave the weaving village of Lamalera on moonlit nights in order to reach their destination in non-weaving villages before their potential trading partners have left for their fields. This trade is an important source of food for Lamalera, a fishing village that has no agricultural land.

Although the exchange of textiles for food was the most characteristic type of barter on Flores, other commodities including livestock, pottery, plaited mats, palm spirits, and dried fish were also exchanged (FIGURE 2-19). Each of these might be the specialized product of a different village or region. Trade itself was a specialization that sometimes vouchsafed survival in environments unyielding of food crops. A striking example is found on Palu'é, a small island off the north shore of Flores, where men annually sail from their barren island in small craft to seek their livelihood through trade.

In some regions, the division between weaving and non-weaving areas is more complex than solely ecological reasons would dictate. In Manggarai, for example, weaving is restricted to a few small areas. In the Ngadha region, one of the main weaving centers is so high in elevation that cotton had to be obtained from distant villages located on lower slopes. In East Flores Regency, the distribution of weaving villages is highly discontinuous. These cases suggest that historical and political factors are operating in addition to the ecological ones.

Inter-community relationships on Flores are in many ways competitive, based on the zealous guarding and promoting of rights established by one community against encroachment by another. Certainly any group that succeeded in establishing textile production as an important part of its economic relations with surrounding communities would try to protect its position. It is therefore not surprising that a host of cultural conceptions surround the bartering systems. In many non-weaving areas, there are still forceful, culturally framed prohibitions against weaving. For example, women in non-weaving Lio areas say their village would be destroyed by a catastrophic storm if they were to attempt to weave. In the Rembong region of Manggarai, weaving is regarded as a curse visited upon the descendants of an ancestor who committed an incestuous act of adultery and murder (see CHAPTER 9).

Might the division between weavers and non-weavers represent the indigenous non-weaving population, on one hand, and newcomers who brought weaving technology to Flores on the other? Some of the most famous weaving communities, including Mbay and Lamalera, are known to be descended from outsiders who came to Flores only in relatively recent centuries.[12] Such communities may have used their knowledge of weaving tech-nology as an advantage in establishing trade relationships with the pre-existing populations. One version of the oral history of the people of Todo in Manggarai is even more explicit, stating that ancestors coming from overseas were responsible for the introduction of weaving to the region, where it had previously been unknown (Coolhaas 1942:342). A similar myth is found on Palu'é (CHAPTER 12).

Yet in other communities with strong weaving traditions, including those in the Lio and Ngadha areas, weaving is not so clearly linked with recent settlement from foreign shores. In these areas there are few cultural differences between weavers and non-weavers and, furthermore, some of the leading weaving communities are located in, or else trace their ancestry from, the interior. These cases may suggest a more long-standing, indigenous division between weavers and non-weavers.

In either case, the reliability of oral tradition must be considered suspect, because the manipulation of orally recounted clan histories for political gain is a key leadership skill. More complete linguistic and oral historical data might shed new light on these issues, but there can be no real resolution without an archaeological picture of community movements and technological change over a period of many centuries.

Although bartering systems have in most parts of Flores been replaced by cash-based markets, the divisions between weaving and non-weaving areas remain and the underlying ecological factors continue to shape economic relationships. Families in non-weaving villages now purchase their clothing with cash, obtained through the sale of foodstuffs or cash crops. Traditional garments, especially at the lower end of the price range, are actively traded at town markets and in rotating weekly markets that operate on rural circuits.

In many weaving villages, dependence on textile production appears to have only grown greater in recent decades. While agriculture has remained marginal due to inherent ecological limitations, village populations have increased and alternative economic opportunities have remained scarce. Under such conditions, the sale of textiles has become the predominant source of income in some villages. Despite strong cultural conditioning to the contrary, in at least one Lio village a number of men have recently taken up weaving because they feel it offers the best potential return for their labor.[13]

The type of textiles a weaver chooses to make depends on the economic circumstances of her family. Some women concentrate primarily on the production of cloth that can be made and sold quickly, because they have a pressing need for cash. These weavers often take their cloth to market themselves, traveling in small groups. Rather than waiting indefinitely in the marketplace for a direct sale to a customer, they sell to a full-time trader (FIGURE 2-20). The proceeds are used to buy rice and other basic supplies for their families, plus the yarn needed for their next cloth. The women may be back at their looms within a few hours.

Women from families that enjoy better economic positions are less likely to produce quickly made cloths intended for sale. They prefer instead to concentrate on making higher-quality, labor-intensive cloths that will be worn by family members or saved for use in bridewealth exchanges. Such cloths are rarely taken to market because weavers

FIGURE 2-19.
Women in the Lio village of Wolotolo, in the mountainous interior, specialize in the making of pots. Coastal weavers value the large vessels as indigo dye pots. The people of Wolotolo once obtained cloth by bartering directly with the weavers, but today pots are sold at regional markets and the potters buy their clothing with cash. 1991.

FIGURE 2-20.
A trader sells cloth in the weekly market at Wolowaru in 1988. The cloths are purchased from weavers or their husbands, who may bring the textiles to market. A few women act as traders in the markets nearest their homes, but taking cloths to distant markets on a full-time basis is ordinarily a male occupation.

cannot obtain a price that is commensurate with the amount of labor involved. However, some women with reputations as highly skilled weavers routinely sell this type of cloth to customers who come directly to their homes. For diligent, skilled weavers this can be a source of considerable income by local standards; but the volume of this trade is nowhere near as great as that of lower-quality cloths sold in local markets.

Basically, then, there is a two-tiered system governing the sale of textiles, with cloths of lower quality sold in markets and cloths of higher quality sold at home to personal clients. Customers who buy inexpensive cloths in markets are mostly ordinary farmers from non-weaving villages. Only a salaried civil servant, a tourist, or perhaps a well-to-do relative seeking garments for a wedding can afford to buy high-quality cloths from the skilled weavers who sell from their homes.

Individual weavers may participate in both systems or otherwise manage to find a niche that meets their particular needs. Women with children and heavy household responsibilities are likely to spend much less time weaving than unmarried or elderly women. Production is normally organized by individual weavers, although various tasks may be performed by others. In the making of ikat cloths, for example, mature women may perform the complex tying and dyeing processes and then turn the yarns over to a daughter for the weaving. Many women prefer to work together in small groups with their kinswomen. Formally organized village weaving groups are growing in popularity, but there remains a strong preference for women to maintain control over the production of their own cloths. Putting-out systems and wage labor in small-scale workshops are virtually unknown.[14]

TEXTILES IN CHANGE

Weavers on Flores often maintain that their techniques and patterns have been inherited with little change from their distant ancestors, but this claim must be treated with some circumspection. For the period prior to the twentieth century details are scarce, but the widespread adoption of patola patterns indicates that weavers were by no means closed to outside sources of influence. The more ample evidence regarding the twentieth century, in the form of photographs, museum collections, and the recollections of elders, reveals a story of dynamic innovation and adaptation.

One of the most important trends, and the most revealing sociologically, has been the democratization of elaborately decorated textiles that were once a prerogative of the aristocratic class. Where commoners once wore plain garments or even bark-cloth, today elaborately decorated ikat or supplementary-weft cloths are available to all. In many cases it was today's generation of elders, who as youths in the 1920s were the first to be educated in the mission schools, who broke with tradition. The eroding of sumptuary prerogatives must have been one of the most poignantly tangible signs of the weakening of traditional authority under colonial rule. Since political and religious leadership were one and the same in pre-colonial society, there is an element of secularization to this process as well.

Photographs from the early decades of the twentieth century reveal the popularity of Western tailored garments and also of sarongs with plaid or checked patterns (FIGURE 2-21). Despite the greater fame of patola cloths, simple striped, checked, and plaid cottons made up the bulk of textiles imported to Indonesia from India, "just a humdrum, useful, business directed…to supplying cheap cloths to poor people."[15] Checked and plaid sarongs have become an international style, popular from East Africa to the Philippines and often associated with Islam. Regional versions woven in Sulawesi, Selayar, Buton, and Bima were staples of Makassarese and Bugis trade. On Flores, they were eventually copied by local weavers as well. In historical photographs, these sarongs appear among all the various ethnic groups and, in many cases, are the predominant type of dress. Today commercial plaid sarongs, mostly imported from industrial centers in Java, are still widely sold on Flores. With the exception of Todo in Manggarai, local production of this type of cloth has nearly ceased.

The degree to which Western dress has been adopted varies with community and gender. Many village men continue to wear sarongs as everyday garments, but urbanized men are more likely to wear them only at home. Thus a man wearing a sarong in the streets of one of the major towns stands out as something of a bumpkin, perhaps come to town to sell some rural product. For women, urban dress is more mixed. In Ende and Maumere, both of which are surrounded by productive weaving villages, roughly one woman in three wears the sarong and blouse combination. In Ruteng and Larantuka traditional dress is less commonly seen; rural women who visit these towns may be even more careful than their husbands to dress in the Western garments considered appropriate for the modern urban setting. Women from villages in weaving areas continue to show great pride in their traditional dress and are rarely seen wearing Western garments. In non-weaving areas, where clothing must be purchased with scarce cash and inexpensive imported garments often sell for less than sarongs made on Flores, more women have converted to Western dress.

The widespread availability of imported items of dress and the development of a cash economy have altered the mix of garments made by weavers. Flat rectangular cloths are much less in demand now, since they are no longer worn at all as lower-body garments and have largely been replaced as upper-body garments by shirts and blouses. Shoulder cloths have virtually disappeared in the Sikka and Lamaholot areas, although historical photographs and museum collections demonstrate that they were once made. In the case of one type preserved in several museum collections, it is difficult to pinpoint where on the island it was made (FIGURE 2-22). In recent years, weavers in many places have begun to make smaller scarf-like cloths modeled after shoulder cloths. Women use these as often as men, sometimes as a sash in the manner of Indonesian national dress, and they have also become a staple of

FIGURE 2-21.
Checked and plaid sarongs predominate, along with Western styles of shirts, in this early twentieth-century group portrait from Léwotala, East Flores. Koninklijk Instituut voor de Tropen, Amsterdam.

tourist sales. The weaving of headcloths and fabric for blouses, belts, and bags has also come nearly to a halt. In contrast, there has been a greater reluctance to give up the distinctive styles of locally made sarongs, even though commercial sarongs imported from Java and elsewhere are now common too.

Another important trend over the course of the twentieth century has been the adoption of new imported materials, especially industrially spun yarns and chemical dyes. Imported yarns were at first highly valued luxury goods, beyond the reach of ordinary weavers, but the tremendous saving of labor made them extremely attractive. By the 1930s they had become more widely available, particularly in villages like those surrounding Ende that had access to town markets. During the Japanese Occupation, which is keenly remembered on Flores as a time of shortage of both yarn and cloth, weavers in areas that had previously converted to commercial yarns reverted to hand-spinning (Kennedy 1955:221).[16] A considerable amount of hand-spinning continued into the 1960s, due to the economic instability of the Sukarno period, but with the developing consumer economy of the so-called New Order period under Suharto, cotton growing and hand-spinning have nearly vanished in many areas. One may still come across women spinning in any of the ethnic regions, but handspun yarn now accounts for only a small percentage of the total production and can no longer be considered the norm except in a small minority of communities. Currently many types of cotton and synthetic yarns are imported to Flores for sale in markets, including both industrially dyed yarns and white yarns to be dyed by the weavers themselves.

Synthetic dyes quickly became items of international trade following their invention in Europe in the 1850s. Despite the degree of isolation that prevailed on Flores, cloths preserved in museum collections demonstrate that chemical dyes were in limited use there before the end of the nineteenth century. Like imported yarns, chemical dyes were at first luxury goods and the bulk of production continued to rely on natural dyes. A 1950 report from a village near Ende indicates that chemical dyes had by that time largely replaced the

FIGURE 2-22. This cloth, collected before 1887, was probably used as a shoulder cloth, although in that era it may have doubled as a lower-body garment as well. Several cloths with similar patterning exist in museum collections, attributed to Flores in general terms but with no reliable information regarding their specific place of origin. The cloths are no longer recognized by informants on Flores. 204 x 118 cm. Museum für Völkerkunde 25.941, Vienna.

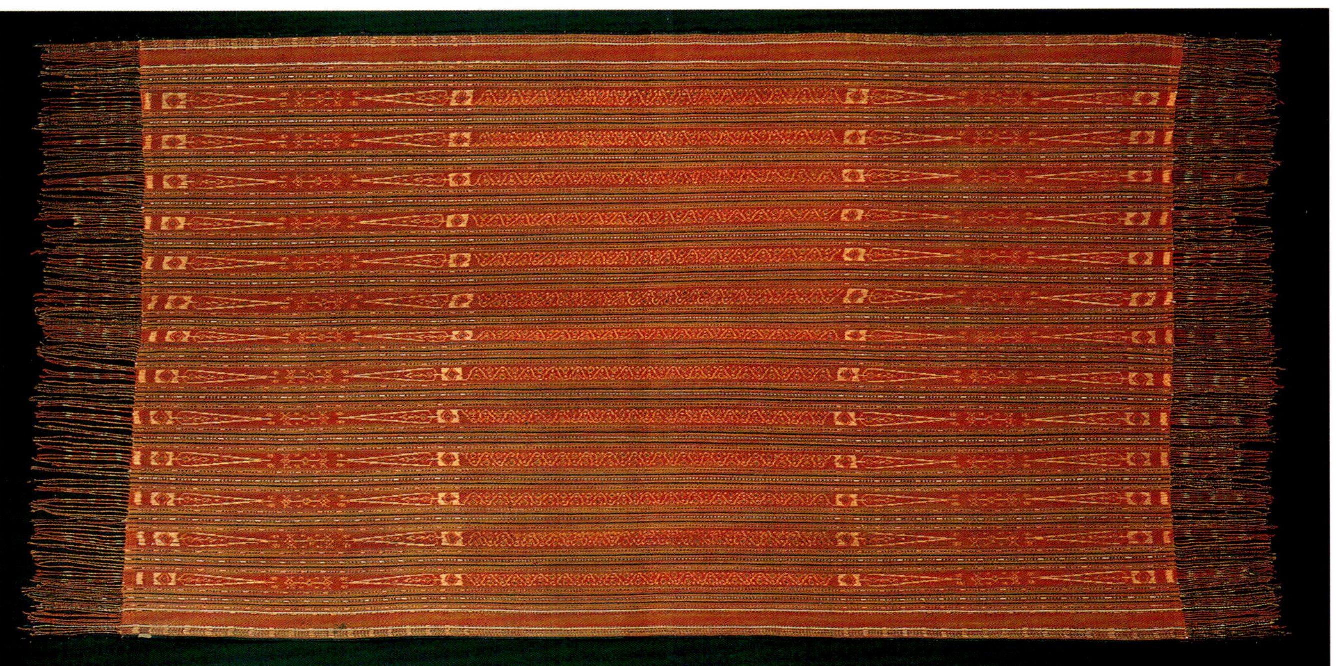

traditional dye for red, while natural indigo was still used for blue-black (Kennedy 1955:23).

The degree to which weavers still command the skills necessary for the complex natural dye processes varies from area to area, but in most communities chemical and natural dyeing continue to exist side by side. Skilled dyers who can afford the investment in labor usually take pride in working with the natural dyes. A commonly heard complaint is that the chemical dyes are not colorfast, but the Department of Industry has made efforts in recent years to train weavers in the use of a new generation of synthetic dyes. The newer dyes are more difficult to use and require greater capital outlay, so weavers are increasingly becoming dependent on small-scale entrepreneurial dye workshops set up in towns and a few of the larger weaving villages. Many weavers who produce textiles for sale continue with the older type of chemical dyes, which they can purchase at low cost in the markets and use in their own homes (FIGURE 2-23).

Cloth production levels are rising in weaving villages where the use of commercial yarns and chemical dyes predominates. These materials have greatly reduced the amount of labor devoted to spinning and dyeing. Interestingly, many weavers seem less willing to take shortcuts in the time-consuming tying of ikat patterns. For a cloth that can be dyed in a matter of days with chemical dyes, rather than months or years with the traditional natural dyes, a weaver may still devote two weeks or more of painstaking labor to the tying of the pattern. As a result, intricate patterns now appear on relatively inexpensive, everyday fabrics. In combination with the democratization process, the result has been a florescence of ikat textile production. This trend is most noticeable in the Sikka, Lio, and Ende ethnic areas, where the towns of Maumere, Wolowaru, and Ende are important marketing centers for ikat cloth. Most rural women in these areas proudly wear inexpensive but elaborately patterned ikat sarongs as everyday garments, whereas in former times much of the clothing would have been plain or decorated with only simple patterns.

Each ethnic group on Flores has a corpus of motifs and design formats that is considered traditional.[17] Weavers in many places still prefer to stick to these traditional patterns. Newer patterns were introduced through increasing contact with outsiders in the early decades of the twentieth century. Among Sikkanese weavers, for example, European-derived floral and bird patterns became quite popular after they were actively encouraged by the missions (FIGURES 7-18, 7-19). In more recent years, there have been additional sources of inspiration (FIGURES 2-24, 2-25). In villages that produce large quantities of inexpensive textiles for market sale, new patterns may be considered a marketing advantage. In the most extreme

FIGURE 2-23.
A woman sells synthetic dye and factory-spun yarn in the Wolowaru market, 1988.

FIGURE 2-24.
This detail of a sarong depicts the sacrifice of the sacred rice mother Iné Paré, whose head is about to be severed by the sword of her elder brother Ndalé in a scene from one of the central creation myths of the Lio people (Petu 1992b:131). Iné Paré's body was cut into pieces, and wherever her blood soaked the soil, rice grew. Similar mythology provides the basis of "rice maiden" cults throughout Indonesia. On Flores the myth was repopularized in the writings of Piet Petu, a priest and textile scholar who commissioned the motif as a textile design based on an illustration that appeared in his 1969 book *Nusa Nipa*. This sarong was made with chemical dyes in the 1980s by a Lio woman living in Ende.

cases, young weavers may derisively say that only old women want to wear the traditional patterns.

Greater mobility is increasing the spread of textile patterns, particularly through women who marry out of their home area. Due to improvements in transportation, more textiles are marketed beyond the borders of the ethnic region in which they were produced. Lio women's sarongs, for example, are now sold in large numbers to Sikka women in the Maumere market. This weakens the tie between clothing and ethnic identity, as does the increasing adoption of Western styles of dress. The Indonesian government now encourages the wearing of traditional costume on national holidays and for activities that promote tourism. At the same time, social and economic forces are propelling more and more Florinese to adopt Western styles of dress.

The export of textiles from Flores to international markets, while not a new phenomenon, increased dramatically in the 1980s. Traders send agents to weaving villages, where they buy used sarongs of mediocre quality at low cost. Most village women find it remarkable that someone is willing to buy their used garments and are eager to obtain cash in this way. The sarongs are sent to Bali, where they are remade into garments or bags to be exported or sold directly to tourists. Judging from the goods that can be found for sale

in European and North American cities, Flores has become the leading source for fabric used in the Bali export trade. Some of the smaller islands in the Lesser Sundas have been virtually stripped of handwoven cloth through this process, but for the moment, production of low and medium quality cloth on Flores appears to be keeping up with exports.

Unfortunately, the demand for ikat textiles in the international art market has led to the disappearance of most old, high-quality cloths. Current market conditions do not reward the production of new cloths of similar quality, as weavers cannot obtain a selling price high enough to justify the amount of labor involved. Local buyers cannot afford such expensive cloths and, if the cloths are exported, middlemen absorb nearly all the profit. As old cloths disappear, an important source of inspiration for weavers is lost.

Mindful of the prosperity that international tourism has brought to Bali, the Indonesian government is now promoting its development in the Lesser Sundas. The natural and cultural assets of Flores may justify such optimism, but infrastructural development currently lags behind ambition. Nevertheless, the number of tourists reaching Flores has risen steadily over the past decade and many visitors are interested in buying textiles. Most tourists willing to face the rigors of travel on Flores are young, intrepid wanderers with limited budgets. They prefer to buy the inexpensive cloths sold in markets. The few who come with a serious interest in textiles, and purchasing budgets to match, tend to seek out skilled weavers at home, just like their counterparts in the upper strata of local buyers. Thus for the most part tourism has not created new marketing patterns, although tourist-directed selling is beginning to appear in a few of the most commonly visited villages. ❖

NOTES, page 269.

FIGURE 2-25.
This shoulder cloth includes bulky anthropomorphic figures representing *ana déo*, the carved wooden ancestor figures found in Lio villages (FIGURE 1-11). The motif was specified by a Japanese visitor who never returned to purchase the cloth. The other motifs, though traditional, are not arranged according to the normal design format. Made by Lucia Seno in Onelako, Ndona District, circa 1980, 219 x 71 cm. Private collection.

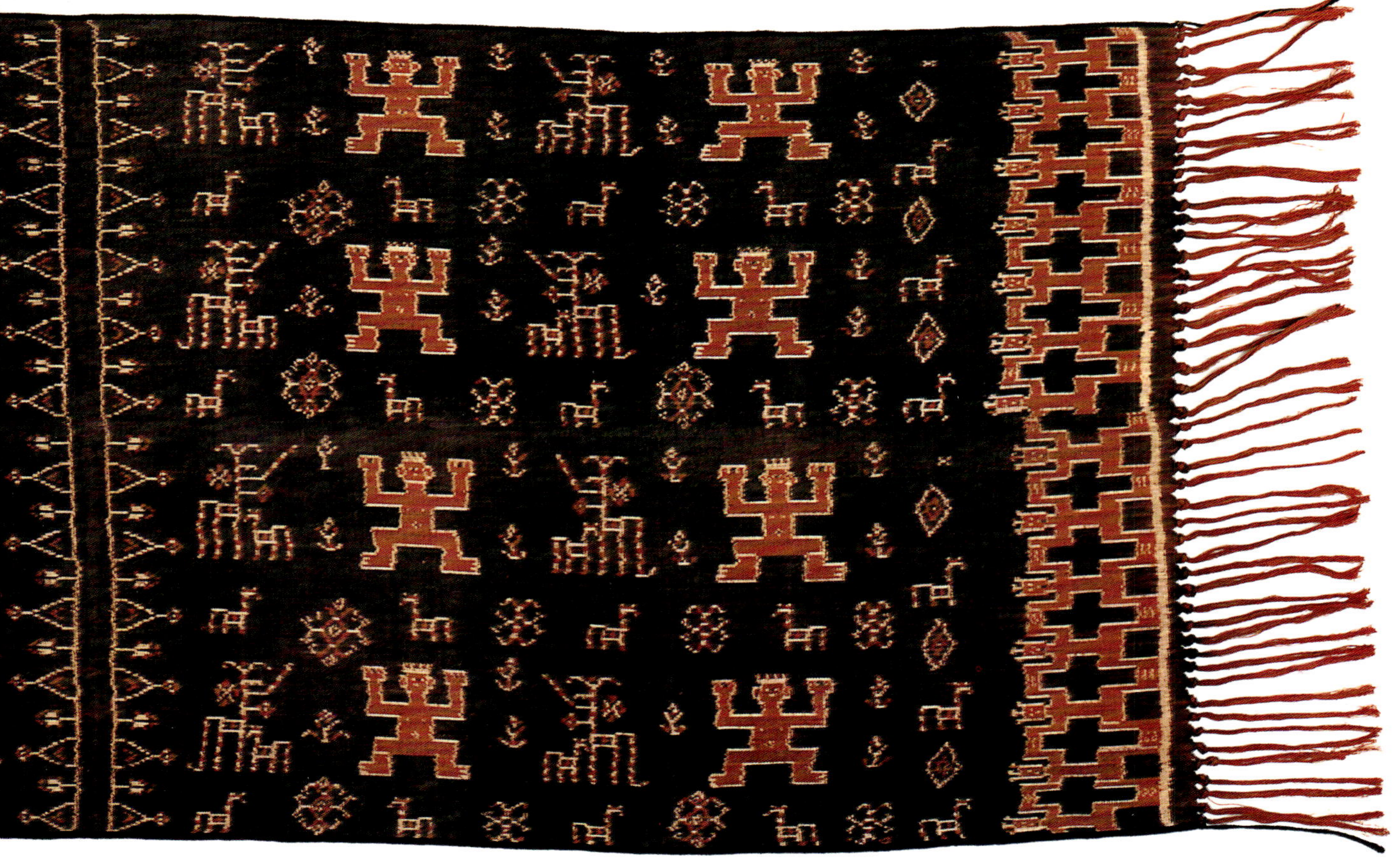

Textile Technology

ROY W. HAMILTON

IN FORMER TIMES, ALL CLOTH MAKING ON FLORES BEGAN with the growing of cotton and the making of yarn, each step of which was carried out by women. Today weavers most often circumvent these laborious processes by buying the imported, commercial yarns that are sold in shops and markets throughout the island. Nevertheless, the production of handspun yarn continues on a small scale in all regencies. For some this is simply a matter of individual preference, but for others it is a means of minimizing cash expenditures. The purpose to which the finished cloth will be put is also a factor. In certain communities, particularly in the Lamaholot areas, only cloths made of handspun cotton are acceptable for bridewealth exchanges. Hand-spinning is less likely to be found where weavers are geared primarily toward the steady production of cloth for sale.

Many villagers can describe several different types of cotton that were once grown. Some are large shrubs that bear bolls sparsely but persistently for a number of years, while others are smaller annual plants.[1] Often the shrubby, longer-lived types are described as indigenous and the smaller annual types as introduced. A few of the cottons grown on Flores have seeds that occur in a single clump rather than being scattered throughout the boll, as is typical of most cottons. This unusual characteristic is believed to have been developed through human selection due to the ease with which the seed cluster can be separated from the fiber by hand.[2] Cottons producing brown fibers are also remembered in parts of Flores, but are rarely seen today.

Cotton has very specific growth requirements, thriving in sandy soil over a long, hot growing season. Ample moisture is required when the plants are young, but the bolls ripen best where there is a pronounced dry season. Thus it is a crop well suited to the hot and seasonally dry coastal regions of Flores. It can be grown in some low-altitude interior valleys as well, but not in the uplands. These climatic requirements are the basis of the division of Flores into weaving and non-weaving areas, although in some cases raw cotton was formerly transported from one area to another.

Until the recent past, each step of the cotton-growing process was accompanied by rites conducted to assure the proper growing conditions and to protect the crop from damage by supernatural forces. According to one report (Tietze 1941), Sikkanese women wrapped cotton bolls, rice, and bits of fish in scraps of ikat cloth, which they tossed into

FIGURE 3-1 (OPPOSITE). Kalsom Memang of Riung, Ngada Regency, removes the seeds from cotton using a wooden mangle. 1991.

the sea while entreating for rain during the early growth of the plants. As the harvest approached a few months later, they returned to the sea again, using their weaving tools as weapons to drive away the "rain serpent" so the ripening cotton would not be ruined.

Some communities celebrated rites involving a "cotton maiden," analogous to the rice maiden cults found throughout Indonesia. The missionary Arndt observed that Ngadha girls whose pure white teeth had not yet been filed (a sign of maturation and marriage-ability) joined the sowing party, laughing and calling out with their mouths open so that the cotton would grow as white as their teeth (1963:146). A more detailed account has been recorded for the Sikka area:

> If a young girl is along for the sowing, who is being initiated for the first time into the work, this is the occasion for a small feast. Everyone dances late into the night to the sounds of the bamboo zither, the goatskin drums and the xylophone. The girl dresses in all her finery because she, especially, must dance by herself. Around her wrists and ankles she wears chains of cotton bolls that rustle softly during the dance; with both her hands she flourishes finely woven cloths. The village girls are wont to blow cotton fluff in her face and ears, to throw it into her hair, and to play other tricks on her. She is sure to find bolls and cotton fluff in her fish sauce; while trying to fall asleep she will leap from her pillow because it has been filled with cotton bolls.... No young man, on the other hand, may dare the slightest affront to the newly initiated girl. For him she personifies the cotton maiden, who assumes a mystical and awe-inspiring relationship to the spirits. However, a young man will try to catch a bit of cotton fluff that falls from her and hide it against his chest as a charm to protect against attack by animals, humans, evil spirits, and angry souls of ancestors.[3]
>
> (Tietze 1941:12)

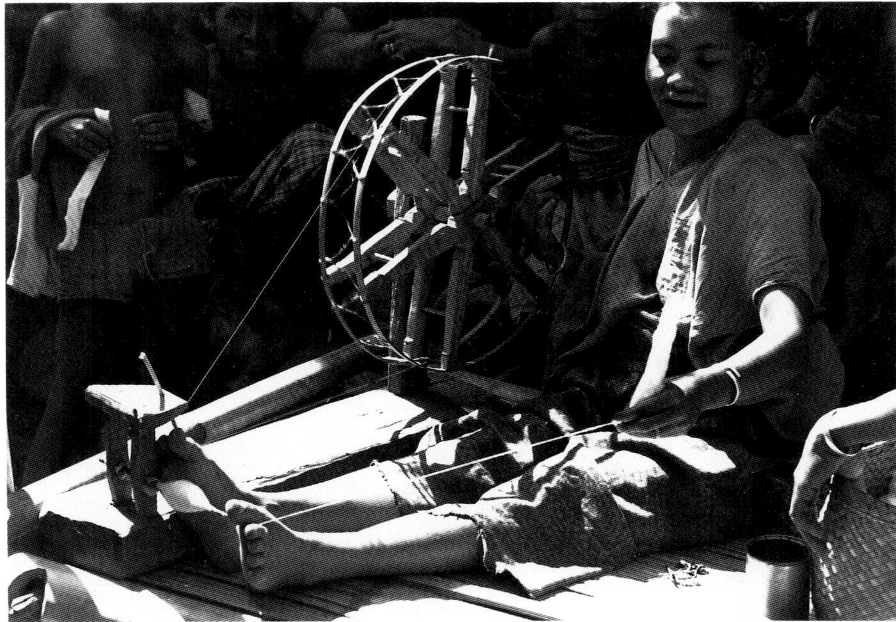

The special status of the girl, and the festive atmosphere, continued as she was instructed by her mother and other female relatives in each successive step of cotton growing and yarn making. The cotton maiden held the promise of becoming a master weaver or dyer of the next generation.

After the harvested cotton is pulled from the bolls and dried in the sun, the seeds must be removed. This may be done with the fingers alone or by using a hand-cranked, wooden mangle (FIGURE 3-1). After the seeds are removed, the fiber is beaten into a fluff, either with a pair of sticks or with a bowed string (FIGURES 3-2, 3-3). In parts of Flores, groups of women continue to gather in groups to fluff and card cotton. Ritual aspects of these tasks may still be observed, including the sacrifice of a chicken or piglet the night before the work is to begin and the performance of a song cycle describing agricultural and textile processes while the rhythmic work progresses.[4]

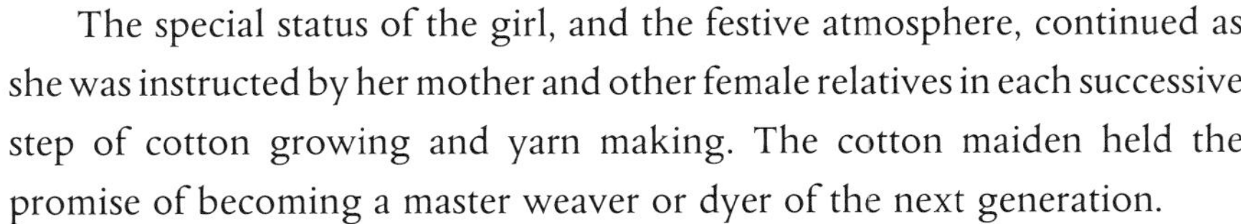

When the fluffing is completed, the cotton is shaped into roves in preparation for spinning. Both drop spindles and simple homemade spinning wheels are used on Flores (FIGURES 3-4, 3-5), but wheels have been increasingly abandoned as the amount of hand-spinning has declined. The drop spindles continue to be valued for their portability. Where hand-spinning is still common, women can be seen spinning as they sit in the market or walk from village to village. After being spun, the yarn is wound into skeins.

DYES

A large number of natural dyes have been used on Flores, but just two of them, indigo and morinda, far surpass all others in importance. These two substances are ranked among the great natural dyes of the world due to their ability to impart rich, lasting hues to cotton fiber. Most natural dyes belong to a group that dye chemists call direct dyes. These are easy to use because the dye molecules react directly with the fiber, usually in a simple hot water bath. Neither indigo nor morinda are direct dyes. Their use

FIGURE 3-4 (LEFT).
A spinning wheel in use in the Lio village of Wolotopo in 1965. Pelzer Collection, National Anthropological Archives, Smithsonian Institution, Washington.

FIGURE 3-5 (RIGHT).
A girl from Lerek, Lembata, spins with a drop spindle while carrying water. Early 20th century. Koninklijk Instituut voor de Tropen, Amsterdam.

FIGURE 3-6.
Yuliana Yuli da Gomez
prepares morinda dye. Léla,
Sikka Regency, 1985.

involves more complex handling, requiring both skill and hard labor. For this reason, on Flores the use of these dyes is the most highly respected aspect of textile artistry. Accomplished dyers are nearly always mature women with many years of experience (FIGURE 3-6).

The indigo used on Flores is processed from the leaves of leguminous plants belonging to the genus *Indigofera*. In some communities two types of indigo are reported, but it is not clear how these are related botanically.[5] Indigo grows at low and mid elevations, planted in small quantities in door yards or more extensively in fields. The plants put on a flush of new growth during the rainy season, but seem barely to cling to life through the dry. For this reason, indigo dyeing occurs mostly during the wet months. Only fresh leaves are processed, which limits trade in the plant, but bundles of fresh indigo are occasionally sold in the markets.

Chemists classify indigo as a vat dye. This is a category consisting of dyes that are insoluble in water and thus unable to bind with the fiber under ordinary conditions. They become soluble only in the specially maintained oxygen-reduced environment of the vat in which dyeing takes place. On Flores the chemical process of oxygen-reduction is produced by natural fermentation, usually in locally made clay pots. The freshly harvested leaves are submerged in water in the pots for a day or two. In the tropical heat they begin to ferment rapidly and the indigo is released into the water. The leaves are then discarded. Sometimes the yarns are dyed directly in the resultant liquid, but often further processing steps are used to concentrate the dye. The indigo can be chemically precipitated out by adding lime and aerating the solution, which returns the dye to its insoluble oxidized state. It can then be filtered out and retained as a paste. This paste keeps indefinitely and can be re-dissolved as needed, providing that fermentation is maintained. For this purpose additional organic materials are sometimes added to the dye pot. Once processed, the indigo is stored in covered, narrow-mouthed clay pots to limit oxidation. The contents form a decidedly organic ooze, often relegated to a shed on the outskirts of the village due to the foul odor (FIGURE 3-7).

This thick solution is kneaded into the yarn. Afterward the yarn is hung out in the sun, which returns the indigo that has bonded with the fiber to its fully oxidized, insoluble state (this is why indigo is so colorfast). The yarn is then washed to rid it of the muddiness caused by impurities and residual indigo. A clear blue color emerges, pale if the yarn has just been dyed for the first time, but growing darker each time the dyeing is repeated. The deep blue-black that is the desired color on Flores can only be achieved through many successive dye sessions.

Morinda dyeing is even more difficult and demanding. The dye itself is contained in the inner root bark of a small tree, *Morinda citrifolia*, which thrives in hot areas near sea level (FIGURE 3-11).[6] This plant is thought to be native to Southeast Asia, but was so highly

regarded by the Austronesian populations that they purposefully carried it as far as Hawaii. The foul-smelling fruits are valued for medicinal purposes in Java and Hawaii, and the roots are utilized in the Pacific for dyeing mats and bark-cloth yellow or red. In India and Indonesia, dyers mastered the complex procedures required to create red or red-brown tones on cotton.

Morinda is a mordant dye, meaning that a special preliminary treatment of the yarn is required before the dye molecules will bind properly with the cotton fiber. Without a mordant, only a fugitive yellow color would be produced. The mordanting procedures required for red are particularly complicated, involving, at the minimum, oil, alum, and an alkali (Kajitani 1980:318). The way in which these ingredients are applied to the yarn varies from place to place. In addition to the essential ingredients, some dyers add extra plant extracts, guarding their recipes as secrets to be shared only among close associates. These secret ingredients, plus differences in water and procedures, may account for the wide range of tones produced by morinda dyeing. In most parts of Flores, rust red is the desired hue. Endenese dyers are known for achieving a color that approaches true red, a feat that is considered difficult, though not necessarily desirable, in other areas.

In the Ende-Lio region, the oil required for the mordant is obtained by pulverizing the nuts of the candlenut tree (*Aleurties moluccana*). The alkali comes from a lye solution made by pouring water through a basket packed with wood ash. The necessary alum is presumably contained in a third essential ingredient, the dried and powdered leaves of the *lobha* tree.[7] Once these diverse ingredients have been assembled, they are cooked

together into a soapy paste and applied to the yarn (FIGURE 3-8). The yarn is then dried in the sun for several weeks until the mixture is thoroughly absorbed into the fiber (FIGURE 3-9).[8]

The preparation of the dye itself is relatively straightforward, but extremely laborious. The roots must first be excavated from the ground, a task for which the help of male relatives is sometimes enlisted (FIGURE 10-4). The entire tree may be uprooted or, alternatively, a section of the root system can be removed and the hole back-filled. This allows the tree to live and the roots to regenerate for future harvests. Once the inner bark of the roots has been gathered, many hours of labor are required to pound it to a pulp in a mortar (FIGURE 3-10). The pulverized morinda is mixed with water to which a small amount of lye has been added. The pulp is gathered up in the hands and wrung to express the dye (FIGURE 3-12). Powdered *lobha* is also added at this time. Some weavers use only the liquid dye, while others submerge the yarn directly into the pulpy mass. The yarn may be beaten with a piece of wood to assure complete penetration of the dye.

The first dyeing with morinda creates only a pale pink color. Weavers usually repeat the process several times over a period of days, drying the yarn in the sun after each session. More hours of pounding are required as new morinda is added to the pulp saved from previous days. The yarn grows darker each day, but is still nowhere near the desired shade. After a few days, it will be put away until the weaver obtains more morinda and begins a new cycle of dyeing sessions.

Morinda dyeing is to some degree seasonal because the hot sun of the dry months is best for curing the mordant, and also because there is less agricultural work to do in this season. Traditionally, yarn for the finest cloth was dyed over a period of many years, carefully stored in a basket in the house between dyeing seasons. Some weavers say that this aging of the yarn is essential to create the rich colors they most admire. Today many women feel that they can no longer afford to work at this pace, unless perhaps they are making a special cloth for bridewealth purposes. The dyeing cycles may simply be repeated as quickly as the weaver can process more morinda, until she is satisfied with the intensity of the color. If the dyeing progresses well, this may take two to three months.

Other natural dyes used on Flores never achieved the status of indigo and morinda, primarily because they are less colorfast. Nevertheless, dyers knew how to utilize a large number of other plants. In some cases these were used as labor-saving substitutes for indigo or morinda. Other dyes created unusual colors, including yellows, oranges, greens, purples, and browns, that were valued as accent colors to be added as fine stripes separating bands of indigo or morinda yarns. With the increasing availability of synthetic dyes, many of these minor dyes have gone out of regular use and are in danger of being forgotten.

Sappan (*Caesalpinia sappan*) is the most important alternative for reddish tones. In most places it is considered a poor substitute for morinda because it is not as colorfast and does not produce as rich a red-brown tone. In the Ngadha areas, where the use of morinda is unknown, alum from *lobha* leaves is used as a mordant with sappan to produce a somewhat

FIGURE 3-10 (LEFT). Martina Minu pounds morinda bark in a mortar. Onelako, 1988.

FIGURE 3-11 (RIGHT). Root, leaves, and fruit of *Morinda citrifolia*. The dye is contained in the inner bark of the root.

deeper and more colorfast shade. In Manggarai, a pinkish red produced with sappan is a favored color for supplementary-weft motifs. Several other plants are used for red in various places, but these have so far been identified only by their local names.[9]

A mud-dyeing process was used as an alternative to indigo in the Ngadha and Lio areas. The yarns were first boiled with various types of bark containing tannin, then submersed in the mud of a buffalo wallow, to which algae or other plant matter had been added (Arndt 1963:150). This is a variant of a dye process found in many parts of the world, based on the interaction of iron in the mud with tannin in the fiber to create a blackish color. The algae presumably enriched the iron content of the mud. Mud dyeing is no longer practiced anywhere on Flores. Yarns dyed to blue-black with indigo are sometimes over-dyed to obtain a true black. This is done by boiling the yarn with various types of bark or wood.[10]

A number of plants can be used for yellow, the most common being turmeric. This dye is fugitive in water, but lasts well when used for bridewealth cloths, which are not ordinarily washed. *Kayu kuning* is another source of yellow, used locally and also exported from Manggarai to Java for use in the batik industry.[11] Morinda (without the complex mordant) and mango bark are additional sources of yellow. Greens are produced by over-dyeing indigo with yellow dyes. Many Sikka textiles contain stripes of bright yellow-green produced in this way. Lio headcloths feature a border of blue-green yarns made by over-dyeing pale indigo with a green dye made from the bark and leaves of mango trees.

FIGURE 3-12.
A weaver in Nggela prepares a dye bath in a container made out of palm spathe. The dye has been squeezed out of balls of morinda pulp. On top of the pile of yarns ready for dyeing are plain white yarns to be dyed for the first time and ikat yarns that have already been dyed with indigo. Underneath are both plain and ikat yarns that are nearing completion, yet still require a few more dye sessions to reach the proper depth of color. 1988.

FIGURE 3-13.
Sisilia Sii works at her loom, making a panel for a man's shoulder cloth (*sémba*). Leaning slightly foreward to reduce tension on the warp, she uses her thumb and index finger to lift the heddle rod, while pushing down with her ring and little fingers on the shed stick. This opens the shed (or gap) between the alternating sets of yarns, allowing her to insert the beater with her right hand. Coordinating these movements requires strength and skill. Onelako, 1991.

LOOMS

Three types of body-tension looms are used on Flores. All are rather similar in terms of their general operation (FIGURE 3-13). They differ primarily in the method of putting the warp onto the loom, which is in turn related to the type of warp beam used and to the presence or absence of a reed, a device that maintains spacing between the warp yarns. Additional variations, such as in the type of back brace or shuttle, are related more to regional preferences than to the functioning of the loom. Some of the decorative techniques, most notably supplementary weft, require additional loom parts.

The most basic of the three loom types has no reed and uses a circular warp (FIGURE 3-14 A).[12] This loom is pan-Indonesian. In the large islands to the west it is now used primarily among the small-scale societies of the interior, having been replaced elsewhere by more advanced types of looms. In the Lesser Sundas it remains the predominant type. It is used in nearly all weaving areas on Flores except in Manggarai and along the north coast of Ngada Regency.

This loom is simple to set up because, at least in theory, the warp is put onto the loom as a single filament, wrapped continuously around the beams.[13] With no reed to maintain spacing, the warp yarns lie closely packed and will completely hide the weft in the finished fabric. This warp-faced weave structure is ideal for cloth that carries its patterning in the warp, because the weft yarns do not interfere visually. Therefore this is the loom of choice for weaving warp-ikat fabrics. It was also once used for heavy plain or striped fabrics, but these types of cloth are rarely made today.

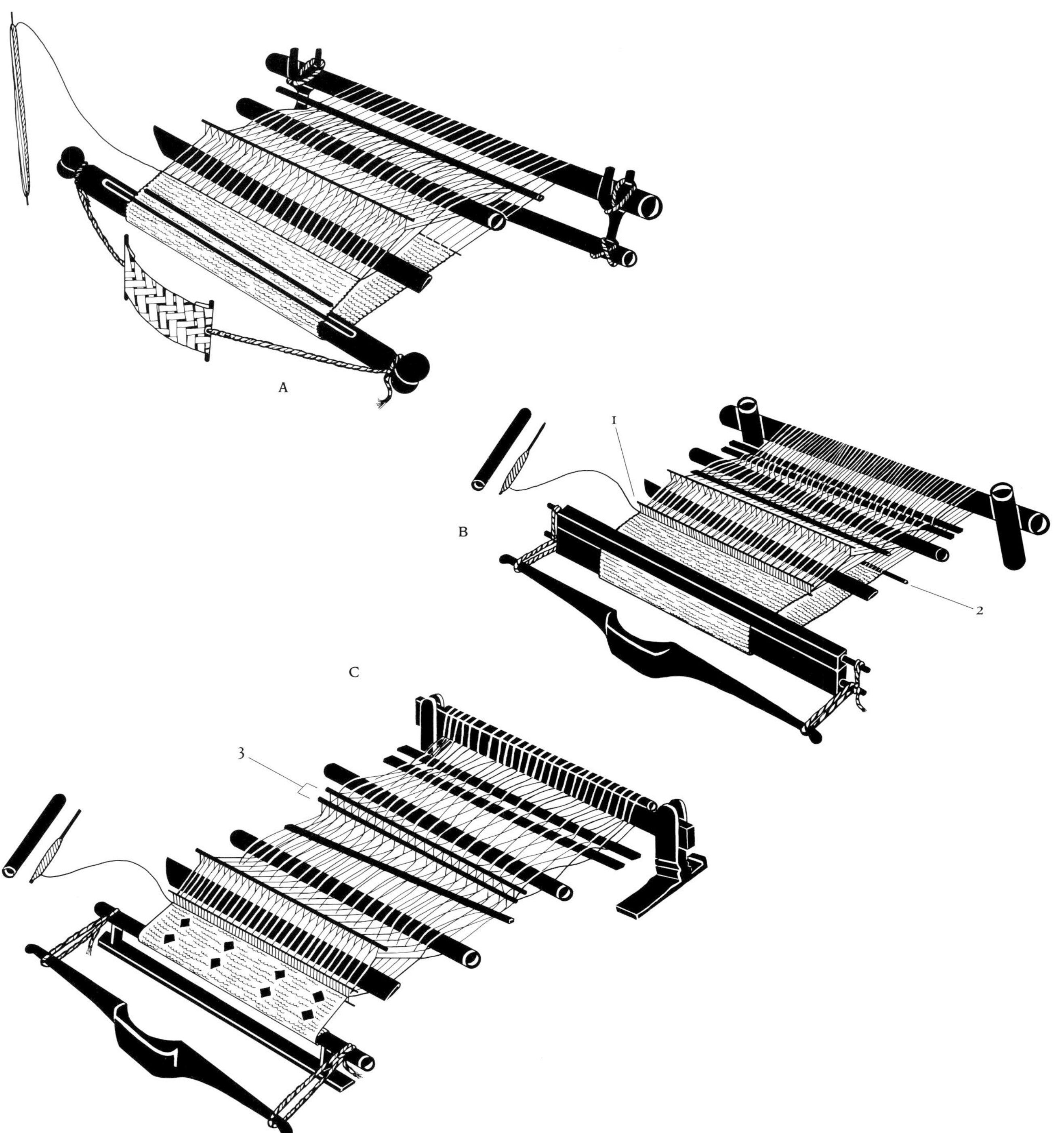

The second type of loom looks very much like the first except for the addition of a reed, which is a rectangular frame holding hundreds of fine slats of bamboo (FIGURE 3-14B). The warp yarns pass through the spaces between the slats. This spacing creates a balanced weave structure, with the warp and weft appearing more or less equally on the surface of the cloth. A reed is therefore desirable if any of the patterning is to be carried in the weft, as in plaid, weft-striped, or weft-ikat fabrics, but such cloth is not very common on Flores.

To warp this type of loom, the weaver must pass the warp yarns through the openings in the reed. Indonesian women have an ingenious system for doing this without cutting the yarn into separate warp ends (FIGURE 4-15). Loops of yarn are pulled through the reed

FIGURE 3-14, A–C.

A. Basic loom with a circular warp.

B. Loom with a false-circular warp, showing the reed (1) and warp connecting rod (2).

C. Loom with a flat warp, showing additional heddles (3) for supplementary-weft weft weaving.

For more details, see APPENDIX B.

FIGURE 3-15.
Rosa Delima layers bundles of warp yarn on a stretching frame (*dao*). Directly in front of her lie four bands of yarn bundles. The bundles were measured out on a warping frame, stretched to even tension, and then counted out one-by-one to assure the correct number for the desired pattern. Now the four bands are about to be layered together, with the corresponding bundles in each group bound together to form the new, thicker bundles to be mounted on the tying frame. The tie in the weaver's hand will remain in place, allowing the four bands to be separated in proper order once the tying and dyeing are complete. Onelako, 1988.

and secured around a connecting rod. The yarn on the other side of the reed is passed around under the loom and secured around the same connecting rod. This produces a "false circular" warp. Although it is not simply wound around the loom like the true circular warp on the first type of loom, it acts the same on the loom because it is held together in a circular form by the connecting rod.

This loom is limited to Sulawesi and other nearby parts of the archipelago that were in close communication with Sulawesi in historical times (Yoshimoto 1991). On Flores it is used primarily by Lio weavers for making warp-striped men's sarongs and in Tonggo for making supplementary-weft sarongs. The use of the reed was presumably brought to Flores when migrants from Sulawesi established coastal communities there.

The third type of loom has a reed like the second, but is distinguished by its warp beam. Instead of a simple round beam, it uses a plank set in an upright frame (FIGURE 3-14C). The warp is wound onto the plank. This is a technological advance that, in theory, allows enough warp for several cloths to be put onto the loom at once. In practice, weight is a limiting factor and on Flores weavers ordinarily make only enough cloth for a single sarong at a time.

As this loom is set up, the warp is passed through the reed in the same manner as with the second type of loom. At the end of the procedure, however, both ends of the warp are secured with separate rods and the connecting rod is withdrawn. The warp can then be stretched out flat to its full length in preparation for winding onto the warp beam plank. This warp structure is referred to as a "flat" warp.

This loom is more widespread than the second type, occurring throughout western Indonesia and on Bali, Sulawesi, and Sumbawa. On Flores it is found only in Manggarai and in the Riung and Mbay areas along the north coast of Ngada Regency. All of these areas were either ruled or settled from Goa and Bima. Because this region of Flores is renowned for making supplementary-weft cloth, the use of this loom is strongly associated with the supplementary-weft technique. The same loom is used in these areas for plain or plaid fabrics, however.

WARP IKAT

Justifiably the most famous textiles from Flores are those decorated with the warp-ikat technique. This is a resist-dye procedure that bears some similarity to the tie-dyeing known in the West, but what is dyed in this case is not the finished cloth but the warp yarns still in their unwoven state. Bundles of these yarns are bound tightly in selected places. The knotted bindings resist the dye, preventing it from reaching the fiber. All elements of the design must be dyed in the proper place on the warp yarns before they are mounted on the loom. Only when the cloth is woven do the designs take on their finished appearance.

It is this demanding procedure that creates the distinctive look of the island's most spectacular textiles. From the territory of the Ngadha people in the west to Lembata in the east, this is the principle means of decorating women's sarongs. Men's sarongs are not decorated with warp ikat except in the Ngadha region, Palu'é, and parts of East Flores. In several regions, however, men's shoulder cloths are made with this technique.

Whether making a sarong or shoulder cloth, the procedure for producing the designs on the warp yarns is identical. The basic steps involve:

1. Arranging the warp yarns on a tying frame.
2. Tying the resist knots.
3. Removing the yarns from the frame and dyeing the first color.
4. (OPTIONAL) Removing some of the resist knots, and in some cases tying additional ones, then dyeing the second color.
5. Removing all ties and arranging the yarns on the loom.

The first step, arranging the warp on the tying frame, is quite complex. Basically, the warp yarns are wrapped onto a warping frame to assure the proper length and then grouped in small bundles, typically consisting of four to eight strands. Each of these bundles will form one unit of the design. The weaver knows how many bundles she will need for each part of the design, depending on its size. Designs that appear on narrow bands in the finished textile will require only a few bundles. More complex designs occurring in wide bands or in a broad central field may require dozens of bundles. These fine bundles are then grouped into larger bundles by folding or layering the warp yarns (FIGURE 3-15). This step is necessary to create a bundle thick enough for the bindings to be properly tied. It also saves work by allowing several identical parts of the pattern to be tied at one time, which accounts for the way designs often repeat geometrically over the surface of the cloth.

The details of how these procedures are accomplished vary considerably from place to place. In some areas all of the bundles that make up a particular pattern are wound onto the frame as a continuous filament. Weavers who use this practice say it is essential for keeping the pattern aligned properly when put onto the loom. In other areas, however, weavers deliberately sever the yarn to make each bundle an independent unit. This gives them flexibility in adjusting the pattern when it is time to arrange the warp on the loom.

FIGURE 3-16.
On the tying frame, resist knots are tied around the bundles of warp yarn, using strips of palm leaf fiber. The pattern for this center panel of a Lio woman's sarong features large elephant motifs (*nggaja*) interspersed with smaller horses (*jara*) and various geometric motifs. The motif consisting of four diamonds (*mata sa liwu*) represents a set of four gold ear ornaments, one of the required bridewealth goods in Lio marriages. Onelako, 1988.

Once the yarns are on the tying frame, the work of tying the resist knots begins (FIGURE 3-16). Fine strips split from the leaf of the *gebang* palm (*Corypha elata*) are the preferred tying material because of their strength. In some places weavers use coconut or pandanus leaves in the same manner. Ngadha weavers choose bast fiber from the *waru* plant (*Hibiscus tiliaceus*), widely used on Flores for making twine. In recent years some weavers have begun to employ strips of the plastic ribbon that is used in shops to tie packages. Whatever the tying material, it is essential that the knot be placed with precision, so that the pattern will be distinct in the finished cloth. The knots must also be tightly tied, so that no dye will seep underneath after months or even years of dye sessions.

Typically the yarns required for a complete garment are prepared at one time. If all will not fit on a single tying frame, some of the pattern bands are tied on a second frame. Because the various bands will later be rearranged on the loom, the weaver has a great deal of flexibility. Sometimes she puts extra yarns on the frame, perhaps to make up for some that did not come out well in a previous project, or to purposefully create extra yarns to save for a future project.

When tying is complete, the weaver removes the yarn from the frame and dyes it with the first color, usually indigo. If only a two-color pattern is desired, then the knots are removed after the first color is dyed and the warp is ready to be arranged on the loom. The natural white of the cotton fiber where it has been protected from the dye constitutes the second color. Ngadha and Nagé ikat work is largely limited to white-on-indigo in this way. A white-on-morinda color scheme is less common, but does occur in some Lio, Sikka, and Lamaholot weaving. Obviously a great deal of effort is saved if the ikat work is limited to a single dye. The finished cloth can be made more colorful by alternating bands of different colors.

More complex color schemes rely on over-dyeing. Typically the first dye is indigo and the second, morinda. For a three-color pattern, some of the ties are removed before the morinda dyeing (FIGURE 3-17). Where the yarn remained tied through the dyeing of both

FIGURE 3-17. Warp yarns, already dyed with indigo, are returned to the tying frame with the resist knots still in place. Some knots will be removed, revealing white spots where the indigo has been prevented from reaching the fiber. These white areas will turn red when the yarns are dyed with morinda, while the areas that are now blue will become nearly black. The ties that are left in place throughout will produce white motifs in the finished cloth. Nggela, 1988.

colors, it retains its white appearance.[14] Where the ties were removed between the two dye colors, the fiber was protected from the indigo but exposed to the morinda, so it takes on a red color. Where the yarn remained untied throughout, it was exposed to both colors and becomes nearly black (the result of over-dyeing blue-black indigo with red-brown morinda).

Endenese weavers rely predominantly on this three-color scheme, but some Lio, Sikka, and Lamaholot cloths are made with four-color ikat. In this case, not only are some ties removed between the two dye colors, but new ones are added as well. Where the new ties were added, the yarn is exposed to the indigo but then protected from the morinda. This leaves small spots of indigo blue in the finished design. The complete color scheme consists of white, indigo, red, and black. This simple list of basic colors, however, does not do justice to the rich variety of shades actually produced.

When the dyeing is complete, the remaining resist knots are removed from the yarn and the warp is ready to be arranged on the loom. If the pattern is a banded one, the bands are organized in the proper order and the narrow stripes of plain yarn that separate the ikat bands are added. The ikat designs are adjusted to make them as clear as possible and the warp is lashed to a cross-stick to hold it in place. The final preparation can now be made for weaving, including tying in the heddles and sizing the warp with starch made from corn, rice, or tamarind seeds.

SUPPLEMENTARY WEFT

Over much of the western part of Flores, the most elaborate textiles are not made with the warp-ikat technique, but rather with supplementary weft. This technique is so named because the yarns that make up the motifs are extra yarns, running in the weft direction, that are woven into the textile in addition to its basic warp-and-weft structure (FIGURES 3-18, 3-19). On Flores supplementary-weft motifs are executed with polychrome yarns on a blue-black or black ground. In some cases the supplementary yarn is continuous, passing from selvedge to selvedge, but more often it is discontinuous, with widely spaced motifs created by the use of separate pieces of yarn worked simultaneously during the weaving process.

Supplementary-weft weavers recognize two levels of skill. The less skilled weavers use a series of pattern sticks or heddles, which raise the proper warp yarns to create the desired motifs. This results in the repetition of rows of identical motifs along the surface of the cloth. A woman who doesn't know the patterns must arrange to have the pattern sticks or heddles inserted in her loom by someone who specializes in this task. Schematic diagrams of patterns are sometimes kept on a banana leaf, run through with bamboo skewers to indicate the correct placement of the pattern sticks.

FIGURE 3-18. Supplementary-weft decoration on a cloth photographed in Mbay, Ngada Regency. The basic warp and weft are black and the colored yarns are worked into the cloth as weaving progresses.

FIGURE 3-19.
Hadija Kambo, wife of Abu Bekar Sepi, works at her loom in Mbay. The back of the cloth faces the weaver, who uses her fingers to insert the colored supplementary-weft yarns. A series of seven supplementary heddles create the simpler part of her pattern (the bands of continuous color). For the larger, more complex motifs, however, she uses only two extra heddles, which provide the proper lifts but require her to create the pattern anew each time from memory. 1992.

More skilled supplementary-weft weavers work without pattern sticks. Instead they use only a single pair of extra heddles, which raise alternate groups of three warp strands each. These provide the proper lifts for inserting the colored yarn but do not program the motif. The weaver can then create from memory whatever motif she desires. This type of work is more highly valued and is readily distinguished from the other because the successive rows of motifs are not identical. Weavers who work with this method can theoretically create free-form, pictorial motifs, although this type of work is a recent innovation. Patterns are sometimes recorded on sheets of graph paper, just as in Western needlepoint. Some of these patterns have been issued by the church-owned publishing house that is the main source of books on Flores.

OTHER DECORATIVE TECHNIQUES

Other decorative techniques used on Flores include supplementary warp, warp float, tapestry, twining, and weft ikat. All of these are of minor importance compared to warp ikat and supplementary weft. They occur only in limited areas or, in some cases, are no longer used at all.

In supplementary-warp weaving, the basic solid-colored structure of the weave remains unchanged and the pattern is carried by additional yarns of a contrasting color, running in the direction of the warp and worked in as the weaving progresses. The finest examples of supplementary-warp weaving on Flores are the Lio bags known as *pundi*, which have not been made for several decades. Supplementary-warp weaving survives most notably in the Lamaholot region, where it is used for making men's belts (FIGURES 3-20, 3-21) and for the decorative bands that appear on some women's sarongs (FIGURES 8-26, 8-27).

In warp-float weaving, the basic structure of the warp is composed of alternating strands of two colors, one of which is made to float over the top of the other out of the normal sequence to create the pattern. The warp-float technique is used to add simple

FIGURE 3-20.
Detail of a man's belt (*mét*) from Léwotala, East Flores, showing the supplementary-warp technique. Both warp and weft are red, with the white supplementary yarns passing from back to front as required to create the pattern. Collection of Penelope Graham.

FIGURE 3-21.
A Léwotala woman puts modern furniture to a novel use, bracing her loom by attaching it to the legs of a table. She is weaving two supplementary-warp belts simultaneously. 1987.

motifs to narrow warp stripes. These are most often found in Lio men's sarongs and also in a distinctive style of shoulder cloth that is known best from Manggarai but also occurs in the Lio and Sikka regions (FIGURE 3-22).

A simple tapestry technique also appears in these same shoulder cloths; it is worked in the form of a row of small triangles along the edge of a solid-colored centerfield. The same technique is also used in Manggarai to create a special border in some sarongs (FIGURE 4-18). Elsewhere it is very nearly forgotten.

The most extensive use of twining is found in vests made of ramie fiber in Ngada Regency (see CHAPTER 5). Twining also appears as a finishing technique on shoulder cloths, to keep the fringe from unraveling. This is usually only a plain double row, but occasionally two colors are used to work simple motifs in slightly wider bands. Weavers rarely bother with this technique today, preferring simply to tie the fringe ends off in groups or perhaps braid them.

Weft ikat involves the resist dyeing of the weft yarns rather than the warp. On Flores this technique is found only in the Sikka region, where it is used in making men's sarongs (FIGURE 3-23). The history of this tradition is not clear, but it is probably of recent origin. The nearest important centers of weft-ikat weaving are on Sulawesi, Bali, and Lombok. ❖

NOTES, page 269.

Garment Assembly

Small textiles such as belts, headcloths, and narrow shoulder cloths consist of single pieces of cloth and are essentially complete when they are taken off the loom. Sarongs and wide shoulder cloths have to be assembled from separate pieces of cloth.

Working with a circular warp, the weaver stops when she no longer has enough room to insert her beater and shuttle. The loom parts are simply withdrawn from the warp, leaving a piece of cloth in the form of a loop, with a small unwoven gap where the weaver was forced to stop weaving. For a shoulder cloth, the weaver simply cuts across the middle of this gap. The cloth can then be opened flat and the cut ends form the fringe. For a wider cloth, two such pieces are sewn together selvedge to selvedge (**A**).

Among most ethnic groups, women's ikat sarongs are made of three panels, woven separately. Each is cut open at the gap, just as for a shoulder cloth, and the panels are then sewn together side by side. This creates a large flat cloth with the cut warp ends running like a fringe down both sides. These are trimmed off and the sides of the sarong are seamed together to form a tube. As the sarong is worn, the warp runs horizontally across the body (**B**).

There are a few exceptions to this basic procedure. In Soa, an area in Ngada Regency, the woman's lower-body garment was once a "mini" sarong made of a single panel. Rarely sarongs are made of four or more panels, a structure occasionally seen in the Lio and Lamaholot areas. In the Nagé area, the panels are sewn together without cutting through the unwoven section of the warp. A gap remains in the finished sarong, but is folded out of sight when the sarong is worn (**C**). This same procedure is followed in some Lamaholot areas if the sarong is intended for use in bridewealth exchange rather than as apparel. There is an ideological aspect of this procedure, as the uncut warp is said to symbolize the bind between the kinship groups organizing the marriage. To cut the warp is prohibited, because it would sever this bond and disrupt the fundamental structure of society.

Two-panel sarongs are sometimes woven on the loom as a single large piece of cloth. In this case, a wider loom and a longer warp are used. The long loop of finished cloth is cut once across the unwoven gap and again across the center of the piece. This leaves two identical pieces which are then sewn together in mirror image (**D**). The end result is wider and shorter than the typical three-panel sarong. This technique is used most often for men's sarongs or for supplementary-weft sarongs worn by either sex. It is used for making women's ikat sarongs only in the Sikka region and parts of East Flores.

Two-panel sarongs made in this way often maintain a design format that is visually tripartite (FIGURE 8-9). This suggests that two-panel construction is a more recent innovation, adopted in areas that once produced typical three-panel sarongs. In the Sikka region, women's sarongs are usually stored and exchanged as bridewealth goods in the uncut form, in which their patterning appears asymmetrical (FIGURE 7-5). Symmetricality is produced only when the two pieces are sewn together in mirror image.

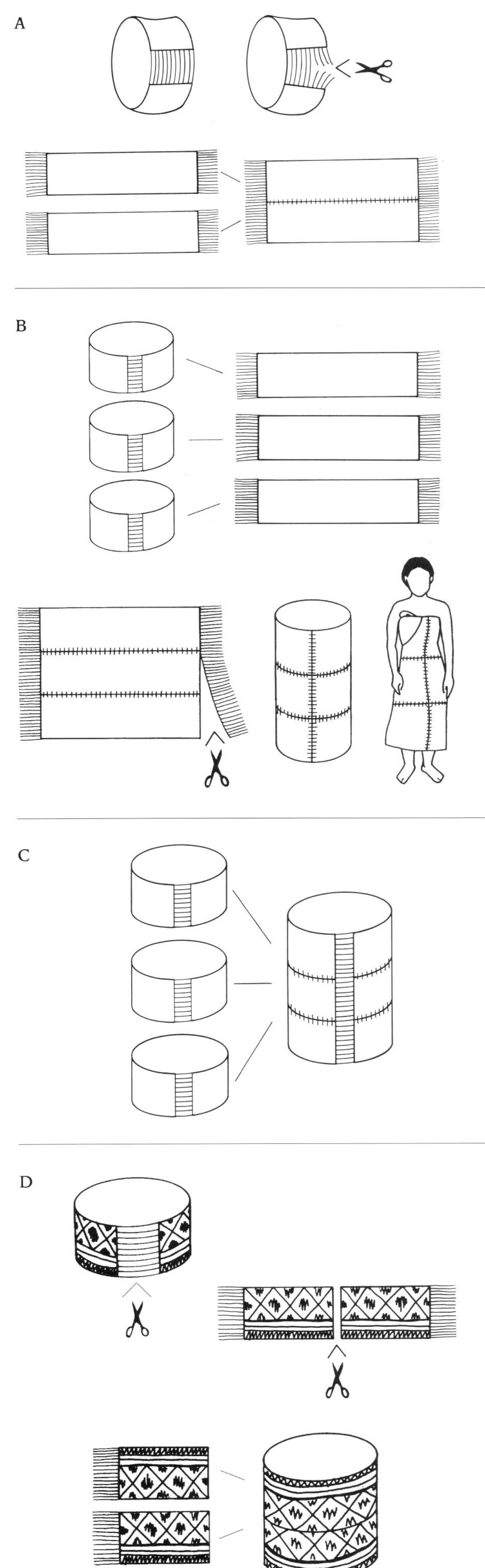

REGIONAL SURVEYS

4

Manggarai Regency

ROY W. HAMILTON

MANGGARAI, WITH A HALF MILLION INHABITANTS, IS THE MOST POPULOUS of the five regencies on Flores. The island is at its widest here and the relatively greater proportion of amply watered upland accounts for Manggarai's reputation as a productive rice-growing region. The landscape is dominated by an extensive volcanic massif that includes the 2,400-meter peak Ranakah, the highest on Flores. From the summit, one can look out over much of central Manggarai. Ruteng, the capital, sits perched on a gently sloping shelf at the foot of the massif. Beyond, the land breaks into a chaotic jumble of mountains cut by deep river gorges. Much of this landscape has been transformed over the past several decades by the building of irrigated rice terraces (FIGURE 4-2). Efforts to build roads into remote sections of Manggarai increased in the 1980s, but many parts of the regency are still without wheeled transportation.

Following the Dutch defeat of Goa in 1669, a protracted struggle for control of Manggarai developed between Makassarese exiles and the Sultan of Bima. In 1722 a son of the sultan married a Makassarese princess, but this attempt at marriage diplomacy failed. In the military conflict that ensued, Bima finally gained uncontested control over Manggarai (Gordon 1975:50-55). The region came to be divided into numerous units called *dalu*, a system that may have evolved as a means of administration and tax collection by overseas rulers. Shifting alliances among dependent *dalu* further atomized the political structure. By the dawn of colonial administration in the early twentieth century, Manggarai consisted of no less than thirty-five separate *dalu*.

The Dutch colonial government elevated the leader of Todo, then the most powerful *dalu*, to the newly created position of Raja of Manggarai. Following Indonesian independence, administration was reorganized to create a system of eight districts under the regency government. Today a bewildering number of overlapping place names are in use. Although the *dalu* structure is no longer operative, *dalu* names are still

FIGURE 4-1 (OPPOSITE).
Detail of FIGURE 4-12.

FIGURE 4-2.
Irrigated rice terraces have almost completely replaced the dry, circular fields divided into wedge-shaped plots that were once a characteristic feature of Manggarai farming.

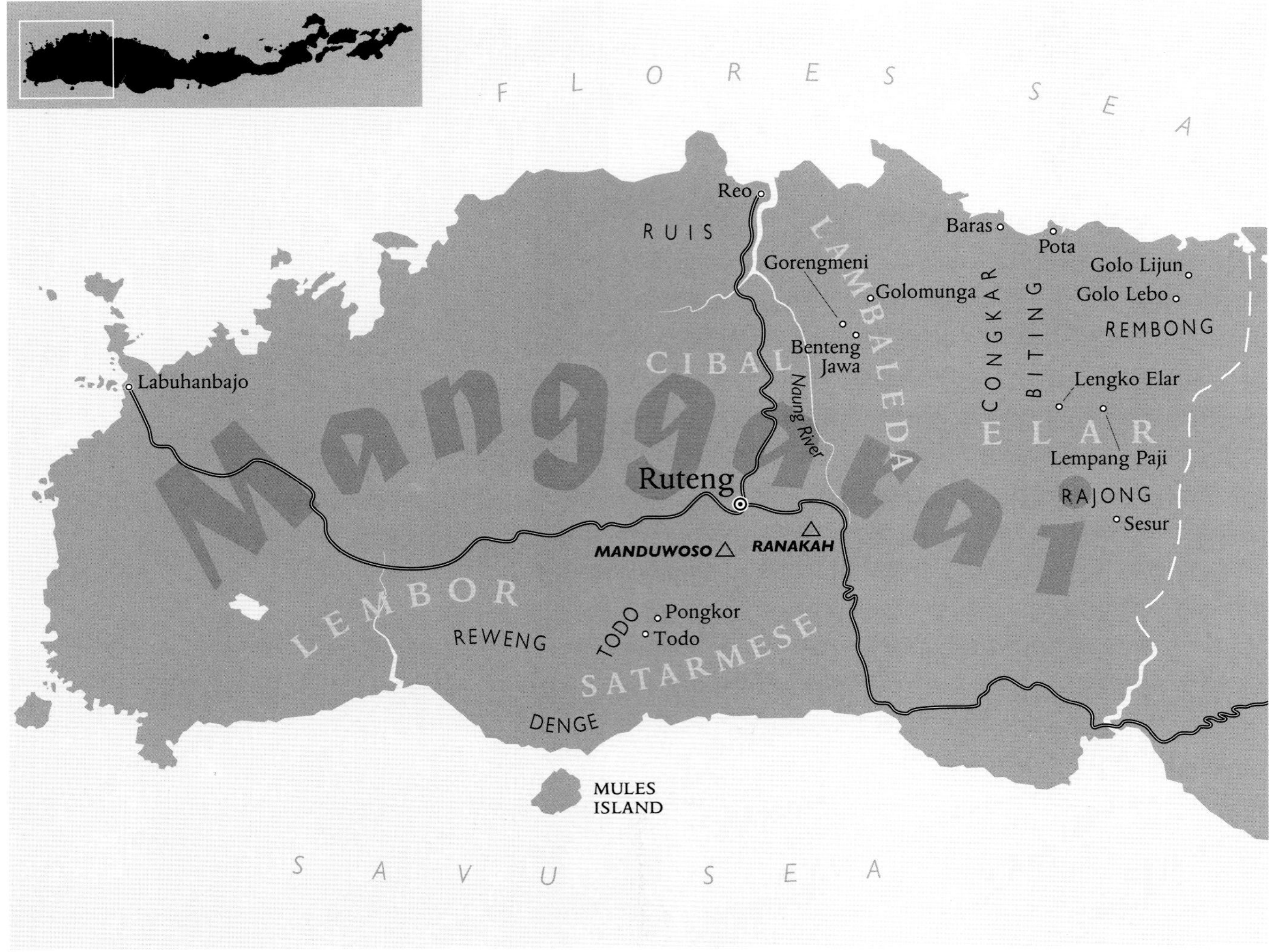

frequently used in referring to different sections of the regency, as are the names of the parishes of the Roman Catholic Church.

In terms of ethno-linguistic classification, the people of western and central Manggarai are relatively homogeneous. The eastern part of the regency is more diverse, with several small language groups living in remote areas. These include the Rembong and Rajong in northeastern Manggarai.[1] Another cluster of small groups is found in the southeast. In some port communities along the north coast, such as Pota, Bimanese is still spoken.

Despite Manggarai's interesting history and ethnic diversity, its textile traditions are rather limited compared to the other regencies. There is no weaving at all in most of the regency and no ikat anywhere. Weaving is found in two separate areas. The smaller of these is centered in the former *dalu* of Todo, located southwest of Ruteng on the slopes above the south coast. The more extensive area stretches from north central Manggarai to the border of Ngada Regency in the northeast. This area includes the former *dalu* of Cibal, Ruis, Lambaleda, Biting, Congkar, and Rembong. Lambaleda is the most renowned weaving area, so much so that the supplementary-weft sarongs (*lipa songké*) produced there are usually considered the archetypal Manggarai textiles (FIGURE 4-3).

The people of Manggarai often like to describe themselves as having a knack for adapting quickly to change. This is evident in the matter of costume. Garments that clearly were not indigenous have been adopted and then abandoned again, scarcely leaving a record. A good example is a type of knee-length pants, constructed of four leg-panels and four large gussets, that were once common in Manggarai (FIGURE 4-8). Tailoring of this sort is not indigenous to Indonesia, but was derived from Islamic garments and widely adopted in western parts of the archipelago. Linguistic evidence suggests it came to Manggarai via Bima, as the term *déko* is used for these garments in both places (Maxwell 1990:413). According to one story (Verheijen 1967:340), an eighteenth-century Manggarai nobleman named Mungkur embraced Islam while residing in Bima and adopted this style

FIGURE 4-3.
Two women from the village of Pongkor wear ceremonial head ornaments (*lando andung*). Their *lipa songké* sarongs are not made in their own village, which is in a non-weaving area. This type of sarong is primarily associated with the distant *dalu* of Lambaleda, although it is made in other areas as well and is worn throughout Manggarai. 1965, Pelzer Collection, National Anthropological Archives, Smithsonian Institution, Washington.

FIGURE 4-4 (LEFT). The striped background fabric of this tunic is similar to the heirloom fragment from Soa (FIGURE 2-16). Both textiles are decorated with appliquéed bands of red trade cloth. The roundels of shell beads, with metal discs at their centers, are the only known Manggarai equivalents of the beaded forms found on Ngadha and Lio women's sarongs (FIGURES 5-14, 10-6). 1993.

FIGURE 4-5 (RIGHT). A young dancer in Manggarai wears a *selémpang* as a shoulder cloth. From Vroklage 1939, fig. 3.

of pants. Afterward, he was known in Manggarai as Keraéng (Lord) Déko. Today, few of these garments survive in Manggarai.

Even rarer today is a type of tunic preserved by descendants of noble lineages in Todo and Ruteng (FIGURE 4-4). According to a report from Todo, such garments were worn by certain nobles who had the right to adjudicate disputes, while in Ruteng it is said that they were worn for warfare or particularly important ritual occasions.[2] The cut of the tunic is an imported style, but warp-striped fabric of this type appears in other parts of Flores and was probably manufactured locally.

The high degree of change has also obscured the history of one of Manggarai's most characteristic textiles, a fringed, rectangular cloth with a solid-color centerfield. In most cases the tapestry technique is used to create a row of tiny triangles where the centerfield joins the borders, but in one unusual example these triangles are imitated using the supplementary-weft technique (FIGURE 4-6). These cloths are clearly modeled after the Bimanese cloth known as *salampé*.[3] In Manggarai today, the term *selémpang*, or its Indonesian variant *selendang*, is normally used. The cloths were used as shoulder cloths (FIGURE 4-5) or wrapped as outer garments over men's trousers, in the Islamic fashion. Some were undoubtedly imported from Bima, but others were made in most, if not all, of Manggarai's weaving

FIGURE 4-6.
This *selémpang,* with supplementary-weft triangles along the edge of the center field, was made in the *dalu* Cibal prior to 1937. Most *selémpang* today have yellow centerfields and red borders (see FIGURE 6-34), but this cloth demonstrates that other color combinations were used as well. 208 x 65 cm. Rijksmuseum voor Volkenkunde 2319-23, Leiden.

districts. Similar cloths were also made at least as far east as the Lio and Sikka regions (FIGURES 6-34, 7-2), although they were used primarily as shoulder cloths in those areas. Today this type of cloth is rarely seen in Manggarai and only the most simplified versions continue to be made.

Selémpang once appeared as part of the costume used for whip-dueling, a traditional form of entertainment in Manggarai (FIGURES 4-7, 9-3), but today the more readily available *lipa songké* are often used instead. Whip-dueling matches are held following the harvest, roughly in August. They remain one of the high points of the calendar in rural Manggarai and attract huge crowds, especially when contestants from neighboring districts compete. Manggarai whip-dueling is but one of several variant forms of ritualized combat common to a number of societies in the Lesser Sundas. It has also evolved into a performance genre, with organized troops performing for visitors or special events. In the contest, the defendant is equipped with a round shield (*nggiling*) that protects the front of the body and a long arching piece of rattan (*agang*) held over the head to deflect the blows of the whip. His opponent takes the whip and tries to strike the defendant. When blood is drawn, the men exchange equipment and the defendant takes his turn on the offense.

TODO

Todo was once the most powerful and highly organized *dalu* in Manggarai. At its center, the village of Todo contained a particularly impressive clan house, surrounded by

FIGURE 4-7. Whip-duelers wearing *selémpang* over trousers prepare for combat in this photo from the 1920s. The defendant, on the left, holds the bent rattan *agang* over his head, while his opponent grips the whip. Several men wear highly decorated head protectors (*panggal*) in the shape of buffalo horns. Koninklijk Instituut voor de Tropen, Amsterdam.

a series of stone constructions. The people of Todo claim they are the descendants of migrants from the Minangkabau region of Sumatra, who introduced iron smelting and cloth weaving to Manggarai (Coolhaas 1942:342). This claim may be plausible, since Minangkabau traders have settled throughout Indonesia, but it must be treated with some skepticism. In the Lesser Sundas, similar legendary accounts of descent from prestigious, distant places are often promulgated in attempt to bolster claims to political authority.

Whether textiles might provide support for this claim is an interesting question, unfortunately with no conclusive answer. The textiles of Todo are unusual in that most are made in checked or plaid plain-weave, as opposed to the supplementary-weft cloths characteristic of other Manggarai weaving districts. Reliance on this form of decoration in Todo could be interpreted as being consistent with the claim to Minangkabau descent, since some Minangkabau groups make plaid cloths similar to the ones produced in Todo, but so do many other Islamic peoples in Indonesia.[4] It seems likely that Todo weaving is more directly related to the former practice of making similar types of checked, plaid, and striped cloths in many other parts of Flores, especially in Islamic coastal areas. At least one elderly informant in Todo maintains that weaving was introduced to Todo only in this century, via Endenese living on nearby Mules Island.[5] It is not clear why this type of cloth continued to be made in Todo, while more highly decorated types of cloth made with more sophisticated techniques prevailed in other places. Perhaps the unique role of the Todo people as an elite in Manggarai was a factor. In the colonial period, the splendor of the Todo nobility was expressed primarily through non-indigenous materials and techniques, such as metallic-yarn embroidery (FIGURE 4-8).

Elders in Todo can still describe the making of a number of types of garments that are no longer produced. Woven cotton loincloths called *tarip* were worn as late as the 1950s by men working in the fields.[6] A flat wrap-around garment called *selendang kerut* was worn for horseback riding. It was made of a single panel of cloth with no fringe, woven in red-and-white plaid and secured around the body with a woven belt, *selendang pesikok*. Plaid headcloths called *sapu curuk* featured fine stripes on a red or white ground, surrounded by a dark border.[7] Unfortunately, examples of these everyday cloths do not appear to have been preserved in museum collections.

The most characteristic Todo cloth, still woven today, is a plaid or checked, two-panel sarong called *lipa curak*, or sometimes simply *lipa Todo*, worn by both men and women. The traditional colors are dark blue, red, and white. In many older cloths the warp and weft stripes are widely spaced, creating a somber open plaid (FIGURE 4-9). Other

FIGURE 4-8.
This outfit of jacket and pants was worn by Todo nobility during the colonial period. The jacket is decorated with couching and the pants with supplementary weft in metallic yarns. Both garments represent imported styles and the techniques are more typical of western Indonesia. Modeled in Todo in 1992.

FIGURE 4-9.
This indigo-dyed, plaid sarong (*lipa curak*) was collected in Todo prior to 1913. Similar plaid sarongs were made in many parts of Flores, but only in Todo have such simple cloths remained the predominant type of weaving. Rijksmuseum voor Volkenkunde 1833-6, Leiden.

cloths, more popular today, feature equal amounts of red and blue appearing in small checks (FIGURE 4-10). The blue color was once dyed with indigo and the red with sappan. Indigo dyeing can occasionally be found in remote villages closer to the coast, but is no longer practiced in Todo village. Even the oldest women in Todo village say that they have always used pre-dyed commercial yarns for any color other than indigo.

Todo cloth was once bartered to non-weaving regions of Manggarai, most often in exchange for water buffalo. Barter for rice was less common, because grain was difficult to transport over Manggarai's relatively long distances. In recent decades buffalo have become less important in the economy, as they have in many parts of Flores. One reason for this is the weakening of the system of traditional religious rites that required the sacrifice of buffalo. Another factor is change in land-use patterns, which put an end to the former practice of running large herds of semi-wild buffalo over the countryside. By 1970 the weaving industry in Todo had nearly died out, perhaps as a result of the lessening importance of cloth as a means to obtain buffalo, and also due to the relatively widespread adoption of Western garments in Manggarai.

In the past two decades, however, weaving has made a substantial comeback as a cash-earning activity. The sale of cloth is now a leading source of village income and weaving is very much geared to the requirements of the marketplace. Todo weavers confess with a laugh that they beat twice after each pick of the weft when making cloth for their own use, but only once if the cloth is intended for sale. This compromises the quality of the cloth, but economizes on labor and materials. Many *lipa curak* are made with new color schemes utilizing the full range of yarn colors available in the markets (FIGURE 4-11). Todo weavers have also learned to make supplementary-weft sarongs modeled after Lambaleda cloth. This borrowed style, which is more marketable outside Todo than plaid *lipa curak*, now accounts for a significant portion of production.

Today the Todo weaving area encompasses about a dozen villages in Satarmese District, which includes the old *dalu* of Todo. These villages are located in two parishes, Todo and Denge. An additional five villages in Reweng parish, located across the boundary in Lembor District, are part of the same tradition. In the late 1980s, the people of Todo proudly celebrated the completion of a road connecting their region to the Ruteng-Labuhanbajo highway. They constructed this rock-bedded road themselves, entirely by hand labor, in a development program led by the parish priest. The weekly market in Todo village is thriving due to this new link and has become an important outlet for Todo textiles. Work continues on the road, now complete as far as the south coast, bringing more of the weaving villages into the modern transportation network.

LAMBALEDA, CIBAL, AND RUIS

The best-known cloth produced in Manggarai is the supplementary-weft *lipa songké* (FIGURE 4-12), a sarong worn by both

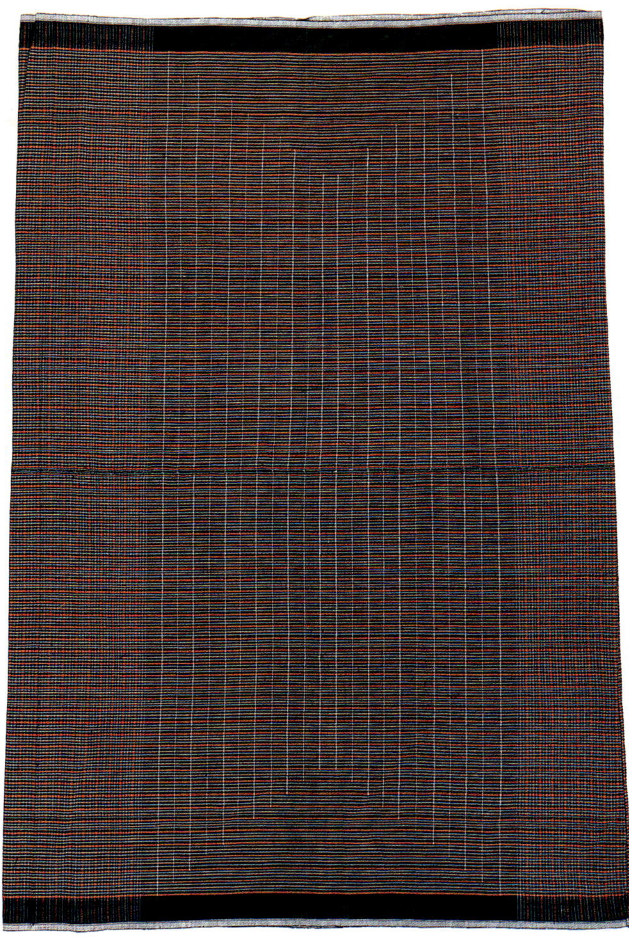

FIGURE 4-10.
Modern *lipa curak* from Todo typically feature smaller, more colorful checks, such as this example made of colored commercial yarns in 1990. FMCH X91.1614, Museum Purchase, Manus Fund.

FIGURE 4-11.
A Todo woman sews together the two panels of a *lipa curak*. This color combination is considered less traditional than indigo and red. Todo, 1991.

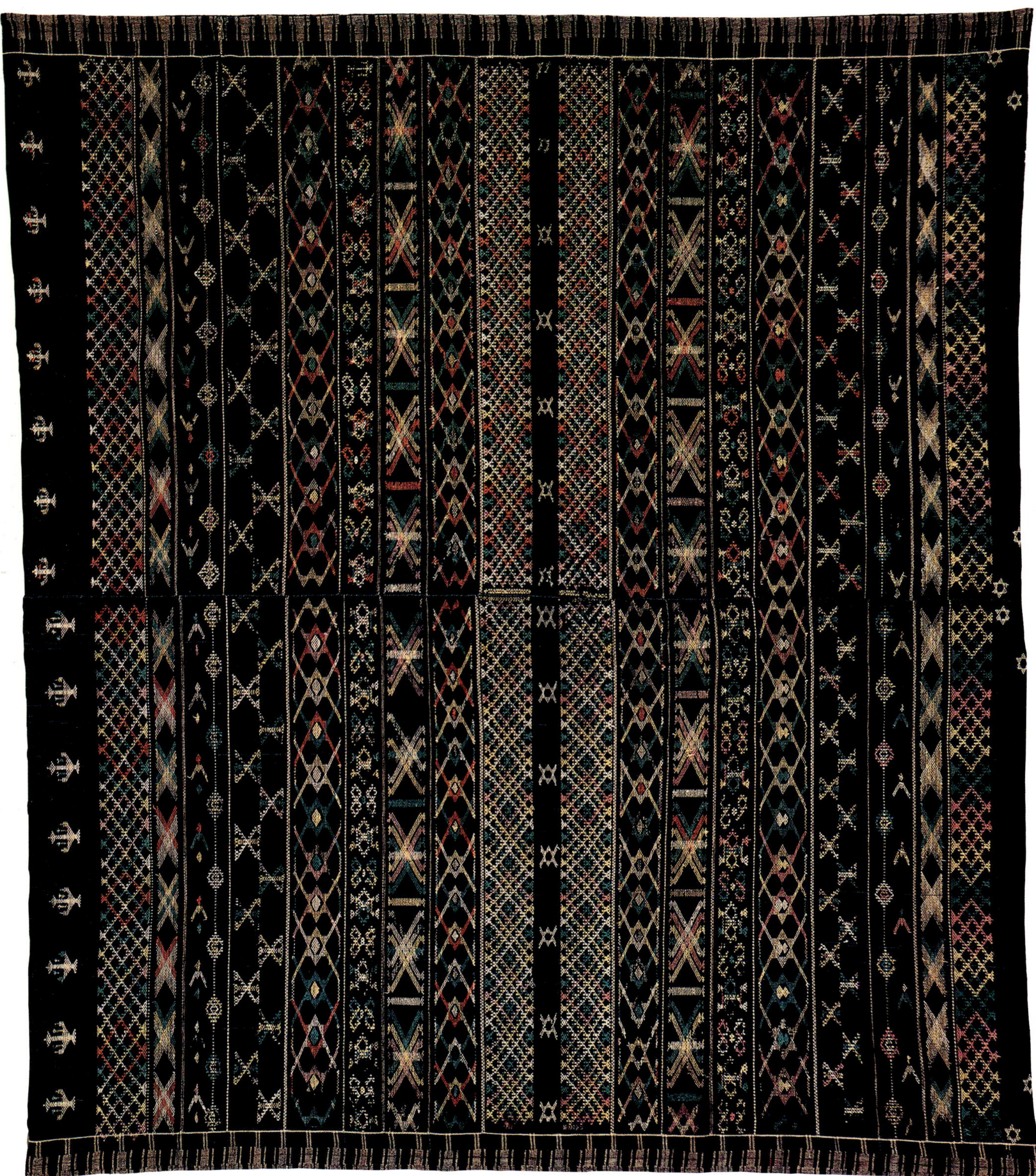

FIGURE 4-12.
Lipa songké sarongs are made
in Lambaleda and a few
neighboring *dalu.* The precise
point of manufacture of this
cloth is unknown. National
Gallery of Australia 1984.1987.

men and women.[8] Visually, the sarong is divided into two sections, one more highly decorated than the other. This design format is common in western Indonesia, where the main section is known as the body (*badan*), and the specially decorated section as the head (*kepala*). In most western Indonesian cloths the head is narrower than the body, but Manggarai weavers say the highly decorated section should cover fully half of the cloth. This is not always done, however, because it is costly in labor and materials.

The blue-black background fabric on the plain side of a *lipa songké* may be entirely unadorned, or it may be decorated with a few widely spaced rows of simple motifs executed in the discontinuous supplementary-weft technique (FIGURE 4-13). The other side of the cloth is densely covered with more elaborate discontinuous motifs, usually interspersed with bands of continuous supplementary weft.

A distinctive feature of high-quality *lipa songké* is a colorful border of small triangles called *jok*, which is worked along the selvedge with the tapestry technique. The *jok* border represents the Manggarai version of the triangular *tumpal* design found on textiles from India and many parts of Southeast Asia. It appears as well in Bimanese textiles and this was presumably the source of its introduction to Manggarai.

Red, yellow, and white are the traditional colors for *lipa songké* motifs. In the past the red was dyed with sappan and the yellow with turmeric, morinda, or *kayu kuning*. These fugitive dyes faded into pastel shades that are one of the delights of Manggarai cloth. The background color was dyed with indigo, sometimes over-dyed with various types of wood or bark to darken the color. Today indigo dyeing and handspun yarns can still be found in some villages, but pre-dyed commercial yarns are always used for the supplementary-weft work.

The recognized center of *lipa songké* production is the former *dalu* of Lambaleda. Within this area, the villages of Golomunga and Gorengmeni include a number of hamlets that are considered to be the traditional heart of the *lipa songké* weaving area. These villages are located near Benteng Jawa, the modern administrative center of Lambaleda District. The Lambaleda weaving region extends beyond this core area and now encompasses a number of other villages stretching from the north coast to mid elevations in the interior. Much of this area is still quite isolated, although the tortuous road connecting Benteng Jawa to Ruteng is now passable by public transportation. There is no weaving in the highest villages in the southern part of Lambaleda District.

Across the deep gorge of the Naung River, and much more accessible to Ruteng because it straddles the Ruteng-Reo highway, lies Cibal District (formerly the *dalu* Cibal). Despite Lambaleda's recognition as the center of *lipa songké* weaving, similar cloths are made throughout Cibal. Leaving Cibal, the highway from Ruteng descends

FIGURE 4-13.
Reverse side of the sarong in FIGURE 4-12. The discontinuous supplementary-weft motifs on the sparsely decorated side are normally spaced in an even grid, but this cloth shows a more open, though not entirely random, arrangement. There is no fixed rule about which way the sarong faces when worn. 130 x 109 cm. National Gallery of Australia 1984.1987.

through a series of gorges to the port of Reo. The surrounding area, the *dalu* Ruis, is also a weaving region.

If there were once traditional motifs or styles unique to each of these areas, it is difficult to distinguish them on the basis of today's cloths. To some extent the style of cloth produced in Lambaleda has become the norm to be imitated in the other districts, and recent innovations have further obliterated regional distinctions. The range of patterning observable in museum cloths may represent localized variations, but unfortunately such cloths are rarely accompanied by reliable documentation regarding their village of origin. Further research is needed to validate the claims some informants make regarding locally distinctive motifs (FIGURE 4-14).

The *lipa songké* is now regarded as the centerpiece of traditional costume throughout central Manggarai. Women wear this garment rolled under their arms, leaving the shoulders bare, or else combined with a long-sleeved blouse. For ceremonial occasions, a head ornament called *lando andung* may be added (FIGURE 4-3).[9] Ceremonial dress for men includes the *lipa songké*, a shirt of Western tailoring, a square batik headcloth from Java, and a shoulder cloth. Currently the most widely used type of shoulder cloth is a narrow, fringed scarf decorated with supplementary weft. This garment is a relatively recent creation, popular with tourists as well as with the people of Manggarai. It is made in all of the *lipa songké* weaving areas and usually referred to as *selendang*, the Indonesian term for scarf-like cloths.

CONGKAR, BITING, AND REMBONG

In the northeastern corner of Manggarai lies Elar District, one of the most isolated parts of the regency. The administrative center at Lengko Elar, in the interior, was only recently connected by a long, rough road to Ruteng. Entry to the northern sections of the district is by boat from Reo to Pota, a port community founded by Bimanese traders, fishermen, and weavers (FIGURE 4-15).

FIGURE 4-14 (OPPOSITE). Some differences in patterning can be observed between this *lipa songké*, which has been attributed to Reo (Gittinger 1979:168), and the one in FIGURE 4-12. Because no comprehensive survey has been made in Manggarai, it is unclear whether these differences represent distinctive local styles or simply individual variation. 175 x 113 cm. The Textile Museum 1978.4, Washington.

FIGURE 4-15 (LEFT). These Bimanese women, photographed in Pota in 1926, put warp yarns through the reed (visible beneath the elbow of the woman at the right). Such weavers presumably served as the link that brought Bimanese textile designs to the weaving districts of northeastern Manggarai. Koninklijk Instituut voor Taal-, Land- en Volkenkunde, Leiden.

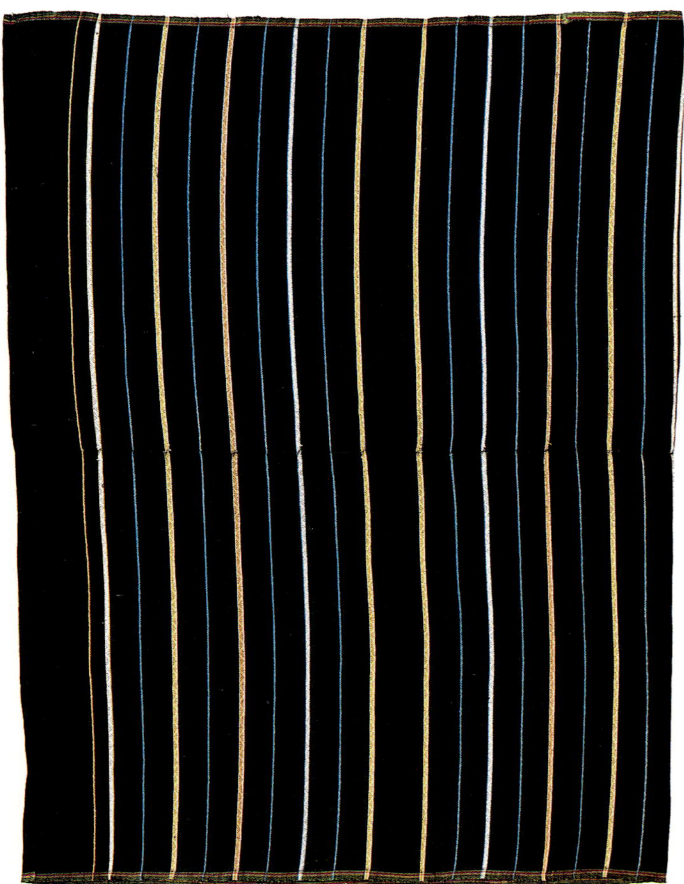

FIGURE 4-16.
Decorations on the characteristic cloth of the *dalu* Congkar (called *naé sudi* or sometimes *kain su'i*) are limited to simple rows of continuous supplementary weft. The back side is plain. Made in Baras in 1991. 133 x 97 cm. FMCH X91.1616, Museum Purchase, Manus Fund.

The district encompasses the former *dalu* of Congkar, Biting, Rembong, and Rajong. There is no weaving in Rajong, which is located high in the interior, but the other three *dalu* are known as traditional weaving centers. The sarongs produced in these areas are different from those of Lambaleda, although they are generally based on the same techniques and on a similar division of the sarong into two differently patterned sections. Each area is associated with its own types, although these have yet to be thoroughly documented. A number of different design permutations can be found and it appears that some types are made in more than one area.

The type of sarong most identified with Congkar is called *naé sudi* and is decorated with only a few narrow bands of continuous supplementary-weft work spaced across one side of the sarong (FIGURE 4-16).[10] The other side shows only the plain blue-black ground. Although simply decorated, these sarongs are distinctive when worn because of the strong vertical orientation of the design. The motifs that appear in the supplementary-weft bands are very simple, created with a small number of pattern sticks (*téti,* "to lift").

The bands themselves are called *punca téti*, stripes made with pattern sticks. Traditionally only one color was used, a light blue known as *ula* dyed with indigo. This accounts for an alternative name applied to these cloths, *punca ula*. Commercial yarns in other colors, especially yellow and white, have long been available and are now commonly added to the color scheme.

The Congkar terminology strongly reflects the influence of Sulawesi in the textiles of this region. *Punca* is a variant of the Makassarese *puncang*, which designates the more highly decorated "head" section of a sarong. *Sudi* is derived from *subi*, a Sulawesi name for the supplementary-weft technique (Kartiwa 1986:62–62).

In Biting, the predominant type of sarong is somewhat more complex (FIGURE 4-17). The warp is blue-black with widely spaced stripes of light blue. On one side of the cloth these intersect with plain-weave weft stripes, creating a grid of large open squares. On the more highly decorated side, the plain-weave stripes are replaced with bands of continuous supplementary weft. These are of the same simple patterns and limited colors as in the Congkar sarongs.

In Rembong, a number of different design formats are produced. The plainest are blue-black sarongs entirely undecorated except perhaps for a tapestry-weave border, which in Rembong is called *kaet* rather than *jok* (FIGURE 9-7).[11] Another simple style, called *lipa léleng lauk*, is plain on one side and has only a few light blue plain-weave weft stripes on the other (FIGURE 9-6). Rather than the *kaet* border, a plain warp stripe of light blue runs along the selvedge.

The type of sarong for which Rembong is best known, however, is closely modeled after the Bimanese cloth *weri* (FIGURE 1-22).[12] It is the most elaborately decorated sarong made in Elar District. The background fabric has plain-weave stripes running in both warp and weft directions, creating a grid structure like that found in the sarongs of Biting. These stripes are composed of yarns of both light and medium shades of blue. This accounts for the name *lipa pungsa ula zua* (sarong with stripes in two shades of blue) often applied to these sarongs. On the more highly decorated side, the spaces within the grid are filled with discontinuous supplementary-weft motifs. Rembong weavers call these "stars," *talaq* (FIGURE 4-18). They are created with pattern sticks, known in Rembong as *ghun*, and weavers refer to the various motifs according to the number of pattern sticks required.[13] Rembong women are permitted to weave these motifs only after the final stage of their marriage rites has been performed, which may not take place until middle age (see CHAPTER 9).

Because each area of northeastern Manggarai is associated with particular styles of sarongs, it is often possible to tell at a glance where a person has come from. The best opportunity for observing this is at the weekly market at Pota, which draws participants from all over northeastern Manggarai (FIGURE 4-19). In recent times, however, many weavers have learned to make styles that originated in neighboring districts. This is particularly true in coastal settlements, where newcomers from various hill communities have sometimes settled side by side. The movement of women upon their marriage is a particularly important factor in the spreading of patterns.[14]

All across the supplementary-weft weaving areas of Manggarai, from Cibal to Rembong, the communities considered to be the original centers of weaving are located in the mid-elevation hills several miles inland from the coast. Higher mountain areas, such as Rajong or the southern portions of Lambaleda, are non-weaving. In villages immediately on the shore, where weaving is now common, weavers invariably trace their descent from inland weaving centers. This is because the low coastal hills and plains were largely depopulated due to the ravages of the slave trade. Bimanese trading and fishing communities such as Reo and Pota developed on the coast, but the indigenous communities were located inland for safety. Only after pacification in the early twentieth century did groups of people from the interior hills begin to settle in new communities on the coast, bringing with them the textile designs of their natal villages.

Although historical factors have thus played a role in the distribution of weaving communities, the underlying basis for the division between weaving and non-weaving populations is ecological. Weaving villagers in the mid-elevation hills were dependent on the bartering of textiles for food produced higher in the mountains, in non-weaving areas. Such a relationship prevailed, for example, between Rembong and Rajong (see CHAPTER 9). When settlements developed on the coast in this century, they were even more dependent on trade relationships due to the extreme harshness of the coastal climate.

FIGURE 4-17.
The patterning of this sarong is regarded as a Biting style (see also FIGURE 4-19), but this example happens to be worn by a woman in Cibal. 1991.

An example can be found in the coastal community of Baras, a few kilometers walk along the beach from Pota. Baras is now an active weaving community, but women acknowledge that their weaving industry was transplanted from the original centers inland. Though Baras is technically in Congkar, it has been settled by people from Biting as well. Both Biting and Congkar styles of sarongs are made today and some weavers imitate Lambaleda styles as well. Until very recently, Baras was a difficult area for farming. Only cotton, and perhaps corn if the rains were good, could be grown on the dry coastal plain. Surplus cotton was traded inland to the main Congkar weaving centers. Finished textiles were bartered for rice or, more often, corn. The measure used for corn, equal to fifty bundles of twelve ears each, was *ca lipa*, literally "one sarong." Today Baras has a reliable rice crop, but only because an irrigation system was completed in the early 1980s.

The making of supplementary-weft textiles, and the underlying social and economic conditions that have shaped production and trade, do not come to a halt at the border between northeastern Manggarai and Ngada Regency. The many similarities that prevail across that border, in Riung and Mbay, will be explored in the next chapter. After an examination of those traditions, some further conclusions about the place of supplementary-weft weaving on Flores will be drawn. ❖

NOTES, page 270.

5

Ngada Regency

Roy W. Hamilton

THE SPECTACULAR CONES OF TWO VOLCANOES, INERIE AND EBULOBO, dominate the landscape of Ngada Regency. In general terms, the Ngadha[1] people (FIGURES 5-2, 5-3) live in the west in the area surrounding Inerie and the Nagé-Kéo live in the east around Ebulobo. However, this is a somewhat oversimplified picture that does not do justice to the high degree of ethnic diversity in the region. Recent field research has uncovered so many localized cultural differences in the Ngadha areas that it is now difficult to speak of Ngadha customs in a general way.[2] The same is true of the Nagé-Kéo, whose very name is a compound uniting the Nagé, who live around the town of Boawae on the north side of Ebulobo, with the related Kéo, who live on the southern slopes.

During the colonial era, the Ngadha and the Nagé-Kéo were under the authority of two separate rajas, at Bajawa and Boawae respectively. The territory of the Raja of Boawae (FIGURE 5-4) stretched from coast to coast and encompassed a variety of different peoples,

FIGURE 5-1 (OPPOSITE). Detail of FIGURE 5-17.

FIGURES 5-2 (LEFT), 5-3 (RIGHT). The ceremonial costume for Ngadha men (LEFT) includes a shoulder cloth (*lu'é*) folded across the chest and a hide bag (*lega*). Ngadha women of the same period (RIGHT) wear head ornaments and wrap their hair over a large gourd (*kobho*). Circa 1920. Koninklijk Instituut voor de Tropen, Amsterdam.

who have sometimes been lumped together misleadingly as Nagé-Kéo. Some groups, such as the people of the Ndora region east of Boawae, are closely related to the Nagé, but others are more distinct. The south coastal community of Tonggo developed after Endenese settlers intermarried with the up-slope Kéo population. On the north coast, the mixed Islamic community of Mbay was historically predominant, but in the surrounding area are several other small, inadequately known groups.[3] The patterns of barter in this part of Flores were unusually complex, involving a high degree of interdependence across ethnic lines. For example, Mbay cloths were used by all groups in the region. Yet Mbay itself was not self-sufficient in textiles, for it relied on Nagé cloth for bridewealth and funeral exchanges.

The territory of the Raja of Bajawa stopped short of the north coast, but did encompass a broad interior valley known as Soa. In the northwestern quarter of the regency, at Riung, the Dutch recognized a third raja. Riung, like Mbay, is an historically important community of mixed Islamic descent. In the sparsely inhabited and roadless hills surrounding Riung, language and customs appear to differ from one community to the next; the cultural affinities in this region remain poorly known.

Given the extreme degree of ethnic variation throughout the regency, the distribution of textile styles is one of the best keys to understanding the relationships among groups. The textiles of the Ngadha people represent a distinct tradition, typified by warp-ikat cloths

FIGURE 5-5 (OPPOSITE, LEFT).
This woman's sarong illustrates the white-on-indigo color scheme and bold sense of design characteristic of Ngadha ikat work. Red is uncommon in the cloths of the Ngadha, who never mastered morinda dyeing. The *kondo* strings used to tie the sarong closed at the shoulders are visible at the top (see FIGURE 5-13). 174 x 79 cm. FMCH X92.354, Gift of Frank R. Wiggers.

FIGURE 5-7 (ABOVE).
The ikat work in Nagé textiles is also limited to indigo dyeing, but plain morinda-dyed bands are interspersed when the warp is arranged on the loom. Men's rectangular cloths (*sada*) were worn as hip-wrappers or as shoulder cloths. They may also have been used as saddle blankets (Maxwell 1990:69). Purchased in Ende in 1929. 216 x 108 cm. Museum für Völkerkunde 27558, Frankfurt.

FIGURE 5-6 (OPPOSITE, RIGHT).
The supplementary-weft cloths produced in several coastal areas of Ngada Regency differ radically from Ngadha and Nagé textiles. The most famous center of supplementary-weft production is Mbay, where this shoulder cloth (*sapang*) was made. In the early 1980s it was obtained by a man from Raja in exchange for antique coins (*dinar*), then given to his wife-takers near Boawae as a funeral gift. 314 x 70 cm. FMCH X91.1621, Museum Purchase, Manus Fund.

with simple white motifs on an indigo ground (FIGURE 5-5). Nagé weavers produce a different style of cloth, separating bands of indigo-dyed ikat with bands of plain red (FIGURE 5-7). In the mixed Islamic coastal areas, including Mbay, Riung, and Tonggo, the supplementary-weft technique predominates (FIGURE 5-6).

NGADHA

The town of Bajawa, located in a mountain bowl, is the urban center of the Ngadha people and the capital of Ngada Regency (FIGURE 5-8). It is the highest town on Flores and also the smallest of the regency capitals, with a population of only 10,000. Prior to Dutch administration there was little sense of political unity in the surrounding region. Despite the high degree of cultural variation, in general terms the Ngadha peoples can be defined by a few shared cultural traits that set them apart from their neighbors. The most obvious of these are the distinctive *ngadhu* and *bhaga* ceremonial structures found in the village plaza (FIGURES 5-9, 5-10).

Ngadha villages range in elevation from sea level to nearly 6,000 feet. Localized variation in climate influenced textile production, especially in the past when all cloth was made from home grown cotton and natural dyes. Cotton was cultivated at low elevations, especially along the south coast and in the Soa valley. Indigo was grown throughout the

FIGURE 5-8.
The Dutch developed Bajawa as an administrative center in part because of the temperate climate of its mountain setting. As in many communities on Flores, the Roman Catholic church is the predominant structure.

FIGURE 5-9 (OPPOSITE, BELOW). Umbrella-like *ngadhu* are prominent ceremonial structures in Ngadha villages. *Ngadhu* are "male"; their "female" counterparts are the small house-shaped structures called *bhaga*, one of which can be seen in the background between the two *ngadhu*. Both types of structures serve as focal points of clan ritual. Beneath the *ngadhu* on the right is a small temporary *bhaga*, used until the clan is able to mobilize enough resources to construct a full-scale one. Wogo village, 1965. Pelzer Collection, National Anthropological Archives, Smithsonian Institution, Washington.

low and mid elevations. Nevertheless, some weaving was practiced even in high mountain villages such as Mangulewa, the highest settlement on Flores. The people of this village grew cotton on land they owned in nearby Soa and produced plain garments dyed with mud instead of indigo.

The more important Ngadha weaving villages were located where indigo could be grown and Ngadha informants today usually list three areas as the traditional centers of ikat production.[4] Two of these, Jerebuu and Langa, are parishes located in a valley that runs under the east flank of Inerie. The third area, sometimes said to be the original home of ikat weaving in the Ngadha region, is called *gholé*, meaning "behind the mountain." This refers to a pair of hamlets, Lopijo and Teni, located behind the highest peak on the rim of the mountain bowl that surrounds Bajawa. These hamlets are today the most isolated communities in the Ngadha region and, in terms of textile production, the most conservative. The use of locally grown cotton and indigo is still the norm. Cloths are made in a number of traditional styles no longer produced in areas more geared toward selling in the Bajawa market. The pace of production is leisurely and the product is a heavy, dark cloth with small, rather indistinct ikat motifs, admired for its authenticity throughout the Ngadha territory.

Textiles in the Ngadha region were once ranked according to the age and status of the wearer. Upon initiation, and then again later in life with the hosting of community feasts, individuals earned the right to wear progressively more elaborate types of cloth. The most costly types of feasts were only within reach of the upper strata of society, so the garments associated with these events were essentially markers of aristocratic status. Today informants are reluctant to talk about such class distinctions, which no longer carry the weight of traditional law, but there is still a sense in some communities that the most prestigious garments are appropriate only for individuals of high social standing.

This system seems to have functioned throughout the Ngadha region, although there were many variations in the types and names of the cloths involved and in the forms of the rituals that qualified individuals to wear them. In Lopijo and Teni such rituals have become rare, but they were common until fairly recently and informants can still describe the various stages involved. A male child wore a plain sarong called *ragi mbiri*.[5] When he became a teenager, and demonstrated his competence by working his own garden, he joined other youths in a series of initiation and circumcision rites called *rupa*. Following circumcision, the initiates were isolated in the forest for a period of up to three months. They returned to the village dressed in new garments referred to collectively as *isi wio ghi'u*. *Isi wio* was the shoulder cloth and *ghi'u* the sarong. Both were dyed with indigo and featured rows of simple ikat motifs. These garments signaled marriageability and later remained a man's daily dress well into married life.

When a man reached mature status in the community and was in a position to host a traditional feast requiring the slaughter of buffalo, he was entitled to adopt a new set of garments, *sapu lu'é* (FIGURE 5-12). These garments, still made in Lopijo today, are decorated with narrow bands of simple horse (*jara*) motifs. Separately, the sarong is referred to as *sapu jara* and the shoulder cloth as *lu'é jara*.

Headcloths (*boku*) and belts (*keru*) are part of the man's costume. The *boku* is a rectangular cloth, dyed with sappan. Supplementary-warp belts are made to wear with *isi wio ghi'u* (FIGURE 5-11), while ikat belts with matching horse motifs are made to wear with *sapu lu'é*. As belts are now becoming rare, they are no longer necessarily matched with the proper corresponding garments. The *lu'é* is often folded and worn crossed across the chest. A common way of wearing the *sapu* is with a small flap, called *lema lako* (dog tongue), folded down at the front.

Young girls traditionally wore two-panel sarongs called *lawo wa'i manu* (chicken-foot sarong), which are rarely made now. These are indigo-dyed garments decorated with small three-pronged ikat motifs resembling chicken feet. When a girl matured she participated in a tooth-filing ceremony and graduated to a three-panel sarong called *lawo wua wera*.[6] This garment marked her marriageability and was decorated with the same motifs as the corresponding men's garments, *isi wio ghi'u*. When a mature women assisted her husband in hosting a traditional feast, she could then wear the sarong *lawo jara*. This garment has the same horse motifs as her husband's *sapu lu'é*, arranged in bands across the surface of the sarong (FIGURE 5-13).

As a couple's status grew with the hosting of additional feasts, women's garments progressed through at least two more levels.[7] As only couples of the highest social standing could accomplish this, these garments were effectively limited to the aristocracy.[8] The *lawo sora* has a number of additional ikat motifs, including *tubha* (spear), *lengé tubha* (spear

FIGURE 5-10 (ABOVE). *Ngadhu* post in an abandoned hamlet, Toda village, 1965. With its thatched roof rotted away, the forked top of the post is revealed. Related forms occur among several ethnic groups (FIGURE 5-33). Pelzer Collection, National Anthropological Archives, Smithsonian Institution, Washington.

haft), *nggaké* (butterfly), *faga* (mantis), *ika* (fish) and *rogo* (crab), all arranged in bands. The highest status woman's sarong, *lawo kéto*,[9] features horse motifs arranged not in bands but in a broad field covering the entire center panel of the three-panel sarong. The value of the sarong was calculated in accord with its status level. A *lawo wua wera* traded for one pig. A *lawo jara* was worth one horse. A *lawo sora* was worth a buffalo with horns half as long as a man's arm. A buffalo with horns fully the length of a man's arms was equivalent to a *lawo kéto*.

With the exception of the plain *ragi mbiri*, all these garments are still made in Lopijo and Teni today. They are not ordinarily worn as everyday garments, but are in demand as ceremonial wear in Bajawa and throughout the Ngadha region. Ceremonial costume today appears at church rites, as well as at more traditional celebrations such as *reba*, the major agricultural-cycle rite that takes place in Ngadha villages during the rainy season, or *ka sa'o* (to feed the house), the dedication ceremony for a new lineage house.

Further research is needed to determine to what degree there may have been regional differences in the motifs of the various Ngadha weaving centers. Cloths preserved in museum collections are of little use in addressing this question, because the precise point of origin is rarely documented (FIGURES 5-14 through 5-17, 5-5). A few old cloths known to be from Jerebuu and Langa demonstrate that these areas once produced very fine textiles, some of them much more boldly designed and clearly dyed than the cloth made in Lopijo and Teni today. In the past, Lopijo and Teni cloth probably equaled this standard as well. Some traditional production continues in both Langa and Jerebuu, but Langa in particular has in recent years become a center of modernized production. Weavers there now make large quantities of chemically dyed sarongs with bands of small horse motifs. These are sold as everyday garments in the Bajawa market.

An unresolved question regards the presence of motifs representing elephants. In Lopijo and Teni weavers say they never had an elephant motif, but some Bajawa informants disagree. There are indeed Ngadha sarongs and shoulder cloths that include a stick figure zoomorph identical to a motif found on Endenese textiles, which is invariably identified in Ende as an elephant (*nggaja* in Endenese). Ngadha weavers are less certain, often identifying the motif as a horse. In Ende this motif is quite standardized, but in the Ngadha region it varies enough to remain open to differing interpretations (compare FIGURES 5-5, 5-14, 5-16, 5-18, 5-19).

A published account of Ngadha textiles mentions two distinct categories of high-status sarongs, *lawo nggaja kedhi* (little elephant sarong) and *lawo nggaja mézé* (big elephant sarong), based on this motif (Maxwell 1983). According to some Ngadha informants, however, *nggaja* is an Endenese word. The proper Ngadha textile name, they say, is *gaja,* which does not mean elephant, but simply denotes something superlative or extraordinary.[10] In Jerebuu, elders sometimes identify cloths belonging to the highest status individuals in the community as *lawo gaja* or *lu'é gaja* even though the motif in question is absent. The name in this case refers to the status of the cloth rather than its patterning. Garments of this sort garnered great respect. In Mangulewa it is said that clan leaders were able to put a stop to warfare by spreading open their *lu'é gaja* shoulder cloths for all to see. If this gesture was disregarded, it was believed that a terrible catastrophe would ensue.

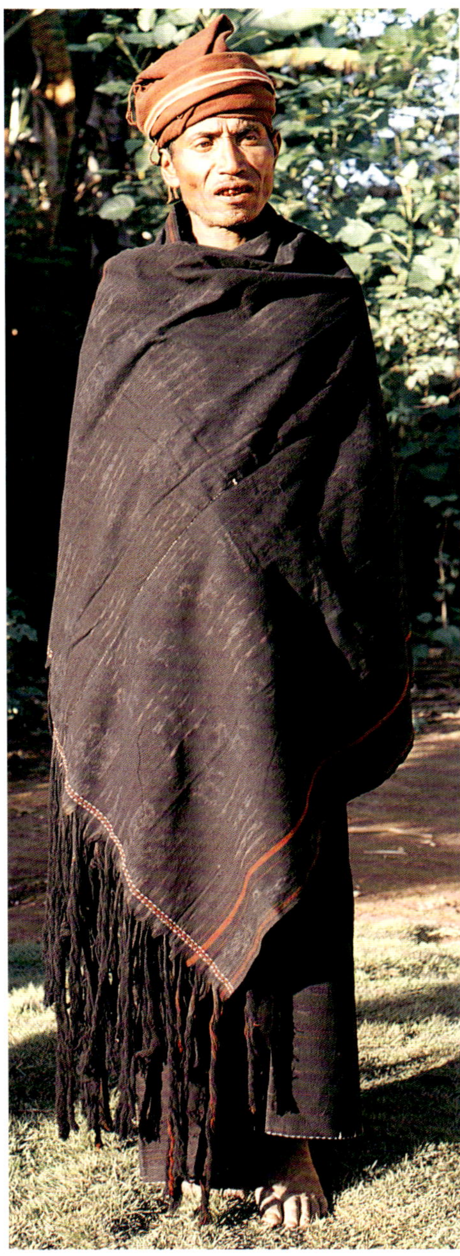

The Magical Origin of Beads

Elders in Lopijo tell the legend of *Ana Kola* (The Orphans), which explains the origin of the beads used for making *lawo butu*. It equates beads with other forms of valuables like gold and cloth, and at the same time offers wry comment on the supposed wealth of far-off Java. As is common with such legends, villagers today can still point to places in the landscape where the events are said to have occurred.

Ana Kola

(THE ORPHANS)

❧*Wea and her brother Landa, orphans from Nua Keli, went fishing in the river. They caught only two tiny fish, but because they were so poor, they decided to take the fish back to the village to raise in a fish pond until they grew big enough to eat. One fish died but the other grew into a pig that the orphans could call to the surface of the pond by singing. The people of the village became suspicious of this magic and killed the pig. When the pig was butchered it was discovered to have the bones of a fish. The villagers ate the meat and scattered the bones around the village.*

❧*The orphans painstakingly gathered the bones together and buried them in the kitchen ashes, where they soon began to sprout. A tree grew from the ashes and was transplanted by the orphans to a nearby mountain top. When the tree matured, all manner of wealth grew from the branches, including gold, beads, money, and cloth. Only the orphans, using a magical knife, could harvest this wealth. If anyone else tried, the tree only grew taller, out of reach. Enraged, the villagers stole the magical knife and chopped down the tree to get at the wealth. When the tree fell, the tips of its branches reached all the way to Java. All the gold and other forms of wealth were lost to Java, except the beads. These remained on Flores and were used to make* lawo butu.[11]

FIGURE 5-14: Ngada woman's beaded sarong, *lawo butu*. 177 x 78 cm. The Textile Museum 1986.26.1, Washington.

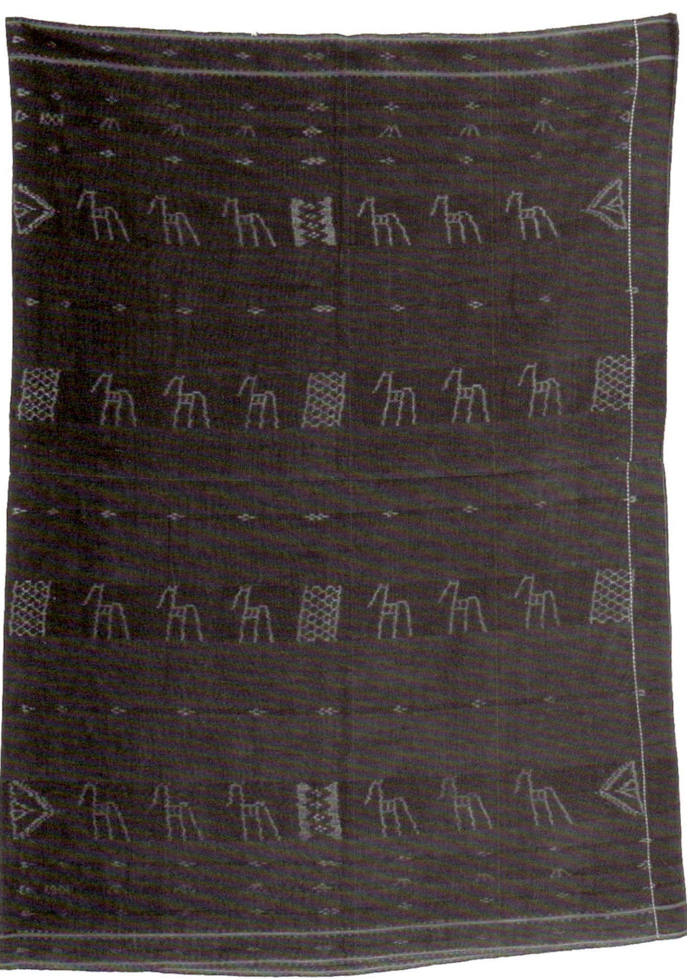

The most famous of all Ngadha textiles are the beaded sarongs called *lawo butu* (FIGURE 5-14). Most beaded sarongs have a centerfield format, but in some cases banded sarongs were beaded as well. Beaded sarongs were created to be clan heirlooms and were worn by women on only the most sacred occasions. In Lopijo they are associated particularly with the ceremony *bhéi ngadhu*, conducted when a newly cut tree was brought from the forest to the village for the construction of a *ngadhu*.

Beaded sarongs were commissioned by clan leaders of particularly high status before they died. The beading was done by men. After the clan leader's death, the cloth was known by his name and stored in the clan house with the other clan treasures. This accounts for an alternative name sometimes applied to these cloths, *lawo ngaza*, meaning "named sarong."[12]

SOA

The ethnic affinities of the people of the various villages in the Soa valley have yet to be thoroughly spelled out, but it is clear that although they were under the authority of the Ngadha raja at Bajawa, their language and customs are in many ways more closely related to those of the Nagé. They participated in a barter system that included other ethnic groups under the authority of the Raja of Boawae and they share a tradition of boxing and hunting rituals with the Nagé.

FIGURE 5-15 (ABOVE, LEFT).
The two-panel *lawo wa'i manu*, worn by girls before reaching marriagable age. Collected prior to 1890, exact place of manufacture unknown.
115 x 73 cm. Rijksmuseum voor Volkenkunde 804-171, Leiden.

FIGURE 5-16 (ABOVE).
This *sapu jara* has unusually large and distinct horse motifs. A distinctive feature of Ngadha *sapu* is the vertical row of red and white twining (*sawé rawé*). The red yarns are dyed with sappan and are normally the only red in the garment. Village of manufacture unknown. 128 x 90 cm. Collection of August Flick.

FIGURES 5-17 (TOP), 5-18 (DETAIL). The human motifs and extensive use of red (from sappan) mark this as an exceptional *lu'é*. The motifs include three different sizes of quadrupeds, the largest of which resembles the Endenese elephant motif. In the stance of the body and the elaboration of the mouth parts, it also recalls the creatures carved on wooden panels beside the entrances to Ngadha houses (FIGURE 5-19). 217 x 134 cm. FMCH X93.26.32, Gift of Anne and John Summerfield.

FIGURE 5-19. The carved figures are called *kata beva* (*kata*, pheasant or wild chicken, and *beva*, the breaking or surging of waves; Djawanai 1983:32) and may be compared to other mythological figures such as the *naga* of Java and Bali and the *aso'* of Kalimantan. Koninklijk Instituut voor de Tropen, Amsterdam.

Soa's textile traditions are distinct from those of both the Ngadha and the Nagé, although weaving is no longer practiced in the valley. Girls in Soa once wore single-panel sarongs called *nai do'i*. These garments were made of yarn dyed black with a mud-dye process. A narrow stripe appeared at the top and bottom edges, dyed light blue with indigo, red with sappan, or yellow with morinda. After a girl reached puberty and participated in a tooth-filing ceremony, a matching sleeveless blouse called *kodo do'i* was added (FIGURE 5-20).

Male children went naked until puberty signaled the time for circumcision. The Soa circumcision ceremony was called *woé sada*, "to wrap a loincloth." The *sada* was a narrow rectangular cloth of undyed cotton. When working in the fields men wore only this garment, but for more formal occasions a two-panel sarong called *nai élu* was added. These sarongs were made of undyed cotton, with thin, evenly spaced stripes of mud-dyed yarn running in the warp direction. More valuable examples were indigo-dyed with white or red stripes.

These simple garments were made locally in Soa and worn on a daily basis by individuals of ordinary means. Aristocratic or ceremonial dress relied on garments traded from neighboring regions. Women wore Ngadha *lawo,* known as *bhago* in Soa. Men wore Ngadha *sapu lu'é* or supplementary-weft sarongs made in Mbay. Soa was an important rice and cotton growing region with strong trade relationships to both of these areas. Raw cotton from Soa sustained the weaving industry in high-elevation areas of the Ngadha territory. Soa rice was critical to Mbay, where the hot, dry landscape prohibited crop production. Until recent decades, there were no permanent markets. Traders would agree to meet at a future date, using a series of knots on a string to mark the passage of days leading up to the promised meeting.

Weaving was abandoned in Soa in the 1950s. The building of irrigated rice terraces, which made women's labor more valuable in agriculture, provided the main impetus for this change. Today Soa women occasionally order *nai do'i* from Ngadha weavers in Langa, but on a daily basis Western styles of dress or commercial sarongs predominate. The striped men's cloth has completely disappeared except for rare pieces preserved as heirlooms (FIGURE 2-16).

NAGÉ

In the colonial era, the Dutch selected the most prominent clan leader in the village of Boawae to become raja in the Nagé region. In the intervening decades, the small town of Boawae has grown up nearby as a district administrative center. The Nagé weaving tradition encompasses more than the core area of Nagé villages surrounding Boawae, however. At Raja, a few kilometers to the east, only the names applied to some aspects of cloth making differ from those in Boawae. Similar textiles are made as far east as the Ndora area, which is in fact a second major production center of "Nagé" cloth. The Kéo, it appears, may not have shared in this Nagé tradition. The history of weaving in the up-slope Kéo villages is poorly known. Kéo weavers may once have made plain cloth, but the only weaving in this region today is the quite different coastal tradition associated with Tonggo.

In Nagé villages, three types of women's sarongs (*hoba*) were once produced. *Hoba do'i* were plain garments. *Hoba niko nako* had plain colored stripes, sometimes alternating with narrow bands of ikat dyed with indigo.[13] *Hoba pojo* had broader ikat

FIGURE 5-20.
A woman from Bogoboa in the Soa region models the *nai do'i* and *kodo do'i* (1991). The garments shown were ordered from Langa and made with chemical dyes. The earlier mud or indigo-dyed versions have not been made in Soa since the 1950s.

FIGURE 5-21.
Woga Dapa, the third wife of Raja Oga Ngole of Boawae, poses with her daughters circa 1920. The girl on the left wears a Javanese batik. Second from left is a locally made striped sarong, *hoba niko nako*. Only the woman in the center wears a Nagé ikat sarong, *hoba pojo*. The two women on the right wear plaid sarongs with supplementary-weft motifs. The Nagé normally obtained supplementary-weft cloths from Mbay, but these more closely resemble the sarongs of Rembong or Bima. Koninklijk Instituut voor de Tropen, Amsterdam.

FIGURE 5-22 (LEFT).
A Raja village woman models a *hoba singi pojo*. Today Nagé women embroider their blouses (*kodo*), but this is a recent development. The blouse's central motif represents a *péo*, the forked ceremonial pole found in Nagé villages. 1991.

FIGURE 5-23 (RIGHT).
The unwoven section of the warp of this Nagé *hoba pojo*, visible at the right edge, was cut open when the cloth entered the international art market. Many sarongs from Flores have been cut in this manner because art dealers sometimes consider them more salable as "blankets." This cloth is shown re-folded to approximate its original proportions. 227 x 176 cm. FMCH X70.120, Museum Purchase, Manus Fund.

bands, sometimes in the form of a central field, alternating with bands of morinda-dyed yarns (FIGURE 5-21).[14] Only *hoba pojo* are made today and they have become the characteristic Nagé woman's garment.

Only a limited number of design formats and motifs appear on *hoba pojo*, which may be constructed from two panels or three.[15] In *singi pojo* sarongs, the widest ikat bands are located near the outer ends of the sarong (FIGURE 5-22). In *singi to* (red end-panel) sarongs, the outer ends consist mainly of red stripes while the most elaborate ikat work is located in the center of the sarong (FIGURE 5-23). Central field motifs are limited to rows of dots, wavy lines, and simple rectangular forms.

A significant portion of Nagé *hoba* are still made with handspun yarns. Even the best old cloths in museum collections are rather coarsely woven. The ikat work is limited to one dye, indigo. Morinda is used only to dye plain yarns. A few supplementary-weft yarns dyed bright yellow-orange add a vertical accent to the finished sarong.[16] The unwoven section of the warp is never cut, but simply folded out of sight when the sarong is worn. Nagé women wear their sarongs with blouses (*kodo*) now made of imported commercial cloth. These are often decorated with embroidery, a technique originally learned from the mission sisters.

At one time Nagé men also wore locally produced ikat cloths called *sada* (FIGURES 5-24, 5-7). When worn as a wrap-around lower-body garment, they were referred to as *sada géa*; when worn over the shoulder, they were *sada bhago*. A number of these cloths survive in museum collections. The design format recalls the *hoba* centerfield, but the ikat motifs are more intricate and the cloths more finely woven.[17] Early in this century changing standards of propriety dictated that these garments be replaced by tubular sarongs. Supplementary-weft sarongs made in Mbay, which had formerly been used in the Nagé region only for ceremonial purposes, came into common usage as the standard Nagé male sarong.[18]

Today the only ikat cloths that Nagé weavers make for men are fringed scarf-like cloths, which are also sometimes worn by women (FIGURE 5-22).[19] Many of these are made with

FIGURE 5-24.
Nagé man's cloth (*sada*). Comparing this cloth with the one in FIGURE 5-5 gives an idea of the rather limited range of variation in Nagé ikat work. 190 X 92 CM. FMCH X70.125, Museum Purchase, Manus Fund.

FIGURE 5-25.
Front view of the twined ramie vest *dhu*, produced only in the Ndora region. The heavy black line that encloses the designs is called the "path" (*zala*). Across the shoulder and lower edge are two identical bands of connected triangles, called the "snake's back" (*logo nipa*). The small circles inscribed with a cross are "eyes" (*mata*); according to local belief there must be an uneven number of these (in this case, four on the front and five on the back) if the vest is to be magically powerful. Made in Pagomogo in 1991. 120 x 48 cm. FMCH X91.1629, Museum Purchase, Manus Fund.

FIGURE 5-26 (BELOW, LEFT).
Plied ramie cordage is twined on a frame, using two alternating shuttles. This piece will make the side panel of a vest. Pagomogo, 1991.

FIGURES 5-27 AND 5-28 (BELOW, RIGHT).
Designs painted on two *dhu* made 40 years apart are nearly identical, excepting the motifs on the side panels. LEFT, a vest collected before 1952 bears a long centipede-like figure of unknown meaning. Detail of Tropenmuseum 2104-3, Amsterdam. RIGHT, the motifs on a 1991 vest include a chalice inspired by the Catholic church and a pair of gold ear ornaments intended as a symbol of ethnic-group pride. Detail of vest in FIGURE 5-25.

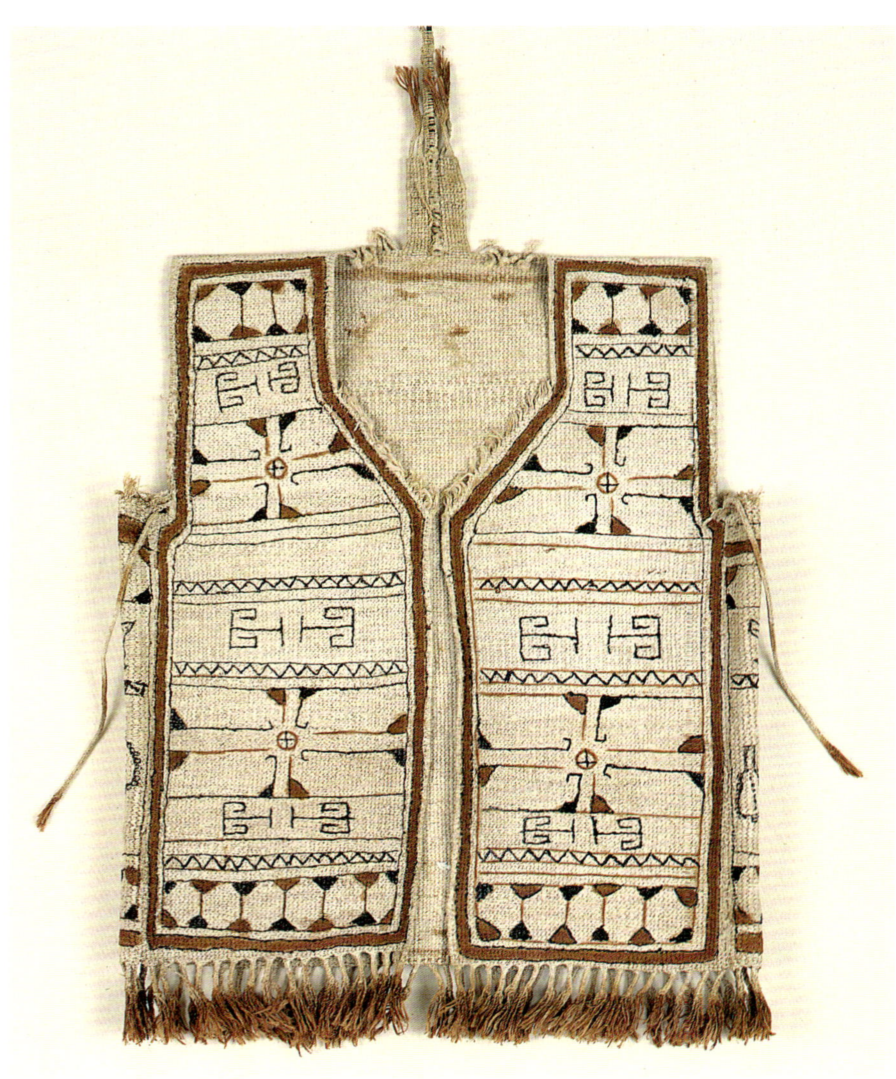

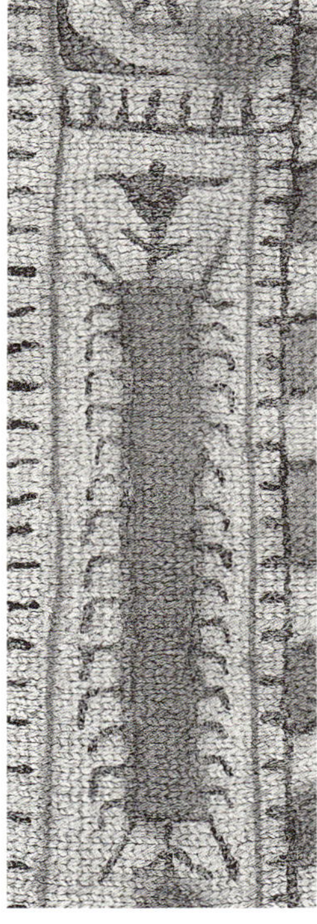

modern, European-influenced motifs. They do not compare in value with supplementary-weft shoulder cloths obtained from Mbay, which are highly prized in the Nagé region as marriage and funeral goods.

The most unusual garments that once entered into the complex exchange system in this part of Flores were men's vests with painted designs (FIGURE 5-25), made only in Ndora. Only three old men currently know how to make the vests, which are no longer widely traded. The vests are made of ramie fiber and are twined rather than woven. They are the only traditional items of clothing made by men on Flores. In Ndora these unique garments are called *dhu*, but they are known by different names in each area to which they were once traded.[20]

Ramie (*Boehmeria nivea*)[21] is planted in gardens and harvested at the end of the rainy season. The inner bark fiber is laboriously stripped from the cut stems with a knife, then dried, split finely, and plied. The twining is accomplished on a simple frame, using two shuttles alternately (FIGURE 5-26). One warp is put on the frame to produce the front and back of the jacket, while a second, narrower warp is used to make the two sides. When the twining is finished, the pieces are sewn together. The vest is washed in water and then fulled by vigorous pounding with a log. Before painting, it is hung in the sun to bleach. The red pigment is made from sappan and the black from dried animal blood (FIGURES 5-27, 5-28, 5-29).

These vests are strongly associated with notions of masculinity. In former times women were not allowed to touch them. A purification ritual was required if the vest came into contact with a menstruating woman. Their primary use must surely have been in warfare, although this is not acknowledged today. In more recent times they have been used for boxing and deer hunting, activities that are now the main foci of masculine bravado.

Boxing matches in Soa and the Nagé region are roughly equivalent to whip-dueling in Manggarai. The matches are held from April to June, moving through a circuit of village

FIGURE 5-29.
Three men cooperate to finish the painting of the vest shown in FIGURE 5-25. The designs have already been painted once and are here being painted over to deepen the colors. Pagomogo, 1991.

FIGURE 5-30.
At a 1991 boxing match in Boawae, referees restrain the combatants as the action intensifies. The weapons visible in the boxers' hands are made of twisted sugar palm fiber. Only one of the boxers wears the *dhu* vest, as they are now scarce.

sites.[22] The day of a boxing match is preceded by a night of dancing, conducted in fire-lit circles in the village plaza. Village elders sing songs in archaic language to accompany the dances, commemorating the dead and offering praise for the harvest. These songs reveal the sacred aspects of the evening, while the drinking of distilled palm spirits and the exuberant dancing of the younger generation characterize its social nature.[23]

The dancing breaks up at dawn. At midday, after a few hours of rest, the crowd reassembles in the plaza, where a rectangular space has been cleared for the boxing. Matchmakers hustle from one end of the field to the other, arranging bouts between suitable opponents. The atmosphere becomes heated when strong and evenly matched boxers are paired, especially if they hail from rival regions. At either end of the field, groups of men chant songs to encourage their favorite while insulting the prowess of his opponent.

The wearing of a painted ramie vest adds a special air of bravado to the occasion (FIGURE 5-30), although not all boxers wear them today. The boxers are provided with a weapon of knotted sugar palm fiber strapped to their palms. They jab at each other with these, aiming for the face. The bout is closely regulated by referees and halted as soon as blood is drawn from superficial wounds. Today both participants and observers insist that boxing matches are purely for entertainment, but ritualized combat and the symbolic drawing of blood, with attendant notions of sacrifice, are concepts deeply rooted in Austronesian societies.

The vests also appear at ceremonial deer hunts (*to'a lako*), held from August to October in the same regions as the boxing. The hunting of deer assumes cult-like proportions throughout central and western Flores and deer meat is eaten with greater relish than any other. More than just a means of obtaining food, *to'a lako* is an integral part of the annual cycle of religious ceremonies.

Men from hamlets throughout the region gather at night and proceed on horseback to the hunting grounds by torchlight. The actual hunt takes place on the following two days. Dogs are an essential part of the hunting party, responsible for cornering the quarry until it can be killed by the mounted hunters with harpoons and

FIGURE 5-31.
Following the annual hunt, the head of a deer is placed at the ceremonial meeting place (*loka*) in a hamlet near Boawae, 1991. The mixed dress, including commercial plaid sarongs, is typical of everyday clothing.

spears. At the conclusion of the hunt, the heads of the deer are placed in the *loka,* the ceremonial meeting ground outside the village (FIGURE 5-31).

An ornament consisting of a long forked pole of rattan decorated with chicken feathers is sometimes attached to the back of the vest (FIGURE 5-32). This ornament (*lado manu*) was worn only by the most skilled hunters and is said to have signaled their determination to pursue the hunt to a successful conclusion. Under traditional law, such a hunter was required to sacrifice a buffalo if he returned to the village without a deer head. The *lado manu* is no longer worn for hunting, but villagers can still name the individuals who were bold enough to wear them in the past. The agility on horseback that was required, as well as the appearance of the tall ornament moving across the open landscape, was greatly admired.

In 1992, the regency government, acting in part through channels of traditional law, enacted a ban on the burning of forest lands. Such burning has been an integral part of the annual hunt, used to control the underbrush and flush the game. Many people speak in favor of the environmental goals of the new ban, but opinions are now divided as to whether the annual hunt can continue.

FIGURE 5-32.
In Boawae, the ramie vest is called *désé.* Here it is modeled as it was once worn by the most skilled deer hunters, complete with the rattan and chicken feather ornament *lado manu.* This ceremonial garb is rare today and no longer ordinarily worn for the hunt.

MBAY, RIUNG, AND TONGGO

The region known as Mbay consists of an alluvial plain formed by the river Aesesa. According to the oral history told by today's elders, the Mbay people are the descendants of Keraéng Jogo, who came to Flores from Sulawesi. A marriage was arranged between Supi, his daughter, and Tuju Bae, a man belonging to the indigenous Dhawé ethnic group. As bridewealth, Keraéng Jogo requested a piece of land the size of a buffalo hide. When this was granted, the hide was cut into the finest possible strand and stretched across the countryside. All of the land enclosed between the line of buffalo hide and the sea was thereafter claimed by the descendants of Sipi and Tuju Bae, who became the Mbay people. The original Mbay hamlet was located inland at the base of the hills backing the plain. The site is still marked by the *ngandung,* a monument said to symbolize the community's origins (FIGURE 5-33).

Mbay is one of the most famous weaving communities in western Flores, a reputation earned over generations based on the high quality of the supplementary-weft cloth woven there. Mbay cloth was once in demand throughout the region, equivalent in barter to a water buffalo or up to ten Nagé *hoba*. Ceremonial dress for men over a wide area, including Soa and the entire Nagé-Kéo region, depends on cloth made in Mbay styles. Although Mbay was historically the leading center of production, today similar cloths are made in a number of other communities as well.

The most important Mbay garments are supplementary-weft sarongs, *lipa dhowik* (FIGURE 5-34), and shoulder cloths, *sapang dhowik*. The motifs, traditionally in yellow and orange, appear on a black ground. As with Manggarai supplementary-weft sarongs, one side of the cloth is more highly decorated than the other. The sarongs may be further categorized as *lipa dhowik punsan*, in which the motifs are entirely limited to one side (leaving the plain side completely blank), and *lipa dhowik sewekkin*, in which even the plain side has some widely spaced motifs. The techniques used in Mbay are the same as in Manggarai, but Mbay cloth is readily distinguished from Manggarai cloth by its color scheme. The black background color of Mbay cloth, produced by over-dyeing indigo with the inner bark of the *rengit* tree (*Acacia glauca*), does not fade to blue as is common in Manggarai cloth. Today Mbay weavers have adopted new colors for their motifs, including red and yellow-green, but they shun the white and pastel shades favored in Manggarai. The best Mbay cloths are characterized by differing motifs in successive rows, indicating that they were created without the use of pattern sticks.

Traditional ceremonial dress for men in Mbay consisted of a *lipa dhowik* and *sapang dhowik*, plus a plaited belt made of *waru* (*Hibiscus tiliaceus*) fiber and a batik headcloth. This style of dress was once restricted to men of high status, whereas ordinary men wore plain black sarongs, *lipa mité*, and plain white shoulder cloths, *sapang bhakok*. Women wear the same sarongs as men, frequently knotting them over one shoulder, and sometimes adding a shoulder cloth (FIGURE 1-2). In a manner typical of the ethnic interdependence of this region, Mbay bridewealth and funeral exchanges required not local cloth, but Nagé *hoba*.

Weaving was an indispensable part of this community's adaptation to its environment. Prior to the 1950s, Mbay was a thirsty plain sparsely dotted with lontar palms, too dry for the growing of crops. Men in Mbay raised livestock and women wove. The products of these two activities were traded to the inhabitants of other regions, especially the Soa and Nagé areas, for rice and other food.

Man-made environmental changes have in recent decades altered the place of weaving in the local economy. In the 1950s a dam was built on the Aesesa and the lontar plain began to give way to irrigated rice fields. After a larger dam was constructed in 1969, the irrigation system expanded rapidly across the level terrain. Once shunned except by its hearty population of weavers and herders, the Mbay plain now attracts newcomers to work the irrigated fields, especially from the overcrowded Ende-Lio region. Women's labor has become valuable in the fields and the looms of Mbay have very nearly fallen silent. Only a few elderly women continue to produce the traditional high-quality cloth that was once the lifeblood of the community.

FIGURE 5-33. Many villages in Ngada Regency have some form of forked ceremonial pole in the village plaza, such as the *ngadhu* found in Ngadha villages (FIGURES 5-9, 5-10) or their Nagé equivalent, the *péo*. At the abandoned site of the original hamlet of the Mbay people, this takes the unusual form of the *ngandung*, a living tree growing from a pile of rocks. According to Mbay elders, the tree represents the penis of Tuju Bae and the circle of rocks the vagina of Supi, symbolizing the original union that produced the Mbay community. 1992.

FIGURE 5-34.
This *lipa dhowik sewekkin*, made in 1991, demonstrates the skill and fine sense of design that have made Mbay's textiles the most highly prized in the region. Today's weavers do not have names for the individual motifs or any explanation of their history. Similar motifs are widespread in coastal Islamic portions of the archipelago. 141 X 110 CM. FMCH X91.1620, Museum Purchase, Manus Fund.

Stretching east and west along the coast beyond the confines of the Mbay plain are a number of other communities in Aesesa District that make cloth in styles similar to Mbay but without the outstanding quality or sense of design. These communities have been less affected by the development of irrigation and have now become the leading producers of cloth in Mbay styles, especially inexpensive sarongs with yellow motifs made with pattern sticks. These cloths are made in large quantities and are sold throughout Ngada Regency and beyond. If there were once distinctive motifs made in the various villages, knowledge of this has been lost to standardization based on popular, simplified Mbay motifs.

Further west along the coast is Riung, a mixed community whose clans trace their ancestry to Sulawesi, Bima, and the Moluccas. Prior to pacification, the single hamlet of Riung was located on a hilltop site a few kilometers inland from the coast. In 1910, the community moved to a more accessible location at the base of the hills. The new mosque built then still stands at the heart of the hamlet.

Riung's textile traditions have not been adequately studied, but it is clear that they combine elements from both Mbay and Rembong. The most highly decorated garments are *lipa kaet sewekkin* and *lipa kaet punsan* (FIGURES 5-35, 5-36), which are analogous to the two types of *lipa dhowik* in Mbay.[24] The highest status cloths, however, and the ones required for bridewealth exchanges, are sarongs with light blue weft stripes called *lipa punsa bulung*, identical to the *lipa léleng lauk* of Rembong (FIGURES 9-6, 5-35). That such plain cloths are more highly esteemed than decorated ones suggests that the supplementary-weft technique is a relatively recent introduction, not yet sanctioned by the experience of generations of ancestors.

A number of more simple cloths were once made as well. Roughly in order of decreasing status, these included plaid sarongs, plain sarongs, plain flat wrap-around cloths without fringes, and plain loincloths. The lower the status of the garment, the more likely it was to be worn in non-weaving mountain areas or, if on the coast, for work or everyday wear by common people. In addition to Riung itself, a number of other villages in the lower and mid-level hills are weaving communities. Today these make simple versions of Mbay-style sarongs indistinguishable from those produced in other areas.

The transitional nature of Riung's textiles, part Rembong and part Mbay, points to a critical observation about the distribution of supplementary-weft weaving on Flores. The region where this technique predominates forms a continuous zone, running from Congkar in Manggarai eastward across the border of Ngada Regency to Mbay. The textiles produced all across this region are closely related. Taken as a whole, they stand in strong contrast to the cloths produced in nearly all Flores' other weaving areas, where the warp-ikat technique predominates.

The use of the loom with the plank type of warp beam throughout this region, plus the known history of communities such as Riung and Mbay, leads inescapably to the conclusion that this is essentially an alien tradition, brought to the north coast of Flores by migrants from Sulawesi and Bima in relatively recent centuries. Not only technique and equipment set these traditions apart, but also usage and nomenclature. In the supplementary-weft areas, sarongs are "unisex" while throughout the rest of Flores men's and women's sarongs are sharply distinguished. *Lipa*, the term used from Congkar to Mbay, is the same term that is used in southern Sulawesi and Selayar (Maxwell 1990:293). The motifs and design layouts of the supplementary-weft cloths would not appear out of place in Bima, Sulawesi, or for that matter, many parts of the Islamic Malay world.[25]

There is one additional supplementary-weft weaving area in Ngada Regency that is not

contiguous with this north coast zone. It is located on the south coast, in Nangaroro and Mauponggo Districts. Tonggo, in Nangaroro District, was historically the most important community along this stretch of coast. Mauponggo weavers acknowledge that their weaving industry is derived from that of Tonggo. Due to its location within Ende Bay, Tonggo had strong connections to Ende. Indeed, the people of Tonggo represent the inter-marrying of the up-slope Kéo population with the Endenese. An Islamic culture similar to that of Ende has developed. Weaving in this region is limited entirely to coastal villages, as it is in Endenese weaving areas.

Tonggo women weave yellow-on-black supplementary-weft cloths that are today indistinguishable from the Mbay-style cloths widely produced in Aesesa and Riung Districts. Weaving is the main eco-nomic activity of women in this area, where farm land is limited. Many hamlets have organized cooperative groups and Tonggo has become one of the major sources of this type of cloth. Although Tonggo weavers claim they once had their own distinctive motifs, this is no longer the case.[26]

Two unusual features of Tonggo weaving suggest strong influence from Ende. One is the use of the circular warp loom rather than the loom with the plank-type warp beam found in all other supplementary-weft areas. The other is the use of an Endenese name for sarongs, *zuka*, rather than *lipa*.[27]

Today Tonggo cloths are made for sale or for use in marriage exchanges. For everyday garments, Tongga men wear Western styles of clothing and women wear primarily Endenese ikat sarongs. In the past, a greater variety of cloth was produced for everyday wear, including *kain bira*, a plain warp-striped cloth that was used for sarongs, trousers and even shirts (FIGURE 6-2). ❖

NOTES, page 270.

FIGURE 5-36.
The base fabric of this *lipa kaet sewekkin* from Riung hamlet is handspun cotton, dyed with indigo and then over-dyed with a combination of additional plant materials to produce a true black. The supplementary-weft yarns are commercial. The motifs are said to be unique to Riung, but it is unclear to what degree the differences between this cloth and the one in FIGURE 5-34, for example, result from regional as opposed to individual variation. 143 x 99 cm. FMCH X91.1619, Museum Purchase, Manus Fund.

6

Ende Regency

ROY W. HAMILTON

ENDE REGENCY IS SHARED BY THE ENDENESE AND LIO ETHNIC GROUPS, who are so closely related that the compound term Ende-Lio is often used. The main urban settlement is the town of Ende, which occupies a low isthmus of land connecting the volcano Iya to the southern coast of Flores. From the town pier, one has a commanding view around Ende Bay and across the water to Ende Island.

These shores are the home of the Endenese people, born of the intermingling of Islamic seafarers with the indigenous inhabitants of the region. From 1570 to the 1630s the Portuguese struggled to maintain a foothold at their fort on Ende Island, but finally conceded to growing Islamic power. Ende developed as an independent state, with its own raja and unique Islamic culture, including a written alphabet based on the script of the Makassarese. The Endenese became the major regional trading force in the Savu Sea. Ende is now the largest town on Flores and the Endenese are the only major ethnic group whose orientation is as much urban and seafaring as rural and agricultural.

Today a precise boundary separates the Endenese from their Lio neighbors. In addition to the town of Ende, the Endenese areas include the districts of Nangapanda and Ende. The Lio population inhabits the remaining four districts of the regency (Ndona, Detusoko, Maurole and Wolowaru). In the colonial era, the Dutch at first recognized two rajas in the Endenese areas, at Ende and Nangapanda (FIGURE 6-2), and two more in the Lio areas, at Ndona and Wolowaru. In the 1920s each ethnic group was consolidated under a single raja, at Ende for the Endenese and at Wolowaru for the Lio.

These various administrative schemes have tended to oversimplify the cultural relationships in the region. The Endenese and Lio languages share 86% of their vocabularies (Aoki 1988:203). Interior villages in the Endenese districts, less influenced by Islam and trade than the coastal areas, have social structures similar to those of Lio villages. Within the Lio regions there is considerable cultural and linguistic variation. Ndona District in particular resists easy categorization. The people there are ethnically Lio, but have long maintained closer ties with their Endenese neighbors than with the other Lio districts, from which they are separated by extremely rugged topography. This is reflected in Ndona's textiles, which more often resemble the cloths woven by Endenese women than the typical Lio styles made by weavers in Wolowaru District.

FIGURE 6-1 (OPPOSITE). Detail of FIGURE 6-22.

In addition to ethnic divisions, the regency is also cut across by a boundary dividing weaving from non-weaving areas. Weaving takes place only in villages located on or near the south coast. There is no weaving at all in Maurole and Detusoko Districts. The same ecological constraints are at work here as in other parts of Flores. Many of the strongest weaving communities face extremely harsh agricultural conditions; income from textile sales is vital to household budgets.

ENDENESE WOMEN'S SARONGS

Today Endenese weavers concentrate primarily on the making of women's warp ikat sarongs (*zawo*), which display myriad combinations of motifs within a rigidly structured design format. The sarongs are always made of three panels. The two end panels (*singi*) are identical, forming mirror images of each other when assembled in the finished sarong. They always contain a plain black band called *mité méré*. The center panel (*ora*) is more variable and Endenese women's sarongs can be divided into three general categories based on its structure and color. Most sarongs belong to the category *zawo kabhi* (FIGURE 6-4), in which the center panel consists of a single large field of ikat motifs (*kabhi*, undivided) rather than a number of separate ikat bands. The motifs are red and white on a blackish, over-dyed ground. Sarongs in the second category, *zawo mangga*, have center panels composed of separate ikat bands, divided by series of narrow ikat stripes and plain black lines (FIGURE 6-5). The motifs are white on a blue-black ground, with red appearing only in a few narrow accent bands. The third category of sarongs, called either *zawo ngéra* or *zawo gézo*, also features banded center panels, but the ikat motifs in these bands are red and white on a black ground, as in *zawo kabhi* sarongs (FIGURE 6-6).

In all three categories, the end panels of the sarong contain the *mité méré* plus a large number of ikat bands of varying widths, separated by fine stripes of plain black. Each ikat

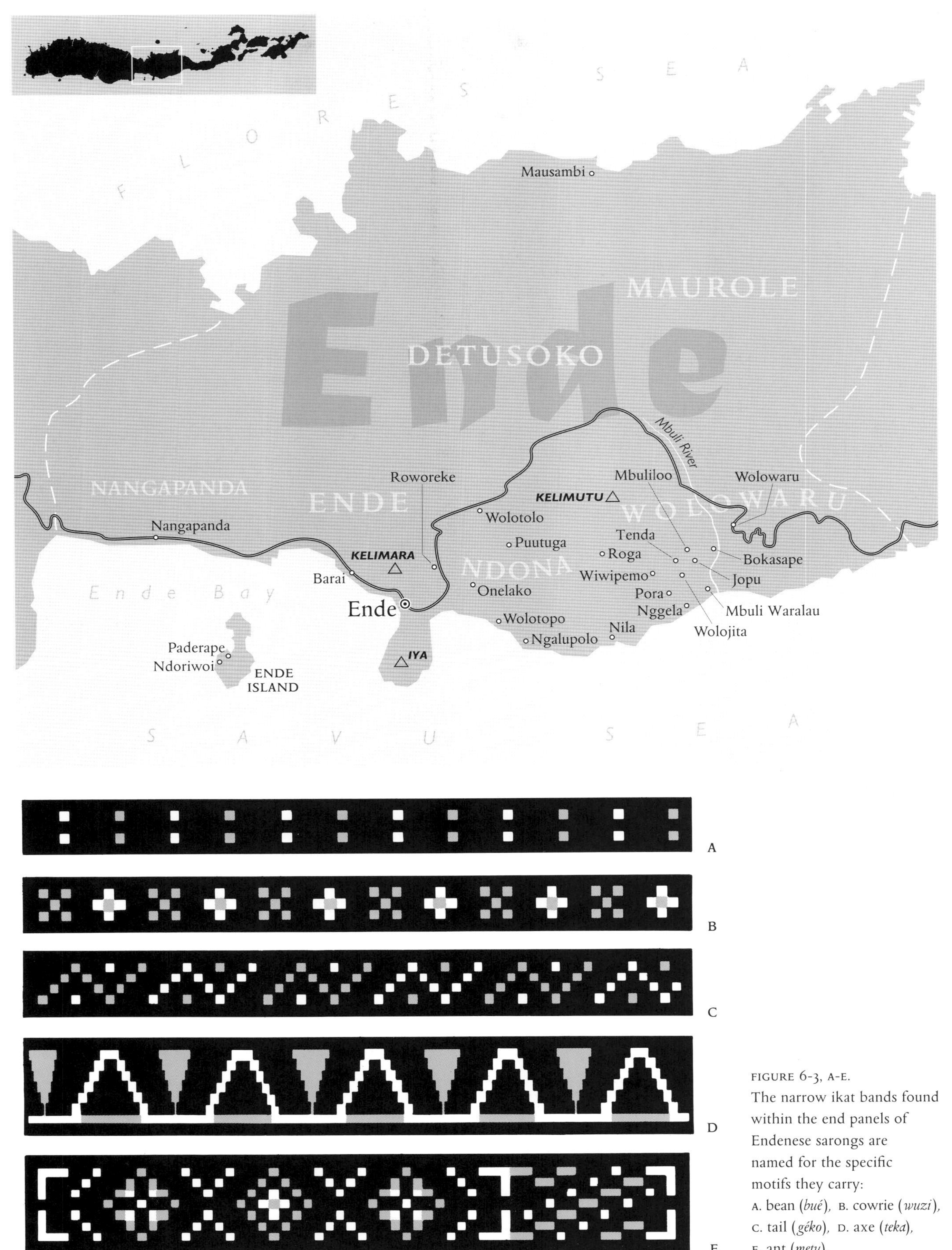

FIGURE 6-3, A-E.
The narrow ikat bands found within the end panels of Endenese sarongs are named for the specific motifs they carry:
A. bean (*bué*), B. cowrie (*wuzi*), C. tail (*géko*), D. axe (*teka*), E. ant (*metu*).

band has its own name. The wider ones (*foko* and *gha'i*) usually replicate a portion of the center panel motifs. The narrower bands (*metu, teka, ghéko, wuzi,* and *bué*) are named after the specific motifs they carry, which normally vary little from sarong to sarong (FIGURE 6-3). The prescribed band widths are expressed as the number of individual ikat bundles required to make up the motif. The arrangement of bands in the end panel is also strictly regulated, usually conforming to one of two possible structures depending on the type of sarong (FIGURES 6-8, 6-9).

Zawo kabhi. This category can be subdivided into many distinct types, named according to either the predominant motif or the internal structure of the central design field. Today four types (*zawo nggaja sendetu, zawo nggaja tendo, zawo jara,* and *zawo péa*) form a distinct subgroup, sharing certain design characteristics and always listed by weavers

OPPOSITE PAGE:

FIGURE 6-4 (LEFT).
A sarong belonging to the *zawo kabhi* category. More specifically, this sarong is called *zawo mata roté* due to the network of *roté* lines enmeshed in the central field. The intense shade of true red evident in this sarong is difficult to obtain with morinda and is the mark of particularly skilled Endenese dyers. 169 x 647 cm. FMCH x88.1261, Museum Purchase, Manus Fund.

FIGURE 6-5 (RIGHT).
The name *zawo mangga* is applied both to the general category of sarongs with banded centerfields and mostly indigo dye, and also to this specific type (with the widest ikat bands carrying a diamond pattern). 156 x 73 cm. FMCH x88.1257, Museum Purchase, Manus Fund.

THIS PAGE:

FIGURE 6-6 (LEFT).
A sarong belonging to the category *zawo ngera/zawo gézo*, collected in 1929 by Ernst Vatter. Museum für Völkerkunde, Frankfurt.

FIGURE 6-7.
Siti Habibah, creator of the sarongs in FIGURES 6-4 and 6-5, poses with her ikat tying frame in Paderape, Ende Island.

as being among the most traditional sarongs. *Zawo nggaja sendetu* (FIGURE 6-10) and *zawo nggaja tendo* (FIGURE 3-16) exhibit, in differing arrangements, the elephant motif (*nggaja*) discussed in the previous chapter. *Zawo jara* have horse motifs instead of elephants. *Zawo péa* feature an hour-glass shaped motif, to which present-day weavers are unable to attribute any particular significance.[1] In all four types, the motifs are rather boldly arranged in rows within the central field.

Weavers today attach little special significance to these four types of sarongs, beyond admiring them as traditional.[2] They are not associated with any particular social standing nor are they considered more appropriate than other sarongs for bridewealth exchanges. It seems likely that this subgroup once included more than the present four types. A similar Endenese sarong, collected by Max Weber in 1889 and preserved in the Rijksmuseum

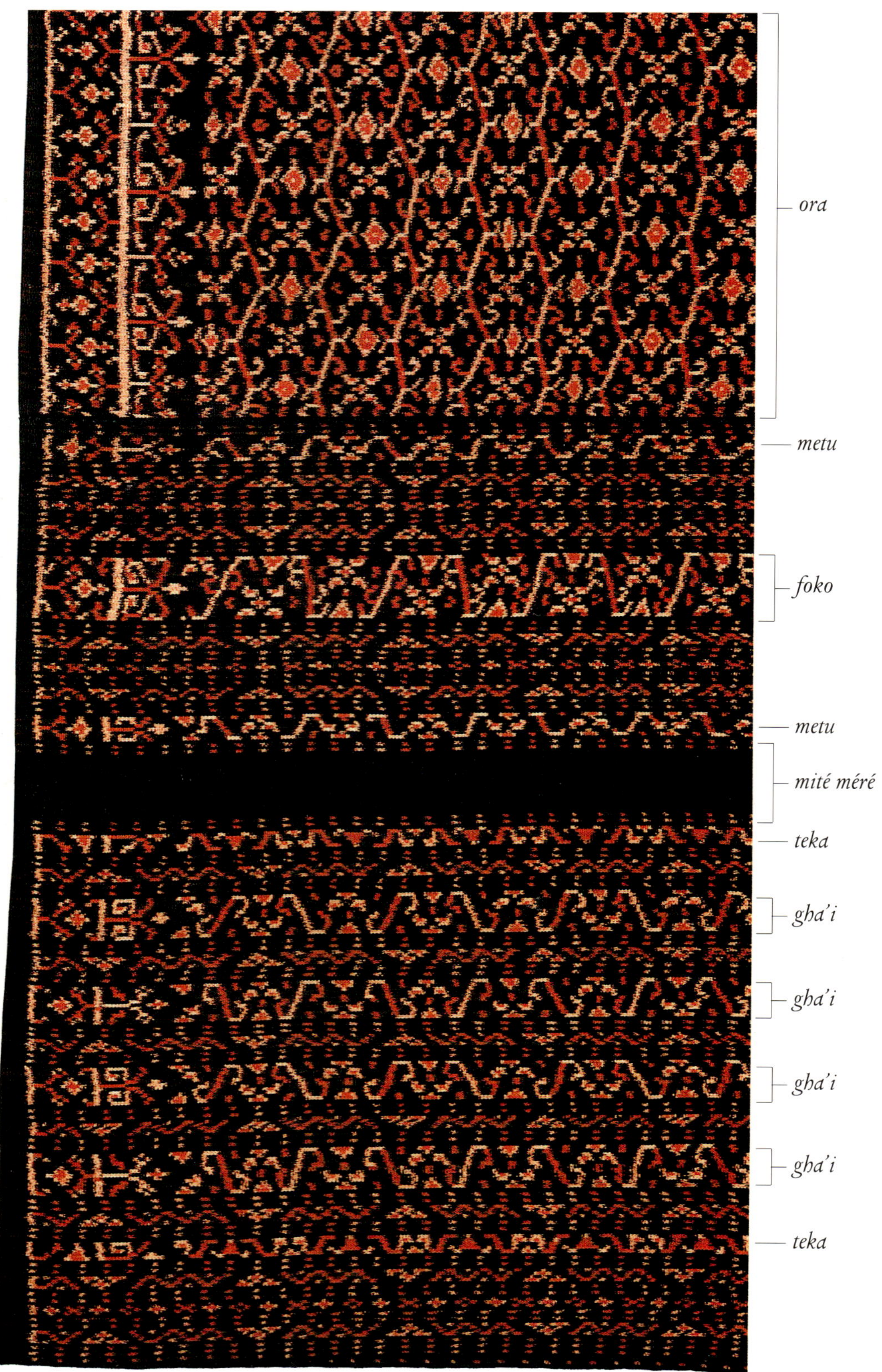

FIGURE 6-8 (DETAIL OF FIGURE 6-4).
Most *zawo kabhi* sarongs have a series of four *gha'i* bands below the
plain black *mité méré*, as in this example. The narrowest bands (*bué, géko*
and *wuzi*) show the standardized motifs (see FIGURE 6-3), but in this
particular sarong the *teka* and *metu* bands, as well as the *foko* and
gha'i, replicate part of the design of the central field.

FIGURE 6-9 (DETAIL OF FIGURE 6-10).
This sarong has one *metu* and two *gha'i* bands below the *mité méré*,
an alternative end-panel structure that is characteristic of sarongs
belonging to a special subgroup of four *zawo kabhi* types. Another
characteristic of this subgroup is the *timbu*, the specific arrow-like
motif seen projecting from the border into the central field (*ora*).

FIGURE 6-10.

Zawo nggaja sendetu sarongs bear the elephant motif (*nggaja*) interspaced with a patola-derived floral diamond (*soké*). This example was made on Ende Island circa 1940. 161 x 70 cm, FMCH X88.1260. Museum Purchase, Manus Fund.

FIGURE 6-11.

The pattern shown on this sarong in the *zawo kabhi* category, made prior to 1889, is no longer produced today. It appears to consist of chickens (*manu*) alternating with elephants (*nggaja*). Although the chicken motif is no longer made, some Lio-speaking informants in Ndona District still use the term *lawo manu nggaja* for sarongs that have elephants alternating with other motifs. 180 x 71 cm. Rijksmuseum voor Volkenkunde 804-202, Leiden.

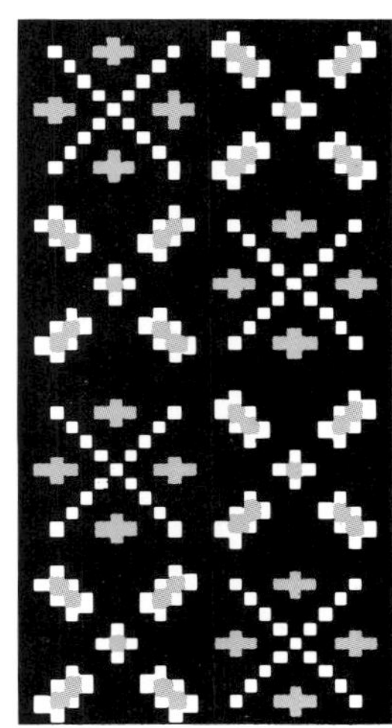

voor Volkenkunde, includes both elephant and chicken motifs (FIGURE 6-11).[3] A cloth at the Deutsches Textilmuseum includes human figures as well (Kahn Majlis 1991a: fig. 139). In minor details these sarongs differ somewhat from today's sarongs in this sub-group, suggesting that the rules of design were perhaps once more flexible than they are at present.

The many other named types of *zawo kabhi* sarongs demonstrate a far greater amount of variation and innovation. Nevertheless, they are also organized according to strict design principles. The centerfield consists of rows of often quite small motifs, which may be arranged in various configurations. Extremely common are several named versions of a motif known as *soké* (FIGURE 6-12), derived from the eight-pointed patola rosette. When a single predominant motif is repeated in simple rows, the sarong is usually named after the motif itself. In other cases the motifs may be enmeshed in a web of interconnecting lines known as *roté*, in which case the sarong is named after the type of *roté* pattern (FIGURE 6-13). The side borders of the center panel take on a variety of shapes, usually echoing the form of the major motif in the central design field. In certain *zawo kabhi*, the borders are replicated within the central field, dividing it into vertical sections. These sarongs are named according to the number of times the border is repeated (FIGURES 6-14, 6-15, 6-16).

The close relationship between the patterning of Endenese sarongs and imported patola has long been recognized. The basic motifs, the connecting and border elements, and even the overall design format and color scheme of *zawo kabhi* draw their inspiration from patola. The limitless variety evidenced in these sarongs in fact represents the experimental reshaping and reorganizing of the patola elements.

Zawo mangga. Wherever a group of Endenese women gather, a few stand out because the predominant color in their sarongs is blue-black rather than red. These women are wearing sarongs belonging to the *zawo mangga* category, which includes three named types common today.[4] Most frequently seen is the type simply called *zawo mangga*, which has a center panel of three or four wide ikat bands separated by a variety of plain stripes and narrower ikat bands (FIGURE 6-5). In *zawo mangga jara*, these bands are replaced with rows of horse figures. The result is a sarong very much like the Ngadha *lawo jara*, although the end panel structures of Endenese sarongs are more complex. In *zawo mangga metu dhiki*, the center panel has only narrow bands like the *metu* bands of end panels.

FIGURE 6-12, A-C.
Three patterns featuring variants of the patola-derived motif *soké*.

A. *Soké mata méré* or "large *soké* pattern" closely resembles the original patola design. This pattern can be seen in the sarong in FIGURE 6-16.

When patterns incorporate smaller *soké* motifs, they may become reduced to their most essential geometric form.

B. *Soké gami zima* features simplified *soké* alternating with small diamond forms called *gami zima* or "five ikat bundles".

C. *Soké bezé azé*, the pattern of the sarong in FIGURE 6-14, alternates small *soké* with a motif called "fly wings" (*bezé azé*).

FIGURE 6-13, A-C.
Three variants of *roté* patterns.

A. *Raza kuma* or "path of a snail"
is the meandering pattern
seen in the sarong
in FIGURE 6-4.

B. *Siku zako* or "leg of a dog"
refers to the zig-zag lines
connecting a variety of
other motifs, including
small *soké* and "fly wings"
(*bezé azé*). They can also be
seen in the sarong in
FIGURE 6-15.

C. *Mata dhiki* or "little motifs"
is another common
roté variant.

Zawo ngéra / zawo gézo. Sarongs in the third category, called *zawo ngéra* in some places and *zawo gézo* in others, are routinely made of ikat bands left over from the making of *zawo kabhi* category sarongs.[5] *Ngéra*, meaning "separated," refers to the banded structure of the center panel. In some sarongs the widest bands in this panel all carry the same motif (FIGURES 6-17, 6-18). In other cases alternate bands carry different motifs, indicating that the weaver has used leftovers from two different sarongs (FIGURE 6-6).

This classification of Endenese women's sarongs reveals a tremendous wealth of variation in both motif and overall design format, which might well be expected to provide the foundation for an extensive vocabulary of social meaning. Thus it is striking that in Endenese society today this sort of meaning is almost entirely absent. Quality of materials and workmanship aside, all of the named types of sarongs are valued equally and used in the same way. Garments dyed with morinda were probably once a prerogative of high-status individuals, but today the color distinction between the *zawo kabhi* and *zawo mangga* categories has no social correlation. If Endenese motifs once encoded meanings, these have been stripped away in favor of an egalitarian experimentation in which designs are appreciated on the basis of aesthetics alone. It seems reasonable to assume that this is related to Ende's prolonged contact with Islam and the outside world, which has secularized the textiles by weakening the socio-religious aspects of traditional society.

OTHER ENDENESE TEXTILES

Museum collections contain many old Endenese shoulder cloths called *sémba*. The finest of these are large cloths constructed of two panels, although single-panel cloths were made as well. Best known are *sémba* that feature a patola-derived ikat pattern related to the *soké mata méré* motif still used today for women's sarongs (FIGURE 6-19).[6] Occasionally museum collections contain two-panel *sémba* with other patterns, which suggests that the full range of Endenese sarong designs may once have been used for shoulder cloths as well. An unusual feature of most *sémba* is the lack of side borders, contrary to what would be expected based on patola design.[7]

Endenese *sémba* from a particular period often bear a resemblance to Sumbanese men's cloths, including similar zoomorphic motifs and even modified versions of the Sumbanese skull-tree motif. These cloths appear to date mostly to the 1920s and 1930s, a time when

Sumbanese cloths were quite popular in Europe (Adams 1969:96). Endenese weavers were exposed to the patterns because their husbands participated in the Sumba cloth trade. It appears that they began to imitate the Sumbanese patterns in an effort to capitalize on the popularity of the cloths abroad. As on Sumba, the demands of the trade brought about a general simplification of motifs and opened new avenues of experimentation (FIGURE 6-20). The economics of production during this period may explain the predominance of design formats without side borders, since less labor is required if the borders are omitted. This production factor also favored single-panel cloths.

The production of two-panel shoulder cloths stopped at the time of World War II and never resumed in Ende, although it continues today in Ndona. The only shoulder cloths made now by Endenese weavers are scarf-like cloths consisting of a single panel (*sa nai*[8]), which feature the same motifs as contemporary women's sarongs. Those with *roté* lines are particularly popular. Today these cloths have become multi-purpose. They are worn as festive dress for women as well as men and have become standard items of the tourist trade.

No other men's garments are made by Endenese weavers today. Many Endenese men routinely wear Western styles of dress except when going to the mosque, when they don commercial plaid sarongs. Indeed, a visitor to an Endenese village quickly notices that none of the weavers working at their looms are making men's sarongs, while this activity is ubiquitous in most Lio weaving communities.

Plain, striped, and plaid cloths were made in the past, but all of these have vanished today. The photo of Raja Kakadupa (FIGURE 6-2) shows a checked headcloth and sarong

FIGURE 6-14 (LEFT). Here the border motif is replicated within the central field, dividing it into two vertical sections. Such sarongs are referred to as *zawo zombo so* (*zombo*, border; *so*, divided). Made in Ndoriwoi village, Ende Island, in the 1980s. 166 x 73 cm. FMCH x88.1258. Museum Purchase, Manus Fund.

FIGURE 6-15 (CENTER). *Zawo zombo wutu* or "four border sarong," with four borders dividing the central field into three sections. 162 x 149 cm, shown folded in half. The Museum for Textiles R81.864, Toronto.

FIGURE 6-16 (RIGHT). *Zawo zombo zima* or "five-border sarong." 177 x 70 cm. Collected in 1929. Museum für Völkerkunde 27562, Frankfurt.

FIGURE 6-17.
A typical sarong in the *zawo ngéra* category, with several wide bands in the center panel all bearing the same motif. 177 x 73 cm, FMCH X91.1628. Museum Purchase, Manus Fund.

FIGURE 6-18.
This *zawo ngéra* category sarong is unusual as it has no wide bands at all. Instead, a series of identical narrow *metu* bands fills the center panel. Patterning of this type, called *metu dhiki* or "little ant," is occasionally seen in sarongs in both the *zawo ngéra* and *zawo mangga* categories. 166 x 68 cm, FMCH X88.1255. Museum Purchase, Manus Fund.

worn with a tailored shirt made of striped fabric. Kakadupa's sarong is no different from the *lipa curak* sarongs made today in Todo, while the fabric of his shirt is identical to the striped *kain bira* of Tonggo, as well as to the striped fabrics once made in the Lamaholot region. In the past, such fabrics must have been made throughout much of Flores. Today's village weaving industries have become more specialized, concentrating on the items that are the most highly decorated and the most specific to single ethnic groups.

NDONA DISTRICT

Ndona District includes several weaving villages, the most important being Onelako, Wolotopo, and Ngalupolo. In Onelako, which is closest to Ende, most cloths are made in Endenese styles and are named according to the Lio language equivalent of the Endenese name. As far east as Ngalupolo the Endenese styles predominate, although the Lio styles associated with Wolowaru District appear more frequently. The villages between Ngalupolo and Nggela are not important weaving centers, but from Nila eastward all cloths are made in the Lio styles.

FIGURE 6-19.
Two-panel Endenese *sémba*
with a patola-derived pattern,
made prior to World War II.
246 x 126 cm. FMCH X70.104,
Museum Purchase, Manus Fund.

FIGURE 6-20.
This two-panel *sémba* displays a Sumbanese-like usage of zoomorphic images, but the individual figures are stylistically more a product of European influence. Note the inscription "Sinbad the Sailor" and the depiction of the roc, a gigantic bird that transported Sinbad to a valley filled with diamonds. 223 x 136 cm. Museum für Völkerkunde IIc 18684, Basel.

Two types of cloths now unique to Ndona District have interesting histories. One is the two-panel man's ikat shoulder cloth *sémba*, earlier described as an Endenese style. Now that these cloths are no longer made in the Endenese areas, they have become a specialty of Ndona. The Ndona cloths still have side borders, which vanished in Ende by the 1930s (FIGURE 6-21), but the range of diversity once displayed by the Endenese cloths has been lost and today all Ndona *sémba* are made with only slight variations of the same central motif. The people of Onelako say that Endenese women who married into their community early in the century introduced this pattern.

The other cloth unique to Ndona District is a type of woman's sarong known as *lawo oné mésa*, in which the entire surface of the garment is covered with a single pattern. This design format, which represents a radical departure from the banded or centerfield structures of other Ende-Lio sarongs, is attributed in Ndona to a weaver named Theresia

Sue. The reputation of this woman as the leading weaver of her generation was based in part on her aristocratic standing, but also more directly on her extraordinary determination and skill. She was the first woman in Onelako to attend school, completing three grades at the mission in the 1920s. She created the *oné mésa* format in the 1930s, at first filling the newly opened surface of the sarong with traditional motifs derived from patola and from *mboko wéa*, the gold ornaments used in Lio bridewealth exchanges. By 1940 she had experimented with other motifs drawn from her school experience, including rosaries and the letters of the alphabet (see dedication photograph). A group of kinswomen surrounding her began to make *oné mésa* sarongs, particularly with the *mboko wéa* motif (FIGURE 6-22). In the fifty years since its creation, the *lawo oné mésa* has spread only within a group of closely related weavers in the single hamlet in which it was created.

LIO TEXTILES

East of Ende the coast is so rugged that the highway makes a long detour inland, rising up through the spectacular Wolowona River gorge and around the north flank of the volcano Kelimutu. Sixty-eight kilometers from Ende, it reaches the market town and district center of Wolowaru. There a spur road branches off, descending the slopes of the Mbuli Valley and eventually terminating at the village of Nggela on the south coast. This populous valley was administered from Wolowaru in the colonial period under the Raja of Tana Kunu Lima (Domain of Five Clans). Of the five constituent communities, the three nearest the coast (Nggela, Wolojita, and Mbuli) were the weaving areas. In the areas higher into the interior, weaving was forbidden by traditional law, a prohibition that remains unchallenged today.

The Nggela community (which encompasses the modern villages of Nggela and Pora) was historically the most prominent, renowned for its elaborate cycle of annual rituals and for its weaving. A more thorough discussion of Nggela textiles can be found in CHAPTER 10. The Wolojita community (consisting of the present-day villages of Wolojita, Tenda, and Wiwipemo) has never been as famous as Nggela, but in fact the textiles of the two areas have much in common, with only minor differences in patterning and terminology. In both areas, the demands of modern market production are bringing about changes, but there is still a substantial body of traditional expertise, as well as a great wealth of textile design.

Textile patterns in the Mbuli community (including the villages Mbuli Loo, Mbuli Waralau, Jopu and Bokasape) differed more sharply from those of Nggela. Unfortunately the stylistic differences from hamlet to hamlet have yet to be thoroughly documented and the high degree of recent change in the Mbuli region now obstructs a ready understanding. The village of Jopu in particular has become a producer of large quantities of inexpensive women's ikat sarongs. These are sold in weekly markets throughout the Lio region and beyond.[9] Jopu church and women's organizations have played an active role in promoting new materials and patterns. Today all production relies on synthetic yarns and chemical dyes. Perhaps more than any other place on Flores, there is a conscious effort to produce new designs as a marketing strategy (FIGURE 6-26).

Lio women's sarongs (*lawo*) are readily distinguished from their Endenese counterparts by the absence of the plain black *mité méré* band. The motifs are more intricate and sometimes new reserve knots are tied between the indigo and morinda dyeings, producing

FIGURE 6-21 (LEFT).
The two-panel *sémba*, derived from Endenese cloths, has now become a specialty of the Lio weaving communities of Ndona District. Made in the 1980s by Sisilia Wunu of Wolotopo. 226 x 123 cm. FMCH X88.1276, Museum Purchase, Manus Fund.

FIGURE 6-22 (RIGHT).
Lawo oné mésa with the motif *mboko wéa. Mboko wéa* is a general term for gold ornaments, whereas names such as *omé mbulu* (see FIGURE 1-1) designate specific shapes and sizes. Made circa 1980 by Bernadetta Wea of Onelako. 159 x 77 cm. Private collection.

small blue accents that are not found in Endenese cloth (FIGURES 6-24, 6-25). The design formats are also more varied. In banded formats, the widest ikat band may occur in the end panels rather than in the center (FIGURE 6-27). Some Lio sarongs are made of four panels, with two narrow panels together producing the centerfield design. In other cases, the centerfield design spills over into the end panels (FIGURE 6-28). The central field may be divided vertically and sometimes adjacent sections carry different patterns (FIGURE 10-12).

In rare cases, bands have been done away with altogether, creating sarongs with overall patterning like the *lawo oné mésa* of Ndona District.[10] As in Ndona, this format appears to be a twentieth-century innovation. Sometimes traditional motifs are used, but the open format has also lent itself to the development of innovative pictorial motifs (FIGURES 6-29, 6-30). Such sarongs occur, with different motifs, in both Mbuli and Nggela, indicating that experimentation was carried on separately in each area.

In addition to women's sarongs, many other types of textiles were made in the Lio areas. The most highly valued men's garments during the early part of the twentieth century were huge sarongs made of indigo-dyed yarns, with a few narrow lines of morinda red carried in both warp and weft to create a subtle plaid. These sarongs are no longer made but are still in use in Nggela, where they are called *luka ria* or "great sarong" (FIGURE 10-14). In Ndona similar sarongs were named according to the span of the fabric used, expressed as a number of *siku* or "elbows" representing the distance from the fingertips to the elbow. The *luka siku lima* or "five elbow sarong" was a sarong of ordinary dimensions considered appropriate for commoners. The *luka siku tera esa,* or "nine elbow sarong," was an oversized garment reserved for men of aristocratic standing at ceremonial events.

For everyday dress, men in weaving villages during this period most often wore plain sarongs or black-and-white plaid sarongs called *luka bara mité* (FIGURE 6-31). In non-weaving interior areas, many men wore plain white sarongs of voluminous dimensions. Cloth for these was sometimes produced in weaving villages and obtained through barter, but today many people recall that imported commercial cloth was also used. This suggests that possibly as early as 1920, in interior areas imported cloth was economically competitive with cloth produced on the coast.

Since the 1960s the predominant type of men's sarong in the Lio areas has been a dark blue garment decorated with bold bands of warp stripes (FIGURE 1-7). These sarongs are generally called *luka* in Ndona District and *ragi* in Wolowaru District. The popularity of this style today is based on the ready availability of pre-dyed cotton-polyester yarns, which are marketed in large quantity in Lio weaving areas. Although the yarns are no longer dyed by the weavers themselves, a strong preference remains for the dark blue color that recalls the indigo-dyed yarns of the past. The stripes are usually white, pale blue, and yellow, although new colors have been accepted for these accents. Sometimes simple warp float patterns are worked into the widest stripes, and in a few rare examples warp ikat bands have been added.

Additional items of men's costume include headcloths, bags, and shoulder cloths. The Lio headcloth is a square piece of red fabric decorated

FIGURES 6-24 (LEFT) and 6-25 (RIGHT).
These sarongs, both identified as *lawo sindé* and both made in Wolojita, illustrate the range of individual variation that may occur within a single named type of cloth. *Sindé* is the Lio name for Indian patola. Locally made sarongs that bear this name always show strong patola influence. LEFT, 174 x 70 cm, FMCH X88.1271. Museum Purchase, Manus Fund. RIGHT, 188 x 134 cm. Collection of Kent Watters.

with fine yellow checks (FIGURE 1-7). Its double blue-green border is made of yarns dyed lightly with indigo and then over-dyed with a green dye produced from mango leaves, mango bark, and turmeric. The resulting color is called *mbopo* and the cloth is called *lésu lobo mbopo*, or "headcloth with *mbopo* border." This type of cloth, identical to the Todo headcloth described in CHAPTER 4, was quite possibly used over much of Flores at one time. It is sometimes referred to as *lésu Eropa*, betraying its ultimately foreign origin. It is rarely made today and most Lio men now purchase a batik head-cloth if they need one for ceremonial dress.

Observers in the colonial period noted that Lio men were rarely without their bags, used to carry betel-chewing supplies and other personal possessions. Men of ordinary social status carried bags plaited from strips of pandanus leaf. The aristocratic and ceremonial bag (*pundi*) was made of woven cotton, decorated with white supplementary-warp motifs on an indigo ground (FIGURES 6-32, 6-33). *Pundi* are made of a single length of fabric, folded in half and stitched closed along the sides. The top of the bag slides into a heavy silver clasp, sealing it closed. *Pundi* have not been made for several decades and are now extremely rare on Flores. Those that remain are guarded as clan heirlooms, taken out of storage only at major ritual events.

Lio men used several different types of shoulder cloths. In the 1920s married men of middling social standing wore shoulder cloths like the *selémpang* of Manggarai, with a tapestry join along the edge of a plain central field (FIGURE 6-34). The crowning glory of aristocratic ceremonial dress was an ikat shoulder cloth. Except for the Ndona District *sémba* described in the previous section, Lio ikat shoulder cloths normally consist of only one panel. Today most rely on a single patola-derived pattern and are called *luka sémba* (FIGURE 6-35). Occasionally one comes across shoulder cloths with other patterns, suggesting that a greater variety of designs may once have been made.[11] Some beautiful examples bearing ship motifs, called *sémba kapa* or *luka kapa*, have been preserved in museum collections (FIGURE 6-36).

FIGURE 6-26. Although this sarong was made with synthetic fiber and dyes, great effort was expended in the tying of such an intricate pattern. The design is not indigenous, but was adapted from a Javanese batik cloth in the weaver's possession. Because the new design is highly admired, its creator doesn't wear it often for fear that the design will be copied by other weavers. Jopu village, 1980s. FMCH X88.1264. Museum Purchase, Manus Fund.

FIGURE 6-27 (LEFT).
The *lawo mogha mité* is a popular banded sarong in the Lio areas. This example is from the village of Tenda. 196 x 140 cm, half shown. FMCH X81.1497, Gift of William Lloyd Davis and Mrs. W. Thomas Davis.

FIGURE 6-28 (RIGHT).
The *kéli mara* pattern of this unusual sarong more commonly appears in the widest end-panel band of a banded sarong (FIGURE 10-15). In this version, it recalls patola patterns and also includes a motif that can be interpreted as an anthropomorphic figure. 172 x 128 cm, folded. Museum for Textiles R79.380, Toronto.

FIGURE 6-29 (BELOW, LEFT).
This design features a variety of bird and human images, spread in a continuous pattern over four panels of cloth. Field photograph of a cloth made circa 1960 in Bokasape village.

FIGURE 6-30 (BELOW, RIGHT).
Another pictoral sarong includes a highly idiosyncratic range of images. Timothy and Tuti Manring Collection, Seattle Art Museum L90.3.344.

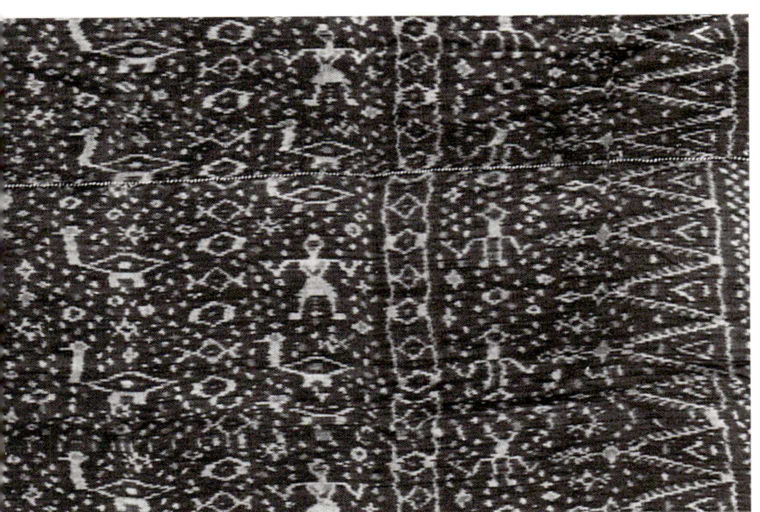

FIGURE 6-31.
A group of men from Tana Kunu Lima, circa 1920, wearing a mix of dress. Some of the plain sarongs are white and others appear to be dyed with indigo or perhaps mud dyes. The black-and-white plaid sarongs (*luka bara mité*) were popular during the colonial period. From Suchtelen 1921, plate 62.

OPPOSITE PAGE:
FIGURE 6-32 (LEFT).
The Lio men's ceremonial bag *pundi*. The supplementary-warp technique is no longer used in the Lio areas. Tropenmuseum 1329-1, Amsterdam.

FIGURE 6-33 (RIGHT, TOP).
Lio elder with a *pundi* bag draped over his shoulder. From Heerkens, 1943.

FIGURE 6-34 (RIGHT, BOTTOM). This type of cloth is known as *sa nai poké dubu* (loosely, "single-panel cloth with tapestry technique") in Ndona and *luka bara lombo* (man's cloth with white border) in Nggela. Onelako, 1988.

SOME COMPARISONS

The Lio men's shoulder cloth called *luka sémba* provides the clearest example of an essential principle of textile design on Flores that deserves special note. The design format of men's ikat shoulder cloths and their female counterparts, ikat sarongs, are transformations of one another. The counterpart of the *luka sémba* is a common Lio sarong type called *lawo luka sémba*, a name that clearly reveals the close relationship between the two cloths. Both may also be seen as transformations of the design format of patola (FIGURE 6-37, A-C). A similar relationship between the design formats of men's and women's ikat cloths can be seen in other ethnic areas as well, for example Ngadha *lawo* and *lu'é*.

Another interesting feature of design layout is the distinction between cloths with centerfields and those with patterns that are banded throughout. According to an interpretation developed by Bühler (1959:13), the banded format predates the centerfield format, which was adopted later from patola.[12] The design formats of Ende-Lio banded sarongs do not contradict this interpretation, but suggest that it be applied with caution. To begin with, even sarongs with banded centerfields have the specialized ordering of bands in the end panel, echoing the transformed side borders of patola. Furthermore, the major ikat bands in the center panels terminate in specific motifs, often in triangular forms, that are analogous to the end borders of patola. While it may indeed be true that banded sarongs of some sort (including those with plain warp stripes) pre-date centerfield sarongs, it would be a mistake to conclude that sarongs identical to today's banded types were being made in pre-patola times. Nor can it be ruled out that today's banded sarongs might have developed secondarily from centerfield designs as a labor-saving short cut (like *zawo ngéra* made of leftover yarns). In reality, it is not even certain that the ikat technique and the secrets of morinda dyeing were known on Flores prior to the advent of the patola trade or even later.[13]

A similar difficulty occurs with Petu's (1977) interpretation of the origins of specific categories of Flores textile motifs, which follows lines similar to Heine-Geldern's influential analysis of Southeast Asian design elements (1937, 1966). Certain motifs, including both figurative and abstract representations of humans, animals, and plants, are classed as Neolithic motifs invested with symbolic meaning. Geometric motifs, such as diamonds, spirals, meanders, swastikas, and triangles, are considered purely decorative and attributed to the Bronze Age. All these motifs are indeed present in Ende-Lio textiles, but they have also echoed throughout India, Southeast Asia and the Pacific, appearing in a variety of media, including tattoo, ceramics, basketry, carving, and bark-cloth painting. One must not conclude, for example, that the geometric motifs appearing in the bands of ikat sarongs have been made in similar form on Flores since ancient times. Today's designs, both in their overall format and in the shape of their specific motifs, must be seen as hybrids resulting from a long period of cross-fertilization and evolution.

A potentially more productive kind of comparative analysis involves the spread of patterns through neighboring groups within a limited area. For example, Nggela and Wolojita weavers sometimes make sarongs with animal figures similar to the Endenese elephant (*nggaja*) motif. They may even copy the plain black band in the end panel, leaving no doubt about the source of inspiration. The elephant motif is often simplified somewhat and Nggela weavers, like their Ngadha counterparts, identify it as a horse. This motif presumably originated with the elephant that appears on a rare type of patola, although it has been drastically transformed from the rotund original to the stick-figure that appears on today's sarongs. That Endenese weavers are aware of the identity of the creature portrayed, while Ngadha and Nggela weavers are not, suggests that the motif was first copied in Ende and then spread into the hinterland. Certainly this is consistent with Ende's role as the major entrepôt.

Unfortunately, broader comparisons of this sort quickly become problematic. Looking over the design formats of Nagé, Ende, and Lio sarong styles, it is clear that there are a large number of structural similarities (for example, compare the over-all structure of the Nagé *hoba* in FIGURE 5-23 to the Endenese *zawo kabhi* in FIGURE 6-4). Many such similarities extend to the Ngadha, Sikka, and Lamaholot areas as well. The Nagé and Ngadha design

FIGURE 6-35.
Men's shoulder cloth,
luka sémba. 228 x 87 cm.
Private Collection.

FIGURE 6-36. Detail of a men's shoulder cloth with ship motifs, *sémba kapa* or *luka kapa*. Dallas Museum of Art 1983.102.

structures are notably more simple than those found in Ende, which again suggests that coastal originals may have been copied in the interior, losing some of their detail in the process.

Overall, the evidence repeatedly leads to the conclusion that textile trends originated on the coast and spread inland. With the exception of the supplementary-weft tradition, however, weavers of all ethnic groups were primarily drawing on the same source of inspiration (Indian trade cloths) and using the same technique (warp ikat), making it difficult to trace specific inter-group relationships. The most productive ikat weaving groups, including the Ende-Lio, the Sikkanese and the Lamaholot, all appear to have been experimenting with this body of knowledge more or less independently and simultaneously. ❖ NOTES, page 271.

FIGURE 6-37, A–C (BELOW). These schematic drawings illustrate the similarities in design structure among patola, shoulder cloths, and sarongs.

A. Patola, based on FIGURE 7-9.

B. Lio men's shoulder cloth, *luka sémba,* based on FIGURE 6-35.

C. Lio women's sarong, *lawo luka sémba,* based on FIGURE 10-10. This sarong is turned on its side to match the orientation of the other cloths.

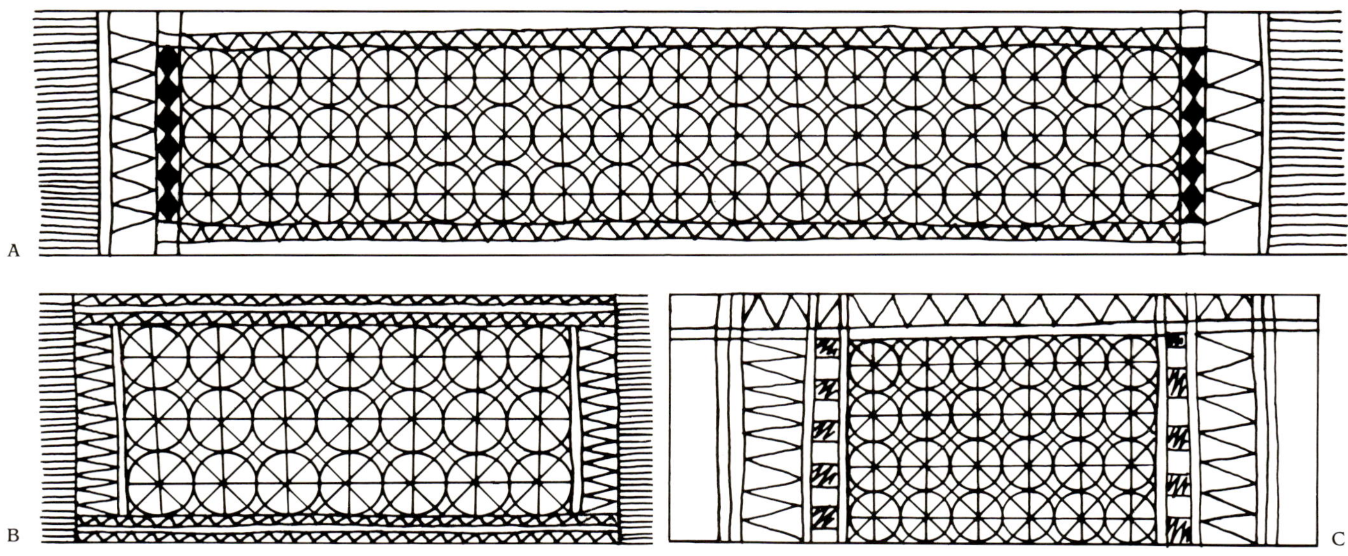

Sikka Regency

E.D. Lewis

KABUPATEN SIKKA, THE REGENCY OF SIKKA, IS HOME TO SOME 300,000 PEOPLE, the majority of whom speak dialects of Sara Sikka, the Sikkanese language. Throughout the regency, textiles play important roles in ceremonial exchanges between the groups which make up a community, especially on occasions of marriages and deaths. Because of differences in the design traditions between localities, every cloth signals its own origin. And, because each group within a community has its own designs, it is frequently possible to identify not only the weaver's place of origin, but the group to which she belongs. The use of cloth as a marker of social identity and social status is thus one of the intriguing features of textile making and use in Sikka.

The most prominent community in the history of the region is Sikka Natar, the "Village of Sikka" on the south coast from which the regency takes its name. Sikka Natar was home to a Catholic population in the seventeenth century and perhaps as early as the second half of the sixteenth century. Before the second half of the nineteenth century, when the Dutch established indirect rule in the region, Sikka Natar was the seat of a local state, or rajadom, ruled by the people of Lepo Geté ("Great House"), a royal family that had adopted the Portuguese name da Silva perhaps as long ago as the sixteenth century. The da Silva family maintained an unbroken dynasty of eighteen rajas that came to an end in the 1950s. During the era of the rajas, Sikkanese rule expanded throughout a large area of eastern Flores and, with this expansion of political power, Catholicism spread from Sikka Natar westward to the coastal community of Léla, eastward to Bola, and, later, into many of the communities of the interior (notably, Nita and Koting).

In the late nineteenth century, the Dutch located their center of the subdivision (*onderafdeling*) of Sikka in the small settlement of Maumere on the north coast, in a sparsely populated area with good access to the main lines of communication and shipping in the eastern archipelago. The Raja of Sikka soon moved his administration to Maumere and in the 1920s, by which time the Catholic Church had established a large mission in the town, Maumere became a center from which social, economic, and political influences emanated throughout the district. With the cooperation of the Dutch, the Raja of Sikka controlled trade in the district through the port of Maumere. And from Sikka Natar, the rajas and the thirteen noble houses of Sikka Natar traded with the Dutch and contracted

FIGURE 7-1 (OPPOSITE). Detail of FIGURE 7-5.

FIGURE 7-2.
Don Thomas Ximenes da Silva (circa 1900-1954), Raja of Sikka, poses with his ceremonial regalia, including a golden helmet of Portuguese manufacture and a gold-headed staff of office (*tongkat*). The elephant tusks were part of the ceremonial wealth of Lepo Geté, the royal house of Sikka. Koninklijk Instituut voor Taal-, Land- en Volkenkunde, Leiden.

OPPOSITE PAGE:
FIGURE 7-3 (TOP LEFT).
Dated 1954, this photo of Don Thomas Ximenes da Silva is believed to be the last taken of the raja before his death. It evokes a strikingly different image from FIGURE 7-2, suggesting that the power of the rajas of Flores depended in part on their ability to fulfill, or even exploit, the divergent demands of office in a time of great social change.

FIGURE 7-4 (TOP RIGHT).
Sacks of rice piled on the beach at Sikka Natar were brought by boat from distant fields in the Tana 'Ai region. 1920s. Koninklijk Instituut voor de Tropen, Amsterdam.

affinal and political alliances with other major and minor rajas on Flores and in the Lesser Sunda Islands. While Sikka Natar was no longer the seat of government, it continued to provide ministers and officials to the raja's government and to be recognized as the main source of power and authority in the rajadom (FIGURES 7-2, 7-3).

From the late nineteenth century to the present, hundreds of people from Sikka Natar became teachers, government officials and Catholic priests. In the days of the rajas, these functionaries were appointed to posts in villages throughout the rajadom and it was principally through them and their families that Sikkanese political hegemony, Catholicism, and Sikkanese culture came to permeate the region. It was also through them and the women of their households that the style of textile making indigenous to Sikka Natar spread throughout the region and to a large extent displaced what may have been a number of different styles indigenous to larger villages of the Sikkanese hinterland (FIGURES 7-5, 7-6).

This, at least, is the tale told by the contemporary people of Sikka Natar, the Ata Sikka, to explain the predominance of their style of textile design in the region. While they recognize the worth of the textiles of Léla, Nita, Koting, Bola, and those made by expatriate Ata Sikka residing in Maumere (especially descendants of the royal and noble houses), the people of Sikka claim that their textiles are superior to all others in the region. To some extent other peoples of the regency agree, and for this reason an account of the textiles of Kabupaten Sikka can reasonably begin with those of Sikka Natar.

FLORES SEA
PALU'É
PULAU BESAR
SIKKA
KIMANG
Maumere
Kéwapante
TANA 'AI
Nita
Geliting
KROWE
'IWANG GETÉ
EGON
Dokot
Nalé
'Ili
Héwoklo'ang
Koting
Watublapi
Halé
Tilang
Hébing
Léla
Bola
Klo'angpopot
Paga
Sikka Natar
(Sikka Village)
SAVU SEA

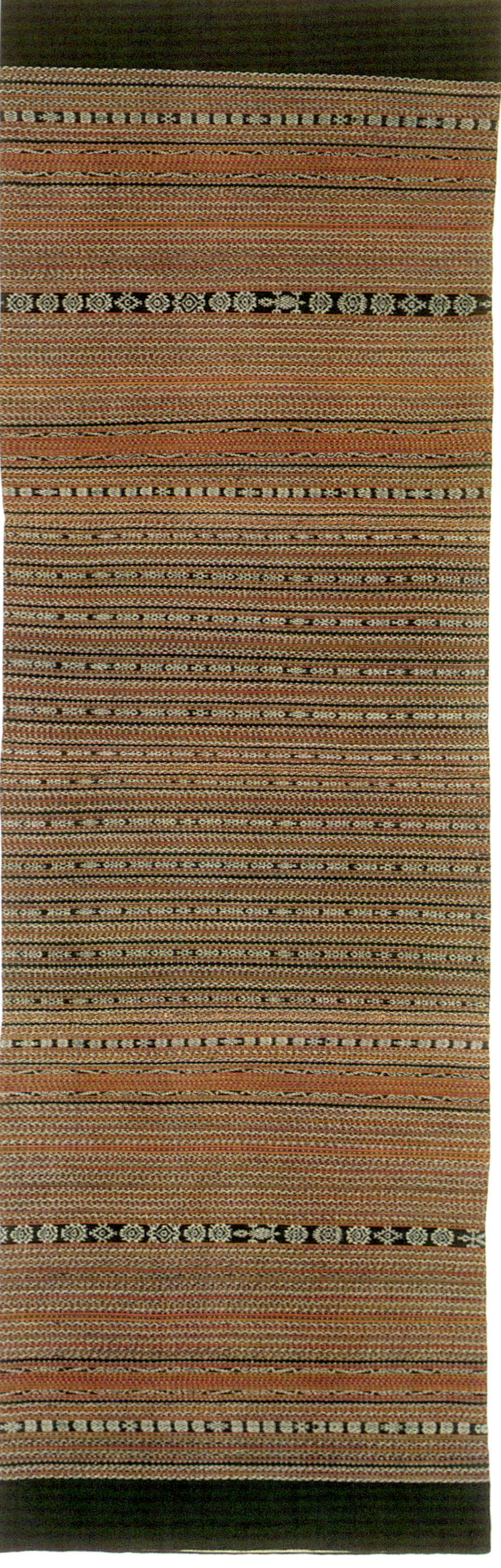

FIGURE 7-5.
This exceptionally fine cloth in the Sikka Natar style, features a motif in the wide pattern section that is associated with the ruling house of the Sikkanese rajas. Valued Sikkanese cloths are stored and exchanged in the form in which they come off the loom, with the fringe uncut. In this form, the banded patterning of the cloth is asymmetrical. Only after the cloth is cut in two and the two panels rejoined (side by side and in mirror image) does the ultimate symmetry of the tubular sarong emerge. 160 x 84 cm. Collection of E. D. Lewis.

FIGURE 7-6.
This four-panel bridewealth sarong from 'Iwang Geté represents an older tradition, consistent with the practice in most parts of Flores of making women's sarongs from separately woven panels. The motifs are much simpler than those of Sikka Natar (see Maxwell 1990:89). 219 x 68 cm. National Gallery of Australia 1981.1144.

Sikka Natar is built on a narrow sandy strand, a coral shelf bounded by the Savu Sea and a steep escarpment of barren hills (FIGURE 7-4). In the early 1980s the village consisted of some 150 households and perhaps 1,200 people, although the population fluctuates because many men work away from the community during parts of the year. In spite of its small size and barren setting, Sikka Natar is unusually wealthy by the standards of Flores.

Although Sikka Natar is unprepossessing in size and appearance, its social order is complex. Until the 1950s the Ata Sikka were ranked in a social hierarchy that consisted of the royal house, thirteen noble houses, free commoners, and people indentured to the noble houses. While indentureship was abolished after World War II and the rajas no longer rule the district, social identity remains informed, at least in part, by this old hierarchy. Everyone in Sikka Natar belongs to his or her father's house, which provides a person's primary social identity. Houses are exogamous; and cross-cutting the old hierarchy of classes is a complex system of marriage alliances among houses which is as important today as ever in the past. Marriages are contracted not between individual men and women but between houses. When a man and a woman decide to marry, the people of the groom's house present a gift called *ling wéling*[1] to the people of the bride's house. This gift creates a debt, and thus an alliance, between the two houses.

Through time, all of the marriages in the village have brought about a complex alliance system within which wife-givers, who receive bridewealth, are ritually superior to wife-takers, who give bridewealth. The system is in principle (but not always in practice) asymmetrical, which means that two groups cannot exchange bridewealth (and wives) directly. Before an item given as bridewealth can return to its source, it must pass through a third group. Thus, goods given as bridewealth may return to a house, but not before they have passed though one or more intermediate groups. One result of this rule is that each individual and house in the community can count at least one other as wife-taker (bridewealth-giver) and at least one other as wife-giver (bridewealth-taker). Since the latter are ritually superior to the former, everyone is both superior to some and inferior to others in the community with respect to ritual status and in terms of affinal relationships. Textiles enter into this system in a highly significant way, for every installment of bridewealth elicits a return gift of cloth.

The patterns of ceremonial and social exchange found in Sikka Natar are also found in the communities of the central hills and among the Sara-Sikka speaking peoples of the north coast. In referring to the other peoples of the district, the Ata Sikka distinguish the peoples of Krowé and those of the area they call 'Iwang Geté. Krowé is the region of the central saddle of the district which includes the villages of Nita, Koting, Nelé, Tilang, Ribang, Dokot, 'Ili, and Kéwapante, and which extends to Bola on the south coast. 'Iwang Geté, which translates as "the great interior" or "the great highlands," includes the villages of Watublapi, Héwoklo'ang, Klo'angpopot, Halé, and Hébing.[2] Embedded in the distinction between Krowé and 'Iwang Geté is a significant classification: the peoples of Krowé were ruled by the Raja of Nita (a rajadom under the Raja of Sikka created by the Dutch), whereas the people of 'Iwang Geté were not part of an indigenous polity.[3] Nevertheless, in all three areas – Sikka Natar, Krowé, and 'Iwang Geté – textiles are among the most important goods given as gifts in the obligatory ceremonial exchanges that take place on the occasions of marriage and death.

The valley of Tana ‘Ai (literally, Forest Land) in the far eastern region of Kabupaten Sikka constitutes a fourth area of importance in a survey of textile traditions of Sikka. The Tana ‘Ai region is divided into seven ceremonial domains or *tana* (earth, land, domain), each headed, in ceremonial and ritual matters, by a man who is always a descendant through women of the founding ancestors of the domain. He is known as *tana pu'an* (source of the earth).[4] While the Ata Tana ‘Ai (People of Tana ‘Ai) speak a dialect of Sara Sikka and their culture bears affinities to that of Sikka Natar, Krowé, and ‘Iwang Geté, the society and history of Tana’Ai differ in significant respects from those of the peoples to the west. Unlike Sikka and Krowé, the Tana ‘Ai region was never ruled by an indigenous raja and, indeed, sovereignty over Tana ‘Ai was a point of dispute between the rajas of Sikka and Larantuka until quite late in the region's history. Whereas the central Sikkanese reckon descent through men, the Ata Tana ‘Ai calculate descent through women. Furthermore, in contrast to the Catholics to the west, the Ata Tana ‘Ai retain their indigenous religious and ceremonial systems.

The Ata Tana ‘Ai say that by *hadat* (tradition, custom, propriety), their women did not in the past weave ikat textiles. Instead, they were acquired through trade. Today, however, young Tana ‘Ai women produce ikat textiles in the central Sikkanese style although the finest ikat cloths in Tana ‘Ai are those purchased in markets on the coast or acquired through trade with Sikkanese and people from East Flores. The traditional textiles of Tana ‘Ai are not ikat. Men's cloths, *sa'en* (FIGURE 7-7), have alternating white and red stripes sometimes separated by black threads. Women's cloths, *nénang*, are indigo-black with a single wide band made up of thin stripes of red, russet, and white, which are sometimes separated by other colors – mainly blues. The Tana ‘Ai *nénang* is thus of a style more commonly associated with East Flores (FIGURE 7-8). Women in Tana ‘Ai have long produced cloth in the style of the Lamaholot peoples of East Flores, but without ikat bands. Nowadays some *nénang* produced in Tana ‘Ai include narrow ikat bands. Most women's ikat cloths are still obtained by trade, however.

As in other parts of Sikka, cloth in Tana ‘Ai has a special significance in ritual. In the past, the most valued textiles in Tana ‘Ai were the *tipa tola* or *'luhen tola*, patola cloths that found their way into the mountains of Tana ‘Ai through trade (FIGURE 7-9). Patola cloths or, in later years, fragments of them, were buried with the dead. As a result, only a few fragments of these highly valued textiles remain in Tana ‘Ai

FIGURE 7-7.
Man's sarong, *sa'en*, from Tana ‘Ai. 115 x 83 cm.
Collection of E. D. Lewis.

(FIGURE 1-4). Today, batik purchased in markets on the coast is used in mortuary rituals.

In Tana 'Ai, marriage is not marked with ritual and, in contrast to other Sikkanese, the Ata Tana 'Ai do not give bridewealth on the occasion of marriage. Nevertheless, cloth is classified as a feminine good and the giving of cloth expresses social obligation. In particular, the death of a man initiates a number of exchanges between his wife's and his own people. The most important of these is the return of one of his daughters from his wife's clan to his own, when the husband and wife are from different clans. In return for the daughter, who is said to replace her father's blood in his clan, the deceased father's sisters give his wife's people gongs and elephant tusks. A counter-prestation in the form of cloth is made by the wife's sisters to their affines. Thus in Tana 'Ai, as everywhere on Flores, the exchange of textiles is a principal medium for the expression of alliance.

THE SOCIAL MEANING OF TEXTILES IN SIKKA

It is in Sikka Natar that textiles most fully express social relationships among the groups who make up the community. There, as throughout the Sikka region, weaving is done exclusively by women and the largest numbers of cloths are produced by married women. Girls begin helping their mothers, aunts, and older sisters with weaving at an early age and older unmarried girls and young women spend much of their time producing cloth. Because mastery of dyeing and weaving requires much experience, years can pass before a young woman begins producing cloth sufficiently valued for exchange in the ceremonial system. Older Sikkanese women say that an industrious young woman who spends much of her time weaving can get a husband more easily than a lazy one. Indeed the sound of the loom, which rattles during use, is incessant in the village during daylight hours and is said to attract bachelors.[5]

Completing a cloth can take as long as twenty years and weavers say that a minimum of ten or twelve years is required for the finest textiles. This is because the threads require many separate dyeings between which they must rest for months while the dye sets properly. The finest red cloths require more than a dozen separate dyeings spaced at least eight to ten months apart. As a result, most mature women have dozens of partially completed cloths stored away. In 1979, one prodigious master weaver, whose house had relatively few exchange obligations over the years, had more than two hundred cloths in various stages of completion. As finished cloth is required — for daily wear, for formal

FIGURE 7-8.
Woman's sarong, *nénang*, worn in Tana 'Ai. This cloth, with its narrow ikat bands, was acquired by trade with people from Boru in East Flores. 137 x 62 cm. Collection of E. D. Lewis.

attire, or for exchange in bridewealth or funeral transactions — prepared bundles of threads are taken from storage and woven into completed cloths. To understand what happens to all the cloths lying about in the storage baskets of Sikkanese weavers, we must know something of the social meaning of textiles in Sikka.

The Ata Sikka divide the world into two principal realms. *Wawa tana*, "down on the ground," is the domain of men, who spend much time away from the village in order to make a living. *Réta uneng*, "up inside (the house)," is the domain of women. Items of real and ceremonial wealth are also divided into two categories. Elephant tusks, gold coins, and horses, which are given as bridewealth, are classified as men's goods. Women's goods include pigs, rice, bananas, household furnishings, kitchenwares, and cloth. Wife-givers give these to their wife-takers as a counter-prestation to bridewealth. Textiles are preeminent among feminine (as distinct from masculine) goods, and they are the true measure of a woman's wealth.

Elephant tusks and gold coins are in principle durable goods. They are, however, non-renewable and, as tusks have become smaller and scarcer, their ceremonial value has inflated. As a result, the velocity of their movement through the exchange system has increased

FIGURE 7-9. Detail of an Indian patola belonging to a Tana 'Ai clan. The full cloth measures 349 x 91 cm. Courtesy of E. D. Lewis.

considerably in recent years.[6] Textiles, in contrast, are renewable consumables. Unlike bridewealth goods, which circulate, cloth is only given once, as a counter-prestation to bridewealth. Women who receive cloths must cut them, sew them into sarongs, and wear them. The Sikkanese point out that as bridewealth goods have increased in value, so too have the numbers of textiles required for affinal exchanges. Given the industriousness of Sikka weavers, the supply of ceremonial textiles is continually renewed. Even educated women who work as teachers or government officials still produce at least a few cloths to help offset the exchange obligations of their kinsfolk.

Within the system of symbolic classification, whereby elephant tusks are masculine and textiles feminine, the Ata Sikka distinguish two sorts of cloth. The first is '*utang*, cloth worn by women (FIGURES 7-10, 7-11); the second is *lipa*,[7] cloth worn by men (FIGURE 7-12). Within these categories, there is a further distinction between ordinary, everyday cloths[8] and ceremonial ones.

Women's cloth, '*utang*, may be black or red. Widows wear black cloth ('*utang mitang*) in which the major motif panel is rendered as ikat against a background of indigo. Only red cloths ('*utang mérang*) can be exchanged in ceremonial transactions. The major motifs

of red cloth are executed in deep russet background produced by indigo over-dyed with morinda. All *'utang* carry the ikat motif on the warp; that is, the warp threads are resist-dyed to produce the pattern of the cloth.

Men's cloth, *lipa*, are rare nowadays and are worn only on occasions of important ritual. In contrast to women's *'utang*, the patterns of men's cloths are carried by the weft, which requires a loom arrangement and weaving technique different from that employed in making women's cloth. In *'utang*, the only visible threads are those of the warp, which are spaced closely together and carry the ikat pattern. In the weaving of *lipa*, a reed is placed in the loom to separate the warp threads so that the ikat pattern carried by the weft threads will be visible. This results in a looser weave that drapes more delicately. But it is very difficult to maintain the precise alignment of the weft threads necessary for sharply defined motifs. As a woman once told me, the only thing more difficult to manage than a man's cloth is the man himself.

Both technically and in terms of Sikkanese symbolic classifications, the warp threads, which are categorically feminine, are seen to bind together the weft threads, which are categorically masculine. This is, of course, precisely what women do in marriage: they bind together Sikkanese houses which are defined by groups of agnatically related men. It is not surprising that the vocabulary of weaving provides metaphors for speaking about the complexities of the Sikkanese system of affinal alliance.

TEXTILES IN A FRAME OF ALLIANCE AND SOCIAL IDENTITY

The primary social identification of an Ata Sikka is by his or her membership in a paternally ordered kin group. That is to say, all Sikkanese, whether male or female, are affiliated primarily with the kin groups of their fathers. These groups are called *kuat wungung*[9] and are divided into *lepo*, or houses, which have some of the characteristics of lineages. Groups of paternally related men are responsible for assisting their members with the bridewealth necessary for contracting marriages. When a woman marries, she retains her paternal identification (she does not give up her father's family name, for example), but she moves from her father's to her husband's father's house and, with her husband, eventually constructs and inhabits a house of her own.

The first ceremonial transaction required for a marriage is the delivery of a number of elephant tusks, horses, gold pieces, and an amount of cash as an installment toward the total bridewealth which the wife-takers and wife-givers have negotiated. The goods in the first gift are transferred from the house of the man to the house of his bride. Bridewealth prestations in Sikka Natar are much larger than in other regions of Sikka. One, contracted in 1978, consisted of twelve elephant tusks of a specified size, twenty-two horses, eight gold coins of nineteenth-century Dutch mintage, and several hundreds of thousands of rupiah in cash. In monetary terms, such gifts are quite valuable but the principle is that bridewealth is never actually paid in full, for full payment would sever the alliance between the two houses. The bridewealth-paying house is conceived to be perpetually in the debt of the bridewealth-receiving house for the gift of life – the fertility – of the woman who has married out of her paternal house. Rather than paying completely, the wife-taking group makes a series of payments to the wife-giving group throughout the lifetimes of the two people who have married. In some cases, these payments continue after the deaths of the husband and wife.

With every installment of bridewealth, the woman's people make a counter-prestation called *'utang labu wawi paré*, "(women's) cloth, blouses, pigs, and rice." Of these goods, the most highly valued are the textiles, which must be of a certain quality. The women of the man's house who receive the cloth have the right of refusal, which is exercised when they feel the cloth they are offered is of inferior quality or when they wish to communicate something in particular to people who are, as wife-givers, their ritual superiors. On one occasion, for example, a prestation of cloth was refused by a wife-taking group who were mindful of an old dispute with their wife-givers. On that occasion, a spokeswoman for the receivers of the cloth made a long speech, in the most politely formal language, the basic message of which was:

> You pitiable people bring us such sad rags. Indeed, we empathize. But
> we wish not to remove the sarongs from the waists of your own women.
> Our honor would suffer from their lack of clothing and your honor
> would suffer should the meagerness of their cloth storage baskets

> become known. Rather than forcing upon you, by receiving your cloth, such indignity, we shall take our wealth and return home. Perhaps another day, after your looms have sounded industriously, we shall meet again and exchange the felicitations that should pass between in-laws.

With the delivery of this remarkable insult, the wife-takers packed up their tusks, unhitched their horses, and departed. Relations between these two houses were still strained many years later.[10]

Goods received by a group as bridewealth and goods received as counter-prestations of bridewealth are redistributed to members of the recipient groups. Tusks and other masculine goods can be used in fulfillment of other bridewealth obligations and masculine goods thus circulate through the community. But cloth cannot be used in this way; it must be worn – that is, consumed or "eaten," as the Sikkanese express the idea – by the women of the recipient group who, in turn, must give to other groups cloth which they themselves have produced. Before it is exchanged, the ceremonial cloth must be kept intact, as it comes from the loom, but once given, it is cut and sewn into a tubular sarong by the recipient, to be worn at events similar to that on which it was received.[11]

In this manner, textiles, which are women's goods, carry social meaning and are marked socially in a way that items of bridewealth – men's goods – are not. Men's goods circulate generally through the community, and thus mark only in the most general way the complex web of alliances that bind the Ata Sikka into a single community. Women's goods, in contrast, identify specific dyads of houses linked by particular marriages. The receiving of bridewealth and the giving of cloth contract not so much the marriage of a particular man and woman, but the undertaking of mutual responsibilities between two houses that endure beyond a single lifetime.[12]

DESIGN ELEMENTS
IN SIKKANESE TEXTILES

Both the origins and the meanings of the motifs of Sikkanese cloth were once encoded in a complex oral and mythic tradition which has now, for the most part, been lost. Nevertheless, from examining the major patterns and structures of the principal motifs, it remains clear that the cloths reproduce to some extent the motifs of patola cloths. While other peoples in eastern Indonesia, such as the Rotinese, Ndaonese, and Lionese, preserve patola panel structures in their contemporary textiles, the Sikkanese do not. Instead, they have preserved some patola-inspired design elements, but, like the people of Savu, they weave the patola motifs into bands rather than in full panels. Why the Sikkanese employ bands, while others in the archipelago preserve the panel designs of the original patolas, is a question that may not be answerable. It is certain, however, that the bands in Sikkanese cloths encode a range of meaning related to the identities of the cloths and their makers.

In addition to distinguishing women's cloth as red or black and ordinary or ceremonial, the Sikkanese also classify cloths according to the origin of the motifs they bear. One category consists of cloths which bear designs that girls have learned from teaching sisters in the Catholic middle schools. The other category of cloth bears motifs native to Sikka. Only these indigenous designs, of which there are many named kinds, can appear on cloths intended for ceremonial exchange. These are the true *'utang* of Sikka, which are used only for ceremonial exchanges within the community. They are the subject of a complex typology by which textiles are classified according to the motifs they bear and the structure of the bands in which they appear.[13]

The basic structural unit of an *'utang* motif is a *siwang*, a group of six contiguous warp threads. By tradition, six is the smallest number of threads tied together in the ikat process. The *siwang* is thus the basic or smallest significant unit, a digit or a bit, in a digitally ordered design system that produces complex analogical discriminations, or messages, about the social world.[14] Wider bands are built up from *siwang*, and various multiples of *siwang* units are named and defined in terms of what can and cannot be carried by them in the way of a motif; that is, as messages in a system of communication. As will be seen, these messages, the arrangements of motifs and bands, communicate the social identity of the weaver and, by extension, information about the position of the cloth's wearer in the system of affinal alliance in the community.

Women's cloths suitable for exchange are identified according to two major features of their design and structure. The first is *kélang*, literally "writing" or "picture." In the context of textiles, *kélang* are the names of the motifs, the number of which is finite in cloths used for ceremonial exchange. The production of these motifs is restricted by rules and influenced by the values according to which they are judged: the accuracy of their reproduction of ideal motifs and the skill of their execution in the cloth.

The second criterion for classifying *'utang* is *hura*, a word denoting order and sequence.[15] In cloth, *hura* is manifested in the sequence of motif-bearing ikatted bands, each of which is set off from its neighbors by one or a few threads of solid color – white, red, blue, yellow, or green. The ikat bands are ordered according to complex rules governing the types of motifs that can border one another.

In short, a cloth is identified first by the name of its *hura*, the name of the particular sequence of bands it displays, and, second, according to its *kélang*, the name of its principal motif. We can think of *kélang* and *hura* as distinguishing the motif and the design structure of the cloth. As in a language, in which the meaning of a sentence varies as words are substituted for one another paradigmatically, and as word order changes according to shifts governed by syntax, differences of both *kélang* and *hura* affect the messages of social identity encoded in the cloth. These carry essential information that identifies both the cloth's maker and its wearer in social terms. The meaning of design

FIGURE 7-12.
Man's cloth, *lipa*, with weft-ikat decoration. Sikkanese weavers make *lipa* using a variety of other techniques as well. Weft ikat sarongs are called *lipa peténg*. Sarongs with continuous supplementary weft are *lipa prenggi* and sarongs with discontinuous supplementary weft are *lipa songké* (Petu 1992:94-95). 117 x 81 cm. Collection of E. D. Lewis.

elements in a Sikkanese ceremonial cloth is thus located outside of the cloth itself, in the rules governing its manufacture, its use, and the social practices of exchange that encompass it.[16] To understand this point we must examine, at least briefly, the major features of the band sequences which are the most striking characteristic of Sikkanese textiles.

HURA: THE DESIGN STRUCTURE OF SIKKANESE TEXTILES

The pattern of a Sikkanese cloth inheres in bands laid into the warp. Bands may consist of ikat threads, solidly colored threads dyed with morinda (*bur*) or indigo (*tarong*), or monochromatic threads of other colors, which are usually brighter than the ikat bands. Ikat bands range in size from more than half the width of the whole cloth on the loom to a width of only a single *siwang*. In all cases, bands of ikat threads are separated from one another by bands of monochrome threads.

The monochrome threads are called *perung*, which is also the word for "thread" in general. They may be of several colors, including *heret* (yellow, from dyes made of turmeric or mango bark), *mérang* (red, from morinda), *mérang linok* (bright red or orange resulting from morinda over-dyed with turmeric), *da'ang tang* (green, from indigo over-dyed with turmeric), *da'ang linok* (blue or light blue resulting from a single or two dyeings of indigo), *mitang* (indigo black), and others. Multiple thread bands of the unelaborated, predominant color are *mérang natar* (literally, village red) in red cloths and *mitang natar* (village black) in black cloths.

More than merely traditional, the bright, monochrome threads and their arrangements relative to the ikat bands produce intricate and subtle symmetries that locate a cloth in a complex system of textile classifications. Just as the motifs are geometrically symmetrical, so too are the sequences of bands. Indeed, the bands of Sikkanese cloths manifest a strict, if not apparent, order and it is this order that is of paramount importance to a Sikkanese weaver. The presence or absence of a single thread can affect the pattern of symmetries that lend form to the cloth's design and thus alter the classification of a cloth.

The major band of a cloth, although not always the widest, is the *'ina geté*, a phrase meaning literally "great mother" and, in the relationship terminology of Sara Sikka, "mother's elder sister." The *'ina geté* carries a motif (*kélang*) which, together with the band sequence (*hura*), identifies the cloth. Thus, when a weaver names a cloth, she mentions both its *hura* and its *kélang*. In cloths of certain types, the motif of the major band also appears in a narrower version, in the band called *'ina kesik*, literally "little mother," a phrase that in the relationship terminology denotes a mother's younger sister.

In cloths suitable as prestations in bridewealth exchanges, the motif of the *'ina geté* appears on a background of dark brownish purple or *wungung*, a color that results from one or two indigo dyeings over-dyed with morinda. The *'ina geté* can carry up to four colors: purple (*wungung*); red (*mérang*), resulting from morinda alone; blue (*da'ang linok*), resulting from indigo alone; and white (*bura*), the original color of the thread.

The bands of a Sikkanese cloth are of a number of named types. They are distinguished in terms of their width and their location relative to other named bands in the overall sequence of bands which defines the design structure of the cloth. The names of the commonest ikat-carrying bands are detailed in the list (OPPOSITE).

The sequence of a cloth's bands, its *hura*, is such that every band bears a spatial relationship to others on the cloth, producing strictly bilateral symmetries with single bands at their centers. These symmetries overlap along the width of the cloth; centers with small symmetries are nested within larger symmetries, each with its own center. Single cloths incorporate from ten to more than sixty overlapping symmetrical clusters of bands.

The central band of a symmetrical cluster can be either ikat or monochrome. The clusters range in magnitude from three bands, in which the central one is flanked on both sides by single identical bands, to as many as seventy-seven. In no case, however, do all of the bands of a cloth belong to a single symmetrical cluster; in other words, in no Sikkanese cloth is there a single central band around which all other bands of the cloth are arrayed symmetrically.[17] This means that all cloths consist of a number – sometimes, a large number – of overlapping and nested symmetries.

FIGURES 7-13 through 7-17 demonstrate the symmetries found in a sample of women's textiles from Sikka Natar. In every case it is apparent that the weaver has devoted painstaking care to the construction of symmetries. Errors are rare and even the smallest can give cause to reject a cloth as a gift in a ceremonial exchange. While the number of *hura* is limited, it is sufficiently large to allow for the many different types of cloth

Named Bands in Sikkanese Cloth

'ina geté – "mother's elder sister," the band bearing the main motif of the cloth, by which the cloth is identified. In red cloths of the best quality, the background color of the *'ina geté* is purple (*wungung*).

'ina kesik – "mother's younger sister," a band narrower than the *'ina geté*, carrying a fragment of the motif of the *'ina geté* (usually the central figures) and, in the best red cloths, also bearing the background color purple (*wungung*).

renda – a wide band at the bottom of the cloth. The *renda* can be the widest band on a cloth but is always red (*mérang*) or indigo (*mitang*) in color and never purple (*wungung*).

ési – a narrow band, usually no more than 7 *siwang* (42 threads) wide. The most common *ési* motif is a repeated "lazy s" figure. Its background color in the best red cloths is purple (*wungung*).

tokang or *likeng* – a narrow band, usually similar to *ési* in width, but with a simpler motif. Its design may be a fragment of the *renda* motif or reminiscent of it. In a red cloth the background color of *tokang* and *likeng* is normally red (*mérang*) rather than purple (*wungung*), but in a black cloth it is the same indigo black as the *'ina geté*. Weavers say the terms *tokang* and *likeng* are synonyms; but *likeng* are usually slightly narrower than *tokang* and are further designated in terms of the number of *siwang* from which they are made, for example, *likeng siwang telu* (*likeng* of 3 *siwang*), *likeng siwang lima* (*likeng* of 5 *siwang*). Cloths do not ordinarily contain both *likeng* and *tokang*.

bueng timu – an ikat band narrower than a *likeng*, usually 6 to 12 threads wide. *Bueng timu mérang* and *bueng timu mitang* are the *bueng* that appear on red and black cloths, respectively. The word *bueng* in Sara Sikka means "seed" or "nut," and the designs of *bueng* bands consist of a row of bead-like dots.

bueng sang – the narrowest ikat band; similar to *bueng timu*, but commonly 3 to 6 threads wide.

produced in the village. The cloths in FIGURES 7-13 through 7-15 are examples of more common cloth designs while those in FIGURES 7-16 and 7-17 are less common.

Inspection of the cloth in FIGURE 7-13 reveals that the *'ina geté* is the center of the largest symmetrical cluster and is at the bottom half of the cloth. In other cloths, the largest symmetrical clusters are centered in the top half of the cloth around bands other than the *'ina geté.* The modest size of the symmetries which often center on the *'ina geté,* which is otherwise the most important band of a cloth, is explained by the need for them to be fully visible when the cloth is cut and sewn into a sarong. When it is worn, the *'ina geté* appears at the bottom of the sarong while the symmetries of the lesser bands are lost in the folds a woman makes in the cloth when wearing it.

As a general rule, clusters of medium magnitude have wider bands of ikat at their centers, whereas clusters of the greatest magnitude have small, unprepossessing, and almost hidden bands at their centers. Single threads are frequently at the centers of small clusters that are nested within larger clusters. This is significant because it reiterates a point made repeatedly by weavers themselves: the small bands of monochrome threads or single monochrome threads in the band sequence of Sikkanese textiles are the defining elements of the textile tradition of Sikka. Although at first inspection they may appear to be anomalous, extraneous, and whimsical, and while to Western eyes their colors may seem to clash, they are (1) what define the Sikkanese textile tradition and style and (2) what define a particular cloth as an example of a class of cloths within that tradition. Far from being randomly inserted into otherwise attractive ikat motifs, these colored threads and dull monochrome bands are the sources of the order and pattern of Sikkanese cloths. They define the secret symmetries at the heart of the aesthetic system of Sikkanese textiles.

THE INVOLUTION OF A TRADITION

In Sikka Natar, the social order is manifested in relations between paternally organized groups and women move between groups of consanguineally related men in marriage. But textiles, the principal medium of cultural expression, are the products of women who possess and control a large corpus of specialized knowledge. While it is difficult to explain *why* women's goods serve as the expressive vehicles for messages about alliance, it is easier to show *how* textiles serve this end. Every established house of Sikka Natar is associated with a number of particular *hura* – that is, a particular ordering of bands in the structure of cloths worn by the women of the house.[18] These *hura* are exclusive, proprietary, and, once their underlying principles have been learned, allow anyone to identify the house of the weaver. In some cases, a house has more than one set of *hura*, as when a house has more or less segmented into two or more separate yet related houses.

In contrast to the messages of social identity carried by *hura*, which are associated with and passed through groups of men (albeit expressed in the work of women), the motifs of the cloths themselves belong to and are transmitted by lineally related women. Women pass on to their daughters, sisters' daughters, and, in some cases, their brothers' daughters, particular motifs and the right to weave them. From childhood, a woman learns the motifs of her mother, her mother's sisters, and her grandmothers. Before marriage, she weaves and wears these motifs in cloths whose structures are in accord with the *hura* of her father's house. After marriage, however, she begins weaving the *kélang* of her

OPPOSITE PAGE:
FIGURE 7-13 (LEFT).
Cross-section of a woman's red cloth, *'utang mérang*, showing its *hura*, or band sequence, oriented the way a finished sarong is worn, with the lower edge at bottom and the center seam at top. This *hura* has 175 individual bands arranged in 55 symmetrical clusters. Here, the bands are numbered starting at the botton edge; the names of the major bands appear beside the corresponding number. To describe this cloth fully, a Sikkanese weaver would give the name of its *hura, mérak sogé* or "red of Ende," plus the name of its *kélang* (the motif of the *'ina geté* band), *naga lalang* or "the path of the naga serpent." Collection of E. D. Lewis.

CHART (RIGHT):
In this graphic analysis of the *hura* of the cloth shown in FIGURE 7-13, each of the 175 bands is represented by a horizontal line numbered in the order it appears on the cloth. Diagonal lines indicate the 55 inter-nesting symmetrical clusters; the apex of each set of lines points to the number of the band that forms the center of the cluster. The length of the diagonals is a measure of the number of bands involved in the cluster (rather than an indication of the width of any particular band).

171. likeng siwang telu
158. ési / tokang
145. likeng siwang telu
141. mérang natar
140. likeng siwang telu
124. ési / tokang
108. likeng siwang telu
107. mérang natar
103. likeng siwang lima
90. ési / tokang
77. likeng siwang telu
70. renda temang
58. ési
46. 'ina geté
(kelang: naga lalang)
34. ési
22. renda temang
10. likeng siwang telu

165

FIGURE 7-14.
Detail of a typical woman's red cloth ('utang mérang),
showing the names of the major ikat bands.
Collection of E. D. Lewis.

FIGURE 7-15.
Detail of a woman's black sarong ('utang mitang).
Collection of E. D. Lewis.

FIGURE 7-16.

Detail of FIGURE 7-1. The widest section of ikat, which in this case is not the *'ina geté,* occupies nearly half the cloth. No special name has been recorded for this section, which will form a broad centerfield when the cloth is sewn into a sarong. The banded sections show a series of symmetries almost as complex as those of cloths that are banded throughout. Collection of E. D. Lewis.

FIGURE 7-17.

Detail of a woman's sarong, *'utang moko,* with an unusual arrangement of bands for a Sikkanese cloth. Indeed, it resembles an Endenese cloth, with its horse motifs and plain black band. The design was likely brought to the region by a clan with Endenese origins. The finished garment will be constructed in typical Sikkanese fashion, with two panels rather than three. Collection of E. D. Lewis.

mother and mother's kinswomen according to the *hura* of her husband's house. Thus, each cloth made by a married woman carries information of two kinds. First, through its *kélang*, it identifies the natal group of its weaver and a group of maternally organized women to which the weaver belongs, who share knowledge of and rights to particular motifs. Second, through its *hura*, each cloth identifies the house into which the weaver has married.

The ultimate consumer of a ceremonial cloth is a woman other than the weaver, who has received the cloth by way of an exchange between alliance groups. In such a case, the wearer advertises her affinal relationship to the weaver each time she wears it. The total ensemble of cloths worn by the married women of a paternally organized house thus records the history of affinal alliances to which that house is a party.

In the past, Sikkanese textiles carried information about two major realms of Sikkanese culture. The social information encoded in the design and design structure of a cloth has been described here. Until recently, the motifs of the cloths themselves carried names that recalled the major events, personages, and creatures of Sikkanese myths. The names are retained, but the myths are now almost completely lost and it has proven impossible to reconstruct the meanings of the textile motifs in relation to Sikkanese mythology.

Even though textiles no longer serve as a vehicle for communicating meaning in relation to myth, which must have been in the past a major domain of Sikkanese expressive culture, the textile tradition of Sikka continues, and can be said to thrive. The tradition has become, however, exceedingly involuted. Within the traditional textile system, the weavers of Sikka are not free to innovate and create new meanings for their work, something that was almost certainly possible when the referent of the designs was a corpus of manipulable mythology. Rather, contemporary weavers are constrained to reproduce unchanged a

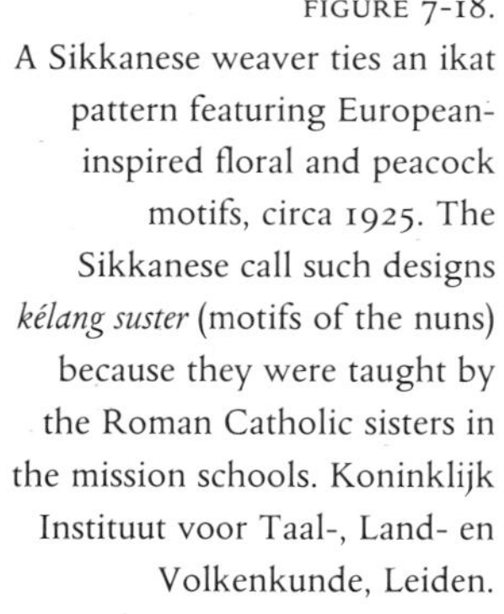

FIGURE 7-18.
A Sikkanese weaver ties an ikat pattern featuring European-inspired floral and peacock motifs, circa 1925. The Sikkanese call such designs *kélang suster* (motifs of the nuns) because they were taught by the Roman Catholic sisters in the mission schools. Koninklijk Instituut voor Taal-, Land- en Volkenkunde, Leiden.

tradition that reached its most impressive florescence just as its underlying rationales vanished. Today, individual creativity in weaving can only be expressed in the second-order cloths, the *kélang suster*, or "motifs of the nuns," which include representations of flowers, deer, birds, and other animals, often copied from cloth imported from Europe or Asia. Such cloths cannot enter the ceremonial exchange system and are therefore less highly valued (FIGURES 7-18, 7-19).

This artistic involution parallels what can be characterized as the increasing complexity of the ceremonial exchange system centered on bridewealth transactions, the general inflation of value of the goods classified as masculine goods, and the increasing legalism and scholasticism with which the Ata Sikka conduct the negotiation of bridewealth within the alliance regime of the community. The Ata Sikka are an extraordinarily well-educated, wealthy, and progressive people when compared to their neighbors on Flores. They possess sufficient means to preserve what the government and the Church have, in the past, attacked as wasteful and atavistic social practices. But with the disappearance of the mythic dimension of their world and that part of culture for which textiles served as the major vehicle of expression, the Ata Sikka increasingly judge cloth on the basis of its technical merits. This involution of a tradition can be seen almost every time a woman sits down to tie a skein of white thread for the making of a ceremonial cloth. Often the weaver takes an old cloth and "reads" exactly the pattern of knots that produced its design. This she then reproduces with complete precision in her new cloth, excluding any embellishment or fancy that would mark her creation as uniquely her own, and the piece that results is a perfect copy of the older cloth. Thus, the social textuality of Sikkanese textiles is preserved and transmitted from generation to generation, but no fundamentally new texts are produced.

In Sikka, textiles are crucial in the representation of both individual and group origins. Since identity is calculated in terms of origins, textiles are texts in which are inscribed both one's own identity and one's relatedness to others. As long as the weavers demand of themselves the degree of technical skill required to produce fine cloth, the textile tradition of Sikka will survive. But the tradition can also be said to have become frozen. It is not now an artistic tradition, if by art we mean a system for the individual expression of not only traditional, but innovative cultural values. However we may judge Sikkanese textiles as objects of art, the tradition must, in its own terms, be seen as the expert exercise of technique in the service of social relations. ❖

NOTES, page 271.

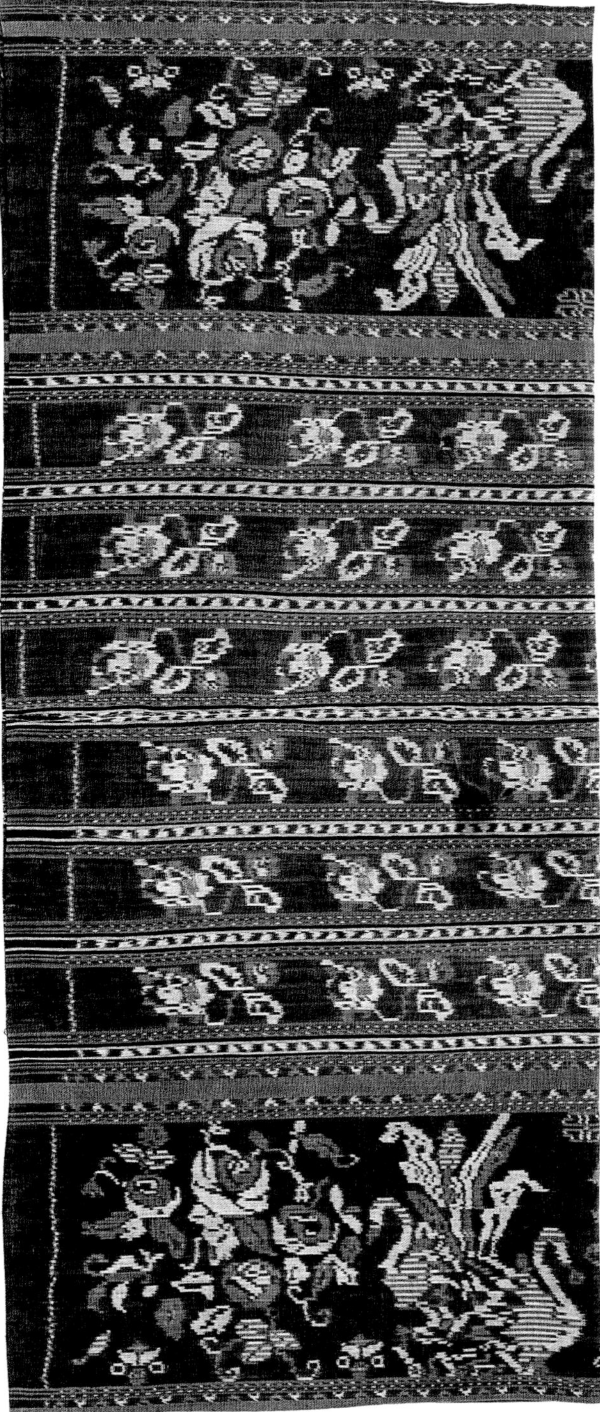

FIGURE 7-19.
A Sikkanese sarong with a *kélang suster* floral pattern. Such sarongs are popular for daily wear and for sale, but more traditional motifs are required for cloths used in bridewealth exchange. 147 x 62 cm. FMCH x81.1448, Gift of William Lloyd Davis and Mrs. W. Thomas Davis.

8

East Flores Regency

R UTH B ARNES

T HE HIGHWAY FROM MAUMERE TO LARANTUKA TRAVERSES A MODERATELY TROPICAL upland region of green and fertile forests and fields. Just before the twin peaks of the Lobe Tobi volcano, the road turns sharply to the north and the land mass of Flores recedes, revealing an island world of great beauty. As the coastline winds toward the north, Solor appears on the right, Lembata with its high volcanic mountains behind it, and Adonara across the Solor Strait. The landscape is dominated by volcanoes that rise straight out of the sea: the nearest is Ili Mandiri on Flores (FIGURE 8-2), while in the distance are Ili Boleng on Adonara, and Ili Api and Labalekang on Lembata. The terrain is drier now, the trees shorter, and the closeness of the sea gives a different color and atmosphere.

This is the Lamaholot region, an area that is linguistically and culturally distinct from the Sikka region. In general terms, one can speak of a coherent Lamaholot culture. At the same time, though, the notion of coherence has to be qualified. The Lamaholot language is spoken on the East Flores mainland and on Solor, Adonara, and Lembata, with the exception of Kédang, which is linguistically independent although culturally related (R. H. Barnes 1974a). There are three distinct Lamaholot dialects, however, with further linguistic subgroups (Keraf 1978). Although people can understand each other throughout the region, words and intonation vary greatly, often from village to village.[1] This diversity is also reflected in the interpretations of similar customs, beliefs, and manifestations of material culture. Visually this is nowhere more apparent than in the textiles of the region. The indigenous dress for both men and women is a tubular sarong. Although the form of garment is universal, the designs that decorate it are specific to particular areas.

FIGURE 8-1 (OPPOSITE). Detail of FIGURE 8-15.

FIGURE 8-2. The volcano Ili Mandiri rises over the waters of Solor Strait. The regency capital, Larantuka, stretches along the strand where the mountain meets the sea. Beyond the limits of the town, the Ili Mandiri weaving district consists of a chain of villages surrounding the mountain.

As has been stressed in CHAPTER 1, for much of Flores the most important social unit was traditionally the village. To a large degree this is still valid for the Lamaholot region. Warfare between villages, although now mostly part of the historical past, is well remembered and still influences social relationships.[2] Nevertheless travel between the islands is common, and local trading is important both in traditional and contemporary economies (Barnes & Barnes 1989). It is probably precisely the balance between village-based societies and inter-regional relationships that has supported the development of visually distinct dress and the adherence to regionally specific design. The most elaborately developed and locally differentiated textile is not used as daily dress, but is given as part of the bridewealth exchange, passing from the bride's lineage to that of the husband. It takes the form of a woman's cloth, and it also is the appropriate dress for special occasions. The distribution of this textile is the primary focus of discussion here.

Bridewealth textiles are used throughout the Lamaholot region. Most widespread are versions of a woman's red cloth, *kewatek*[3] *méan*, which in reality has the brownish red color achieved when dyeing with morinda. In western Solor there is a cluster of villages around Tanaléin where the bridewealth cloth is a "black" cloth, *kewatek kemetā*, which means that much of the thread is dyed with indigo. The thread is dyed to a dark blue, but the textile is referred to as "black." In Kédang, as well, a black bridewealth cloth is used. Both red and black versions must be woven from locally grown, handspun cotton and are dyed with plant dyes locally procured. There is a strongly pronounced ideology of the bridewealth cloth as an indigenous product. This stands in contrast to the main gift presented from the groom's lineage to the bride's, which is an elephant tusk formerly traded from mainland Southeast

Asia or, ultimately, India or Ceylon. In some Lamaholot areas, a third component of the gift exchange is a set of five ivory or shell bracelets. These accompany the textiles and are therefore part of the wife-givers' prestation.[4] In Kédang the wife-takers give either a tusk or gong, the latter imported from Java. This is in reciprocation for the textile gift.

A consideration of Lamaholot textiles should begin with one observation: weaving is not found everywhere in the region, and not all weaving centers produce elaborate ikat textiles. There are even some areas where weaving has been traditionally prohibited (Ruth Barnes 1987). On Lembata, in particular, Mingar at the western end of the island was affected by a prohibition on producing textiles. Kédang also followed this restriction, to the degree that no loom parts were allowed to enter the old hamlet, the ceremonial focus of each community. Yet even in non-weaving areas bridewealth textiles, traded from certain weaving centers, have been part of the exchange of marriage gifts for a long time indeed. It is possible that the prohibition against weaving developed in areas that were settled by people who did not use the backstrap loom, but depended on bark-cloth, instead.[5] Bark-cloth is not made now, and all non-weaving areas depend on a local trade in textiles for their indigenous clothing and bridewealth cloths.

Altogether six areas produce the finest ikat textiles, or did so formerly.[6] Two of these are the districts surrounding the peaks Ili Mandiri and Lobe Tobi, on the East Flores mainland. Three more (Lamalera, Atadéi and Ili Api) are located on Lembata. The sixth ikat weaving area covers parts of central and western Solor. Weaving is an important industry in other areas as well, including Adonara, northern Solor, and Kalikur in Kédang, but these areas do not produce the elaborate ikat bridewealth textiles.

EAST FLORES (ILI MANDIRI AND LOBE TOBI)

In East Flores, the villages around the Ili Mandiri volcano are well known for the quality of their weaving. Three types of women's cloth are still produced and have roles in ceremonial exchange: *kewatek méan*, *kewatek makasar*, and *kewatek kenumak*. A fourth type, *kewatek ketipa* (FIGURE 8-3), is now rarely found (Maxwell 1981:48). *Ketipa* is a generally recognized Lamaholot name for Indian patola, which had a lasting effect on local textile design (Ruth Barnes 1991a).[7]

FIGURE 8-3.
The influence of patola design is evident in the design format of this rare *kewatek ketipa*, held by two villagers in the Ili Mandiri region in 1981.

FIGURE 8-4.
Shell beads called *kinga*
(Maxwell 1981:50) have been
added to this *kewatek méan*
(woman's red cloth) from the
Ili Mandiri region. The widest
ikat band, the *kenirék bélén*,
stands out due to its darker,
over-dyed color. 157 x 59 cm.
FMCH X88.1285, Museum
Purchase, Manus Fund.

Of the cloths made today, the *kewatek méan* or "woman's red cloth" (FIGURE 8-4) is the most prestigious. It is entirely covered with narrow ikat bands, and close to the border is a wide pattern, called *kenirék bélén*.[8] The design shown in this wide band varies, although it seems to be most commonly a version of a rhombic shape or eight-pointed star. Its presence in similar form on the *kewatek ketipa* suggests that the *kenirék bélén* is inspired by patola designs (cf. Bühler & Fischer 1979: pls. 40, 51). Maxwell also relates the patterns to carvings on the posts of village ceremonial houses (1981: figs. 14-17). These designs are said to "belong" to specific lineages, which means that they are only made by the women of these lineages. This theme of pattern "ownership" recurs with other Lamaholot textiles as well, and will be discussed below.

Lamaholot weavers make a distinction between textiles where the ikat design is colored with only one dye, hence yields white on either a red or dark blue ground, and those dyed first with indigo and then over-dyed with morinda. This over-dyeing is called *belapit*. The bridewealth cloth inevitably has to include at least some over-dyed ikat bands.[9] The indigo and morinda together produce a brownish red, with the depth of the color varying according to how many times the indigo dyeing was repeated. Ideally, it is said, no indigo-blue should show in the finished cloth.[10] Even the (invisible) weft has to be red, a practice that among the Lamaholot is confined to East Flores; elsewhere the weft is usually dyed with indigo. By contrast, the other two textiles, *kewatek makasar* and *kewatek kenumak*, prominently feature ikat bands that are dyed with indigo alone (FIGURE 8-5). Their widest ikat bands are less elaborate than the *kenirék bélén* of *kewatek méan,* and red thread is restricted to plain bands.[11] Although both types of cloth may be included in the gift exchange, they have a lesser role than that of the bridewealth cloth. Other cloths dyed entirely with indigo and called *kenirék mitén* are intended for everyday wear and are not suitable for gift exchange (FIGURE 8-6).

The districts near Ili Mandiri are the only areas where the men's cloth, *senai*, includes some ikat (FIGURES 8-7, 11-10). Also unique to these areas is the making of men's belts, *mét*, decorated with supplementary warp (FIGURE 11-11). In most other Lamaholot areas, the

FIGURE 8-5 (LEFT).
Maria Somi Doren wears a *kewatek kenumak*, with a *kewatek méan* over her shoulder. Wailolong, Ili Mandiri region, 1982.

FIGURE 8-6 (RIGHT).
Kenirék mitén are women's sarongs dyed entirely with indigo and intended for daily wear. Most have simple banded center sections, but out of individual preference some are made with patola-inspired centerfields of simple rhombic forms. 114 x 64 cm. Collection of August Flick.

FIGURE 8-7.
Although it has simpler patterning than a woman's sarong, the Ili Mandiri men's sarong, *senai* (CENTER), nevertheless stands out compared to non-ikat styles of men's dress in East Flores. Many early 20th-century sarongs were plain (LEFT) or plaid (RIGHT), the latter shown with a supplementary-warp belt, *met*. Koninklijk Instituut voor de Tropen, Amsterdam.

men's cloths are decorated with plain warp stripes, produced by mounting different colors of warp threads on the loom.

While ikat production and the weaving of red bridewealth cloth is found throughout East Flores, Lobe Tobi was formerly the second important ikat-weaving area. This tradition seems to have weakened considerably, and although much weaving is still done, complex and fine cloths are no longer produced. The only examples of the old Lobe Tobi bridewealth textiles survive in the Museum für Völkerkunde in Frankfurt, Germany, in a collection of material gathered by the ethnologist Ernst Vatter (see OPPOSITE). The cloth in FIGURE 8-8 is extremely close to the *kewatek ketipa* of Ili Mandiri. The main difference is in the border bands at either end. The Ili Mandiri cloth also shows an angular precision in defining the eight-pointed stars of the central field; the Lobe Tobi cloth is by comparison slightly more curvilinear. It is impossible to say now whether these small differences are due to individual or regional distinctions. Also remarkably similar are the specific names cited: Vatter recorded *tenepa*, and Maxwell gives *kwatek méan tenipa*. However, from his collection it is apparent that another version of the traditional Lobe Tobi bridewealth cloth was visually closely linked to textiles from the Sikka region, and was quite distinct from the Ili Mandiri textiles. While the latter show small-scale designs in geometric precision, the Lobe Tobi cloths often have elaborate floral patterns (FIGURE 8-9).

FIGURE 8-8 (LEFT). The most elaborate of the known extant Lobe Tobi bridewealth sarongs (*tenepa*) features a patola-inspired central field similar to the *kewatek ketipa* of Ili Mandiri (FIGURE 8-3). 158 x 65 cm. Museum für Völkerkunde 27742, Frankfurt.

FIGURE 8-9 (RIGHT). Other Lobe Tobi *tenepa*, such as this example with floral motifs from Lewo Awan, bear a stronger resemblance to Sikkanese textiles. 134 x 65 cm. Museum für Völkerkunde 27771, Frankfurt.

The Pioneering Work of the Vatters

Many of the textiles illustrated in this chapter belong to the Museum für Völkerkunde in Frankfurt, Germany.[†] In 1928-29, a curator at this museum, the ethnologist Ernst Vatter, traveled for eight months through East Flores, the Solor Islands, Pantar, and Alor. Vatter was accompanied by his young wife Hanna, to whom he had only recently been married. The Vatters collected over 1,250 items for the museum. Although roughly 200 were destroyed during the bombing of Frankfurt in World War II, the collection remains the most comprehensive ever made in the eastern Lesser Sundas.

Vatter was an exceptional collector for his day. He not only selected objects that represented the full range of material culture among the various ethnic groups, but he also provided extensive documentation. Many of the issues that have remained unresolved in this book would not have done so had other collectors been as careful as Vatter to record simple details such as the names of the villages in which items were obtained. He also had an exceptional eye; the textiles he collected, especially those from Lamalera, provide an unmatched testimony to the artistic skills of the region's women.

Although the islands the Vatters visited are remote even today, they managed to transport heavy motion picture equipment, which they used to film scenes of daily life as well as special costumes and dances. This footage has been preserved at the Institute for Scientific Film in Göttingen and provides a unique record of many items of dress that have now nearly vanished. The ethnographic account that Vatter published in 1932 (*Ata Kiwan: Unbekannte Bergvölker im Tropischen Holland*) remains a valuable resource today.

Ernst Vatter was only 40 years old when he went to Flores, but his name drops from sight in the anthropological literature after the mid 1930s. Because Hanna was Jewish, Vatter was forced to retire in 1937. The couple emmigrated to Chile in 1939 with their three sons. Abandoning his promising career as an ethnologist, Vatter supported his family by running first a chicken farm and then a children's home. He died in 1948. Hanna Vatter returned to live in Germany in 1970.

TOP: Ernst and Hannah Vatter.
Courtesy of Hannah Vatter.

MIDDLE: Hannah Vatter with village women on Adonara. Courtesy of Hannah Vatter.

BOTTOM: On Solor, these men posed for the Vatters in their warrior costume. From Vatter 1932.

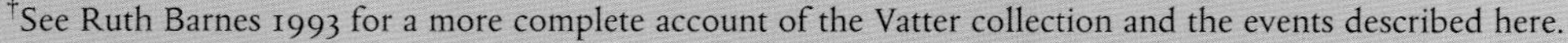

[†]See Ruth Barnes 1993 for a more complete account of the Vatter collection and the events described here.

The link to Sikkanese textiles is also confirmed in certain technical aspects of weaving. In general a Lamaholot textile is made up from two circular cloth panels sewn together into a tubular sarong. An exception exists in southern Lembata, where the most prestigious version of the bridewealth cloth is made up from three panels. While usually the warp setup on the Lamaholot loom corresponds to one cloth panel, the Lobe Tobi cloth is woven as a double length, as is commonly done in Sikka. The entire length is then cut into two panels which are sewn together to complete the textile. This technical characteristic of using a long warp, incidentally, also spread to southwestern Solor.

SOLOR

Solor, the smallest of the three Lamaholot-speaking islands, is also smaller than mainland East Flores. Yet historically it was once of greater importance than any of these other areas. On the northeastern coast, just inside the Solor Strait, both Portuguese and Dutch had at one time established settlements with fortifications, and used to harbor their boats during the worst of the west monsoon. Here they restocked their supplies before they continued their journey from Timor to the Moluccas. Timor was the primary source of sandalwood, and the Moluccas, of course, provided cloves and nutmeg. It is Solor, therefore, that was first visited and written about in Portuguese and Dutch sources. The first Europeans were following a well-established route, and they found Chinese and Islamic merchants already present in the sixteenth and early seventeenth century. Cloth traded from India was much in demand, and both here and across the strait in the coastal settlements of Adonara the imported patola cloths were used as bridewealth until the early twentieth century, instead of locally made cloth.[12] In southwestern and central Solor, however, red bridewealth cloths were, and still are, produced.

Ernst Vatter, when he visited western Solor in 1929, reported that he found many cultural similarities with Lobe Tobi. As far as weaving is concerned, the use of the double-length warp is an indication of this. The patterns of the textiles, however, do not have the same wide, floral design as was once common in Lobe Tobi. Instead, the cloth is divided into bands. Again, as in the Ili Mandiri textiles, there is a wide ikat band near the border. Vatter reported that the arrangement of patterns was linked to the lineage of the weaver (1932:223-224). The collection in Frankfurt has several very fine textiles from Solor that have become rare in the area. They are all distinguished by an extremely wide ikat band at either end of the textile, with designs that are usually influenced by patola (FIGURE 8-10). The center of the cloth is covered with narrow bands of simple ikat patterns. The reason for this curious arrangement may have had to do with the way the textiles used to be worn. Formerly, a married woman fastened the long sarong over her shoulders with wooden pins, and also gathered the cloth at the waist, presumably with a belt. Vatter illustrates this manner of dress for Lobe Tobi, as well (1932: pl. 22.2); in effect the central part of the textile was hardly visible, as the cloth was draped from the shoulders over the waist belt. This made the wide, patola-inspired ikat designs visually most prominent.

As recently as the early 1980s a small number of similar textiles could still be seen, but they were no longer in circulation as bridewealth textiles. Instead, they had become lineage heirlooms.[13] The bridewealth cloth now made in western Solor is called *kewatek temodol belapit* (FIGURE 8-11). It is more modest in appearance, but it nevertheless has certain

characteristics in common with the cloth previously used. Again it is a *red* cloth, which means that all parts that are not patterned have a solid reddish-brown color. The name *belapit* indicates that the ikat bands are dyed with both indigo and morinda, especially in the wide border designs. This clearly distinguishes the textile from the *kewatek temodol biasa*, in which the ikat is only dyed with indigo.[14] This later textile is used for daily wear. As in Ili Mandiri, there also exists a cloth called *kewatek makasar*.[15] This cloth is used as festive wear; it has plain red bands alternating with very narrow ikat bands.

The region around the villages of Tanaléin and Lewokukung has an altogether different textile tradition. All cloth is deeply dyed with indigo, a color that is called *kemetã*, "black." Two versions exist, *kewatek kemetã* (woman's black cloth) and *kewatek mowa* (woman's cloth with ikat). Both have red bands at the border, as well as some ikat. For the black version (*kemetã*), this band is dyed with indigo only, while the *kewatek mowa* has a few narrow bands of over-dyed (*belapit*) patterns (FIGURE 8-12). The main surface, from the borders inwards, has small bands of color, but the overall impression is dark and muted. These cloths are the standard bridewealth textiles, although their value in the local economy is not very high.[16]

LEMBATA

(LAMALERA, ATADÉI AND ILI API)

Lembata still is the least accessible of the three Lamaholot islands. Its main market town and administrative center, Lewoleba, is in daily contact with Larantuka, but it is difficult to reach other parts of the island. Especially southern Lembata depends on contact via the sea, as the island can only be crossed on foot or, with difficulty, on horseback. Yet the southern part of the island has been involved in inter-island and, indirectly, international trade from before the arrival of Europeans in the area. The small Islamic merchant enclave of

FIGURE 8-10 (TOP).
Detail of a woman's red cloth, *kewatek méan*, formerly used as bridewealth cloths in western Solor. Ritaebang, 1982.

FIGURE 8-11 (MIDDLE).
Detail of a *kewatek temodol belapit*, the bridewealth cloth currently in use in western Solor. Ritaebang, 1982.

FIGURE 8-12 (BOTTOM).
Woman's cloth with ikat, *kewatek mowa*. Lewokukung, 1982.

Labala provided a contact to maritime trade links for the villages of the interior of the Atadéi peninsula, while the coastal village Lamalera did the same for the hinterland of villages on the slopes of the Labalekang and Mingar volcanoes.[17]

The textiles produced in Lamalera and on the Atadéi peninsula are of outstanding quality. Here an unusual version of the bridewealth cloth stresses a tripartite division (FIGURES 8-13, 8-14, 8-15). In Lamalera this textile is called *kewatek nai telo*, in Atadéi *petak harén nai telo*.[18] The cloth always has a central panel that displays a large, continuous design field, while the two outer panels are divided into ikat bands of various widths. The central panel usually shows very strong patola influence (Ruth Barnes 1989a:82-87; 1991a). To some degree, these central designs are linked to particular lineages.

Both weaving areas have much in common and even share some patterns, most prominently the manta ray, *moku* (FIGURE 8-16), but also a boat representation as well as several patola-related designs (Ruth Barnes 1989a:98). The reason for the similarities is likely to be found in the history of Lamalera. The village was supposedly settled by refugees from Lapan Batan, an island to the east of Lembata which is said to have been destroyed by a natural disaster, probably a tidal wave caused by submarine volcanic activity. Other widely dispersed clans and communities in the Lamaholot region also claim descent from Lapan Batan, and there is little doubt that the story is based on fact (see also Vatter 1932: 9-10; R. H. Barnes 1982:410; Dietrich 1984:322). Ultimately, however, the ancestors of Lamalera claim to have come from Sulawesi. Their first attempt to settle on Lembata was on the Atadéi peninsula, near Mulan on the side of Labala Bay. It is said that here they were introduced to Lamaholot language and culture. Interestingly enough, the language of Lamalera is closely related to the dialect spoken in Mulan today, unlike the villages that surround Lamalera (Keraf 1978: Appendix VI). If the

FIGURE 8-13 (LEFT).
Three-paneled bridewealth cloth, *kewatek nai telo*, Lamalera. 168 x 72 cm. Museum für Völkerkunde 27997, Frankfurt.

FIGURE 8-14 (CENTER).
Three-paneled bridewealth cloth, *kewatek nai telo*, Lamalera. 155 x 69 cm. Museum für Völkerkunde 28664, Frankfurt.

FIGURE 8-15 (RIGHT).
Three-paneled bridewealth cloth, *kewatek nai telo*, Lamalera. 177 x 68 cm. Museum für Völkerkunde 28108, Frankfurt.

introduction to Lamaholot textile design also occurred here, it would not be surprising that Lamalera weavers were influenced by the ikat textiles of Atadéi. Weaving itself was possibly already known to Lamalera's ancestors prior to their arrival on Lembata (Vatter 1932:205).

Atadéi bridewealth cloths are often exceptionally long and derive their appeal from bold, strong shapes with contrasting red and black. Areas dyed with indigo are never allowed to remain blue; they are always over-dyed with morinda. While this is also the case in Ili Mandiri *kewatek méan*, in Atadéi the effect is stronger, because repeated indigo dyeing yields a very dark blue, which in combination with the morinda creates a black tone. Since not all parts of the design are colored with both dyes, there are red areas as

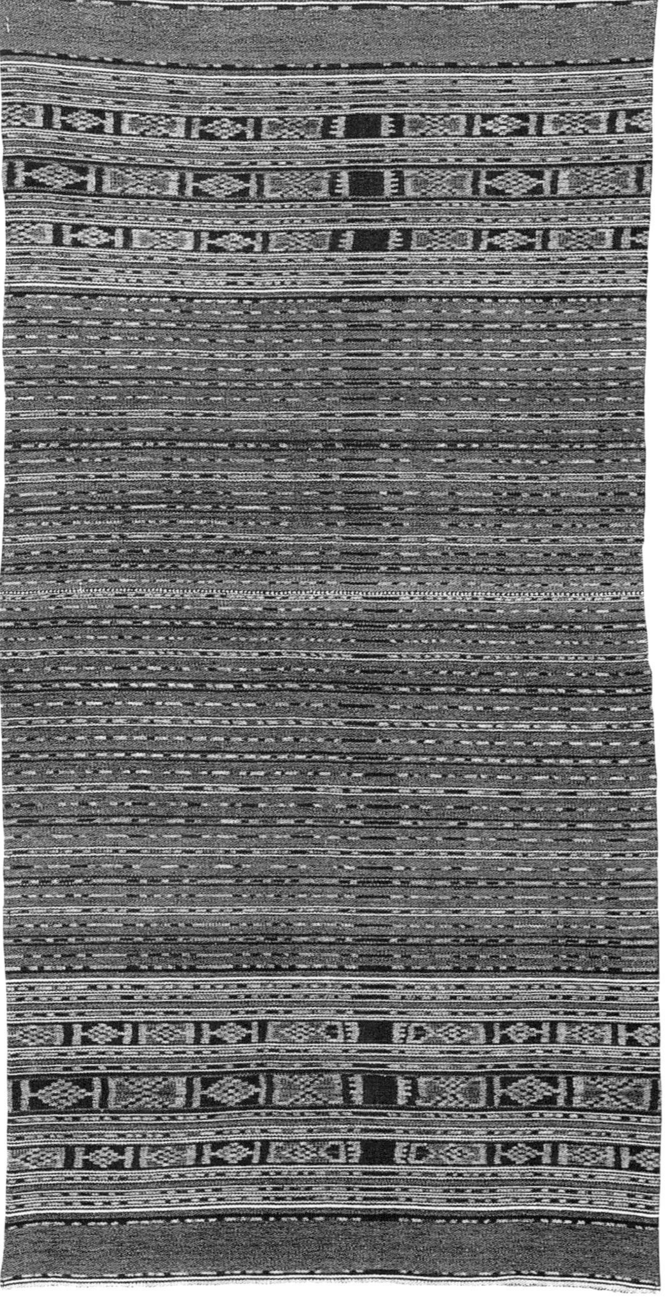

well within any ikat band and these stand in dramatic relief against the black of the over-dyed areas.

What most consistently distinguishes Atadéi cloth from Lamalera cloth is that in Lamalera parts of the design in each band are dyed only with indigo and are allowed to remain blue. Therefore the finished Lamalera cloth shows a greater range of colors, including the natural color of the cotton, plus red, blue, and dark (over-dyed) purple or black. The central panel also is treated slightly differently in the two traditions. In Lamalera the continuous design fills the entire panel from one selvedge to the other, while in Atadéi additional bands are inserted near the selvedge. One could say that Lamalera makes more of the continuous design and sets the entire central panel apart.

Lamalera also has a two-panel version of the bridewealth cloth, the *kewatek nai ruã* (FIGURE 8-17). This has very narrow ikat bands throughout, flanked on either side by thin, colored bands. Close to the borders of the completed textile are wide ikat designs. The women's textiles woven in Lamalera for daily or festive wear are often very innovative in their ikat designs. They may combine indigenous patterns with recently introduced European motifs, and they often use bright store-bought dyes (FIGURE 8-18). By comparison, the utilitarian cloth produced in Atadéi tends to be more conservative (FIGURE 8-19).

The men's cloth in Lamalera is a two-panel tubular sarong with warp and weft bands creating a tartan-type design (FIGURE 8-20). The term *senai*, sometimes used for men's cloths in western Lamaholot, is replaced as one moves east by the term *nowi* (or *nofi*). Here *senai* becomes the word used for shoulder cloths instead.

The third weaving area on Lembata is in the north of the island, in the villages surrounding the Ili Api volcano. The bridewealth textiles have narrow ikat bands throughout the textile (FIGURE 8-21), usually arranged in groups of three, with two identical bands on either side of a different central band. Again, a wide band is placed near the border. As in all other parts of the Lamaholot region, with the exception of southern Lembata, the cloth is usually made up from two panels. However, some rare Ili Api cloths have three panels, the central one showing strong patola influence (FIGURE

OPPOSITE PAGE:

FIGURE 8-16 (TOP).
Border detail of an Atadéi sarong showing the manta ray motif, *moku.* Museum für Völkerkunde 28040, Frankfurt.

FIGURE 8-17 (BOTTOM).
The two-panel bridewealth cloth, *kewatek nai ruã,* from Lamalera. 177 x 68 cm. Museum für Völkerkunde 27992, Frankfurt.

THIS PAGE:

FIGURE 8-18 (TOP).
Detail of a Lamalera woman's festive cloth, *kewatek menikil,* showing a traditional border design dyed with bright, commercial dyes.

FIGURE 8-19 (MIDDLE).
Border detail from an Atadéi woman's cloth dyed entirely with local plant dyes. Collection of Ruth Barnes.

FIGURE 8-20 (BOTTOM).
Two Lamalera men plaiting sails for their fishing boat wear the tartan-style men's cloth, *nowi.*

FIGURE 8-21 (LEFT).
A typical banded, two-panel bridewealth cloth from the
Ili Api district. 156 x 69 cm. Timothy and Tuti Manring
Collection, Seattle Art Museum L90.3.346.

FIGURE 8-22 (CENTER).
Three-panel Ili Api bridewealth cloth with a broad central
field. 136 x 67 cm. Collection of Kent Watters.

FIGURE 8-23 (RIGHT).
Cloth of the type made in the Ili Api region for trade to
Kédang, where they served as a bridewealth cloths. The
design format differs sharply from the bridewealth cloths that
Ili Api weavers made for use in their own communities.
170 x 67 cm. Collection of August Flick.

8-22). Like the *kewatek ketipa* of Ili Mandiri, this type of cloth has virtually disappeared, to be replaced by the two-panel cloth. The Ili Mandiri cloth (FIGURE 8-3) is certainly sewn together from two panels, despite the visually tripartite division of its design. In contrast, the Ili Api textile is actually made up from three panels. Thus it shows complete agreement between visual and technical construction, as was also noted for the bridewealth cloth of Lamalera.

In addition to the red cloth, Ili Api produces "black" (actually dark blue) textiles for daily wear. Indigo-dyed cloths were also once important for the export trade to Kédang, where

a prohibition on weaving exists, and where red is not acceptable as a color for bridewealth textiles. The older versions of the cloth had wide ikat designs near the borders, with golden-yellow silk bands set along either side. The center of the textile, which was sometimes a separately woven panel, was dyed a very dark blue (FIGURE 8-23). These black bridewealth cloths were apparently exported to Alor as well, where many of them were recently bought by art dealers. It is very likely that the early export market was also largely supplied by the Islamic weavers of Kalikur in Kédang and the coastal communities on Adonara, where a commercial textile production had developed. They now have taken over the trade entirely.

ADONARA, NORTH SOLOR, AND KALIKUR

Descriptions of Lamaholot weaving usually only address the areas that produce fine ikat textiles. This leaves out a tradition that, visually at least, is prominently present wherever one travels in the area. It concerns the textile production of Adonara's coastal villages and, to some degree, similar communities on the northern coast of Solor. Islamic weavers provide much of Adonara's interior with textiles, and may have done so for centuries. Like men's metal working, women's weaving is a major economic factor in these coastal communities.

However, there is no red cloth made, and no recollection of its former production. The textiles are primarily decorated by single-color bands. Up to World War II, silk was imported and included into the band structure (FIGURES 8-24, 8-25); nowadays metallic thread is frequently set into the warp. Supplementary warp is also common, a technique that is not part of the Lamaholot weaving tradition, with the exception of the *mét* belts from East Flores (FIGURES 8-26, 8-27).

Coastal Islamic weavers also produce ikat, but the designs are much simpler than those made in the more important ikat areas. If a natural plant dye is used, it usually is indigo, and now this is often replaced by commercial dyes. As mentioned above, patola cloths were formerly used as bridewealth gifts in the coastal communities of Adonara and

Solor, and possibly in other parts of the two islands as well. They are no longer available; but as the area has no tradition of using red or black bridewealth textiles, a great variety of cloths are now acceptable, all made by the Adonara weavers. While at present it is common to see rather garish color combinations that include much pink, purple, and fluorescent green, some of the older textiles with silk bands appeal through their rich luxuriousness (FIGURE 8-28). The success of the Islamic coastal weaving centers is certainly closely related to the geographical distribution of weaving and non-weaving areas referred to at the beginning of the chapter. They historically supplied areas where little or no weaving was done, and still continue to do so.

It also happens that these production centers were once part of a powerful political league, the *lima pantai* (Malay, five coasts). This was an alliance of five Islamic settlements, each with a leader who claimed the title of raja: Terong and Lamahala on Adonara, Lohayong and Lamakera on Solor, and the most powerful Muslim political leader, the Raja of Adonara. These communities were already important when the first Dutch transactions were carried out in the area early in the seventeenth century, but their histories may go back much further (Dietrich 1984:318, 321).

There can be no doubt that political and economic influence were closely related. All the coastal settlements were involved with the inter-island and (ultimately) international transfer of merchandise. Through their trading connections the export of local products took place, and foreign goods could pass into the mountain villages. In Kédang, this role was played by the community of Kalikur: "That Kalikur had by itself partly succeeded in establishing its suzerainty over the rest of Kédang is due to its control of trade with the interior" (R. H. Barnes 1974a:11).[19]

The textiles woven in different Islamic coastal communities cannot easily be distinguished from one another. They are not made to identify the wearer with a specific locality, but are made to be widely acceptable for marketing purposes.

THE "OWNERSHIP" OF PATTERNS

Much has been made of the supposed ownership of particular patterns, an issue that will be reconsidered briefly here. The ethnographic fact is certainly well established. Several different sources report that certain patterns are associated with particular clans and that women may only produce and wear designs that are appropriate to their lineage.[20] A girl learns patterns from her mother, but she also becomes acquainted with the patterns of her birth-lineage (her father's clan), and may use other lineage designs as well, providing there is a genealogical link. Since descent is patrilineal, the actual lines of transmission must soon become confused.[21]

Maxwell (1981:57) has suggested two possible mechanisms for how ownership might nevertheless be maintained. The first is based on the marriage rules of the region, which are guided by an asymmetric prescriptive alliance system (R. H. Barnes 1977). If this were followed strictly, then successive generations of women marrying into a given patrilineage would come from the same wife-giving group (which would also be patrilineal). Alternatively, she suggests the possible presence of matrilineal descent in addition to the patrilineal structure, which might manifest itself in the continuity of textile patterns through the female line.

FIGURE 8-26 (LEFT). Supplementary-warp sarong from Adonara. 141 x 66 cm. FMCH x88.1283, Museum Purchase, Manus Fund.

FIGURE 8-27 (RIGHT). Collected in 1929 by Ernest Vatter in Atanila (south coast of Kédang), this sarong may have been imported from Adonara, or produced in Kalikur. Both areas share the same patterns and supplementary-warp technique. 144 x 73 cm. Museum für Völkerkunde 28096, Frankfurt.

So far, neither hypothesis has been shown to be verifiable. Even in Lamaholot communities that show concern about following the marriage rules strictly, there is in fact a great deal of personal choice involved, as there are always several lineages that are potential wife-givers (R. H. Barnes 1977). There is by now not even agreement about the correct pattern a woman should learn: that of her own lineage, or her husband's.

In the meantime, the link between patterns and lineages has taken on a life of its own in the literature.[22] The ethnographic evidence, on the other hand, shows a certain degree of ambiguity. In Lamalera, for example, it is possible for a woman to learn a variety of patterns, all linked to specific lineages. She will choose a pattern which relates to her own line of descent through her mother, mother's mother, father's mother, etc. In fact, her choice is wide. There are many instances where women have learned several patterns from different lineages, and used them in different textiles in equally prominent positions. In some cases sisters have chosen to learn different designs from their own, common, genealogical descent lines. At least in Lamalera, the link of pattern to lineage is clearly expressed, but it cannot be seen as a genealogical calling card. It does seem to be closely related, though, to the ownership of patola cloths, as the designs that are explicitly linked to specific lineages also often bear close comparison to patola owned by those lineages (Ruth Barnes 1989a: 75-76). However, it must be stressed that at least in this century it has not been the norm for a woman to focus specifically on learning the design that reflects the patola her own or her husband's lineage may own.[23]

There is a further complication as well. In western Lembata, Lamalera is the village where the best ikat textiles are produced. In the mountain villages to the north, weaving and ikat work are done, but they are not usually of good quality.[24] To the west, in Mingar, weaving is traditionally prohibited. Lamalera textiles are an important trade item in both areas, and in the case of Mingar, the women of Lamalera are the major suppliers of indigenous cloth. That includes the bridewealth cloth, with patterns that are supposedly owned by clans. Yet these textiles are, and have been for a long time, perfectly acceptable as cloth gifts, and they circulate freely.[25] On special occasions, they may even be worn by the women who own them. It is obvious, therefore, that people distinguish between a textile's origin and its circulation. The woman who makes a red bridewealth cloth may use patterns that she claims refer to her line of descent. For this we have sufficient evidence from various parts of Lamaholot culture. However, the cloth's circulation is not restricted by its origin.

COMMON THREADS

This survey of textile traditions found among the Lamaholot reveals a great deal of diversity for the region as a whole. Is it then useful to consider the material in its entire spread? Such an effort only makes sense if there are shared similarities. One common concern, certainly, is the requirement to use a specific color. Areas with strongly developed ikat traditions all produce red bridewealth cloth. The term used, *mean*, has superlative associations that go beyond the color reference. In related languages of Flores, the word can mean "extraordinary" and may in part refer to "extraordinary wealth, such as golden objects" (R. H. Barnes 1974:106; Ruth Barnes 1989b:50). However red is also an ambiguous color. As the color of blood, it stands for fertility, but it also represents warfare. Some areas may therefore reject the red bridewealth cloth and prefer a textile that is predominantly dyed with indigo. Only in Adonara and northern Solor, where imported rather than locally made cloth was traditionally used as the major gift, is there apparently no color restriction.

The making of a red cloth is to some degree age-related (Maxwell 1981:53). Throughout East Flores and the Solor Islands, in contrast to Savu and Sumba (Maxwell 1985, Hoskins 1989), secretive behavior concerning the manipulation of dyes concentrates, in general, not on indigo but on the morinda dye bath preparations. Sometimes, as in Lamalera, women speak about the process as a dangerous undertaking, safe only for older women who no longer bear children (Ruth Barnes 1991b:100-101). It is explicitly the making of the red cloth that requires caution, not the use of specific patterns. This confirms that the redness, *mean*, is potentially ambiguous and needs to be handled with care.

A close relationship between technique and meaning is a common theme reflected not only in the dyeing of threads, but also in the tying of ikat designs, and in their arrangement

on the cloth. For example, the cloth production emphasizes a constant interplay between odd and even numbers. The patterns are built up from small units, *kenumak*, each made up of six warp threads (i.e., an even number), while the pattern itself has a prescribed width that must be made up of an odd number of *kenumak*. The bundle of six warp threads may be said to combine odd and even, as six is made up of either three times two, or two times three. Odd and even numbers, however, have a symbolic meaning that refers to life and death, to transition and completion. Previous publications have described how the entire ikat process consists of different stages that emphasize symbolic meaning (Ruth Barnes 1989a:40-41, 94-95 and 1989b:51-53). Such notions also play a role in the particular size that is appropriate for a pattern, as well as in the number and arrangement of design bands covering the cloth surface.

The spatial treatment of patterns on the textiles shows certain similarities. There is strict adherence to symmetry in all Lamaholot traditions. There always is a single central band, and moving outwards from it in either direction, band after band is reflected in its mirror image on the other side of the center. This is most clearly expressed in the tripartite structure of the three-panel cloths from southern Lembata, but as a design principle it applies everywhere.

Finally, the link of the textile to fertility and well-being is obvious, as it is part of the wife-givers' gift. The laying of the warp in its continuous, circular form can become a symbol for the "thread of life." The continuous warp of the cloth often may not be cut if it is to be used as bridewealth. The patterns that are represented can also refer to the lineage's wealth, by quoting designs from the patola treasure (Ruth Barnes 1991a:15-16).

Furthermore, there is an aesthetic approach that is common to all areas. Weavers often state that the quality of the cloth depends on the precisely defined designs. A good textile is judged by the clarity of outline, and the small, separate units (*kenumak*) that together make up the complete pattern are emphasized. The result is in direct contrast, for example, to the textiles of Sumba, which display large, bold forms. When Lamaholot women describe their ikat designs, they often refer to the size appropriate to each pattern, and counting the design is an important aspect of correct production. It is this that is checked when the textiles are evaluated as potential bridewealth gifts, along with the skill displayed in the precision of outlines and appropriate color combination. Another aspect commented on as the characteristic of a good textile is its strength, hence durability. It is said that a correctly made textile will last, while one that includes mistakes, such as the wrong pattern (Maxwell 1981:62) or an inappropriately tied design will be destroyed by mice. The same may happen to a cloth that has been dyed too hastily. There is no doubt that the weavers attempt to overcome through skill the difficulties inherent in ikat production. Potential fragility is contrasted to the desired durability. In verbal exchange and transmission of technical knowledge from mother to daughter, ikat weavers emphasize the difficulties of their efforts and insist on laborious over-dyeing of indigo with morinda (*belapit*).[26]

These shared approaches towards cultural and technical aspects of making and using textiles, in particular the bridewealth cloth, must not be allowed to conceal the surprising variety found in the area. Common themes can be recognized almost everywhere, in more or less elaborate form. But differences also crop up, and just as the dialect of Lamaholot may change from one village to the next, so the interpretation of the form and function of ikat textiles can be equally varied. ❖ NOTES, page 272.

FIGURE 8-28 (OPPOSITE). One of the oldest surviving textiles from Flores, this sarong was presented to the Rijksmuseum by the physician and Asian scholar von Siebold in 1837. It was recorded as coming from Larantuka, but this may only signify where it was acquired. Stylistically it belongs to the tradition of colorfully banded sarongs with silk yarns and limited use of ikat, now associated with the coastal Islamic weaving districts of Adonara and the related *lima pantai* areas. Although it is not therefore part of the Lamaholot bridewealth tradition, it is unusually luxurious and finely made. 134 x 63 cm, top edge folded behind. Rijksmuseum voor Volkenkunde 1-134, Leiden.

191

PART THREE:

CASE STUDIES

The Curse of the Cooked People

Weaving in Northeastern Manggarai

M ARIBETH E RB

G IVEN THAT HANDWOVEN TEXTILES REPRESENT AN ESTEEMED TRADITION in many Indonesian societies, it is perhaps surprising to find a people, in northeastern Manggarai, who are not particularly proud of their weaving. They have practically no indigenous special designs and produce simple cloths that are frequently unadorned, with few sacred meanings or uses. This is not to imply that cloth or weaving itself does not have a prominent place and rich symbolic meaning; it is only to point out that the view of cloth and in particular of weaving itself is rather singular in comparison to many other societies in Indonesia. The Rembong and their neighbors in northeastern Manggarai see weaving as hard work and an unfortunate economic necessity. This view is tied to the notion that those who weave are cursed. The curse originated at the beginning of the world, when all the customs of the ancestors were first laid down. As will unfold below, it is not weaving itself that originated in a golden ancestral age, but instead the curse that makes weaving necessary. Weaving is in some ways likened to the sinful deeds that engendered this original curse.

According to the people of northeastern Manggarai, the beginning of the world was a time when all distinctions and oppositions were created. Originally the sky (father above) and the earth (mother below) were bound together by a vine. Out of their original union life on earth sprang forth. From that time onwards, however, things started to split apart. Oceans receded and boundaries were set up between land and sea. Because of a dog fight, the vine was bitten and earth and sky flew apart. These separations are symbolic of the most fundamental opposition, that between male and female, and the distinction that is the foundation of Manggarai social order, that between *anak rana* and *anak wina*. The Rembong tell that in the beginning brothers and sisters married one another. As these unions were not very fertile, it was decided instead that a brother would give his daughter to marry the son of his sister, and hence the alliance between the children of men (*anak rana*) and the children of women (*anak wina*) was initiated.[1] Along with these other separations, the division between life and death also began. While at one time the dead remained with the living, due to the mistake of a human being they became separated

FIGURE 9-1 (OPPOSITE). A Rembong man wearing a supplementary-weft sarong does a special dance at a ritual sacrifice to further his power and influence. Lempang Paji, 1984.

195

and now the dead must go to their own village on the top of a mountain, and ultimately return to the sea.

The time when all distinctions and separations were created is called *nguza watu, lalak tana,* when "rocks were young and earth was soft." The world at that time is said to have been malleable, and all happenings to have left their imprint on the landscape. Odd-shaped rocks are said to be proof that a particular occurrence took place. Symbolically this means that the customs of the ancestors were first created in this impressionable time, but were afterwards hardened and solidified, and hence have descended to human beings in subsequent ages as formed and permanent regulations. This is what is called in northeastern Manggarai, as elsewhere in Indonesia, *adat,* customary laws and traditions that have been inherited from the time of the ancestors. Following the ways of the ancestors will ensure their protection, while opposing them will bring difficulties and destruction. The rain will not fall; the crops will not prosper; predatory animals will destroy what grows. To fail to follow the ancestors' regulations (or, in a sense, to try to reunite what was separated at the beginning of the world) is to be doomed.

NDIVAL'S CURSE

According to the sacred history told in various forms throughout northeastern Manggarai, in this golden age at the beginning of the world lived two brothers, Ndival and Obak.[2] The two were powerful magicians and together ruled the world. The younger brother Obak, however, coveted his elder brother's wife, the beautiful Bava Ndani. One day when Ndival was out in the forest collecting materials to build a house, Obak visited Bava Ndani and attempted to seduce her. He said, "Let's chew some betel nut" (an invitation to sexual intercourse), but Bava Ndani answered, "Ndival has taken my betel nut bag" (a euphemism for the female genitals). Obak lifted her sarong to see that in fact she was completely smooth. He raised his machete and cleaved an opening in order to copulate with her. Afterward he left her bleeding body on the floor and departed.

When Ndival found out about this betrayal and murder, he interpreted it as a challenge to his authority as the elder brother. He called a contest with his younger brother to determine who was the strongest and had the right to rule. The two prepared to have a feast and summoned all of their subjects to attend. The main sacrifice was Ndival's enormous buffalo Meze Nggoeng. Whichever of them could succeed in killing the buffalo would be the strongest. Obak attempted to kill Meze Nggoeng and failed. Ndival raised his magic sword, telling all of the observers to stand far away. Ndival's own subjects were obedient, but Obak's subjects refused to move. Ndival hefted his great sword and severed the buffalo's head, killing it in one stroke. Due to the power of his sword and the blood of Meze Nggoeng, the heads of all of Obak's followers standing nearby were also sheared off. Ndival challenged his brother again. Could he bring his subjects back to life? Obak tried, but again failed. Ndival waved his sword and all the severed heads were restored to the bodies, however no one got back the right head. This, according to the people in northeastern Manggarai, was the origin of the different languages spoken in the world. More importantly, this cleaving rent a major distinction between the people of northeastern Manggarai, which has in some ways come to be symbolic of all the other separations created at that time, namely, the opposition between "raw people" (*ata taqa*) and "cooked people" (*ata maméq*).

This almost biblical tale of brotherly rivalry, envy, and greed signals the end of the golden age in the eyes of the northeastern Manggarai folk. Ndival, disappointed with his brother, left Manggarai forever and took all of its wealth with him. With his departure, where there had once been harmony, sprang discord; where all had once been prosperous, now people had to labor, to plant rice and maize and work for a living. Because of the original sins of incest and adultery,[3] conceit and disobedience, the followers of Obak were especially cursed for all time; these are the people who are "cooked." The followers of Ndival, on the other hand, continued to enjoy some of the primeval prosperity; these are the people who are "raw." This distinction between the cursed and the blessed, the cooked and the raw, is fundamental to understanding the place of weaving in the ideology of the northeastern Manggarai folk.

RAW PEOPLE AND COOKED PEOPLE

The place where these happenings are said to have occurred, now referred to as the Garden of Eden, is in the *dalu* of the Rajong people (FIGURES 9-2, 9-3). The sites where these and other great events of the golden age took place are still visible in the landscape. The Rajong themselves are said to be the descendants of Ndival and their land is still blessed. They live in considerable prosperity, cultivating only small fields, but gaining large yields of rice and maize. According to local belief, they guard the place where the world began and control all the other creatures of the earth. At the great Rajong new year's feast (before the planting season), the other people of northeastern Manggarai must bring raw food offerings. The Rajong return these offerings in cooked form. As the guardians of the place where the world began, they consider themselves to be the source of all other people, and as the inhabitants of this primeval place, they are strictly forbidden to weave. Weaving is considered a potentially dangerous activity, a product of culture as opposed to nature, that brings supernatural condemnation on those who engage in it. Some people say it is precisely because the Rajong do not weave that they have such bountiful produce from their agricultural labor.

The cursed people are their northern neighbors who live in the *dalu* of Rembong. The Rembong are "cooked" people. Cooked things cannot be planted, they are dead. Part of the curse of the Rembong, and their association with death, is the fact that they are weavers. In a not entirely logical way, people

FIGURE 9-2.
Young woman from Sesur, Rajong, 1920s. The plain indigo-dyed garment patterned with a few lighter stripes is still a common style today in northeastern Manggarai and across the regency border in Riung. As the Rajong people do not weave, this sarong must have been obtained through trade, probably from Rembong. Koninklijk Instituut voor Taal-, Land- en Volkenkunde, Leiden.

FIGURE 9-3.
Whip-duelers in Rajong, 1927. Sarongs with a plain white ground color are no longer made today, but they were once common in other interior areas as well (FIGURE 6-34), suggesting that there was a tendency on the part of coastal weavers to retain for their own use the more highly valued cloths dyed by the labor-intensive indigo process. Koninklijk Instituut voor Taal-, Land- en Volkenkunde, Leiden.

say the Rembong's curse is that their fields will produce poorly and their crops will be devastated by predators *because* they are the cooked people, the damned descendants of the followers of Obak. Because they get poor results from agriculture, they are forced to supplement their livelihood by weaving. The indigo-dyed cloths they weave are then traded for foodstuffs with more prosperous neighbors who do not weave. At the same time, however, their cursed status is said to be the *result* of weaving. Weaving itself is seen to be a "hot" activity, which brings predatory animals to the fields and results in poor harvests. This roundabout logic seems to result in a double curse for the Rembong; they are cursed and therefore have to weave, but they are further cursed because they weave. What is underscored is that weaving is a prohibited and damned activity, which brings retaliation from the ancestors.

As an example of how weaving itself brings a curse, people tell of a Rembong woman who married a Rajong man. She brought her loom with her when she moved to her husband's village, and continued to weave there. The first year they planted their crops everything was eaten by mice and wild pigs, while their neighbors' fields were untouched. The following year the same thing happened, so the woman threw away her loom. After that they had no more problems with field predators and reaped the same bountiful yields as their neighbors.

Why is weaving a prohibited activity and why is it seen to bring a curse on those who engage in it? Weaving is not considered a "natural" act, a gift of the gods or ancestors. Rather it is regarded as a man-made activity, not something that originated in the golden age. Weaving is likened to other acts that show trust is not being placed in the ancestors or their regulations, such as building fences to keep field predators away. If one follows the rules of the ancestors – all rituals and behavior set down in the time when rocks were young and earth was soft – then one need not build fences, and by a certain logical extension, one also need not weave. To do so is to put more trust in cultural inventions than in the ways of the ancestors. These cultural acts show, say the Rembong, a certain conceit on the part of human beings. This is why weavers are punished with predators in their fields, and people who build fences find wild pigs will be brazen enough to enter even their villages in broad daylight.

As a prohibited activity resulting in punishment from the ancestors, weaving is analogous to the incestuous and murderous acts that led to the institution of the curse in the first place. Obak's original incestuous act is mirrored in the actions of his followers, the cooked people. By clamoring around the buffalo Meze Nggoeng, Obak's followers showed a desire to "eat their own clan" (*ghan mawa*), a phrase that refers both to incest and to partaking of the meat of one's own sacrificial animal.[4] To be "cooked," therefore, implies that one "eats one's own clan," something raw people would never do. Hence "cooked" is a label that has many references, and as a designation for weavers means that they are associated with all of these sacrilegious acts.

The Rembong readily admit the danger of weaving and their own impertinence in risking it, and yet they continue to weave. Moving away from the mythological realm, there are also ecological and historical explanations for the division between weaving and non-weaving regions. As in other parts of Flores, cloth produced in an agriculturally marginal area (Rembong) is used to procure food by bartering with a nearby area where more regular rainfall provides better harvests (Rajong).[5] Based on oral history, the Rajong consider themselves, and are considered by others in eastern Manggarai, to be the indigenous people of the region. Among the Rembong, despite the mythological tales placing Ndival and Obak together at the beginning of the world, many clans actually claim origin from other places. These clan histories tell of migration (often because of conflicts between elder and younger brothers) from other parts of Manggarai or from Ngada, Palu'é, or Sulawesi. While it is certain that there have been people in Rembong since before the time of colonization by Goa (predating the seventeenth century), the indigenous populations may have been almost entirely eradicated by the slave trade during subsequent centuries. This distinction between a non-weaving people who claim indigenous origin, and weaving peoples who apparently originated from elsewhere, is found in other parts of eastern Indonesia as well.[6] Interestingly, a similar division in eastern Flores and Solor between immigrant weavers and indigenous non-weavers coincides to some extent with the moiety system of Demon and Paji, a classification that is said to have originated in the beginning of the world because of a fight between two brothers over the elder brother's wife (Arndt 1938:1-5, Maxwell 1981:53, Ruth Barnes 1987:18-21).

ANAK RANA AND ANAK WINA: CLOTH AND EXCHANGE RELATIONSHIPS

As the source of all things, the raw people (the Rajong) symbolically give life to all other people in Manggarai. This status equates them with *anak rana*, the "children of men" (also referred to as wife-givers). The gift of a woman, who will bear children to continue another's

descent group, is the gift of fertility and life. By metaphorically saying that they are *anak rana* to all other people, although this is not literally true, the Rajong mean that they give life and blessings to all others. "Raw" has connotations of life and fertility, since raw things can be planted and reproduce while cooked things cannot. The equating of the Rajong with the *anak rana* is evident in the division of labor at various northeastern Manggarai rituals. It is always the task of the *anak rana* to do the cooking, just as the Rajong, at their new year's feast in the sacred source village, receive raw gifts and return them cooked.

Thus there is an analogy between the exchanges that take place between the Rajong and the Rembong and those that take place between the *anak rana* and *anak wina*. In both cases, the flow of goods is specific and theoretically immutable.[7] The raw Rajong may not weave.[8] The cooked Rembong, in their accursed state, must weave. This asymmetry, and the implied notions of superiority and inferiority, life and death, is analogous to the asymmetry that exists in the marriage system. A brother must always give his daughter to his sister's son in marriage; he cannot marry his son to his sister's daughter. This would be incest. As a transgression of the ancestral regulations, it would result in disaster, similar to what would happen if the Rajong were to weave. Founded upon the distinctions and oppositions created in the ancestral time of the golden age, the asymmetry and interdependency between the "children of men" and "children of women" is the same as the asymmetry and interdependency of the raw and cooked people.

The asymmetry that exists in the affinal relationship is also evident in the types of goods the *anak rana* and *anak wina* give to one another. *Anak rana* (children of men or wife-givers) must receive superior "masculine" goods, while *anak wina* (children of women or wife-takers) receive "feminine" goods considered to be of less value. Masculine goods include chickens, horses, buffaloes, short swords, and, in the present day, money. Feminine goods are pigs, jewelry, rice, household utensils, and handwoven cloths (FIGURE 9-4). Store-bought cloth cannot be substituted.

The relationships that these exchanges of gifts perpetuate are those that originated at the beginning of the world, between man and woman, and wife-giver and wife-taker. *Adat,* the ways of the ancestors, dictates that the creation of these relationships is a long process; one exchange of gifts does not a marriage make. Indeed it could be said that far more than marriage is at stake in these ritual exchanges, since the act of marrying puts one on the road to becoming an adult. This sometimes lifelong process unfolds in multiple stages. The exchanges start between the young man and young woman themselves, with exchanges of small gifts. Next the young woman's family becomes involved, lending the relationship some legitimacy. The young man is expected to do labor for them (fetching water and firewood, also working in the fields), while the young woman starts to weave cloth for him. The relationship only becomes formal, however, when the wider families become involved in the exchanges. Each clan must gather the appropriate gifts beforehand (cloths, rice, pigs, and jewelry from the wife-givers; chickens, horses, buffaloes, money, and swords from the wife-takers), and then set a date to meet and confirm the union. At that point the young man moves in with his wife's family; he must live with his *anak rana*. A later exchange will give the young man the right to bring his wife to his own village. This may be many years later, however, and they may already have a number of children. Only once this stage has been accomplished does a Rembong woman have the right to weave supplementary-weft motifs into her cloth. To do so before this stage would be presumptuous, the transgression of a prohibition that would lead to illness or other forms of disaster.

One further exchange is needed before the couple is considered "complete" and gains the full rights of adulthood. They may be quite old by this time, and many Rembong couples never reach the final stage. If they do, they are considered important, powerful people, true adults capable of gaining wealth and prestige through sorcery or other means. It is only at this stage that the most important gift of cloth is bestowed by the wife-givers, *anak rana*, upon the couple, their *anak wina*. The gift indicates the couple's status of completion as adults and also foreshadows their death, for it is the cloth they will be buried in. For the first time they are also given a live pig (in previous rituals they had always been given meat already ritually slaughtered). In the first part of the ritual the couple and husband's wider kin group must go to the house of the woman's father, bringing, as on earlier occasions, horses, buffaloes, chickens, swords, and money, but this time there must be more of everything. Then, after sacrifices are done, and the couple has spent the night there, something happens which was never done at previous rituals: the *anak rana* (the woman's family) accompany the couple back to their own home. When they arrive, the wife-givers confer upon the couple the rights to own their own home, to host large ritual feasts, and thus to become complete adults. For their ritual journey of transition to gain these rights, the couple wear the newly acquired shrouds, drawing a symbolic equation between the journey made through life and the journey made in death (FIGURE 9-5). The next time they wear these cloths will be at their own burial.[9]

FIGURE 9-5.
Procession to the house of the wife-takers (*anak wina*) during the final bridewealth exchange ritual. The woman at the tail of the procession is wearing her burial shroud. Lempang Paji, 1984.

Somewhat paradoxically, the negative assessment of weaving as a cooked product associated with broken prohibitions and death seems to be contradicted by the importance and value that cloth has as a "feminine" gift associated with life and fertility. This paradox may be resolved by saying that many agricultural peoples see death as the source of new life (Bloch and Parry 1982). The woven cloths, as is frequently true about women themselves, are symbolically associated with death, and yet out of death will spring new life. Without these cloths, marriages could not take place, just as without the woman herself life could not continue. The symbolic association

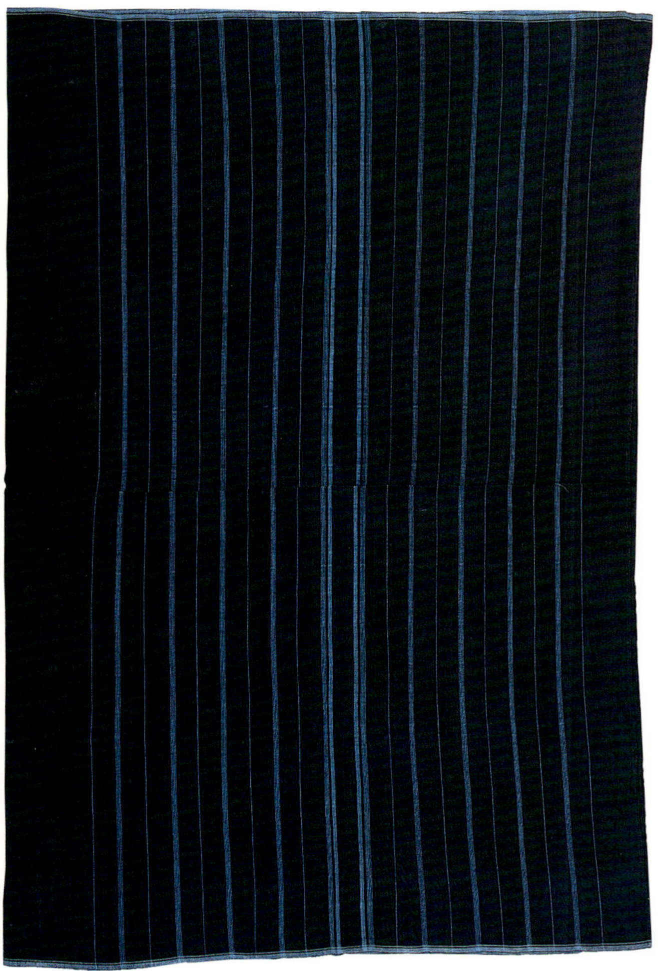

FIGURE 9-6.
A black sarong with pale indigo warp stripes, *lipa léleng lauk*, from Rembong. 140 x 95 cm. Collection of Maribeth Erb.

between women, the earth, the ocean, and death, which is implied in the mythological histories about the formation of the world and its oppositions, is also analogically associated with cloth and "the cooked." The cloth that is given by a couple's *anak rana* at the last marriage stage, as mentioned, is the same one used to bury them, returning the body (tied in a fetal position) to mother earth. This suggests a continuity and cycle between life and death, in which the exchange of cloth plays a major role (Woodward 1980:16).

WOMEN AND WEAVING IN THE REMBONG ECONOMY

Due to its value as an exchange good, and to its portability, cloth served as a kind of currency in the pre-monetary economy. As late as the early 1970s money had not penetrated the Rembong economy, principally because taxes up to that time could be paid in kind. Many exchanges of goods and labor were reckoned in terms of cloth. Particularly in the colonial and early post-colonial circumstances the role of cloth in the economy reached new levels of importance. Labor and goods needed for innovations, such as the building of wooden houses or the terracing of fields for wet-rice cultivation, were paid in cloth. Part of the importance of cloth also had to do with its role as a payment for fines. The Catholic Church adopted the indigenous practice of fining people for improper behavior and instituted a fine for "village" marriage (cohabitation before a Church wedding). The way to discharge this fine was in cloth, possibly because money had no value and this was the only way that foreign missionaries could penetrate the local economy. An influx of cloth, paid as fines, gave the missionaries currency to buy labor, horses for transportation, and other important necessities. The missionary priest living in Rembong related that thread was also used to pay for the performance of a Church wedding. Once the priest had enough thread for several cloths, he would commission a woman to weave for him, her payment being half of the outcome. One cloth would buy a horse, or a week's labor of digging (for road-building or agriculture). Cloth was so important in the local economy that even after 1973, when local government officials demanded taxes in cash, cloth was still the measure by which a cash value equivalent was calculated.

It is evident therefore, that despite its classification as a "feminine" prestation, cloth was in the past, and still is in the present, an important item in the economy of the Rembong and other Manggarai peoples. Because of the value of cloth, it may be understood why, notwithstanding the belief in the accursed status of weavers, the Rembong are willing to bear the consequences and weave anyway.

Although Rembong cloths are vital in exchange relationships, they are very stark and simple in comparison to the textiles produced by many other Indonesian peoples. The traditional cloths were practically unadorned. I was told that the only indigenous designs running through the body of the cloth were pale blue stripes (FIGURE 9-6) or plaid. Many cloths were woven entirely of blue-black threads, with no stripes at all. The only additional design that may have been traditionally used on the plain or striped cloth was the triangular, tapestry-woven *kaet* border (FIGURE 9-7).

The Rembong probably borrowed the *kaet* motif from areas further west in Manggarai before they started using other introduced motifs. All motifs appear to be considered rather special and extraordinary by the Rembong and are imbued with meaning consistent with their whole attitude toward weaving. Unlike supplementary-weft motifs, the *kaet* motif is a public pattern, with no special rights or status needed to weave it. Some Rembong say that it is woven into the cloth as a protective device. The red and yellow colors of this border are said to be an imitation of a noxious glowing trail that emanates from the tail of a deadly bird-like creature as it flies. Humans are vulnerable to these fumes if they are not wearing the *kaet* motif. Imitation in this case is seen as a protection against the poison.

The supplementary-weft "star" (*talaq*) design, also introduced from further west, were a later addition to the inventory of Rembong motifs (FIGURES 9-8, 4-18). Rembong stars are far simpler than the more elaborate supplementary-weft designs found in Lambaleda cloth. According to traditional regulations the right to weave these motifs is only gained after the marriage stage that brings a couple to live in the husband's village. Once a woman is eligible, she still has to buy the right to weave them from an older woman who already has it, by giving her gifts appropriate to their relationship (chickens, horses, buffaloes, and money if she is from a wife-giving clan; pigs, jewelry, cloth, and rice if she is from a wife-taking clan). If she does not have the right herself to weave *talaq* she can invite a woman who does to weave them into her cloth for her. In payment she should give her some "iron" (in reality some kind of metal bracelet or ring), as a protection against the danger of these designs. Weaving the supplementary-weft motifs is thought to be even more dangerous than ordinary weaving, a further indication of human impertinence. The colors are considered dangerous to the eyes and supplementary-weft weaving is said to cause a woman to go quickly blind. In order to protect against this, one should put an old coin (again the notion of metal as protection) on the cloth before starting to weave. The use of specific motifs, therefore, is not the inherited property of a clan or household as in some parts of Indonesia; rather, individual women gain these rights for themselves. Magic associated with dyeing is also the property of individual women, who use it to protect the dyeing process.

It could be argued that because of the important role that cloth has in the Rembong economy, weaving to a certain extent empowers the Rembong woman. She is an important economic asset to her family, since the woven cloths, particularly in the past, were crucial to getting

FIGURE 9-7.
A chicken is sacrificed to the ancestors. The young man holding the chicken wears a plain black cloth decorated only with the tapestry-woven *kaet* border (known as *jok* in other parts of Manggarai). Golo Lijun, 1983.

through the annual period of food scarcity that preceded the new harvest. When produce from the fields ran out, traditional alternatives were only to search for roots and leaves in the forest, or to trade cloth for rice and maize. Women boast that their families depended on them for income, although men counter that it was they who had to make the long journeys to barter the cloth. Now that money has infiltrated the economy and some cash crops like coffee and cloves have started to reap profits for the Rembong, cloth is no longer the only alternative. However, new reasons for needing money, such as the education of children, mean that cloth continues to hold an important place in the search for economic necessities.

In this sense it can be argued that women hold an important role in the household due to their contribution to its maintenance through weaving. At the same time, it must be remembered that what women do is also seen to endanger everyone, as weaving brings a curse to the Rembong. In this sense, one could also say that women are blamed for the accursed state the Rembong inhabit. It could also be argued that the loom is in some respects a woman's prison. She works very hard, almost day in and day out, frequently year round. This is the most regular activity of women in Rembong. They weave in the villages, sitting outside or under their houses, and also in their field huts. Most Rembong still rely on swidden farming (whereas their Rajong neighbors now almost entirely utilize the far more productive wet-rice agriculture). If their fields are far from their houses, they live in their field huts for approximately half of the year, from the November planting to the June harvest. Between work in the fields, women continue to weave.[10]

In the past, the only time that women had a break from their looms was during the dry season, when two special occasions would evacuate the entire community from the villages and fields. One of these was the group hunt, in September and October, when for several weeks whole villages would descend to the meadows to burn the grasses and flush out game. Some Rembong villages still undertake the group hunt, but on a much smaller scale. The other occasion was when there was a need for lime, which is used both for chewing betel and for indigo dyeing. Before there were communities on the coast from whom inland villagers could obtain lime, the entire village would descend to the coast. While the men cut coral to burn for making lime, the women and children caught fish and collected shellfish. On both of these occasions women felt an exhilaration to be free from their everyday work in the field and village, and in particular to be free from their endless task of weaving. The loss of these community activities in the present day, and the loss of leisure time in general in Rembong because of newly discovered necessities, has transformed both men's and women's lives to a certain extent. New activities that both men and women can engage in to improve the family economy (such as planting coffee, vanilla, or cloves) have created more work for all, but have taken away some of the presssure from weaving as an economic necessity.

Considering the importance of weaving traditionally and up to the present day in the Rembong economy, a woman who cannot weave is assessed as a very poor choice of spouse. She is in some way seen as being incomplete. A recent case shows an interesting clash of values between the traditional role of a wife, and the changing expectations of the present.

A Rembong man who had political aspirations to become headman (*kepala desa*), broke off his relationship with a village woman (his mother's brother's daughter) and took instead

FIGURE 9-8.
A Rembong *lipa talaq*. The star motifs are similar to those on the cloth illustrated in FIGURE 1-22, but the format in which they are arranged is somewhat simpler. Golo Lebo, 1992.

a wife who was literate. This seemed a proper choice for a man who wanted to be a member of the government bureaucracy. This man became headman, but after a number of years his dissatisfaction with his wife started to grow. The problem was that although she was literate she could not weave. In order to have access to this important resource of the Rembong economy, the headman returned to his old love. He worked in her parent's garden in exchange for her weaving for him (the prelude to a traditional marriage). Though in the past this budding polygamous relationship would have been quite acceptable for a village leader, under a local government where almost all of the administrators are Catholic, this is now strictly forbidden. The matter became public knowledge when the woman gave birth to a child out of wedlock, an act considered to be dangerous. The affair became a matter of litigation and went as high as the district (*kecamatan*) legislature, starting all of Rembong buzzing with gossip about political intrigue and accusations of sorcery. Although it is clear that this incident shows people caught between changing systems of morality, the interpretation of the Rembong villagers most familiar with the case was that the whole affair never would have taken place if the village headman's wife had fulfilled her role as a woman by being able to weave.

WEAVING: BRINGING INTO EXISTENCE NEW LIFE

Although weaving in Rembong is considered a dangerous, cursed, "hot" activity (and cloths inferior "cooked" products), paradoxically many aspects of weaving are likened to harvesting activities and are seen to be symbolic of the protecting of new life. It can be argued that the threads and the finished cloth, like rice plants, are equated with living beings that have a soul, and are dependent on human beings for their existence and protection. Both rice and cloth might be said to be the children of human beings.[11] Many precautions taken during the harvest and at various steps involved in making a cloth are reminiscent of precautions taken to protect a human infant. If precautions are not taken, then spirits of the dead or evil magicians will hinder the success of these activities, in the same way that they are thought to steal the souls of the rice or bring illness to a human child. Some of these precautions are still taken by many Rembong, though the activities are no longer the full-scale village events of the past.

The most vulnerable times involved in cloth production are the burning of coral to produce lime for dyeing, the dyeing of the threads with indigo, and the actual weaving of the cloth. To produce lime, living coral pried out of the sea at low tide was arranged in alternating layers with firewood on the beach. The leader of the village would take an old piece of smoke-permeated cloth, called *sengi,* which is thought to protect against evil spirits. The same type of cloth is used to wrap an infant on the day he is given a name and brought out of the house for the first time. It is also waved over the pile of rice grains harvested from a field on the last day of the harvest. As the leader waved the cloth over the pile of coral, he called out, sending away the spirits of the newly dead, who might otherwise hover around and hinder proper burning. The burned coral was carried by horse to the village. There it was treated with a solution made by boiling special leaves and roots, which processed it into powdered lime.

When picking indigo, women are forbidden to use coarse language. A similar prohibition is in place during the rice harvest, for fear the souls of the rice will be offended and run away. If a woman swears, the plants will not yield indigo dye, indicating a similar fear that the soul of the plant might depart. In the past, the dyeing of the threads was often a communal activity, with one woman, noted for her magic, serving as the leader. By the use of special phrases, she would chase away evil spirits before the pots were set in place. Under each pot were placed seven threads and seven pieces of "iron," so that if someone had died, his or her spirit would not be able to touch the dye mixture in the pots. Just before the dyeing began, an extra precaution was taken: a piece of *sengi* cloth was waved over the pots. People say the threads will not turn black if the ghost of a person who has just died is hovering around. If anyone's threads were not taking the dye properly, then the leader would use further magic to chase away the spirits of the dead. Communal dyeing is no longer the norm, but some of these precautions are still taken by those women who continue to dye. Certain other things affect the dyeing process and are therefore prohibited. One should not touch any kind of sour fruit (lemons, grapefruits) or meat; the sour juice and grease are said to stop the threads from turning black. It is forbidden to even bring sour fruits near the pots, but if a woman does eat meat before dyeing, then she should wash her hands with ashes before touching the threads. Soap may not be used, it is another forbidden substance which will stop the threads from turning black.[12]

The day before a loom is to be set up for weaving, the weaver takes five balls of the thread she has measured out to use and ties their ends together. This ensures that the threads will not be stolen by evil spirits. The whole notion of "tying together" (*pekon*) is an important one to the Rembong, seen to protect new life against evil forces and the stealing or running away of its soul. The afternoon before the rice harvest begins, in a similar manner some of the rice plants are tied together in the center of the field, to ensure that the rice souls will not be stolen or run away during the harvest. The Rembong believe that if these things are not tied, the soul containing their substance may disappear. Even though one may have been certain that there would be enough thread, and even though it looks as if there is a bountiful yield of rice in the field, if the "soul" is gone, these appearances will deceive; the thread will run out and the rice husks will be empty. A similar precaution is taken for children, around whose wrists a string is often tied, so that one of their souls, located in the pulse, cannot be seen by evil spirits, and will not run off due to shock.

Similarly again, both harvesting and weaving must both stop well before the sun sets. The setting sun is symbolic of death, and hence the precautions suggest a fear that the souls of the rice or the threads are especially vulnerable during these activities as dark approaches. A further prohibition exists when a weaver is ready to cut a finished cloth off her loom. She must not do so near sunset, for this will bring about the death of the person who wears it.

In many ways, then, weaving is seen to be like the harvest; many of the same prohibitions are in force and many of the same precautions must be taken. If the lime, dye, and threads are not protected, much as new rice and new children are protected, then the task will not be successful, and evil spirits will harm the product. The Rembong seem to be making an analogy between cloth and the new life of children and the rice plants, which are vulnerable and need to be protected. Weaving, then, like harvesting and nurturing the young, is the bringing into existence of a new life.

Thus the Rembong seem to hold two rather contradictory attitudes about weaving. On one hand, it is a cursed activity associated with death, while on the other, it is an important and hence vulnerable activity, needing protective measures like other activities dealing with new life. Actually, a similar attitude is held towards rice. Like weaving, the rice plant is considered "hot" and was never in the past kept in the house. The rice chaff is thought to give off a hot glow, which can be dangerous to human beings. The chaff is associated with fertility, but also with heat. It is beneficial, but in excess is potentially dangerous. The ritual to clean out the village of all the sins of the past year, before the new years planting, is called "clearing away the rice chaff." The chaff is symbolic of all the transgressions of the villagers that must be cleared away before the new crops can be planted. At this yearly ritual, the leftover bits of thread used in weaving are also thrown away. When a woman finishes a cloth she must not just toss away the leftover strands. They must be brought to the village center, along with the chicken that each family must bring to be sacrificed, and presented at the village altar to be neutralized before they can be thrown away. These bits of thread, I suggest, are the dead leftovers of a created life, just like the chaff of the rice. As in the case of a dead human being, they will be potentially harmful if not dealt with properly in ritual. The ambiguity associated with all life, therefore, is that it must end in death, and the dead must be dealt with properly lest other dangers arise. This strengthens the suggestion that cloth, like rice and human beings, is alive and must be nurtured, but at the same time like all creatures who live, becomes dangerous and ambiguous after death.

THE WEAVING PROCESS AND CHANGE

Despite the Rembong admonition to the young that custom and tradition are unchangeable, like rocks shaped at the beginning of the world, many things have altered. Influences from the Catholic Church, as well as colonial and post-colonial national governments, have had an effect on many aspects of the ritual life and beliefs of the people

FIGURE 9-9.
A health care worker and her husband, who became village headman. Though a very modern couple, they insisted on performing the final marriage stage ritual. Lempang Paji, 1983.

of Manggarai. Rembong is possibly the most isolated region in Manggarai, but even though change has been more muted than in other areas, it has nevertheless had an effect. Marriage exchanges, and the importance of cloth in them, have perhaps been the most resilient features of Rembong tradition. Despite many changes in other areas of their ritual life, even the most modern of the Rembong folk continue to place importance on completing the full range of marriage rituals leading to "completion" (FIGURE 9-9). Handwoven cloth retains an important role in all ritual activities and exchanges. One could never substitute store-bought sarongs for the indigenously woven indigo-dyed cloths in ritual exchanges, although many people do use them for everyday wear. For people who themselves are put "on stage" at a ritual event, it is imperative to wear the traditional blue-black cloth and not a substitute (FIGURE 9-1). Although the role of the indigenously woven cloth remains important in Rembong ritual life, the process of weaving itself has undergone some shortcuts in recent years.

Up until about fifteen years ago the Rembong performed every step of the cloth-making process. This included the making of lime and the growing of cotton. Villages where the climate was too cold to grow cotton traded to obtain bolls with the seeds still intact. Extracting the seeds was a major task that each woman performed for herself, using a hand-cranked mangle made by her husband. Nowadays the women who do their own spinning are becoming fewer, and even those who do prefer to obtain cotton that is already cleaned and ready to be spun.

Though many Rembong women still use the indigenously spun thread for the warp, the weft thread and the colored thread for the supplementary-weft stars are store-bought.[13] This mixture of thread is seen to have several advantages. The indigenous thread is stronger, so using it for the warp ensures a long-lasting cloth. Store-bought thread is said to be warmer, probably because it is finer and therefore can be woven more tightly. By mixing the two, one gets both strength and warmth. At least one woman in Rembong still weaves cloth entirely from indigenous thread, but most other women prefer this mix. In other areas of Manggarai women weave entirely from the store-bought thread, and recently some Rembong women have begun to do this as well.[14] The labor involved in preparing and spinning of thread is so time-consuming that they may prefer to compromise strength for faster production. Because much of the cloth made in Rembong still contains some handspun thread, it has became quite popular in other areas of Manggarai. Itinerant traders travel long distances to Rembong to buy the plain Rembong cloth, which is inexpensive compared with cloth from other areas.[15]

Given the amount of hard work involved in making a cloth (work that the Rembong well comprehend, and view as a curse), it is easy to understand why weaving has changed or even disappeared in parts of Manggarai where there are easier ways of making a living. The people of other areas are far wealthier in coffee, chocolate, and clove trees than the more isolated Rembong, and also long ago started cultivating the more abundant irrigated wet-rice. Until the Rembong internalize some of these newer innovations, weaving will continue to be an important part of their life and economy.

Despite its negative connotation, weaving in northeastern Manggarai contributes to the integration of people both through marriage alliance between clans and also across the ethnic *dalu* divisions. The differentiation of weavers and non-weavers leads to an interdependence between peoples living in neighboring regions. The distinction between them is said to be symbolized by "raw" and "cooked," those who give life and those associated with death. This symbolic difference is mirrored at the level of marriage alliance in the interdependence and intertwining of two clans: the *anak rana* who give life through the gift of a young woman, and the *anak wina* who receive her in order to ensure the reproduction of their own group. The cloths that are woven, therefore, play an important part in the exchange of goods and interdependency of people in Northeastern Manggarai, as symbols both of the ancestral curse and death, and of fertility and the new life that emerges from death. ❖ 　　　　　　　　　　　　　　　NOTES, page 273.

10

Cloth Production and Change in a Lio Village

WILLEMIJN DE JONG

N THE LIO VILLAGE OF NGGELA, TEXTILES MAY BE CONSIDERED A SOCIAL SYSTEM in which all kinds of institutions express themselves; in other words they are an instance of what Marcel Mauss, in developing the concept of the gift, called a *fait social total* (1923/24). Textiles provide a key to understanding Nggela society. Not only are they basic for everyday living, as clothing and as objects of trade, but they also serve as prestige goods in several sociopolitical and ritual contexts. Nggela craftswomen have produced a unique cloth system comprised of at least thirty-three specific and distinctly named types of cloth, with ikat and non-ikat designs, about which knowledge is still fragmentary.[1] I chose Nggela as a research site because I was fascinated by these valuable and artistic female products, and impressed by the apparent autonomy of the ikat weavers as well as the singularity of Nggela society and culture.

This chapter will focus on the production of cloth and the way it has changed over time. Specifically, I am interested in how such a rich cloth system developed, what factors influenced change, and how change affected the value of cloth and the position of weavers. To address these topics, I will first outline the relevant features of Nggela society and the technical and social aspects of cloth production. Then I will explore the formal, social, and religious properties of cloth. Finally I will directly address various aspects of change.

NGGELA SOCIETY AND THE IMPORTANCE OF CLOTH

According to local oral history, especially genealogical knowledge, people calling themselves Lio probably settled the south coastal portions of their current territory at the end of the sixteenth century. They brought with them their *adat* (customary laws, institutions, and norms) and the technology of ikat weaving. The founding of the *adat* community of Nggela may have occurred around the end of the seventeenth century. From the beginning, the village was exposed to Portuguese and Dutch colonial influences. Nggela developed a unique culture, more complex and highly ranked than most other Lio communities. This was perhaps due to the wealth of the early immigrants, who may have included Portuguese, Javanese, and Malaccans (Ndate 1981:16; 1988:17).

FIGURE 10-1 (OPPOSITE). Young woman with traditional gold jewelry (*we'a*). This kind of gold jewelry represents one of the male gifts (*belis*) in marriage rituals, such as bridewealth transactions. It is also worn by women at certain rituals, in particular at the rain dance. Nggela, 1988.

The people of Nggela are proud of their cultural achievements, including their gold jewelry (FIGURE 10-1), cloth, and elaborate agricultural rituals. They also take pride in their women, on whom is bestowed the richest bridewealth in the Lio region. Given in return is the largest number of cloths, sometimes up to fifty or more (FIGURE 10-2). Despite the bridewealth system, post-marital residence is matrilocal, rather than patrilocal as in other Lio communities. Seventeen *adat* leaders, instead of the usual seven, were once responsible for settling juropolitical and ritual affairs. The people of Nggela sharply distinguish themselves from the neighboring *adat* communities, particularly Mbuli. They identify themselves as more refined, as evidenced by their speech and their non-violent handling of conflicts.

Nggela's descent system is of the double unilinear type, with hierarchical matriclans (*kunu*), characterized by totems and food taboos, and with patrilineages (*suku*). Clan membership is decisive in determining rank as well as political and ritual rights.[2] Members of the matriclans that founded the village once constituted the nobility. Only they could claim the most important *adat* offices and titles, "lord of the earth" (*mosa laki*) for men and "great lady" (*fai ngga'é*) for women. The skills of good ikat designing were also passed on within the highest ranking matriclans. Matrilineal descent groups of more recent immigrants (*ata mai*) and slaves (*ata ko'o*) ranked lowest. In between were the clans of commoners (*ana fai walu*).

The two most important patrilineages (named Sa'o Labo and Sa'o Ria after their ceremonial houses) are the ones that first organized Nggela's political and cultural institutions. Ranking somewhat lower are the patrilineages of the so-called Portuguese-Java-Malacca group. Because of their wealth, men from these patrilineages were willingly accepted as marriage partners for the daughters of the founding patrilineages. Heirloom treasures including the most sacred type of cloths, the beaded women's sarongs known as *lawo butu*, partly belong to the lineage and are transmitted patrilineally. Rights over land, houses, and children are also reckoned patrilineally.

The people of Nggela subsist mainly on corn, cassava, millet, and rice, grown in *ladang* (dry fields cultivated by shifting agriculture). Formerly they also planted cotton. Men produced coconuts and pigs for trade. Women's subsistence and trade products were, and still are, cloths. Surplus cloths were traded at regional markets.[3] Since the 1980s, they have also been sold directly to tourists who visit the village. Today agriculture hardly fulfills subsistence needs and cloth production offers almost the only possibility of earning cash income. Cloths were once used as currency as well. Even today they may serve as payment (for health services for example) if cash is not available.

Since Indonesian independence in 1945, and especially with the extension of formal education since the 1970s, a class structure based on education, occupation, and income,

FIGURE 10-2. Cloths as female gifts at a bridewealth ritual (*tolo nata*). Women of the family of the bride bestow cloths to male members of the family of the bridegroom, who are invited to the house of the bride. Nggela, 1988.

has emerged. Thus Nggela's population can also be classified as peasants and weavers on one hand and white collar employees, particularly teachers, on the other. Nggela today has a population of about 1,200, not counting the exceptionally high number of people who have left Nggela to work elsewhere – for example, as government employees in Ende or other towns.

A central social institution in Nggela is the giving of gifts at life cycle rituals, especially at marriage and death, between affinal kin groups. "Male" gifts are gold, cattle, and money; "female" gifts are cloths and rice. The giving of cloths has increased

FIGURE 10-3.
Rain dance (*muré*). Young women wearing ritual attire, in particular the sacred *lawo butu*, perform the rain dance for some civil servants from governmental tourist agencies, who aim to promote the tourist industry in the Lio region. Nggela, 1988.

in importance since independence. Gift giving is multifunctional, providing economic benefits, strengthening social ties, and fostering prestige and power.

Formerly twelve agricultural festivals (*nggua*) were performed annually. This cycle culminated in a four-day dance feast called *joka ju*, held to banish evil spirits and illness. Another outstanding ceremony was the four-day rain dance *muré*, performed when new fields were cleared after lying fallow for seven years. The rain dance ceremony has not been performed in its traditional context since independence. Occasionally a short version is presented at national or regional folkloric events or for tourists (FIGURE 10-3). Other annual agricultural rituals were performed regularly until 1980.

The system of agricultural rituals is a creation of men, while the cloth system is a singular female achievement. Weavers discussed with me thirty-three named types of cloths, with different designs and uses. This cloth system demonstrates a high level of female artistic skill and technological knowledge. Like the agricultural rituals, the aesthetics of cloth are intricately connected with the values of the ancestors, i.e. with traditional religious beliefs. Therefore the aesthetics of the "art of ikat weaving," as it is called by native experts on Lio culture as well (Petu 1969, 1976; Ndate 1981), are not fully apparent to an outsider without studying the cloths and their place in Nggela society.

TECHNOLOGY AND LABOR ORGANIZATION

The technical aspects of ikat work in Nggela are similar to those in other places on Flores (summarized in CHAPTER 3). Except for two types of ritual cloth, the *lawo butu* and the *luka ria*, textiles made of handspun thread are no longer found in Nggela. Weavers have used exclusively machinespun thread (in particular, and increasingly, rayon), since the second half of the 1960s. Although Nggela cloth looks naturally dyed (in contrast to the cloth of Mbuli), most of it has been produced with chemical dyes, or a mixture of chemical and natural dyes, since the mid 1970s.

There are two types of chemical dyes. The first, called *celup*, is a composition of naphthol and several other substances, available only in town shops. Only a few women in the village know how to dye with *celup*. The other dye, called *sumba* (actually *kesumbat*), can be purchased locally and is used by all weavers. *Celup* is a better quality dye and more expensive. It is often used as a substitute for indigo. *Sumba* is used for dyeing red or yellow in an ikat warp, or for red or black in the weft. It may also be used in combination with morinda, to shorten the process by "closing" the red color after three sessions of morinda dyeing.

Nggela craftswomen have developed their skill with the various shades of synthetic dyes to the point that it is sometimes difficult for weavers themselves to distinguish cloth dyed with morinda from cloth dyed with synthetic red dyes. The exact procedures are kept secret, even with the synthetic dyes. Especially during dyeing and weaving, Nggela women live in a state of latent anxiety, fearing the destruction of their work by the magical powers of witches. Most witchcraft in connection with cloths is said to be female and based on envy. Women try to counteract this threat with specific gestures or spells and by working in hidden places.

Nggela people say that women have power inside the house, managing family income and expenditure. Men have power outside the house, representing the family to the outer world. Both are said to participate equally in decision-making. Generally, agricultural work is performed by men and cloth production by women. Women control the weaving tools, the raw materials, the production process, the finished products, and the revenues. However, some aspects of cloth production have traditionally required cooperation between husband and wife. Men's tasks include making the weaving tools, providing the coconut leaves used for tying the ikat knots, and digging morinda roots (FIGURE 10-4). Men usually help with winding thread and sometimes with warping (FIGURE 10-5). Formerly men also helped with spinning. Some men, said to be homosexuals, do ikat work and dyeing, although these tasks are in theory exclusively female. Women perform agricultural work particularly during planting and harvesting, but women's ikat labor is valued more highly than agricultural labor by either sex.

Labor patterns also differ according to age. Apprenticeship with factory thread and chemical dyes takes on average two years. At about seventeen or eighteen, a young women

FIGURE 10-4 (LEFT). A husband has the task of digging morinda roots. His wife helps to remove the bark of the roots, which contains the red dyestuff. Nggela, 1988.

FIGURE 10-5 (RIGHT). Cooperation between husband and wife is evident as a husband helps his wife set up the warp (*go'a*) before weaving. Nggela, 1988.

starts to learn the major weaving tasks systematically. First she is introduced to the ikat work, then to weaving. Until she marries, she works on her mother's cloths. After marriage she makes cloth for her own family, although she may continue to live in the house of her parents. Cooperation between mother and daughter is encouraged by the matrilocal residence pattern. Women continue to work their looms until about age fifty, after which they may concentrate more on the less strenuous ikat work.

There is additionally a division of labor according to wealth. Wealthier women may have others do certain tasks for them, such as tying, dyeing, or weaving. Thus some women give orders and others take them. A woman's output increases considerably if she can dispose of the labor of others (including unpaid husband and daughters as well as paid workers). The productivity of poorer weavers is often affected by a shortage of capital for thread and dyes, which can be a major expense compared to the limited cash such women have at their disposal. Often they have to interrupt production temporarily, while they earn cash by selling something or working for another woman.

While some women specialize in certain tasks, all are alike in that they are both subsistence and market producers. Many weavers, but not all, have developed clear strategies of cloth production. They try hard to adapt to market demands, especially for the tourist market. They determine which color combinations and types of cloth will be the most attractive by observing what sells best. In 1990, for example, there was a small revival in producing cloth dyed with morinda, because Chinese traders and Japanese tourists had paid high prices for such cloths on several occasions.

THE CLOTH SYSTEM OF NGGELA IN THE 1970s

CLOTH TYPES	CLOTH NAMES	RITUAL CLOTHS	NO LONGER PRODUCED
IKAT CLOTHS			
WOMEN'S SARONGS			
A. OVERALL CENTER PANEL MOTIFS	*lawo redu*		
	lawo luka sémba		
	lawo wenda jara		
	lawo barai		X
	lawo kapa ria		
	lawo kéli mara té'a		
B. VERTICAL SECTIONS	*lawo jara élo*		
	lawo pundi		
	lawo kapa lo'o		X
	lawo jinga runu		
	lawo rangka / kangga au		
	lawo lima desa		
C. HORIZONTAL BANDS	*lawo népa nua / mité*		
	lawo népa ndu'a		
	lawo mogha		
	lawo gami terasa		
	lawo mangga lo'o		
	lawo gelo		
	lawo keli mara mité		
D. MOTIFS OVERALL	*lawo gamba*		
GIRL'S SARONG	*lawo sulu*		
MEN'S SHOULDER CLOTHS	*luka sémba*	X	
	luka tégé / songgé sindé	X	X
	luka kapa		
	luka gamba		
MEN'S SCARF	*luka leté*		
NON–IKAT CLOTHS			
MEN'S SARONGS	*luka mité / luka lo'o*		
	luka bara mité		
	luka ria	X	X
BOY'S SARONG	*luka sulu*		X
WOMEN'S SARONG	*lawo butu*	X	X
MEN'S SHOULDER CLOTH	*luka bara lombo*	X	X
MEN'S HEADCLOTH	*lésu*	X	X

THE FORMAL PROPERTIES OF CLOTH: TYPES AND MOTIFS

Types. On the basis of information given by weavers, I have been able to reconstruct the cloth system as it existed in Nggela in the 1970s. The table (ABOVE) shows the varieties of cloths, classified according to patterning (ikat or non-ikat), function, and design format, and indicating which are associated with ritual use and which are no longer made.[4]

FIGURE 10-6. Woman's beaded sarong, *lawo butu*. These most sacred of Nggela's cloths are used at the rain dance and at the roof-renewal ritual performed for the most important *adat* houses. The beaded motif, which is similar to the most common motif of Ngadha beaded sarongs, is referred to in simple descriptive fashion as octopus (*kubi*). 197 x 64 cm. National Gallery of Australia 1988.155.

In general, women's tubular sarongs, *lawo*, are characterized by ikat designs; there are at least twenty named kinds. In contrast, ikat never appears on men's tubular sarongs, *luka*, although it does embellish four kinds of men's shoulder cloths, also called *luka*,[5] as well as a large variety of men's scarves (*luka lété*) that are not separately named. The only non-ikat sarong for women is the one most highly valued: it is the outstanding, beaded black sarong with red-and-white stripes, known as *lawo butu* (FIGURE 10-6).

Squares and stripes, rather than ikat, are the distinguishing feature of men's sarongs: a large black one with fine red squares (*luka ria*), a white one with black squares (*luka bara mité*), and a black one with stripes of various colors (*luka mité*). Also without ikat are a red and yellow shoulder cloth with multi-colored borders (*luka bara lombo*) and a red and yellow headcloth (*lésu*) with a plaid pattern, both for men.[6]

Most of the twenty-two named sarongs are claimed by the weavers to be original creations of Nggela.[7] Variants of certain sarongs are the result of altering the ground color from black (*mité*) to "yellow" (*té'a*), which is really red-brown, or of changing the size of the motifs from large (*ria*) to small (*lo'o*). Still other sarongs, not listed in the table, are made by copying motifs and patterns from outside Nggela.

All women's ikat sarongs are composed of three parts: a central panel (*oné*) and two border panels (*gha'i*). They fall into three main types depending on the arrangement of the motifs in the central panel: A) those with motifs spread across the whole central panel, B) those with vertical sections, and C) those banded horizontally. A fourth rather uncommon type with only one example, *lawo gamba*, bears motifs not only on the central panel, but over the entire sarong; it seems to be a rather new creation.

The most highly valued ikat sarongs are those with ikat motifs spread over the center panel, on a red-brown ground. The *lawo redu*, formerly dyed with only a little red, is prized as a bridewealth cloth (FIGURE 10-9). Another sarong of high value is the *lawo luka sémba* (FIGURE 10-10), inspired by the motifs of Nggela's most famous cloth, the men's ikat shoulder cloth *luka sémba* (FIGURE 6-35). Sarongs with vertical sections, characteristically with a red-brown ground, are almost as highly regarded. Of these, *lawo jara élo* (FIGURE 10-11) and *lawo pundi* (FIGURE 10-13) are the most important.

Nowadays, morinda dyeing is mostly restricted to the three most highly valued sarongs — *lawo redu, lawo luka semba,* and to a lesser extent *lawo pundi* — and is a measure of their worth. The patterns of *lawo redu* or *lawo pundi* are those most likely to appear on a girl's sarong, *lawo sulu*.

Horizontally banded sarongs rank lower in the *lawo* hierarchy and are not supposed to be given as a marriage gifts. They are pejoratively called *lawo lélu* (thread sarong), a term that stresses the narrowness and simplicity of the ikat design. On these, bands of fine, simple ikat motifs alternate with narrow plain bands; the ground is black or reddish-brown. Of these the most important are the *lawo népa nua* (FIGURE 10-7), the *lawo mogha* (FIGURE 10-8) and the *lawo kéli mara* (FIGURE 10-15).

Motifs. The principal ikat motifs are geometric or floral, with a few additional zoomorphic and even anthropomorphic forms. More generally, they can be divided into two categories: those that are purely geometrical or, if representative, highly stylized; and those that are figurative and less stylized. Prestigious types of sarongs show only motifs of the first category.

In sarongs with overall center panel motifs and in those with vertical sections, the floral and rhombic motifs show strong influence from Indian patola. The relationship among patola, *luka sémba* and *lawo luka sémba* has already been explored in CHAPTER 6. The rhombic motif is particularly visible on the *lawo redu*. Similar motifs on other cloth types seem to be transformations of the *redu* motif.[8]

Horses (*jara*) appear on *lawo wenda jara* and, in more stylized forms, on *lawo jara élo*. Stylized human motifs occasionally appear on vertical-section type sarongs (FIGURE 10-12). They are likened to the carved wooden figures in the former ancestral council house (*keda*), so they presumably represent ancestors. Less-stylized human figures appear on *lawo gamba* (FIGURE 2-24) and *luka gamba*. Other figurative motifs include ships (*kapa*) and mountains. The ship motif appears on the shoulder cloth *luka kapa* (FIGURE 6-36), and on two ship sarongs, *lawo kapa ria* and *lawo kapa lo'o*. Weavers say that Portuguese ships provided the model for these motifs. This may be true for the shoulder cloths, but the

FIGURE 10-7 (LEFT).
An old woman wears a *lawo népa nua* (alternatively called *lawo népa mité*). Nggela, 1988.

FIGURE 10-8 (RIGHT).
The end panel of a *lawo mogha*. The second widest ikat band (*foko*) includes a diamond pattern (*mata bili*) that is taboo, meaning it may not be tied by all women. Ndate interprets it as the female vulva, symbolizing fertility (pers. com.). Nggela weavers do not know its symbolic meaning. The same band appears in *lawo luka sémba* (FIGURE 10-10), also considered taboo, and in *lawo népa nua* (FIGURE 10-7), which is only occasionally mentioned as taboo.

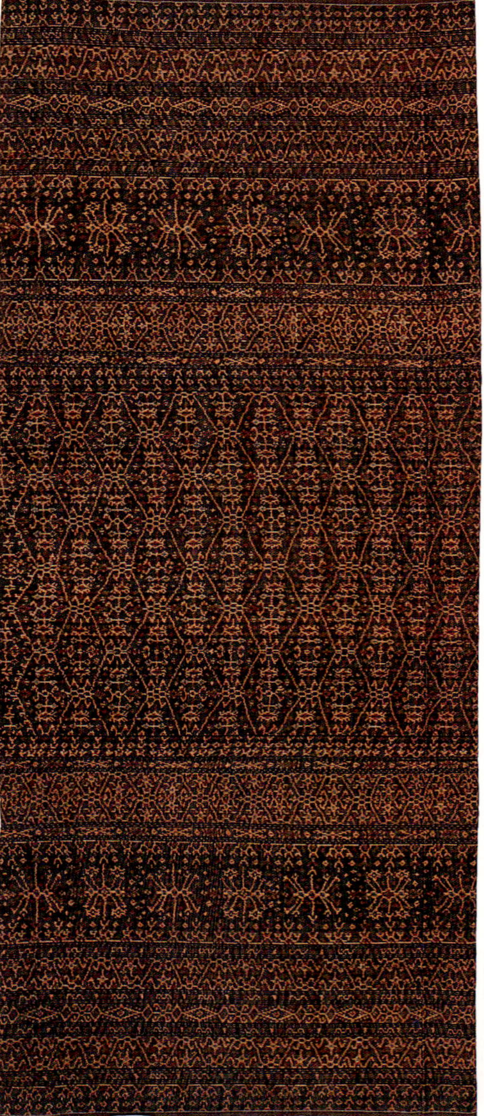

FIGURE 10-9 (LEFT). Cloths of this type with patola-derived motifs are important bridewealth prestations. In Nggela, they are known as *lawo redu.* The example illustrated here is from Wolojita, where they are known as *lawo daki.* Only minor differences between the cloths of the two villages occur in the design that fills the rhombic spaces. 169 x 71 cm. FMCH X88.1270, Museum Purchase, Manus Fund.

FIGURE 10-10 (RIGHT). *Lawo luka sémba,* made in Nggela or perhaps a nearby village. 176 x 70 cm. Collection of August Flick.

motifs on the sarongs actually appear to be variations of the rhombic *redu* motif. A stylized mountain motif appears on two different sarongs named *lawo kéli mara,* one a horizontal-band type (FIGURE 10-15) and the other a center-panel motif type (FIGURE 6-28). It represents Kelimara, a mountain northwest of Ende. A more figurative motif, representing the mountain Kelimutu, sometimes appears on *luka gamba* shoulder cloths. Relatively non-stylized, pictorial motifs are found on *lawo gamba* and *luka gamba.* These include gold jewelry, *adat* houses, aeroplanes, etc.

Most beaded motifs on *lawo butu* resemble the rhombic forms of *lawo redu,* but in this case are called octopus (*kubi*). Less common beaded motifs include fish and human figures with arms raised as if in prayer (Petu, in Ndate 1988:33).

SOCIAL PROPERTIES OF CLOTHS: GENDER, AGE, AND RANK

As we have seen, ikat sarongs (*lawo*) are worn by women and striped non-ikat sarongs (*luka*) by men, thus clothing refers to gender. Ikat designs can be interpreted as female markers, and stripes as male markers. To a certain extent age is also indicated by clothing.

When a boy or girl reaches the age of three and begins to carry out small tasks, a ritual is performed and the child receives his or her first sarong. Children's *sulu* cloth types are small-scale copies of women's and men's sarongs. As adults, many younger women prefer wearing the vertically sectioned sarongs, while older women often wear black versions of the horizontally banded types (FIGURE 10-7).

Nggela cloths also communicate rank. Women told me that it was taboo (*piré*) for younger women to tie certain designs, for they might become barren or die at an early age. Only post-menopausal women were allowed to tie designs of *luka sémba, lawo luka sémba, lawo mogha*, and *lawo élo*. Today younger women are particularly careful when tying these patterns; if they fall ill, they will refrain altogether. In earlier times this taboo was more strictly followed. Moreover not all post-menopausal women designed these cloths. Older noblewomen of the two most important patrilineages, Sa'o Labo and Sa'o Ria, were particularly famous for tying these patterns. Evidently these women had monopolized the production of certain cloths.[9]

Noblewomen were able to create new ikat designs and develop their artistic skills because they were released from the drudgery of other productive (and reproductive) tasks by female slaves. In certain cases, a female slave (*ndu longgo*) was included among the marriage gifts. High-ranking women had control over resources including cotton and labor. They carefully guarded their copyrights by working in hidden places and concealing their cloths after washing so that other women could not imitate them. Thus the taboo against tying certain designs supported a monopoly on the part of the highest-ranking women. These cloths were in fact prestigious luxury goods, the production of which has encouraged the proliferation of a rich variety of ikat cloths.

Certain motifs or cloth types may also have been related to particular high-ranking matriclans. The horse motif may be an example. I have unconfirmed information that women of the noble Nggondé matriclan, whose totem is the horse, used to wear *lawo wenda jara*. However, when these women were also members by marriage of the Sa'o Ria patrilineage, it was (and still is) taboo for them to wear this sarong. My informants could not tell me why. The reason may be that these women, being members of the two founding patrilineages of the village, were obliged to wear only original Nggela sarong designs. Eventually, the noble weavers of Sa'o Ria created a horse sarong of their own, the *lawo jara élo*. A similar situation is said to have existed with the highly stylized zoomorphic motif "falcon wing" (*siku mbira*), a variant of the rhombic *redu* motif. I was told that this sarong was once worn by women belonging to the Mbira Méra (red falcon) clan, which had that bird as its totem.

The importance of rank and prestige can be reconstructed more directly by looking at ritual cloths. In life cycle rituals, particularly at marriage and death ceremonies, *lawo redu, luka sémba*, and *luka ria* are the most important cloths. To begin with, they are bestowed by the family of the bride on the parents of the groom. The *lawo redu* was also traditionally worn by the bride during the wedding ceremony.

In the past, prestige was most visible in the context of the twelve annual agricultural rituals (last repeated in 1987/88). Whereas life cycle rituals only pertain to the kin groups involved, agricultural rituals were significant for the *adat* community as a whole. Cloths with certain motifs were worn to enhance the prestige of the wearer (Ndate 1981:65). The

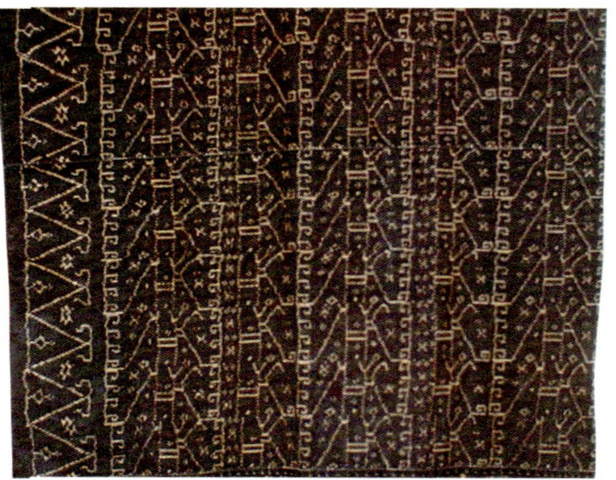 

adat leaders wore *luka sémba*, together with the handwoven headcloth *lésu*. At *joka ju*, the most important feast of the annual cycle, they wore the prestigious *luka ria* as well (FIGURE 10-14). A less prestigious shoulder cloth, the *luka tégé*, was worn by middle-aged men, while the *luka bara lombo* belonged to men who were newly married. The latter two groups wore ordinary *luka mité* sarongs and batik headcloths.

The most sacred ritual cloths in Nggela, the beaded *lawo butu*, derive their meaning particularly from the *muré* rain dance ceremony, where they were traditionally worn by young unmarried women (FIGURE 10-15). *Lawo butu* were also worn by married women from two of the highest ranking matriclans during the ritual for the renewal of the roof of the most important *adat* houses (FIGURE 10-16).

Note that the normal rules of patterning (ikat for women and non-ikat for men) are reversed during the agricultural rituals. The men's ikat *luka sémba* and the women's non-ikat *lawo butu* possess sacred properties. They are associated with the categories of persons who were traditionally believed to be the best suited as intermediaries between the profane world of the village and the sacred world of the spirits and ancestors, namely, the highest ranking, eldest male *adat* leaders and the highest ranking, young unmarried women. The latter serve as symbols of purity and fertility. Thus the most important ritual cloths, with their reversed patterning, publicly communicate the importance of the cosmological order and simultaneously confirm the existing sociopolitical order.[10]

RELIGIOUS PROPERTIES OF CLOTHS: SACREDNESS AND PROTECTION

The use of cloths in agricultural rituals shows not only their importance with regard to rank, but their religious significance as well. This applies to ritual cloths in a narrow sense and also to traditional motifs in general. When asked about the symbolic meaning of the motifs, weavers generally answer that they originate from the ancestors. This applies particularly to all the more traditional motifs, including serpent-like geometric motifs, patola-influenced motifs, horses, ships, and the stylized versions of mountains and human figures. Generally, ikat decorations are seen to provide magic protection and to symbolize the balance of life and the cosmic order.

Weavers sometimes have visions of both old and new motifs in dreams, in which a snake may appear. Lio people, perceiving snakes as metamorphosed ancestors, generally attribute magical power to them and believe they can bring fortune or misfortune. Some geometric motifs, especially those of *lawo népa*, are identified by the weavers as snake-like.

According to Sikkanese priest Piet Petu (1969:66, 94-98, 112-113), the origin of ikat weaving was strongly connected with the snake cult and the sacred snake was the model of the first ikat patterns and colors (black and reddish brown).[11] Therefore the first cloths with snake-like motifs and colors (*lawo népa mité* and *luka sémba* according to Petu) were once *adat* cloths of high value. These cloths gave magical protection against danger. Those who produced or wore them were feared and respected like the sacred snake. Their production regenerated ties with the ancestors and upheld the traditional system of values. Clearly Petu's interpretation has many elements of truth, as the Lio still worship snakes today, but it may be viewed as partly mythological as well.

Ndate, whose classification of motifs is spiritual rather than formal, also mentions the sacred python as the most common and important zoomorphic motif, and maintains that ikat motifs contain values of magical power and purity (1981: 38-46). He points to the role of divine inspiration (*raju ngga'é*) in the tying of motifs, particularly anthropomorphic ones (including the octagons on *luka sémba*).[12] Typically, an old woman past the age of childbearing dreams of a snake, which appears as an intermediary and inspires the dreamer to tie the pattern. Because such motifs symbolize fertility, tying them is taboo for younger women. Other animal motifs with symbolic meaning may be tied, but their shape is never made distinct. They are hidden, as it were, by a supernatural dimension. The indistinct quality of the ikat technique is thus religiously explained and legitimated.

The same applies to floral motifs. The overall aesthetic impression they give, however, is more essential than the clarity of their shape. The eight-rayed floral patola motif is still the most sacred and the most strongly connected with a taboo, although not all younger women respect this to the same degree. Said to represent the inner man or woman, its central part is called the "heart" (*pusu até*).

Of the geometrical motifs, the rhomb (symbolizing combat against calamity and providing healing power) is the most important. It appears in transformed shapes on *lawo redu, lawo kapa,* and *lawo pundi.*

FIGURE 10-13.
Lawo pundi, a prestigious though rather new type of sarong, the main motif of which, the large rhomb, was once allegedly copied from a shoulder cloth from another village. Most *lawo pundi* show combinations of several motifs. The origin of this cloth is uncertain, but it is in the style of Nggela and was produced there or nearby. 164 x 67 cm. FMCH X81.1502, Gift of William Lloyd Davis and Mrs. W. Thomas Davis.

FIGURE 10-14.
Three *adat* leaders (*mosa laki*) wearing the prestigious men's sarong (*luka ria*), shoulder cloth (*luka sémba*) and head scarf (*lésu*) while dancing (*gawi*) during one of the main agricultural rituals, the four-day dance festival to banish the evil spirits (*joka ju*). The other men wear the small sarong (*luka mité* or *luka lo'o*). These ceremonies, regularly enacted until 1980, were reinstated in the ceremonial year 1988. Nggela.

CHANGE

The cloth system in Nggela first developed its richness under the influence of Dutch colonialism, after the founding of the community at the end of the seventeenth century. Noblewomen created new motifs, patterns, and cloths in part by emulating prestigious colonial status symbols. Although they tried to monopolize the new designs, gradually other women would succeed in copying them. This in turn spurred the development of new, more complicated patterns.

According to local *adat* experts, *lawo népa nua*, a horizontal-band sarong with only geometric motifs, was probably the first type of ikat sarong in Nggela. Sarongs with overall center panel motifs may have appeared later. Once *lawo népa nua* and *lawo redu* became accessible to all women, noblewomen presumably created *lawo mogha* with a pattern band (*foko*) that was taboo to all others.[13] (Today *lawo mogha* is no longer prestigious, however.) *Lawo luka sémba* and *lawo jara élo*, the cloths with the most complicated taboo designs, were probably created later.

As already indicated, the designs of *lawo redu, luka sémba,* and *lawo luka sémba* were strongly influenced by patola cloths, which were imported by the Dutch particularly in the seventeenth century and dispensed to reward support from the indigenous elite (Bühler 1959, Bühler et al. 1975:18, Fox 1980b:40-41). Patola may have reached Nggela via the base the Dutch East Indies Company maintained near Ende for the export of cinnamon (Suchtelen 1921:11). As elsewhere in Indonesia (Gittinger 1979:48), they become the highly valued property of the village nobility. During the nineteenth century, however, they disappeared from the southern Lio region, unlike East Flores, where they are still maintained as clan treasures (Maxwell 1981, Ruth Barnes 1991a). Today's weavers in Nggela have never seen patola cloths and know nothing about them. The horse motif may also have been borrowed early in the colonial period, perhaps from Dutch gold pieces, which were also imported as tokens for the cooperation of the local elite. These gold pieces were highly valued on Flores (Gittinger 1979:49).[14]

The nineteenth century was an unstable period in the Ende region, characterized by volcanic eruptions, inter-village warfare and the ravages of the slave trade (Suchtelen 1921:11-12). *Adat* communities like Nggela may have adopted a more inward orientation in this period. If so, noblewomen may have continued to develop their ikat art without further outside influence. Many of the most important cloths, particularly the prestigious ikat sarongs with horizontal bands and overall center-panel motifs may have been created during this period.

Dutch political control, established only at the beginning of the twentieth century, had a rather strong impact on Nggela culture and economy. The levying of taxes (Suchtelen 1921:13) produced a shift toward a monetary economy. Factory thread became available, but at first only the wealthiest, highest-ranking women had sufficient capital to purchase it. Low-ranking weavers of modest means, increasingly forced to produce surplus non-ikat cloths for trade to pay taxes, must have had little time to devote to ikat designing. Women, like men, mainly wore the white sarongs with black squares (*luka bara mité*) during this period. They also wore plain black sarongs made of factory cloth (*kai beku*). Most had only one ikat sarong, reserved for feasts. Insolvency among poor families seems often to have led to indebtedness or enslavement.

Nggela was placed under the authority of the Raja of Tana Kunu Lima (the Lio domain centered at Wolowaru) in 1914, but this seems to have had little influence on the village's autonomy. However, pacification may have increased the opportunities for trade in locally produced cloth. At that time Nggela was considered one of the more developed areas. With more than 1,300 inhabitants, it was one of the larger villages in the district of Ende (Suchtelen 1921:57, 476-477).

Weavers began to routinely use factory thread for the warp in the 1930s, whereas handspun thread was still produced for the weft. By the end of the colonial period they had already developed most sarong types with horizontal banding and overall center-panel motifs. Human motifs are also said to have been tied by the mothers of today's high-ranking senior weavers (i.e. during the 1930s), combined with horse-motif variants of *lawo wenda*. The increasing importance of Catholicism in Nggela led gradually to the erosion of the indigenous religious system. The rain ceremony lost its importance toward the end of the colonial period. With its demise, the beaded *lawo butu* have not been produced since the 1930s.

FIGURE 10-15.
Young woman in ritual attire for the rain dance. She wears a *lawo butu* with a *lawo kéli mara* underneath. A *luka sémba* is tied around the waist. Formerly the *lawo butu* was presumably worn without another *sarong* underneath. Nggela, 1988.

FIGURE 10-16.
Three women of two of the
most important matriclans
wear *lawo butu*, red blouses,
and old gold jewelry during
the ritual of the renewal of the
roof of an important *adat* house
(*até sa'o*). Nggela, 1988.

Indonesian independence in 1945 effectively subverted the traditional sociopolitical structure of the *adat* community. Feudalism and the rank system were officially abolished. The *adat* leaders lost their formal political functions in village affairs, and with them a part of their legitimacy in judicial and religious matters. Noblewomen lost their monopoly of certain types of cloths. In a sense, Nggela's cloth system became more egalitarian.

A few of the best known types of sarongs were created in the post-independence period. The sarong with the stylized mountain motif *kéli mara* was created in the 1960s by an elite Nggela woman who had lived in Ende for a time. This sarong has achieved rather high status nowadays and is worn in combination with the *lawo butu* when the rain dance is performed. At about the same time, the creation of the *lawo pundi*, allegedly inspired by a shoulder cloth from the village of Wolotopo, may have initiated the popularity of vertical-section designs. These two sarongs, plus the *lawo jara élo*, are examples of Nggela designs that have become famous and are now widely imitated. In the post-independence period, such prestigious new designs can no longer be monopolized through taboo restrictions.

The New Order (as the Suharto government is called) began in 1966 and has also had important economic consequences in Nggela. With factory thread widely available, the production of handspun thread has stopped altogether, and with it the making of the ritual sarong for men, *luka ria*. The use of synthetic dyes has been promoted by the regency government through subsidies aimed at increasing the productivity of weavers.[15] Weavers tie more layers of warp threads at once, producing more cloths in less time. Since the 1970s there has been an increasing need to adapt cloth production to the exigencies of the growing cash economy (to pay for education, supplementary food, etc.). Together with the expanding tourist industry in the Ende area in the 1980s, this has resulted in perhaps the most far-reaching changes in cloth production in Nggela's history.

Formerly ikat sarongs were rather rare, but now most women own at least two or three. Production has increased, but partly at the cost of quality. Weavers feel that the ikat work itself has improved, at least for the cloths they make for their own use, but that the quality of the colors has declined. The traditional process of learning weaving skills first and then ikat skills is now reversed. Men have become less involved in cloth production, in part because some of the tasks with which they assisted (including the digging of morinda root and the spinning of thread) have decreased in importance. Of all the steps in cloth making, only the actual weaving on the loom has remained essentially unchanged.

Beginning in the 1970s, and increasingly through the 1980s, skilled women know how to tie almost all of the existing designs, regardless of their descent, and can also create new motifs. These are mostly less stylized, figurative forms used primarily in the production of shoulder cloths for the tourist market. The *lawo gamba*, with motifs spread over the entire sarong, also belongs to this category.[16] Ikat artists still attempt to monopolize their creations as in former times, being generally unwilling to show them to other women for copying. Ikat designing is obviously still connected with prestige, but weavers have also become business rivals who try to defend their potential for sales.

In order to shorten the ikat work, there has been a tendency to create larger motifs. Some small motifs are considered out of fashion today, such as the *barai* motif (a smaller version of rhombic motifs seen on *lawo redu*) and the ship motif called *kapa lo'o* (smaller than *kapa ria*). The same applies to the very fine motif of the prestigious men's shoulder cloth, *luka tégé*, which is no longer produced. The motifs on the *luka sémba* have also become larger and the motifs of recent *luka gamba* are rather large and dispersed across the cloth.

Recently Nggela weavers have begun manufacturing cloth made to order with particular motifs or combinations of motifs. These are then sewn into jackets. By 1991 new cloth types with variations of the *sémba* motif had appeared. These include a new type of *lawo luka sémba* and also tablecloths called *blangkit*, constructed from two panels similar to *luka sémba* sewn together.

It is perhaps not surprising that most ritual cloths have fallen casualty to the economic, sociopolitical, and cultural changes that have taken place since the beginning of the twentieth century. The rank system and the traditional religious beliefs that defined their place in Nggela's cloth system have lost their importance. The production of ritual cloths also depended upon spinning, which weavers now consider old-fashioned as well as time-consuming. Most important in the minds of weavers, however, is that the production of ritual cloths no longer yields either prestige or cash. Existing beaded *lawo butu* and *luka ria* are still in use, but most other ritual cloths are no longer to be found. The *luka sémba* is an exception, because it developed as the most important export cloth during the 1970s and 1980s. In addition to ritual cloths, the *sulu* cloths for children also nearly vanished by the 1980s. Today the main arena for displaying cloth, and for achieving prestige via cloth production, is the system of gift giving at life cycle rituals. These have outstripped the agricultural rituals in importance. In this context, especially *luka ria, luka sémba,* and *lawo redu* are still important.

Perhaps an indicator of the decreasing value of cloths as ritual and sacred objects is that weavers can give only sparse information about the religious meaning of the motifs.[17] Nor have I been able to obtain empirical confirmation that belief in a divine being is still a part of the art of making ikat cloth, as stated by Ndate (1981:39). Certain elements of the snake cult and of ancestor worship are still alive, but have been superimposed with the Roman Catholic belief system. This can also be seen in the rather low evaluation of the *lawo népa mité,* which was once a prestigious sarong with its snake-like motifs.

Cloths that were once the mainstay of the traditional local trade in textiles, especially *lawo redu* and *luka mité,* have lost this function, although they remain important as gifts in life-cycle rituals. Under the influence of the growing tourist market, production of cloths for sale concentrate on *luka sémba, luka gamba,* and, since 1989, the men's scarf, *luka lété.* A further item important in the export trade is used ikat sarongs, which are processed in Bali into purses, belts, bags, jackets, and so forth.

CONCLUSIONS

The sociopolitical restructuring of the post-independence period, the erosion of the traditional belief system over the course of the twentieth century, and the economic influences of the New Order have effected many changes in cloth production. Traditionally production was oriented toward the needs of everyday dress, ceremonial wear, and regional trade. Today it is oriented toward prestige based on the system of life cycle rituals and toward profit from the tourist market. Weavers have responded to these changes with rational and innovative production strategies.

In the sense that the largest number of cloth types were used in the 1970s, Nggela's cloth system can be said to have reached its culmination at that time. Now, although cloths are still highly valued female goods, the richness of this female cultural system has diminished. The value of cloth has to a certain extent shifted from sacred to profane, from cloth as a sociopolitical and religious resource to cloth as an economic resource. The *luka sémba* exemplifies this best. As this cloth evolved to become the most important export commodity of Nggela during the 1970s and 1980s, its status and its sacredness decreased. However, that women continue to tie the motifs of this cloth with special care suggests that it has not entirely lost its traditional sociopolitical and religious significance.

The cloth system in Nggela has always expressed the labor, knowledge, and power of women. Due to technological innovations and the loosening of cultural restrictions, Nggela weavers seem to have achieved greater autonomy since independence, particularly since the 1970s. With the role of men in cloth production decreasing, women who are skillful and have access to sufficient capital can, if market conditions are favorable, become almost completely independent petty entrepreneurs. Furthermore, the capital they require is earned through their own efforts, primarily selling cloth. By producing more cloth for sale, women have achieved greater economic power.

Beyond controlling the process of cloth production, Nggela women have achieved a deciding say in the distribution of their products, both in trade and in ritual exchange. Since the advent of the tourist market, women sell more cloths directly without petty traders as intermediaries. Whereas male agricultural products are now largely restricted to subsistence, female-produced textiles have become the leading market products. The demands of the tourist market are rather fluctuating, however, and cloth sales have not grown proportionally to the increase of tourism in the region. Meanwhile, the amount of cloth bestowed in the prestige system of gift giving has strikingly increased since independence, due to sociopolitical factors connected with the former rank system on the one hand, and to the greater productivity of the weavers on the other hand.[18] This has given women additional social and political power.

FIGURE 10-17.
Waiting for tourists to buy cloths. Nggela, 1988.

In the past, noblewomen created an outstanding part of Nggela culture and achieved prestige through the female cultural system of cloth wealth, while high-ranking males achieved prestige through the system of agricultural rituals. Both were tied to the system of rank and both expressed the indigenous religious beliefs. The existence of such parallel prestige systems for women and men is common in many parts of the archipelago (e.g. Vogelsanger 1980). The two systems reinforced each other in certain ways. Overall, the cloth system was perhaps secondary in importance to the agricultural ritual cycle, because the latter presented the main political arena for gaining prestige and power in the village community. However, men needed women to produce the prized cloths they displayed as markers of authority, and women gained prestige on the one hand through the cloths their husbands wore, but on the other hand through their own cloths and their management.

Since the disappearance of the agricultural system, prestige is derived both through the male/female system of ritual exchange and through the female cloth system, which again are closely interconnected. Furthermore, the production of cloth is economically indispensable in today's cash economy. Significantly, this cultural heritage is now common property. Nggela women, no matter what their social standing, have the potential of earning cash income, prestige, and power through cloth production.

Will the increase in power and autonomy of women in Nggela since Indonesian independence (and particularly since the 1970s) be only temporary? Their position may be threatened due to increasing dependence on the tourist market, with its unsteady demands (FIGURE 10-17). Perhaps only by continuing to produce for a diversity of purposes — for their own use, for gift giving, and for sale — can they maintain their strong position and at the same time guarantee the further development of the cloth system and the high quality of Nggela cloth. ❖   NOTES, page 274.

11

Vouchsafing Fecundity in Eastern Flores

Textiles and Exchange in the Rites of Life

P ENELOPE G RAHAM

"LARANTUKA IS THE END OF THE WORLD...."

S O OBSERVED AMERICAN ANTHROPOLOGIST RAYMOND KENNEDY (1955:37) in his fieldnotes during a brief period of research in Flores from late 1949 to early 1950. Indeed this port town, together with its environs populated by speakers of the Lamaholot (or Solorese) language, marks the eastern extremity of the elongated island of Flores. Yet, Kennedy's impression notwithstanding, Larantuka's very proximity to sea routes frequented over centuries by both Asian and European merchants provided access to trade goods for the Lamaholot communities in its hinterland. A nineteenth-century Dutch account describes inter-island trade in this area as follows:

> In the months of December, January, and February the Makassarese come bringing spices, arak, knives, tusks, cloth, etc., which they sell to local people on credit. In June, July, and August they return from Timor and other islands and receive in exchange wax, coconut oil, turtle, whale oil, sharkfins, birds' nests, etc.; while the Butonese in exchange for their cloth receive cotton, maize, or rice. The tobacco from Geliting on the north coast is mostly taken to Kupang, Alor, and Atapupu; last year the export to these places alone was around 450 pikols; how much was exported to Makassar I do not know. The trade consists, therefore, for the most part of barter exchange. The Solorese themselves also take their oil and cloth to Kupang, Alor, or Atapupu.

> (Kluppel 1873:387-388)

Current social and ritual practice in Lamaholot communities often engages textiles from such early trade, sometimes alongside more recently introduced items. Thus, in upland villages old Butonese textiles may still be seen, worn as hipcloths forming part of

FIGURE 11-1 (OPPOSITE). A male elder displays a woman's red tubular cloth of the top grade, called *kewaték mé'an*. Here the folded cloth decorates the stone backrest of his clan seat on the low wall of the village ceremonial plaza, during a festival for the adjacent temple of the ancestral religion (*koko*). Léwotala, 1987.

229

FIGURE 11-2.
For a harvest celebration, a woman wears an indigo trade textile from the island of Buton as a hipwrap over her locally made, top-grade red tubular cloth. Léwotala, 1988.

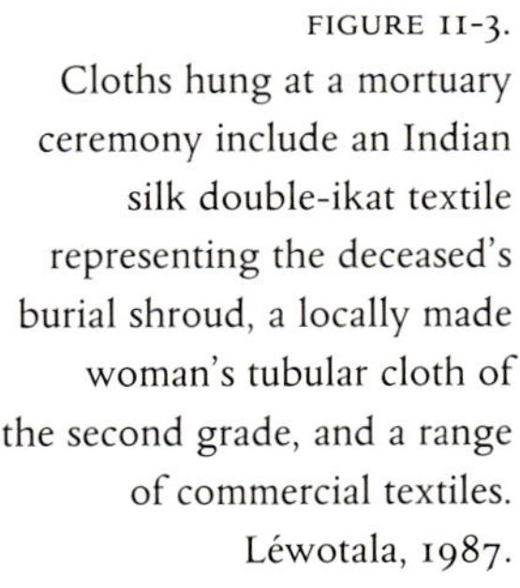

FIGURE 11-3.
Cloths hung at a mortuary ceremony include an Indian silk double-ikat textile representing the deceased's burial shroud, a locally made woman's tubular cloth of the second grade, and a range of commercial textiles. Léwotala, 1987.

FIGURE 11-4.
Dressed in red tubular cloths, two female elders sit ready to offer betel nut and palm wine to guests outside Lamahéwén's clan house. The women are acting as hosts during a ritual to terminate a period of *post partum* taboos for a young mother and her firstborn child. Lamatou, 1986.

a woman's ritual attire (FIGURE 11-2). At the main mortuary ceremony an Indian silk patola cloth is displayed as a represention of the ideal shroud. Beside it hang a locally made cloth and various commercial textiles of the kind generally used nowadays to wrap the corpse (FIGURE 11-3).

In the changing circumstances of village life, some locally made textiles regarded as traditional ritual apparel are now deemed appropriate not only to ancestral rites but also to novel situations consequent on the introduction of formal schooling and Catholic religiosity. So, for example, the high-grade cloths worn by female elders acting as hosts for clan rites (FIGURE 11-4) are also regarded as proper formal attire for women sponsoring children about to receive the sacrament of First Communion. Drawing on notions of Indonesian cultural identity, promulgated from the political center, in this latter context the cloth is worn as a tubular skirt topped with a Javanese-style bodice (FIGURE 11-5). Similar attire may be chosen by a young bride having a church wedding, although the more delicate negotiations necessary for the marriage of a man and woman from different villages might entail taking on all the sartorial trappings understood to be associated with nuptials in the Western world.

Despite the wide range of textile products available to villagers in eastern Flores, specific configurations of imported and indigenous items have precise symbolic connotations within Lamaholot cultural constructions of fertility. Here I examine one such instance through a consideration of exchanges marking significant transitions in the life-cycle of human beings within the domain (or traditional district) termed Léwoléma, literally "five villages." Since the central village of Léwoléma has developed into two virtually self-sufficient settlements, this domain actually subsumes six communities known as Léwotala, Rian Kotek, Lamatou, Kawaliwu, Léworahan, and Bélogili (see MAP, CHAPTER 8).

FIGURE 11-5.
For ritual occasions of relatively recent advent (e.g. sponsoring a child for First Communion in the Catholic Church), many women choose to pair an Indonesian-style bodice with a top-grade local textile worn as a skirt. Léwotala, 1986.

FIGURE 11-6.
The adjacent settlements of Léwotala and Rian Kotek nestle at the base of hillsides that are burnt off to form swidden fields. In the distance to the southeast lies the neighboring domain of Baipito with its imposing volcano, Mount Mandiri. Léwotala, 1986.

LOCAL IDEOLOGY

My research was concentrated for the most part in two communities, Léwotala and Rian Kotek (FIGURE 11-6). There, as elsewhere in the Lamaholot region, the communal temple of the ancestral religion, and through it the ritual collectivity concerned, is oriented to a nearby mountain associated with the origin of life. For specific clans this mountain represents the place from whence their clan ancestor emerged; for other clans with different ancestral origins it still represents a link to the source of life in Divinity. In many rituals, the correct orientation of the participants vis-à-vis the mountain is vital, especially in sacrificial rites, transition rites, and the conferring of blessings understood to entail the saliva of ancestors and Divinity. The district of Léwoléma lies immediately to the northwest of Baipito, the neighboring domain made up of villages ranged around the slopes of the volcano, Mount Mandiri. In Baipito, this one imposing mountain is regarded as the origin place of the ancestor whose offspring founded most of the villages in the domain. In Léwoléma, by contrast, a series of smaller peaks are recognized as the origin places of ancestors of particular clans, although such clans often no longer have even ritual precedence in the village communities separately oriented to one or other of these mountains.

The mythology and ritual practice of villagers in Léwoléma suggest that the fecundity of women is crucial not only to the reproduction of human beings but also to the regeneration of cultivated crops. This linkage is made explicit during the planting ceremony held annually in the ritually most significant gardens of the village. On these occasions, the seed rice to be distributed in the ash-fed earth is first poured into a large plaited container, then covered with a woman's red cloth and an embroidered blouse (FIGURE 11-7). A woven belt completes the clothing of this cylindrical container of seed, now identified with the maiden of mythic accounts from whose dismembered body rice and other crops are said to originate. While women sowing the rice are free to wear lightweight work cloths from the trading communities of Solor and Adonara, fine locally made textiles form the ritual attire of those women designated to keep the rice-maiden company at the ritual center of the field. A vertical pole behind the container of seed rice and a horizontal beam on the ground in front of it are seen as backrest and footrest for the mythic maiden, who is described as weaving in the coming months while the seed germinates and the crops grow.

Read as a sociological statement, this image condenses the culturally conventional view of women's tasks and represents them as reproduction and weaving. Indeed, in more prosaic characterizations, women's work focuses on child rearing and household provisioning, including barter trade, together with the processing of home-grown cotton into woven textiles for clothing and exchange. In ritual speech, a young woman's ability to warp a loom and weave a cloth is counterpoised with a young man's productive gardening and tapping of lontar palms. In former times, these phrases designated adolescents' coming-of-age and articulated their acquiring the status of marriageable adults. This juxtaposition highlights important aspects of local cultural identity, but if it once encapsulated the full range of male and female tasks, it certainly does not encompass them today. The contemporary complex division of labor spans a range of activities, increasingly pursued by women as well as by men, from subsistence gardening and cash crop cultivation through to circular migration (providing laborers for plantations in the states of East Malaysia) and salaried positions in the service of the Catholic Church or the Indonesian government. The effects of these varied life styles, combined with a rigorous modernization drive conducted by officials of the local government in the 1970s, disrupted the transmission of textile skills, such that many women under forty years of age have not mastered the full set of cloth production techniques. Nevertheless, women's high quality textile work remains prestigious as a cultural ideal. Furthermore, some younger women rightly see the production of indigenous textiles using locally grown cotton and natural dyes as a future cottage industry, catering to an anticipated tourist market as well as the demands of village ritual and exchange practices.

FIGURE 11-7.
On the day of ceremonial first planting for the agricultural season, seed rice is set in a large plaited container at the ritual center of the field. Conceptualized as the mythic maiden from whose dismembered body rice and other cultivated crops originate, the container is clothed in a red tubular cloth and black embroidered blouse, both placed on top of it, and a supplementary warp belt tied around its middle. Léwotala, 1986.

TEXTILE TECHNIQUES

Cotton is picked during the early months of the dry season around May and June. The seeds, removed using a cotton gin, are saved for the replanting of annual cotton varieties in gardens and house-yards. The cotton bolls are dried in the sun, then fluffed with a bow (FIGURE 3-2) and carded prior to spinning. Virtually all village women know how to spin cotton and many do so regularly using a spindle. The spinning wheels available are said to be faster in producing thread, but they break down very readily. Indeed, I never saw a spinning wheel in good working order, although I came across a few in need of repair.

Most mature women can prepare indigo dye, which is generally done under the eaves at home or beside the household granary on an individual basis. Both the learning of ikat motifs and the exacting process of red dyeing are usually carried out under the direction of a woman highly skilled in these regards. In Léwotala and Rian Kotek, with a combined population in 1985 of 1,541 people of all ages, there were to my knowledge five active women's groups for collaborative work of this kind. Older women indicated that this represented about the same number as when they were growing up. If so, it appears that top quality ikat work and the careful mixing of red dye ingredients were always the prerogatives of just a few women renowned for their expertise, around whom others gathered for these purposes in each village. Nowadays at least, these groups are based on women's social relations rather than any particular ties of kinship or marriage. They are, however, exclusive in the sense that younger women learning the skills of master craftswomen in one group do not participate in the activities or know the motifs and dye practices of other groups.

233

Although, in my limited experience, there are some differences between groups, both their motifs and their methods are variations on design elements and dye techniques (see also CHAPTER 3).

In the Lamaholot language, bundles of thread decorated using the ikat tying method are termed *mowak*. For the women with whom I studied, a minimal skein of threads to carry a single ikat pattern is a grouping of four threads. Such a single ikat skein or *kenuma*, once it is placed in a cloth, gives the appearance of a row of identical dots or dashes reserved against the indigo or red color in which the skein was dyed. More significant broader bands of decoration in the finished cloth are built up from a series of *kenuma* placed side by side, such that their differing arrays of dots and dashes combine to generate larger motifs. Bands of ikat built up in this way are named after the number of *kenuma* they comprise, thus bands are referred to as "*mowak* twos" (*mowak rua*) or "*mowak* threes" (*mowak telo*) and so on. The more prominent bands of ikat decoration are the wider "fives" (*léman*) and "sevens" (*piton*) respectively, while the major band for the top-grade women's cloth should consist of at least fifteen or seventeen *kenuma* and is referred to as the "big motif" (*kenirék bélén*).

The process of preparing red dye is a complex one. Used together with from ten to fifteen other plant materials, masticated candlenut provides the basis for a mordant. A smaller set of ingredients, prepared in particular ways over a whole day, mix to form the red dye bath. Those cited as crucial are the water infused with bark from the root of the tree *Morinda citrifolia* (known in Lamaholot as *keroré*) and at least three other substances which are added to it. In preparing these materials, the *keroré* root bark is washed and scraped clean, dried in the sun, repeatedly pulverized and soaked in the water in which it is then pressed by hand, before the resulting liquid is strained and set aside. To this is added a quantity of fine powder attained by pulverizing and sifting the dried leaves and bark of the plant *lou* (which must be requested of travelling merchants from Maumere and further west in central Flores, who obtain this material in the Lio area where the plant, there termed *lobha*, grows); a little *gamé* dissolved in water, taking advantage of this plant extract's availability in the commercial form (Indonesian *gambir*) in which it serves as an ingredient for the chewing of betel-nut; and finally a measure of water filtered through the ashes of specially burned ironwood bark (*kebahi*).

When these ingredients are mixed to obtain a liquid of the proper color, skeins of thread are immersed in it over two nights and the intervening day before being hung out to dry in the sun. This dyeing process should be repeated an uneven number of times (for example 9, 11, 13) during the dry season over each of three to five years for the skeins to acquire the desired depth of color. After the dry season, skeins in varying shades of red are stored away until the next year, when textile work of this kind is once more concentrated into the lull in agricultural labours which occurs between the harvest and the following planting of the fields.

Women who work together in procuring and preparing morinda and the other red-dye ingredients all know their own bundles of thread and store them individually at the end of the communal dye work. The *mowak* is stored with its ikat knots intact. For a top-grade women's textile, the many single skeins or *kenuma* (the minimal skein of four threads) necessary are batched together with, but separable from, the other *mowak* suitable for just one cloth. When a woman wants to weave such a cloth, she takes out a set of the morinda-dyed *mowak* intended for this purpose and, putting aside the *kenuma* skeins, ties a second set of knots (*lapit*) over some of the red sections in the broader ikat bands before immersing the *mowak* – usually the whole set – in an indigo dye-bath. This overdyeing of most (if not all) of the decorative scheme deepens the exposed parts of the relevant *mowak* to a more blackish red. The depth of color sought, the extent to which indigo overdyeing is applied to *mowak* of different dimensions, and the selection of areas of the major motif band to be tied off before overdyeing all vary regionally as well as with individual taste, skill, and patience. After this overdyeing, both sets of knots are untied and the warp for that particular red cloth is then ready to be placed on the weaver's loom.

Warping a loom and weaving a textile are skills ideally acquired in late adolescence, but nowadays, given their added responsibilities in the agricultural and commercial sectors of the economy, few women attempt to master these processes until after marriage and the early years of child rearing. Even then, the work is only attempted initially under the watchful eye of a master weaver, until sufficient competence allows the younger woman to work independently at her own home.

TYPES OF CLOTH

In Léwoléma, all the textiles that local women produce are worn on appropriate occasions, from the top-quality red cloth, marked as women's attire for ritual purposes, to the striped cloths that constitute everyday working garments. The more prestigious kinds of textiles also have symbolic significance. Thus, when a village girl leaves her family home to live with her husband, or when a pregnant woman dreams or fears a miscarriage, her natal clanspeople clothe her in a ritual context by placing a fine local textile over her right shoulder. This protective gesture expresses their commitment to the well-being and continuing vitality of both the woman and her offspring. In bridewealth exchanges, particular types of locally made cloth combine with imported Indian textiles to reciprocate elephant tusks. In so doing, they vouchsafe the fecundity of women bestowed by their natal line on men of another clan. Before saying more about the nature of these rites of life from conception through to mortuary exchanges, I set out the main types of cloth produced in Léwoléma. I then mention the imported textiles and tusks, also involved in affinal exchange, commenting briefly on the question of their origin.

The most prestigious locally made women's textiles are two-panel tubular cloths termed *kewaték*, a category which is subdivided into ranked grades as follows. The top grade is the "red *kewaték*" (*kewaték mé'an*, FIGURE 11-1). The ikat bands arrayed across this cloth are all morinda-dyed and at least in part overdyed with indigo to put elements of the decorative scheme into stronger relief. The distinguishing features of this textile are its all-over red color and its design layout, ideally featuring the full inventory of ikat bands (numerous *kenuma*, a pair of "twos," multiple "threes," and either a "five" or a "seven" if not both) as well as the major motif (*kenirék bélén*) in each of two mirror-image panels. The second grade women's textile is the *kewaték pasan* (FIGURE 11-8), a name local people said has no meaning. In my view, the phrase is probably indicative of this textile's complementary role (cf. Indonesian *pasang*) with respect to the top-grade *kewaték*. As such, the cloth is clearly inferior, having no major motif, but rather a series of indigo-dyed lesser ikat bands ("twos," "threes," and "fives") and numerous morinda-dyed single ikat skeins (*kenuma*) arrayed across the red

ground of the textile. For both these types of textile the plain warp threads and notably also the weft are morinda-dyed.

By contrast, the wefts and the warp ikat bands on the *keriot* types of cloths for women are all indigo-dyed, which marks them as less sumptuous items. The term *keriot* refers, I gather, to the design layout which these textiles share. *Keriot* cloths have a blue and red striped or plain indigo centerfield and an obligatory section of indigo-dyed ikat rows at each end of the two-panel tubular textile. If the dots in the central area form a pattern of diamonds or the like, this optional characteristic attracts the designation "illustrated" or "patterned" (*kenirék*, from *girék* to draw or write). The *keriot kelaor* or *keriot kenirék* (FIGURE 11-9A) has a plain red warp ground featuring indigo *kenuma* stripes in the center-field, while the identical design in a purely indigo version is termed "blue-black *keriot*" or "blue-black patterned" (*keriot mitén / kenirék mitén*, FIGURE 11-9B). This indigo version is a textile for women to wear as everyday apparel. The further designation *keriot kenuma* ("ikat skein" *keriot*), which can also be applied to these textiles, might stem from the indigo-dyed *kenuma* featured in the centerfield of such cloths, although no local person attested to this derivation.

Male ceremonial attire consists of two-panel men's tubular textiles with a design format akin to the women's *keriot*. These are of two kinds: one, featuring a red weft and warp centerfield enlivened by thin plain indigo stripes (*senai mé'an*, FIGURE 11-9C), is now very rare, although it was supposedly once quite common. The more prestigious men's cloth, according to most of my informants, and certainly the one favored by Léwotala elders of the present generation has a more heavily striped warp of red and blue, invigorated by indigo *kenuma* and supported by an indigo weft (*nowin*, FIGURE 11-9D). These kinds of textiles have identical sections of indigo-dyed ikat rows at each end of the completed cloths. By contrast, a man's indigo textile for daily wear does not feature any ikat decoration, just a single white warp thread appearing at intervals through the field and usually a yellow warp thread before each selvedge end of the finished textile (*senai mitén*, FIGURE 11-10). A woven belt (*mét*, FIGURE 11-11), decorated using the supplementary-warp technique, although categorically a man's textile, may occasionally be worn by a woman. Nowadays, the small loom used in weaving such a belt is sometimes braced at its far end by a piece of household furniture, such as a table (FIGURE 3-21).

Textiles of local materials made to any of these specifications all take a great deal of time to produce and the higher the quality of the finished item, the more time and skill has gone into it. Such a cloth, if worn as apparel, should not, I was told, be treated

carelessly or roughly. Village women nowadays also make a range of work cloths considered more suitable for rugged wear and tear. These have no ikat decoration and require considerably less dye preparation to achieve the various stripe effects involved. Chemical dyes have a place in their production (see Graham 1991:161).

TRADE TEXTILES AND ELEPHANT TUSKS

Through trade, these Léwoléma communities acquired not only the Gujerati silk double ikat patola (*ketipa* in the Lamaholot language), but also Indian mordant-painted cotton cloths, which in Léwotala are known as *réda* (FIGURE 11-12). In exchanges of the life-cycle, these imported items are combined with high-grade local textiles to reciprocate prestations of elephant tusks. The origin of the tusks and the dating of their initial entry into the Lamaholot region are issues to some extent unresolved. Like the Indian textiles, they may well have been introduced to the area through the Asian trading network, prior to European contact. On the other hand, one Florenese oral tradition describes them as an import from Malacca, which perhaps supports the view that they were introduced into Flores by the Portuguese (Hens 1916, 2:59). In a recent article, Barnes and Barnes make the following salient points:

FIGURE 11-9, A-D.

A. Detail of a woman's third-grade cloth, called *keriot kelaor* or *keriot kenirék*, showing the decorated edge of one panel. Rian Kotek, 1987.

B. Detail of a woman's blue-black cloth, *keriot mitén* or *kenirék mitén*. Rian Kotek, 1987.

C. Detail of a man's cloth for ceremonial or recreational wear, *senai mé'an*. 71 x 112 cm. Collection of Penelope Graham.

D. Detail of a man's cloth for ceremonial wear, *nowin*. Rian Kotek, 1987.

FIGURE 11-10.
A woman clad in a cloth from the Sikka area in east central Flores shows a man's indigo cloth, *senai mitén,* fresh from the loom with its warp still uncut. Léwotala, 1986.

Ivory and silk cloths were mentioned as trade items in the Moluccas by Tomé Pires in his *Suma Oriental* of 1512 to 1515 (Pires 1944:198). Lamaholot interest in patola and ivory was mentioned as early as 1624 (Basilio de Sá 1956:480) (for a summary see Barnes, Ruth 1989:126-29). They continue to be mentioned from time to time in historical documents thereafter. Of interest is Rademacher's report (1786:181) that at the end of the eighteenth century Makassar ships included elephant tusks in the goods they traded on Flores for, among other things, slaves, oil and rope. Hogendorp (1780:427) describes great trading in the same century on Solor of iron, elephant tusks, silk patola and other cloths which the islanders obtained for slaves, wax, ambergris, birds' nests, fish (i.e. whale) oil, and other products. Beckering (1911:178) supposed that the elephant tusks brought into the islands in former centuries derived, like the patola, from India. According to Cornelis Speelman's 1670 report on Makassar trade, the Makassarese acquired the elephant tusks they brought in to Flores and Timor from Siam and Cambodia (Noorduyn 1983:119).

(Barnes & Barnes 1989:409-410)

Tusks appear in the shipping lists of the Dutch at Batavia (Jakarta) from 1665 onwards (for earlier years there is no information) and were transported from there to the eastern islands (Dietrich 1984:323). Van Lynden reports that a tusk of thirty to forty pounds could be acquired for "three good slaves" (1851:323). Both the Portuguese and the Dutch sought slaves as a profitable item of trade from the Flores/Timor area (Biermann 1924:14-15; Boxer 1947:11). In Léwoléma, tusks and textiles, although readily convertible to other kinds of capital, retain importance as clan heirlooms and items of affinal exchange (Graham 1991). In this respect, they form a link between the one-time practice of taking slaves for the purpose of participation in external trade and the internal circulation of prestige goods exchanged for the life of human beings in a variety of ways. As Barnes and Barnes point out,

> Bridewealth objects are generally not items of utility, but stores of wealth and prestige. The silk cloths and the tusks derive from outside, in fact international, trade. Their acquisition originally took place in the same context as barter for utility goods. In this way they link the internal values of the community, in particular marriage alliance and its exchanges, with this foreign trade.
>
> (Barnes & Barnes 1989:10)

RITES OF CONCEPTION AND MATURATION

In Léwoléma, a ritual may be held with the intention of clearing the way for a couple to conceive a child. The aim is to make amends for any disrespect the man or woman has previously shown to Divinity and/or to those regarded as intermediate sources of life.

FIGURE 11-11.
A man's woven belt (*mét*) showing supplementary-warp decoration. 16.5 x 145 cm. Collection of Penelope Graham.

FIGURE 11-12.
One end of an Indian trade textile, approximately three arm spans long overall. These mordant-painted cotton cloths, known in Lamaholot as *réda*, are now rare but were once used for ceremonial attire and are still reckoned in calculations of bridewealth and its reciprocation. Léwotala, 1988.

Whichever party is deemed the focus of the conciliatory ritual must seek the intercession of a representative of some clan they regard as a progenitor (*belaké*), that is, a clan which stands in a "life-giving" relationship to an individual or another clan having conferred upon them life in or through the person of a linking woman. For this ritual role, the couple usually call on the brother of the woman, if the problem is regarded as on her side, or the mother's brother of the man, if the fault is identified as coming from his side.

At the request of the couple, this representative of a progenitor line goes some way up the mountain to which the village community is oriented. He carries with him and brings back again a whole betel catkin and an unopened areca nut. Returning to his clan house, he presents them to the woman who is seeking a child. He also gives the couple his blessing by anointing both the woman and her husband with his own saliva, imbued with masticated candlenut. This intervention, in which both the progenitor and the mountain are intermediaries to Divinity, is expected to wipe away any past error impeding the couple's fertility and, in so doing, to confer upon them the fruitfulness they seek. In return for the saliva blessing, the couple give the progenitor, who performed the rite, a pair of silver earrings (*belaon*).

If this ritual is not efficacious, then the couple may repeat it on any number of occasions. Each time they do so, they will ask a representative of a different progenitor clan (progenitor to the woman or the man and/or their respective clans) to intercede by going to the mountain on their behalf. If and when a pregnancy does occur, the progenitor who last performed the ritual and gave the couple his blessing is accorded credit for facilitating this flow of life towards them. To repay his efficacy, they should present him with an elephant tusk. A tusk of up to half an arm span in length is considered appropriate. If a longer one is provided, then the progenitor must give the couple a high-grade woman's textile in return. Should the couple be unable to provide a tusk at this time, the obligation may be deferred for an extended period, so long as they inform the progenitor of the child's birth before performing the rites associated with it some days later.

A canonical four days after a woman's giving birth, rites of bathing and anointing mark the newborn baby as a separate person and allocate it a place in the clan structure of the Lamaholot world. The clan that hosts the rites, usually that of the infant's father, thus constitutes itself the baby's genitor, but it must also pay due respect to the progenitor lines involved. Without the fecundity of other clans' women a generation ago in bringing forth the present infant's parents, there would not be any newborn for the host clan to incorporate today. Thus, the clans of the infant's mother's mother and father's mother are regarded as progenitor lines of the baby's mother and father respectively. Each is acknowledged with a pair of metal earrings (*belaon*), given to their representatives present at the birth rites. Should either of these progenitor lines wish to do so, they may exercise their prerogative to receive, at the bathing rite, an elephant tusk rather than merely the subsidiary gift of earrings. If so, they are required to reciprocate with a high-grade local textile. Indeed, by letting it be known in advance that they plan to "dress the child," which entails placing such a cloth on its head and shoulders during the birth rite, a progenitor is in fact giving notice that the host clan must have an elephant tusk ready for the exchange.

Information gathered in Léwotala by an Indonesian research team indicates that there used to be stipulations about who should cut a young child's hair. According to these researchers (Departemen Pendidikan dan Kebudayaan 1984:179-183), the hair of children under the age of five was not to be cut by the child's own mother or father. Rather it was tended by the child's mother's brother, who would come to his sister's child's residence for this purpose on the invitation of the child's parents. The mother's brother then used his lontar-slicing knife as a razor to shave the head of the boy or girl child, leaving only a shock of hair at the sister's child's crown. This was left to protect the fontanelle. The mother's brother's wife would collect the hair trimmings, take them away and deposit them between a leaf and the trunk of a banana plant. Disposal of the trimmings in this way was said to keep the head of the sister's child "cool" like the trunk of the banana palm, so the child's hair would grow thick and healthy. Following the haircut, the mother's brother would symbolically clothe the sister's child by presenting a woven textile. The authors conclude (Departemen Pendidikan dan Kebudayaan 1984:189) that this haircutting marks the transition from infant to childhood and that the mother's brother shares in moral responsibility for the child. In my view, the mother's brother's prerogative to cut the child's hair must be interpreted as indicating more than passive moral responsibility, in as much as the mother's brother effects the transition and thereby guarantees the integrity of the child undergoing it.

MARITAL EXCHANGE

In principle, bridewealth in Léwotala consists of five elephant tusks, collectively termed *nolé*, for which the reciprocal prestation, known as *ohé*, comprises textiles of four different kinds. This exchange transfers rights in a woman which are specifically concerned with her fecundity. Local proverbs attest to the fact that bridewealth does not have to do with acquiring a woman's body or her labor in any general sense. Rather, it is about gaining the means to procreate.

The five bridewealth tusks are individually known by terms that indicate their place in the series, often with reference to the reciprocal prestation required for each of them. The first and largest tusk is specifically the tusk exchanged for the woman. It can be referred to as "the price of a woman" or, on analogy with other transactions to acquire rights over persons, as "the price of a slave." There is, thus, no *ohé* reciprocation in the form of a textile for this initial tusk. The second tusk in the series requires an Indian silk patola, locally termed *ketipa*, in exchange. This tusk may therefore be referred to as the *ketipa* tusk or simply as the tusk that "follows on" after the initial one. The third tusk obliges an Indian cotton trade textile (*réda*) in return and is, thus, known as the *réda* tusk. The fourth and fifth tusks are each reciprocated with locally woven textiles and embroidered cotton tops. Both of these tusks are referred to as cloth and blouse tusks. These five tusks are of decreasing size, from more than a full arm span (the distance measured between the central fingertips of the left and right hands of a person's outstretched arms) to just half this length (FIGURE 11-13).

Qualitative as well as quantitative measures affect the exchange values of tusks and textiles alike. Thus everyone agrees that, of locally woven textiles, the kind termed *kewaték mé'an* is the highest grade and the type known as *kewaték pasan* is the next level. On any given occasion, however, negotiators may reject as inadequate the specific *kewaték mé'an* offered and request different one(s) to reciprocate their particular tusk(s). Indeed, the views of elders I spoke with occasionally diverged in specifying the number of cloths they would require for a given prestation. Different elders stipulated variously one to three *kewaték mé'an* as necessary to reciprocate the fourth tusk of the bridewealth set, and one or two *kewaték pasan* in exchange for the fifth tusk in the series. Exchange values in practice, it seems, depend on the exact quality of the specific tusks and textiles offered, as well as on the skill of the negotiators and the precedents they are able to cite to make their case.

Each tusk in the bridewealth set is, however, ideally expected to fall within a certain size range when measured against the human body, typically that of the men conducting the negotiations. The first tusk should be in excess of a full arm span. Tusks slightly less may be accepted, so long as they reach at least to within the palm of the far hand. The second in the series should extend to the far wrist. The third tusk must be one of those which reaches to below the far elbow, preferably well into the forearm. The fourth should extend to the far elbow, but any tusk coming within the far upper arm is acceptable. The last of the five should fall within the far side of the torso or reach the mid-point of the chest at the very least. The five individual tusks in the series are, then, each expected to be of a stipulated size, although a tusk which approximates that length will generally be accepted as a substitute if need be.

Earrings (*belaon*) also form part of the bridewealth prestations, as one pair of earrings must accompany each of the five tusks. These earrings are described as the arms and legs of the tusk, constituting its stem and cord. A bridewealth tusk should have these features, both a stem from which it emerges and a cord by which it attaches, so that the two lines involved in the affinal exchange will be linked in perpetuity. The earrings, thus, symbolize a commitment to continue the affinal alliance of which this marriage is a part, so that the relationship does not terminate. The progenitors of the young couple, represented usually by the mother's brother's lines of the bride and the groom respectively, also receive a pair of earrings each. These prestations, which as I mentioned are repeated following the birth of a child to the couple, evoke not only the tusks of which earrings are the stem and cord, but also the crucial role of progenitor lines in vouchsafing the flow of life to any union.

The actual exchange of wealth items (tusks and textiles) in respect of a marriage is, however, quite unusual in Léwotala, unless one party comes from outside the domain. Affinally allied lines in the village or within the domain prefer to regard marriage payments as a structure of debts incurred, which may be defrayed through a cyclic set of nominal prestations. Otherwise, such obligations are allowed to bind affinal units to one another through the generations. In some instances, the debt from a particular union is not paid out until a new marriage, which may involve a child of the initial couple, generates another debt to sustain the affinal relationship between the lines concerned. In any case, wife-givers will not usually seek to collect any of the tusks due to them, unless they are being pressed to supply a tusk they owe to one of their own wife-giving lines. Bridewealth debts are indeed inherited by children and grandchildren and so on indefinitely. Even Church leaders, who are often very critical of local customs, extol the virtues of this debt structure, which they depict as an obligation to mutual assistance whenever necessary, between lines allied across the generations.

The most common form of marriage in Léwotala takes place in anticipation of its forming part of a closed cyclic set of unions, thus transacting bridewealth as a series of debts incurred and credits to offset them. If debts are to be minimized, a cyclic set of marriages arranged simultaneously both incurs and cancels out all marriage payments. This includes any preliminary items, as well as the mortuary tusks which would otherwise change hands, not only at the death of each of the women concerned, but also on the passing of her sons. Such a closed cycle of marriages is termed *kenéuk*, a noun derived from the verb *géuk*, which describes how the bridewealth goes around in a circle. But *kenéuk* marriages do not need to be arranged contemporaneously. As usual, the debts incurred in respect of one marriage may be inherited and eventually defrayed by other marriages, which close the cycle in subsequent generations.

Given this system of continuing debt as regards marriage payments, most people in Léwotala embark on married life without any wealth items changing hands. This is in expectation of their marriage eventually linking up with others to form a closed cycle (*kenéuk*). Meanwhile, clan leaders keep a mental record of all such unions and promote some likely marriages as chances to *géuk*. They do, however, also take full advantage of opportunities to acquire wealth items for their clan, as these arise. Thus, when negotiations over marriage payments occur, those involved must be alert and vigilant to their rights, obligations, and opportunities. A number of factors influence each party's willingness to compromise. First, wife-givers (*belaké*) generally request a tusk only when they need it for a specific purpose, usually to fulfil an obligation to wife-givers of their own who are pressing them for payment. For this reason, the *belaké* can not compromise beyond what they estimate their own *belaké* will accept. Second, the wife-takers (*opu*) offer tusks from among those available to them, usually freshly obtained from their own wife-takers. The *opu* will endeavor to convince the *belaké* that they have nothing better at their disposal, so take it or leave it. Third, the *belaké*'s desire to extract the maximum possible and the *opu*'s attempt to give the minimum acceptable are tempered by mutual concern for the enduring nature of the affinal alliance. Attitudes and strategies are, however, also influenced by recent encounters prior to this one, which may have entailed insults or generated scores to settle. Finally, the astuteness of the respective spokesmen has considerable impact on the nature of the bargain struck.

FIGURE 11-13. An elephant tusk presented to the bride's clan by the groom's line, on the eve of the marriage of a Léwotala woman to a man from a village beyond the domain. Léwotala, 1986.

Greed in demanding tusks is, however, frowned upon. In such cases, social retribution is likely to occur, as everyone owed tusks by the group who have just acquired many would soon start pressing their demands for payment on terms very favorable to themselves. One saying, which refers back to the brother-sister sibling relationship, depicts a wife-giver who extracts too much from his wife-taker, as a brother who impoverishes his sister's husband: "the brother may be laughing, but the sister is crying." Furthermore, excessive demands and tardiness in facilitating the flow of life to others are understood to provoke reciprocal misfortunes in the form of illness and infertility in one's own line.

MORTUARY PRESTATIONS

Reckoning affinal debts in terms of the number of tusks owed, groups of men usually estimate each woman bestowed as calling forth seven tusks. In so doing, they count not only the five tusks of the bridewealth set, but also two tusks constituting the return of the woman's "hair skewers" following her death. In Léwotala, such a mortuary tusk prestation is only made if the deceased person has led a "productive" life. In those circumstances, the relevant *belaké*, who inspects the corpse before giving permission for burial, has a right to elephant tusks represented by the one on which the head of the corpse rests while lying in state. When a canonical four days have elapsed since the death and the corpse has been properly interred, this progenitor provides a saliva blessing to mourners classified as "sister's children" at the deceased's household during the main mortuary ceremony. In return, he receives a pair of earrings. Furthermore, he may then leave the mortuary ceremony, taking with him the tusk prestation, which he will reciprocate with textiles in due course. Most people who complete a normal life span and die a "timely death" in Léwotala do indeed become the occasion for these affinal exchanges during their mortuary rites.

In determining whether a mortuary prestation of elephant tusks is required as regards the deceased, differential criteria apply to the productivity expected of men's and women's lives. These criteria relate to the kinds of fertility privileged in local conventional accounts of the work of men and women. In all cases, however, the prestation involves recognizing the "harvest" from a person's lifetime and apportioning a share to the progenitor line which made that life possible. In other words, this affinal aspect of death returns to the progenitor a part of the harvest, which the flow of life emanating from his line has generated out of the resources of its women's fecundity and their sons' labor. If, however, the specific affinal investment whose outcome is evinced in the life-work of the deceased has failed to bear fruit, then no dividend is payable in that instance.

The phrase "hair skewer," describing the mortuary prestation for a woman, implies that something from the woman herself is being returned to her natal house, where she most likely ceased to reside following her marriage. According to Léwotalan elders, a woman's procreative achievements are the most significant factor in determining whether a mortuary prestation must be made for her. Furthermore, for women, reproductive success entails not just giving birth to children, but also rearing them. In addition to spinsters and married women who remain childless, women who in Léwotala would not occasion mortuary prestations on their death include those whose offspring all died in childhood. Indeed, a married woman's brother can only claim the tusk pillow from her deathbed, if at least one of his sister's children attains maturity.

In contrast to this emphasis on procreative achievements for women, the criteria applying to men explicitly privilege productive over reproductive success. Thus, deceased young men do not necessarily occasion a tusk prestation as part of their mortuary rites, even if they have fathered offspring. The crucial factor as regards men is a record of achievement in agricultural production. So, for instance, a young married man, father of one or two toddlers, with just a few harvests to his credit would not yet have achieved a productive return sufficient to necessitate a mortuary prestation consequent on his death. However, even a bachelor with no children, if he dies an old man after a lifetime's agricultural work will meet the requirements obliging his clan to provide a tusk headrest for his corpse. This same tusk pillow will also serve the corpses of his male siblings until, following the death of the last of them, the tusk prestation is collected by their mother's brother or another representative of that progenitor line.

The mortuary prestation for a woman is two elephant tusks, each no more than half an arm span in length. The reciprocal cloth is a locally made textile of first or second grade (*kewaték mé'an* or *kewaték pasan*). For a set of male siblings, the mortuary prestation consists of one to three tusks, depending on their size. The elders who suggested sample prestations to me would expect reciprocal textiles according to the nature of the tusks offered: for a single large tusk they might hope for an Indian patola cloth, as well as a *nowin* and a *mét*; whereas for other tusk combinations, the more usual mortuary reciprocation of a *kewaték mé'an*, together with a *nowin* and a *mét*, would suffice. As these hypothetical examples of appropriate prestations indicate, there is considerable flexibility in practice and negotiations are the significant factor in determining acceptable tusks and textiles for particular mortuary exchanges. Nevertheless, the return prestation for mortuary tusks given on behalf of male dead stands out among instances of textile reciprocations for its inclusion of men's cloths — *nowin* and *mét* — among those offered to the clan of the deceased sister's sons. In this way, the male subject and his garden labor, which occasions the mortuary exchange, is echoed not only in the "male" tusks that substitute for a share of the deceased's produce, but also in the men's cloths which in this instance form a subset of the categorically "female" counter-prestation of textiles.

Finally, in the Lamaholot oral poetic tradition, it is significant that the same phrase occurs in reference to the mortuary prestations for both men and women: *sogo beliko' lulun ohan*, "dismantle the threshing frame, roll up the mat." As an agricultural analogy, this expression relates the end of the productive life of a man or a woman to finishing the reaping and threshing stage of the seasonal cycle in the fields. The concluding phrase also evokes the mat on which the deceased is laid out in the house. This mat must be cleaned, rolled up and put away as part of the sequence of mortuary rites.

The elders who explained these expressions to me, however, stressed the crucial relevance of this phrase to the progenitor line receiving the mortuary prestations. These words serve as a reminder that having thus attained a share of the harvest, accrued by the recently deceased sister or her sons during their lifetime, the progenitor must now realize that the threshing is finished and the mat is put away. There should be no expectation on the part of the progenitor of receiving any further prestations in relation to the death(s). Or, as one of my informants paraphrased the message more dramatically: "Do not even think about any more tusks on that account; do not calculate further for it is finished there!" This mortuary prestation is, then, a form of closure, returning to the "life-giver" what is rightfully theirs and terminating the obligations incurred by the wife-taker in respect of a particular woman: her marriage, her fecundity, and her sons' productive labor.

VOUCHSAFING FECUNDITY

In conclusion, I suggest that in Léwoléma the range of textiles and tusks available, together with the diversity of institutional forms and practices constituting life-cycle exchange, highlight the creativity with which men and women historically enacted their concern for fertility and prosperity. In rituals of the life-cycle, progenitor lines in the person of maternal uncles vouchsafe the fecundity of their sisters and share in the "harvest" of sisters' sons. In so doing, they motivate a set of graded exchanges testifying to the orientation which in Léwoléma characterizes the greatest gift of all: the gift of life. ❖ NOTES, page 274.

12

Black and Red, White and Yellow

Socio-cosmic Ideas in Palu'é Textiles

M ICHAEL P. V ISCHER

IT IS RARE IN CENTRAL FLORES TO FIND A TEXTILE TRADITION still fully embedded in mythology and cosmology, and to find people who are able to elucidate the meanings of aspects of the cloths they produce. In certain communities on the island of Palu'é such knowledge is still to some degree alive, and therefore I take this opportunity to present some of the ideas connected with Palu'é textiles and with their use in ritual and ceremonial exchange. In doing so, I draw on various myths and cosmological notions with the intention of revealing the relationship between ideas connected with textiles and the remarkably coherent system of Palu'é socio-cosmic thought.

Palu'é or Nua Lu'a, as its twelve thousand inhabitants call it, is a small island consisting an active volcano located some fifteen kilometers off the north coast of central Flores. There is almost no accessible drinking water on Palu'é. For household purposes (including dyeing processes) water is traditionally gathered from banana plants, a method once also employed throughout the drier regions of Flores (FIGURE 12-2), and by the condensation of volcanic steam. For drinking fluid, the juice of the lontar palm (*Borassus flabellifer*) is tapped twice daily.[1]

The people of Palu'é are subsistence farmers; they produce tubers, mung beans, chick peas, and maize through shifting cultivation. During the dry season (March to December) most men leave the island with their boats to fish and trade on the Flores Sea, or to seek work on Flores (FIGURE 12-3). The women remain at home to care for children and elders and tend their crops and livestock – pigs, goats, and chickens. This is also the season when most textile production activities take place.

There are twelve traditional domains (*tana*) on Palu'é, each constituting a separate territorial, political, and ceremonial entity, and in each of which a different dialect of Sara Lu'a (the language of Palu'é) is spoken. Seven of the domains practice water buffalo sacrifice and are referred to as "domains of water buffalo blood." Five practice pig sacrifice and hence are known as "domains of pig blood." All domains are linked by a system of political and

FIGURE 12-1 (OPPOSITE).
A male priest-leader atop the ceremonial courtyard makes an offering of pig meat skewered on a bamboo pole to the Supreme Being. The officiant wears a tucked-up *naé romo* cloth and a Mbay-style supplementary-weft shoulder cloth; the red fabric of his headcloth and waistband is commercially produced. The offering is made following the center's reinforcement with new soil and the ceremonial setting of the "Black Patola Stone." Ko'a, 1987.

247

FIGURE 12-2.
A girl in a Sikka-type cloth extracts banana tree fluid (*waé muku*) through an incision at the base of the trunk; the fluid is channeled into a bamboo container. The yield varies with the seasons and stages of the moon; during the rains and when the moon is waxing a single trunk can yield up to eight liters a day. Kéli, 1979.

FIGURE 12-3 (OPPOSITE).
Two Palu'é men on a trading mission to Maumere, circa 1920s. The man on the right wears a *naé romo* loincloth in tucked-up fashion (*bosi naé*). His companion, left, is clad in a simple black cloth possibly of Ngadha origin. Note the bows and arrows for fishing, the sheathless short sword stuck into the loincloth, and the string of ancestral beads (*tupi*). Both men have the traditional hair style (*lolo éré cepu*). Koninklijk Instituut voor de Tropen, Amsterdam.

ceremonial alliance. Although we are here mainly concerned with the "domains of water buffalo blood," much of the information related to textiles also holds true for the "domains of pig blood."

A domain consists of groups (*kunu*) of individual houses that trace descent through men to a common set of ancestors and recognize a common place of origin. In each domain the houses of two such origin groups claim to have settled there first, and thus claim precedence over later groups. They hold most ceremonial offices and sponsor the large-scale ceremonial cycles; political and ritual leaders are recruited from their most senior houses. Two priest-leaders are the guardians of separate ceremonial centers where ritual contact is established with the ancestors believed to abide inside the volcano.

Through the sacrifice of water buffalo at the end of each ceremonial cycle (every five to ten years), the priest-leaders reach the Supreme Being to gain support for the welfare of the domain. Sacrificial animals are purchased from communities along the north coast of Flores with whom the Palu'é domains maintain relationships of ceremonial alliance. At the beginning and end of every cycle the domain acts as host to its allied domains, who come to dance and chant. Having successfully hosted a cycle, the domain can move into a position of precedence with respect to its allies. Until recently this was expressed in the ability of a domain to raise the support of its allies in warfare against non-allied neighboring domains.

Political alliances evolved long before 1907, when Palu'é was integrated into the Rajadom of Sikka. Until then, the island had never formed part of a larger realm. Rather, the island's domains each maintained separate truce relations with individual groups in south Sulawesi as well as along the north coast of Flores. This enabled them to trade safely throughout the Flores Sea during the months of seasonal migration.

248

FIGURE 12-4.
At a boat inauguration ceremony, two boys and two girls represent the mythical ancestral couples of the domain. The boys hold ceremonial swords (*topo*) and wear *naé romo* cloths tucked up beneath rare ancestral indigo dyed cotton skirts (*héma*), presumably from South Sulawesi. The waistbands (*cindé*) are of Javanese origin. The girls wear different types of traditional Palu'é cloths (LEFT: *wua wela*; RIGHT: *widi mata*). All four wear necklaces of highly valued ancestral beads (*tupi*) together with shirts (*lambu*) and headdresses (*lésu*) of commercial fabric. Keli, 1979.

According to mythical narratives, relations with alliance partners were based on instances of warfare in which Palu'é sorcerers assisted their partners on Flores in battles against western invaders (*Hata Lanu*). These events gave rise to specific ceremonial and economic privileges and modes of interaction. For example, a domain whose production of certain goods was prohibited by ancestral law would depend on trade with an alliance partner where such goods were produced; this secured a peaceful alliance. Some alliances were couched in botanical idioms: thus the Lio Lambo, inhabitants of a region on the north coast of Flores straddling the Ngada/Ende regency boundary, would rely on seasonal Palu'é migrants to plant their coconut trees; some Palu'é domains in turn would have their areca palms planted by men from Lio Lambo.

A similar pattern was established immediately to the east of this region. There most domains adhered to an ancestral prohibition on weaving and relied on outside groups such as those from Palu'é to supply them with textiles.[2] In turn they provided goods such as palm gin and rice, the production of which was prohibited by ancestral law on Palu'é.

Men, being oriented to the outside world, were always exposed to new and foreign ideas and goods, whereas Palu'é women, remaining at home, were only indirectly touched by new developments. In such a situation women took on the role of preservers of ancestral tradition. Although men can be observed as the main actors especially in ritual, it is chiefly women who hold the knowledge of the proper procedure and often of the appropriate ritual speech couplets. This passive and containing function also finds its expression in the quintessentially female realm of textile production. Here women preserve many of the ancestral ideas and values contained in them by faithfully reproducing new cloths from old cloths. It is therefore not astonishing that while women know all the iconographic details of textiles, it is only men who can elucidate the concepts they stand for.[3]

MYTHICAL ORIGINS AND ANCESTRAL HEIRLOOMS

The cosmos of Palu'é is layered. It consists of eight layers of firmament and eight terrestrial layers, whereby the earth's surface forms the eighth. The layers are conceived of as rectangular shapes suspended in the void. Supernatural beings as well as the Palu'é Supreme Being are located at various layers. Palu'é cosmology does not clearly inform us, however, about which beings are located at which layer.

According to the Palu'é origin myth, the first ancestors came from the outermost western rim of the earth. The point of ancestral origin is identified by the couplet "turmeric placenta" and "semen blood," referring to the constituent elements of human beings; then the names of two pairs of mythical ancestors are invoked (FIGURE 12-4). The myth lists chains of paired place names representing stages in their mythical voyage to the island. On their eastbound voyage the first ancestors are said to have brought with them "the stone and the soil," a metaphor that stands for the island and its domains. Once they had reached the present location of Palu'é, "the stone and the soil" are said to have grown to become the island. In ritual speech this primordial substance is also referred to as the "Black Patola Stone" (FIGURE 12-5).

Palu'é is thus believed to be in some sense alive and capable of growth. This notion is reflected in a body metaphor which is commonly applied to the island. The mountain top is classified as the head of the embodied island, and the sea as its feet. The settlements and specifically their ceremonial centers are the navel, which according to Palu'é body concepts represents the locus of growth. The ceremonial center, consisting of named monoliths atop a mound at the center of the main settlement, is the place where a connection can be ritually established with the various layers of the universe and the beings that reside there. As such it represents the very center of the Palu'é universe.

FIGURE 12-5.
In a ceremonial dance, the "Black Patola Stone," representing the primordial substance from which the island is believed to have grown, is attached to a bamboo pole and covered with an Indian trade cloth (or European imitation) to keep it "cool." In the background a Ko'a priest-leader acts as the main chanter, while Ko'a women dance with the pole and chant the refrain.

From their place of origin the first ancestors also brought sacral objects essential for the ritual communication with their Supreme Being (FIGURE 12-6). They brought the bronze gongs and the drums whose sound could reach to the highest layers of the firmament to alert the Supreme Being. They brought the porcelain bowls to hold seeds of charmed rice employed for offerings, the chants containing the corpus of Palu'é cultural knowledge, and the spear and the sacrificial sword to slay the water buffalo. They brought the ceremonial shield and the string of shells from the deep sea to remind them of their alliances and of their mythical voyage. Finally they brought beautiful red silken patola cloths with designs of stars and triangles (FIGURE 12-7). These hang as ceremonial banners during the large-scale ceremonies for the mythical ancestors. They are also used to cover and cool the mythical Black Patola Stone during the reenactment of the myth of origin, when the women of the domain dance with it as others chant place names marking the route of the ancestral voyage.

Just as the mythical stone and soil are represented in ritual by the Black Patola Stone, these objects, which were identified with the very origins of the place, came to epitomize the domain and its progenitors, and are believed to be to some degree alive and to possess inherent supernatural powers. Thus it is said that when in storage the cloths can fight each other, creating holes and tears which at a later moment may heal again and disappear. Due to this potency, individual threads are given on ceremonial occasions as very special prestations to houses of allied priest-leaders as an aid to communication with the Supreme Being.

It is not difficult to imagine the impact and importance of heirlooms such as those brought by the first ancestors. In a world that for a long time produced neither textiles nor metal objects nor porcelain, these objects were extremely rare and highy valued and could only be obtained by way of trade. An important and often told myth explaining the social and ritual order of the domain illustrates the high value accorded to textiles on Palu'é:

One night the first settlers saw gold blinking in the forest on the mountain-top. They rushed up the mountain to get the gold and gathered it in the folds of their bark cloths.

FIGURE 12-6.
At a ritual in the ceremonial courtyard, the son and daughter of the main Ko'a priest-leader wear ceremonial dress. Special objects deemed necessary for communication with the Supreme Being surround them: the ancestral skirt (*héma*) atop a monolith, the shield (*huta*) with a string of shells (*wuli*) leaning against the monolith, and the large drum (*maba ca*), at the right. The young man holds an offering of charmed rice (*piga holoné*) in a Chinese blue and white tradeware bowl. Ko'a, 1987.

But what they had thought was gold was actually fire and it burned their cloths and scalded their hands. In the morning they could see that newly arrived settlers had been clearing the forest. From afar they watched as the newcomers felled large trees with metal axes and cleared the land with fire. Until then, clearing had been done with stone axes and was very slow and strenuous.

Their children were attracted by the delicious smell of cooked food and approached. The new settlers asked them to share their meal and so they came to know cooked food for the first time. Until then food had been eaten raw and tubers were stuck under the armpits to warm them up before they could be eaten. The new settlers also offered them coconuts which they opened with a metal blade. Until then their fathers had always opened coconuts by splitting them with their elbows. And they saw the beautiful cloths the new settlers were wearing – colorful woven cotton with intricate designs. Until then they had only known coarse cloth made of tree bark.[4] The children returned home and told their parents about what they had seen. When the parents went to ask the new settlers to share the things their children had seen, they were refused. There followed a war between those who had brought fire and those who had settled on the island first.

After the war the new settlers moved into the old village where they were allowed to set up their own ceremonial center and conduct their own blood sacrifices. Although not entitled to their own ceremonial gongs and drums, they were put in charge of all the sacral objects of the domain and thus also became the guardians of its gongs and drums. In return, the first settlers received fire, metal tools, and the knowledge of weaving. This is how it came to be.

In this myth textiles are placed on a par with the great technologies of fire and metal. Apart from the occasional fashioning of arrow tips from scrap metal, however, the production and working of metal never took hold on Palu'é. Metal objects traditionally are purchased at allied markets along the north coast of Flores. Unlike metal, the production of textiles was fully integrated and eventually became associated with the island rather than with the outside world where it had originated.

MARRIAGE ALLIANCE
AND CEREMONIAL EXCHANGE

According to Palu'é historical narratives, subsequent settlers were integrated into the domain by way of marriage alliance.[5] In taking wives from the first settling group, all subsequent settlers became subordinate to the first settlers. These new alliances were marked by the exchange of goods between the wife-giving first settlers and the wife-taking subsequent settlers. In this exchange, wife-takers were expected to make prestations of goods they had brought from the outside world: golden ear pendants from the Lio, pigs from the Ngadha, and ancient ivory tusks acquired through trade. Wife-givers would reciprocate with goods associated with the domain and the island. Textiles,

FIGURE 12-7.
A Keli elder looks through a pile of Indian trade cloths and European imitations. Such cloths form part of the ancestral heirlooms of the domain and are believed to be imbued with supernatural powers. Keli, 1979.

FIGURE 12-8.
During the final stage of bridewealth installments, a female member of a wife-giving house reciprocates the prestation of a large pig from a wife-taking house. She gives a Sikka-type cloth and a commercially produced shirt, which are placed onto the pig to be taken home by a representative of the wife-taking house. Ko'a, 1993.

originally associated with the outside world, now featured as important objects associated with Palu'é, together with cultigens, ancestral glass beads, ivory armrings, and household goods.

To this day, marriage alliance is effected through bridewealth exchange – of goods from the wife-taking house which are associated with the outside world and according to Palu'é classificatory thought are conceptually male, and of counterprestations by the wife-giving house which are associated with the island and classified as conceptually female.

As a rule the goods given as bridewealth amount to a total of ten objects of each category, e.g. ten pigs, ten ivory tusks, ten sets of golden ear pendants; the amount of each installment is subject to extended negotiations. The size of counterprestations is always determined by the amount given by the wife-taking house. Ear pendants and ivory tusks are mostly reciprocated with ivory armrings and highly valued ancestral beads, whereas pigs and small amounts of cash are reciprocated with textiles and large baskets of harvest goods (FIGURE 12-8).[6] In everyday life, relations between two allied houses are continuously expressed by the ability of a house to ask for and to receive the category of goods it is entitled to, if the need for such goods arises. Small exchanges over time are not counted as part of bridewealth but are considered part of the proper way of daily interaction between affines. In this way there is a continuous flow of conceptually male goods in one direction and of conceptually female goods in the other, linking the houses and origin groups of the domain into a tight network of interdependence based on marriage alliance.[7]

Every ceremonial occasion is marked by exchange, be it large-scale domain ceremonies or smaller ceremonies restricted to the house or the origin group. Many rituals entail the sacrifice of a pig. On such occasions the house conducting the ritual will always present the head of the pig and a specific amount of cash to one of its wife-giving houses. That house is then obliged not only to accept the prestation but to reciprocate immediately with a cloth and a shoulder band, or these days more often with a commercially produced shirt. If the wife-giving house holds no textiles in stock, its members are forced to turn to one of their own wife-giving houses and pass on the head of the pig in order to receive the textiles needed. The same head may pass through a number of hands before it is finally reciprocated with textiles which then find their way back to the wife-taker who initiated the exchange.

If the search for textiles takes more than a day, then a sum of money is added to compensate for the "stench" (as it is put) of the decomposing pig's head.

In mortuary rituals, which are held on the actual day of death, the ancestors are perceived to participate directly in exchange. Here again, wife-givers bring conceptually female and wife-takers conceptually male goods which are exchanged for gifts of the opposite gender. The goods received from wife-givers by the house of the deceased typically consist of textiles. This type of mortuary prestation is termed "the wrapping" (*poko*), a reference to the custom of wrapping the corpse in multiple layers of textiles before burial; nowadays these textiles are also placed on top of the coffin (FIGURE 12-9). Wife-takers bring ivory tusks as well as golden ear pendants and usually also pigs, which are slaughtered and cooked to feed the funeral guests. The tusks and ear pendants are buried with the deceased: the tusks are placed alongside the corpse and beneath the neck as a head support; the ear pendants are put in the mouth.

According to Palu'é thought, these mortuary prestations accompany the deceased on his voyage to the place of origin of the mythical ancestors. After a voyage of three days he takes up residence in the ancestral abode inside the volcano, where the mortuary prestations are believed to ensure his welcome. It is understood that these objects in turn allow the ancestors to practice ceremonial exchange with the ancestors of wife-giving and wife-taking houses.[8] If the ancestor has been able to establish himself in the society of the dead by means of the goods given to him by the living at his burial, he is in the position in turn to assist the living members of his house and ensure their health and continuing success in all of their undertakings.

SOME CATEGORIES
OF SYMBOLIC CLASSIFICATION

Palu'é classificatory thought is structured by dual partition so that much of the world, and what is in it, can be classified as either male or female. This partition entails a notion of asymmetry in that the conceptually male is defined as superordinate to the conceptually female. Furthermore, classification is mostly relative rather than absolute, and depending on the context the same thing can be viewed as either male or female.[9]

In Palu'é thought a number of classificatory categories are linked to the basic male-female partition. The opposition of inside versus outside, for example, constitutes a set of categories with great relevance to our argument. The inside is associated with the conceptually female and the outside with the conceptually male. Thus the island is female, in opposition to the outside world, which is male. At another classificatory level the villages and the fields of a domain are viewed as being inside and conceptually female in opposition to the forest and the mountain, which

FIGURE 12-9.
A modern cement grave covered with a *naé romo* cloth. The cloth is a mortuary prestation by a wife-giver of the deceased, who is believed to take it with him on his journey to the ancestral abode inside the volcano. Keli, 1985.

are conceptually male. Finally the inside of the house is classified as female, as opposed to the village grounds, which are conceptually male.

Notions of "heat" and "coolness" pervade Palu'é classificatory thought. On Palu'é, men are believed to be conceptually hot, in a state of potential aggression and violence; whereas women, especially young women, are thought of as being conceptually cool, soothing, and placid. Thus men are said to be "burning hot as the sun" and girls "as cool as the light of moon reflected in their cheeks." In a similar way, the domain and specifically its cultivated parts are considered to be cool as opposed to the forest and the outside world which are classified as hot. Disharmony, illness, and danger are all associated with heat, whereas health, harmony, and peace are associated with coolness. Thus a great part of ritual activity on Palu'é is aimed at transforming noxious states of "heat" into a state of beneficial "coolness." The juice of the coconut, for example, is an important ritual cooling agent.[10] Palu'é women's cloths, because of their strong association with the conceptually female, are employed to similar ends in rituals of the domain as well as in the context of healing.

TAMA LU'A: THE CLOTHS OF PALU'É

In the first treatise ever written on the textiles of central Flores, the author only barely mentions the textiles of Palu'é and states that "the inhabitants of the Island of Palu'é only know how to produce very primitive ikat cloths" (Tietze 1941:2, my translation). The statement reflects a former attitude of the Sikkanese administration toward the remotest part of the regency. The implication is of general backwardness and lack of technological sophistication, and perhaps also that Palu'é ikat cloths when compared to the intricate designs and varied colors of neighboring Sikka might appear somewhat less attractive. Tietze was not aware that Palu'é women are extremely skillful in producing cloths in the styles of various Flores groups either for sale on Flores markets or as daily clothing for themselves. They have been doing so for a long time and the fact that some types of Flores cloths currently produced on Palu'é no longer exist in their region of origin proves this point.

Palu'é weavers have never changed the designs and colors of their own cloths, however, to suit the aesthetic sensitivities of a specific period. New cloths have always been carefully copied from old cloths and the knowledge of their manufacture has always been passed on from mother to daughter. Palu'é ikat cloths collected around the turn of the century and now held in European collections show a remarkable continuity with those produced at present (Fischer & Rassers 1924: nos. 1710/34, 1710/35). They are virtually identical in structure and motif. They are, however, up to a handspan wider than present-day Palu'é cloths.

Palu'é ikat textiles are generally called *tama Lu'a*, Lua cloths (after the indigenous name of the island) or *tama koa*, boiled cloths (in reference to the effervescent effect of lime used in indigo-dyeing). In the domain of Ko'a where most of this information has been gathered, a folk etymological connection is made between *koa*, the term for boiling, and Ko'a, the name of the domain; and it is maintained that the correct term for Palu'é cloths is really *tama Ko'a* in allusion to the name of this domain, which according to its own women produces the best-quality cloths of the island.

Most domains take pride in the quality of their cloths, and although the types of cloths and the motifs employed are largely the same in every domain, small differences in their execution can indicate the provenance of a specific cloth. For example, cloths from Keli can be identified by how much red dye is allowed to spill into the white of the motifs. In another domain the red dye is typically kept light and in yet another the central red bands (*hina ca*) are broad compared to those of cloths made elsewhere. These differences allow the wearer to be identified during ceremonial dances; and when the women of one domain link arms to perform circular dances and ceremonial chants, women attending from other domains can often be heard commenting critically on the particularities of the dancers' cloths (FIGURE 12-10). In doing so they emphasize a notion informed by local pride that the only proper way of execution is that of one's own domain, a notion extending to just about any realm of life.

FIGURE 12-10.
Ko'a women dance with interlinked arms atop the central ceremonial courtyard (*togo tupu*). Note the head-strap baskets (*poté lo'o*) decorated with beads, shells, tufts of fur, and strips of red cloth for the final stages of the ceremonial cycle leading up to the sacrifice of water buffalo. Ko'a, 1987.

FIGURE 12-11.
A man's cloth, *naé romo*, sewn
into the shape of a tube.
104 x 122 cm. Collection
of Mary Jane Leland.

TYPES OF CLOTHS

At present there is only one traditional type of cloth for men on Palu'é. Known as *naé romo*, loosely translated as "men's cloth" (FIGURE 12-11), it features a series of evenly spaced red bands set against a black background; simple geometric ikat patterns made up of tiny white dots run between the red bands. When taken off the loom the cloth is cut and sewn into the shape of a tube. It can be worn in three basic styles: tied around the waist and hanging loosely down to the ankles (*kubo naé*); tied around the waist but taken up along the sides and tucked into the back to hang in folds at front and back, leaving the sides bare, *bosi naé* (FIGURE 12-12); and finally, for agricultural work or for work out at sea, as a short loincloth, folded in two and tucked up high into the waist, *cepu éré rétané* (FIGURE 12-13). The *naé romo* is worn for work as well as on ceremonial occasions.

Weavers in the domain of Keli used to produce another type of men's cloth referred to as *naé huta*, designed specifically for work. This cloth, without ikat designs, features only red bands against a black background. Wider than the *naé romo*, it served as a more effective protection against the cold of the mountains. Its width is generally cited as the reason why it is no longer produced: a wide beam stretches the arms of the weaver to the utmost, causing significant discomfort.

Every domain has several types of women's cloths, sometimes given different names from one domain to another, even though they are to a large degree identical. Two basic types are produced in all domains: *widi mata*, "the '[cloth of the] eyes of the goat" (FIGURE 12-14) and *wua wela*, "the candlenut [– cloth]" (FIGURE 12-15). Nearly every domain also produces slight variations of the two basic types, which are often considered separate types and given different names. The cloths are worn on ceremonial occasions as well as for everyday life.

There are two ways of wearing women's cloths. Most commonly, the cloth is folded down and worn on the hips, a style called *kubo* (FIGURE 12-10). During pregnancy, and before and after bathing, it is tied around the breasts and reaches down to mid-ankle (*kubo éré rétané*).

TEXTILE PRODUCTION AND SOCIALIZATION

In everyday life, textile production is highly visible. During the dry season the rattling of the sounding boards of backstrap looms can be heard throughout the settlements and women can be seen engaged in various stages of textile production.[11] The prominence of textile production in the lives of Palu'é women is already highlighted in the very first ritual for a newborn child.

Three days after giving birth, a mother leaves the seclusion of her house and presents her child to the community for its naming ceremony. Objects specific to its gender are

FIGURE 12-12 (LEFT).
During a healing ceremony, an elder wears a *naé romo* man's cloth in the style known as *bosi naé*. He sprinkles charmed rice kernels (*sivé*) onto his ancestors' mortuary monoliths, where eggs have also been offered in hopes of ancestral mediation with the Supreme Being. The proximity of a mortuary monolith to the ceremonial center reflects the status of the origin group of the deceased. Keli, 1979.

FIGURE 12-13 (RIGHT).
A Kéli man wears a *naé romo* in the *cepu éré rétané* style, tucked up high for agricultural work. Kéli, 1979.

placed on a winnowing tray in front of the child. Although the ingredients may vary somewhat according to domain and origin-group affiliations, the tray for a male child typically contains a small knife, and, for a female child, a wad of cotton and a small bow-shaped instrument (*wu kapa*) used to remove seeds and impurities from cotton. Once the child has been given its name, it is instructed in its social role. A male child is told that he will be expected to wield his knife well to construct houses, fishtraps, and boats. The female child is told that she will be expected to work the fields, raise livestock, and produce Palu'é cloths. Then an infant of the opposite gender is brought in and their hands are linked, emphasizing the complementary nature of their gender-specific roles.

During the first few months of life an infant is kept tightly wrapped in Palu'é woman's cloth and for at least a year its mother carries it around inside the folds of the cloth she is wearing. Infants are believed to have "thin skin" which makes them vulnerable to negative outside influences such as witchcraft and harmful supernatural beings, and the woman's cloth acts as a protective device. As the child continues to grow its skin becomes "thicker" and it becomes less vulnerable and can be allowed to move around without cover or clothing. Only once a child has passed through puberty is its skin considered to have the "thickness" of adulthood. This is also the moment when the young person is felt to have reached sufficient maturity to participate as an officiant in ritual activities.

Until the onset of puberty children used to go naked. Then they would be given old rags or discarded cloths to cover their genitalia and only gradually would they begin wearing their own adult cloths. Nowadays this period is shortened to the age of six or seven, when children enter school and are obliged to wear school uniforms. Young men go on to wear commercially produced chequered sarongs and shirts, and young women usually wear the ikat cloths of the neighboring Lio or Sikkanese, and hand-stitched blouses of commercially produced cloth.

As the child learns to walk it begins to observe and imitate its parents as they perform their daily chores. A boy of three or four years can be seen carrying around a bush-knife larger than his own body and while his father fashions planks for a boat he practices chopping on a piece of wood. A girl of the same age may carry a small headstrap basket to collect firewood and leaves for the livestock, just like her mother. She may also begin to learn the rudiments of weaving on a small improvised backstrap loom (FIGURE 12-16) while her mother weaves a cloth next to her.

Most of the instruction in textile production is informal. Girls learn by observing their mothers and elder sisters and the women of their settlement. A young woman becomes proficient in weaving before she begins to learn to tie off motifs. Until the cloth is set up on the loom her seniors will advise and correct at all stages. Nowadays a young woman knows how to tie off the designs of several types of Flores cloths, often before she gets her first opportunity to try a traditional Palu'é cloth. Producing Flores cloths allows her not only to demonstrate her tying skills but also to gain a small income by selling such cloths through her brothers in Flores markets.

As a young woman enters her late teens she avoids the hottest sun, hoping to retain a light skin, which along with the ability to weave Flores cloths is considered attractive to potential suitors. This constitutes a shift in values influenced by the modernity of the rapidly changing Flores mainland. A male elder summed it up by remarking that in the olden days a suitor would first look to see if a young woman had black hands and black teeth. Black hands showed that she knew how to use vegetable dyes; black teeth indicted that she was used to chewing betel and therefore probably didn't consume much food and could tirelessly work her fields. Knowledge of textile production was a prerequisite for marriage and so was the ability to carry out strenuous agricultural work.

At present the art of using vegetable dyes is disappearing on Palu'é. Young women prefer to use chemical dyes not only because they involve a lot less time and effort but also because vegetable dyes, especially indigo, give off an odor considered unpleasant. Nowadays only very little cotton is grown on Palu'é. Women mostly purchase machine-spun thread on Flores and are no longer capable of spinning fine, even thread.

FIGURE 12-14 (OPPOSITE). Woman's cloth, *widi mata*, sewn into a tubular garment. 180 x 67 cm. Collection of Mary Jane Leland.

FIGURE 12-15 (LEFT). Woman's cloth, *wua wela*, as it comes from the loom, not yet cut and sewn into a tube. *Wua wela* cloths feature several fine strands of yellow-orange threads (FIGURE 12-18) not found in *widi mata* cloths. The motifs displayed in the ikat bands of the two types of cloths are nearly the same, although their succession within the "large mother" band may vary. Kéli, 1979.

FIGURE 12-16. A young girl wearing a Lio-type cloth practices weaving on an improvised loom made of twigs, bark, and elephant grass. Kéli, 1979.

Nonetheless, the production of traditional textiles is still alive on most of the island.[12] Every five to ten years, whenever a domain prepares to initiate a ceremonial cycle, its women begin to produce traditional cloths using mostly machine-spun thread and chemical dyes. Those who have never done so before now learn and participate, so that when the allied domains come to the center to chant and dance, the women of the hosting domain can rise together and proudly show off their cloths made in the style of the ancestors.

THE SIGNIFICANCE OF COLORS

The main colors represented on Palu'é cloths are red, black, and white. This color scheme is found on very old types of cloths throughout Southeast Asia and high symbolic significance is generally given to it (Maxwell 1990:58). The dominant background color is black, the series of bands are red, and the geometric ikat motifs are white, the natural color of cotton. On most women's cloths we find yet another color, several fine strands of thread which are dyed to a shade of yellow or orange. Red dye is obtained from the powdered root of the *Morinda citrifolia* tree[13] and black dye[14] from the leaves of the indigo shrub. The yellow-orange color on woman's cloths is produced by mixing powdered turmeric (*Curcuma domestica*) with betel pepper, areca nut, and lime.

In the poetic and metaphoric form of speech generally employed in ritual these colors are always invoked as two couplets. Black, *mité*, is paired with red, *réa*, while white, *pura*, is paired with yellow-orange, *réré*. Palu'é thought makes a number of associations with these colors. Black and red are colors first of all associated with the origins of the island and with the first ancestors (see above). In one category of rituals aimed at removing "heat" generated by discord, long exposure to the outside world, or construction activity, the noxious "heat" is gathered into an egg which is passed across the body. The egg is then disposed of in the direction of the setting sun, at the very moment it disappears behind the horizon. The sun is believed to be taking all the negative influences with it to the place of origin of the mythical ancestors. In allusion to the color of the setting sun, the ritual officiant as well as the person on whom the ritual is performed must wear at least one piece of red clothing (FIGURE 12-17). In this context the black background color of the loincloths worn by the participants stands for "the deep black sea" (*mité ti'é*) which the ancestors crossed in their mythical voyage from the west.

At another level of interpretation these colors also refer to notions connected with human blood. The blood of every group of settlers in the domain is associated with a color on a spectrum that reaches from red to black: at one end of the spectrum are the first settlers whose blood is said to be "as red as the blood of the water buffalo" they regularly sacrifice; at the other end of the spectrum are the newcomers, the bringers of technology whose blood is said to be "as black as the polished wood of the tamarind tree (*kaju malé*)" from which they take their name. In a classificatory sense the opposition of these two colors on Palu'é cloths encompasses all the shades between the two extremes of the spectrum, including the blood types of all other groups represented in the domain. As such, red and black stand for all the origin groups of the domain and for all their constituent houses.

On Palu'é, human conception is thought of in terms of a convergence of two elements associated with specific colors. In intercourse man drips semen onto an ethno-anatomical organ located inside the womb and referred to as the "turmeric placenta" (*kuni*). This organ

FIGURE 12-17.
A female ceremonial officiant and the builder of a house perform a ritual during the inauguration ceremony for the house (*lali nua*). The aim is to rid the builder of "heat" accumulated during construction by dispersing it towards the setting sun. Both participants wear red shirts of commercially produced cloth, an allusion to the setting sun and to the place of origin of the mythical ancestors, believed to lie in the distant west. On the winnowing tray lie scrapings of cement and corrugated iron as well as wood scraps taken from the house. Ko'a, 1986.

acts as a container for the semen which in the process of entering the womb is transformed into that type of blood (*laja*) which is specific to the man's group. The fetus is thought to grow from this "blood-semen"; and with every act of intercourse in which "blood semen" is dripped onto the "turmeric placenta," the fetus is believed to increase in size until it is completed and ready to emerge from its mother's womb and be born. According to one interpretation, the yellow-orange color (obtained from turmeric) of the fine strands of

FIGURE 12-18.
The fine turmeric-dyed strands that separate the larger pattern bands, as in this *wua wela* cloth, are symbolically associated with the "turmeric-placenta."

thread found in the warp of some women's cloths refers to the mother's "turmeric placenta" (FIGURE 12-18). In this opposition, the natural white of the undyed cotton used for the geometric motifs is associated with the color of semen before it is transformed during intercourse into the man's specific color of blood. The colors featured on Palu'é women's cloths thus also refer to the realms of conception and human reproduction.

INTERPRETING BANDS

Marriage alliance is a fundamental theme informing the groupings of evenly spaced warp bands. On women's cloths there are three types of grouped bands. The widest grouping of bands, which contains the broadest series of motifs, is referred to as the "big mother" (*hina ca*), and the slightly narrower grouping of bands is referred to as the "little mother" (*hina lo'o*)[15], whereas all other groupings of bands are referred to as "children" (*hanané*). According to one interpretation, the "big mother" is classified as conceptually male and the "small mother" as conceptually female. At one level the classification of these three types of band groupings simply refers to the stem family of father, mother, and children.

At another level the three band types allude to the alliance established between two houses by way of marriage. Here we must note that the wife-giving house is classified as male and its members are referred to as "brother people," whereas the wife-taking house is classified as female and its members are referred to as "sister people." At this level the broader "large mother" grouping of bands therefore refers to the wife-giving house and the more narrow "small mother" grouping of bands to the wife-taking house.

Ideally, wife-giving houses and wife-taking houses maintain this relationship across successive generations by following the cultural prescription of matrilateral cross-cousin marriage, a form of marriage where a man marries his mother's brother's daughter and a woman marries her father's sister's son. Alluding to the theory of conception outlined above, such a marriage is referred to as a marriage of "turmeric-placenta" and "semen-blood" (*wai kuni laja*) and it is said that with every successive renewed alliance between the houses of traditional wife-givers and wife-takers that "the turmeric placenta is reattached and the blood is brought together anew" (*nuku palu kuni cémo palu laja*). Ultimately this form of marriage aims at a reconnection with the state of origin as expressed in the Palu'é origin myth.

On woman's cloths this form of marriage is represented by the fine strands of threads that run between the individual bands making up the "big" and "little mother" as well as those of the "children." The image of individual houses linked through successive marriages of the "turmeric placenta" with "semen blood" is further enhanced by a category of triangular motifs referred to as "houses" (*nua*, FIGURE 12-18).

Beyond this imagery of marriage and of affinal relations between individual houses, the bands can also be interpreted as an expression of relations at a higher socio-cosmic level. Here the "big mother" grouping represents the central village of the domain, which also contains the central ceremonial courtyard, whereas the "little mother" grouping and those of the "children" represent the domain settlements and hamlets which are oriented towards a central ceremonial courtyard.

Finally, congruence with the pervasive dualistic organizational features of the domain is achieved once the cloth is cut up and sewn into a tube for wearing. In this process the cloth is cut apart across the warp and reassembled in a manner resulting in two "big mother" groupings which are separated by "little mother" groupings, thus mirroring the two separate ceremonial centers of each domain and those settlements that are oriented towards them (FIGURE 12-14).

MOTIFS AND MEANING

With all the ikat motifs as with any other iconographic aspect of Palu'é cloths, there is strict adherence to tradition. No weaver is free to add a new motif or omit one from the range depicted on traditional cloths. In fact, a warp with even the minutest divergence from the traditional model is often disassembled and corrected before it is set up on the loom. In order to avoid mistakes, weavers use old cloths as guidelines and even very experienced women will generally keep a cloth on their knees as a model to follow while tying off the motifs of the cloth they are producing.

According to mythical narratives, women first decorated their textiles exclusively with geometrically stylized representations of objects from their own daily lives. They depicted cultigens such as tubers or maize; things related to animal husbandry such as the pig sty or the chicken's foot; and finally objects associated with body care, such as the fine-toothed comb used for removing nits.

Agriculture represents a nearly exclusively female realm; apart from the clearing of the fields men participate only marginally. This is expressed in the absolute right of women to allocate all harvest goods for consumption, ceremonial exchange, or sale. Although domestic animals are often brought in by men from the outside world and while their disposal remains the privilege of men, their raising, feeding, and tending on a daily basis is again an almost exclusively female domain. Finally, the nurture and care of young children is primarily a female realm in which men only gradually participate as the children grow older.

Upon seeing the motifs depicted on the first cloths, Palu'é men are said to have pleaded with their women for the inclusion of a motif associated with one of their own realms. The women conceded, as it is put, "out of love for their men," and chose a motif from the male realm of hunting. This inclusion of a conceptually male element in a predominantly female field illustrates a general feature of Palu'é dual classification, wherein everything of one kind is believed also to contain a little bit of its opposite.

With respect to textile motifs, women are associated with the cultivated world of the house and the fields, while men are associated with the uncultivated world of the forest and (implicitly) the outside world. Although on present-day Palu'é there is only very little primary forest left and hence only very little game, hunting still constitutes an important male realm. On moonlit nights men still like to venture into the forest with their dogs to hunt the civet cat (*laku*). This form of hunting demands special skills and special rules apply: no lights may be used, and once the dogs have chased a civet cat up a tree, the hunter has to gauge his target by using the reflection of the moon in the eyes of the cat. Hence the pride men take in any catch they can bring home. Often the tail of the civet cat is cured and dried on short staffs which men then carry around with them as fly swats, thereby identifying themselves as keen marksmen. According to some female elders it is for these reasons that

Palu'é women conceded to include the motif referred to as "the trace of the civet cat" (*laku laéné*). And, indeed, the motif consists of groupings of dots portraying the footprints a civet cat leaves on a humid surface.

A number of motifs depict various substances associated either with the cause or the remedy for a given affliction. On one hand they allude to the basic medical knowledge a daughter receives from her mother, which places her in the position to deal with the minor ailments commonly afflicting children, and on the other they allude to the fundamental quality of beneficial coolness inherent in younger women.

The candlenut (*wua wela*), for example, is used as a home remedy for sore throat, a common ailment during the rainy season, and it gives its name to one particular cloth which is customarily worn for ceremonial chanting. Here the implication is that the voice will be as clear for the chanting[16] as if the chanter had been treated with candlenut.

The design called *hua wua* takes its name from the generic term for allergenic seeds and grasses growing along paths and in fields. Young people, especially children, are frequently beset with skin rashes, which in the absence of water can easily ulcerate. The indicated remedy is to apply a mixture of chick pea (*wéwé*), tubers, betel-pepper, areca nut, and lime that has been masticated by a woman. The body is then covered with the textile containing the *hua wua* design; the tubular cloth is pulled up across the head, leaving the arms to hang out at an angle. The body is kept covered for a full day, after which the mixture is washed off in the sea.

A WOMAN'S CLOTH TO PROTECT THE GROWING CENTER

In conclusion we turn briefly to a ritual in which several socio-cosmic levels are merged by means of the body metaphor and where a number of associations with the conceptually female are expressed through the ritual use of a woman's cloth.

The ritual takes place at a final stage of the ceremonial cycle and constitutes part of the reenactment of the myth of origin. After the "Black Patola Stone" has been brought to the ceremonial center and the myth of origin has been chanted, soil from the lower and upper half of the domain is collected by the members of those houses affiliated with that center. This "bringing in of soil" commences after sunset and must be completed before sunrise (FIGURE 12-1). Two large baskets are placed on top of the ceremonial center. They serve as intermediary receptacles for the soil before it can be spread across the center to reinforce it and to cover those stones exposed by rain since the closure of the last ceremonial cycle. Once the center has been fortified, the "Black Patola Stone" is equally embedded in this soil. Only then is the center prepared for the final sacrificial offering of water buffalo to the Supreme Being (FIGURE 12-19).

Throughout the whole procedure, which is marked by feverish activity to accumulate a sufficient amount of soil within the prescribed period, a ceremonial officiant of the first settling group sits on top of the central monolith literally hugging the largest of the two baskets. His body and head are entirely covered with a woman's cloth and throughout the night he remains absolutely motionless and silent until the work has been completed.

As we have seen earlier the island and its domains are believed to be alive and capable of growth. One of the principal aims of the final stages of the ceremonial cycle is to stimulate this growth by reconnecting with the origins of the island and its people through the reenactment of the myth of origin. This reenactment takes place at the ceremonial center of the domain, which in terms of the commonly cited body metaphor is classified as its navel. The navel

FIGURE 12-19.
At the closure of the ceremonial cycle, the main Ko'a priest-leader poses with the carcass of a water buffalo sacrificed as an offering to the Supreme Being. The periodic sacrifice is held to restore cosmic harmony in the domain and to ensure its growth and welfare.
Ko'a, 1987.

represents the central locus of growth of the human body and in many ways the embodied domain and its ceremonial center in ritual are treated just like the body of a growing infant.

We recall that during the first few months following birth a mother keeps her child tightly wrapped in a woman's cloth to protect it from negative influences such as witchcraft and harmful supernatural beings, and to ward off illness by keeping it cool. In a similar manner the ceremonial officiant embraces the basket containing the fresh soil at the most crucial moment of the domain's growth, when its center is similarly vulnerable to negative outside influences. Here the cooling and healing qualities of the woman's cloth he covers himself with provide the same protection and care for the growing center of the domain as that which a mother can give to her newborn child. ❖   NOTES, page 275.

CHAPTER I

1. Each of these groups is further divided into a number of dialects. For example, Nagé-Kéo, the speakers of which comprise a populous and important ethnic group, is classified as a dialect of Ende-Lio. Manggarai, Ngadha, and Ende-Lio belong to the Bima-Sumba Group of the Austronesian language phylum; Sikka and Lamaholot belong to the Timor Area Group (Wurm & Hattori 1981:40).

2. Bellwood (1985) provides a major synthesis of recent developments in the study of the prehistory of island Southeast Asia. In the distant past, the archipelago was inhabited by Australoid populations whose modern descendants include the native peoples of Australia. In Indonesia, the Australoid people were gradually absorbed or replaced by newcomers of Southern Mongoloid stock. Prehistorians now attribute the Southern Mongoloid presence to the expansion of Austronesian-speaking populations from Taiwan, through the Philippines, into Indonesia and beyond. The present populations of Flores and the other Lesser Sundas exhibit a wide range of physical appearances. The genetic mixture in this region has generally been thought to represent a less-than-complete replacement of the Australoid phenotype with the Southern Mongoloid. Despite the apparently mixed genetic heritage, any non-Austronesian languages once spoken on the island have been completely replaced.

3. Proto-Austronesian has been demonstrated through comparative linguistic techniques to have contained a word that is the forerunner of the words meaning "loom" in today's Austronesian languages (Blust 1976:34). Baked clay spindle whorls have been unearthed in archaeological sites on Taiwan belonging to the Yüan-shan culture, which is thought to have been a precursor of the impending Austronesian expansion (Bellwood 1985:216).

4. As Austronesian-speaking populations expanded across the Pacific to Polynesia, weaving entirely disappeared from the technological repertoire. An Indonesian-type loom occurs in only a few locations in the western Pacific (Ling Roth 1977:106, Riesenberg 1952).

5. Bühler believed in the antiquity of ikat in eastern Indonesia, but stopped short of identifying the region as the technique's point of origin. Instead, he labeled it the "most archaic" (1942:1604) because it was in some places applied to bast fiber. In a later article he further spelled out his views, saying that either Indonesia or the Asiatic mainland "might be considered as having independently given birth to the ikat technique." Regarding the possibility of Indian trade cloths having been responsible for the development of ikat in Indonesia, he felt that "if any transfer of such methods can be envisioned, it must have taken place at a much earlier time and in more elementary forms." (1959:11). Most scholars have accepted these opinions, but it does not necessarily follow that the ikat technique was used in all parts of the archipelago from early on. There is no conclusive proof that it appeared in the Lesser Sundas before the period of European contact and this possibility should not be entirely dismissed.

6. Bühler (1941) attributes their origin to the Near East, but it was in India that they reached their most developed and influential forms.

7. The most extensive colonial era works are: Arndt 1929-31, 1932, 1935, 1936-37, 1938, 1944; Suchtelen 1921; and Vatter 1932. Additional sources include: Beker 1913; Bekkum 1944, 1946a-c; Coolhaas 1942; Cornelissen 1929; Elbert 1912; Heerkens 1943, 1944; Nooteboom 1939; Stapel 1914; Staveren 1915; Tietze 1941; and Vroklage 1939, 1940, 1941. World War II and subsequent instability in Indonesia halted the output of ethnographic research, with the exception of Verheijen's early work (1951) and Kennedy's field-notes (1955). Since the 1970s, however, new research has resulted in an increasing number of in-depth descriptions of both traditional society and cultural change, including: Aoki 1988; Robert Barnes 1974a, 1974b, 1977, 1979; Ruth Barnes 1987, 1989a&b, 1991a&b; Barnes & Barnes 1989; Djawanai 1983; Erb 1987, 1991; Forth 1989a&b; Gordon 1975, 1980; Graham 1991; Hamilton 1989, 1990, 1993; Howell 1989; Lewis 1988a&b, 1989; Maxwell 1980, 1981; Nakagawa 1988; Prior 1988; and Yamaguchi 1989.

8. The terms "domain," "clan," "lineage," and "house" can only be used here very generally. The societies of the Lesser Sundas are renowned in the anthropological literature for their numerous complex variations on these themes of social organization; to use the terms more precisely would require a detailed and separate examination of social structure in each community. Among most ethnic groups, lineage membership is calculated patrilineally, but there are notable matrilineal exceptions, such as the people of the Tana 'Ai region of Sikka Regency.

9. In an analysis of Lio village organization, Prior equates the leader who has authority over land with "village cooperation" and "fertility" (1988:62), and the leader who speaks for the community with "cosmic order" and the maintenance of "boundaries." Generally speaking, control over land use rights was vested in the hereditary head of the clan recognized as the village's founding clan. However, oral histories frequently explain how this title, through a sequence of events, came to be passed to another clan. In the Islamic state that developed at Ende, the raja was a passive authority removed from everyday affairs while the *raja bicara* or "talking raja" exercised day-to-day executive authority (Dietrich ms:84).

10. Skill in oratory was an important component of leadership because many rites involve the recitation of the oral histories of clans. These histories were potentially subject to manipulation, providing an important means of asserting a clan's position (Lewis 1988b).

11. Class membership was largely determined by birth, but unusual economic success or marriage to a person of higher status held some chance for upward mobility, while penury, capture during inter-village warfare, or serious violations of community law could result in enslavement. The inherent tendency for junior lines of aristocratic lineages to slip out of aristocratic standing provided motivation for some individuals to establish themselves in new areas. Some village clans were recognized as offshoots of clans with the same name in neighboring villages. Oral histories frequently champion the exploits of an outsider who came to the village, established his clan, and through military courage and well-placed marriage, succeeded in asserting a leading position for his progeny.

12. A seminal work by Wouden (1968 [1935]) discussed this type of social structure in eastern Indonesia, predating the famous treatment of similar themes by Lévi-Strauss (1969 [1949]). A large body of literature has developed since then, giving the societies of eastern Indonesia a significant place in anthropological theory. Fox (1980c) provides a recent compilation of work by researchers who have advanced these and related themes.

13. See Robert Barnes (1974a:28-31) and Howell (1989:423) for examples of this type of ideology.

14. The presence of corn among the leading traditional staples serves as a reminder of the pitfalls of projecting the ethnographic record into the distant past. This crop was introduced to the archipelago from Mexico in the early 16th century (Reid 1988:19).

15. Bellwood believes that "some contact between India and eastern Indonesia ... may have begun by as early as 200 B.C." (1985:302), but "...Sulawesi, the Lesser Sundas and the Moluccas were only affected ... in a most superficial way." (1985:138).

16. Javanese traders, however, may have been visiting Timor and marketing Timorese sandalwood to China, India, and Arabia for several centuries before the first Chinese descriptions of Timor (Ormeling 1956:94-96).

17. The relevant passages appear in Pigeaud's translation (1962, 3:17). A debate concerning various interpretations can be found in Fraasen (1976),

Robert Barnes (1982) and Dietrich (1984).

18. The Portuguese apothecary and diplomat Pires, writing from Malacca in 1512-1515 (Cortesão 1944), provides the most detailed picture of the Malaccan world. His descriptions of the lands within Malacca's sway are quite thorough, but what he was able to learn of the Lesser Sundas was rudimentary, again suggesting that they remained rather isolated.

19. For a more thorough treatment of various Asian influences on textile design in the archipelago, see Maxwell (1990).

20. The history of the Ende fort is given by Rouffaer (1923a, 1923b) and Suchtelen (1923).

21. See Erb (1987:22) for local accounts of the tribute system.

22. Predacious raids by Endenese slave traders decimated coastal sections of Sumba (Needham 1983), while the Bimanese wreaked similar havoc in Manggarai (Gordon 1975:48-50). Many slaves were used within the region as domestic labor. Others were sold through international markets flourishing on Bali and in Batavia (now Jakarta). Most were used for agricultural labor in Java, but some were taken as far as the Mascarene

Islands, Madagascar and Cape Town (Needham 1983).

23. In retaliation for an Endenese raid of a Dutch post on Timor, the Dutch destroyed the town of Ende in 1838 (Dietrich nd:19). In the last quarter of the 19th century, they became enmeshed in festering local disputes and faced persistent problems with rebellious native leaders (Dietrich ms:1983), who are today regarded on Flores as heroes in the struggle against the Dutch.

24. Recorded by Suchtelen (1921:211), translated by Hain (1978:189).

25. Land tenure presents a critical problem. The former system recognized only communal ownership, with use-rights controlled by the heads of the leading clans. Modern Indonesian law allows individuals to claim ownership of land. At least in some communities there has been a successful reconciliation, taking advantage of the new system by claiming land in the name of the clan leaders, while preserving the spirit of the old system by then sharing the land (and the tax burden) within the group (pers. com., Andrea Molnar).

CHAPTER 2

1. Some textile scholars prefer to avoid the term "sarong" because it is subject to variable interpretation. Here it is used as a gloss for the Indonesian term *sarung*, which on Flores is applied to all tubular garments (and only to tubular garments). The local languages of Flores have separate terms for men's and women's sarongs, except where the sarongs themselves are unisex.

2. Ruth Barnes (1989a:50) provides an account of three different ways of wearing sarongs on Solor, each of which was once appropriate for a particular age or status, but this system is no longer practiced.

3. In mountain communities, women also wore shoulder cloths when needed for warmth.

4. Islamic informants sometimes say that their marriage practices do not involve bridewealth, but in rural Islamic weddings a series of payments is due to particular relatives of the bride, just as in non-Islamic wedddings. In Ende's urban setting, this process is somewhat simplified (Fatta 1982:48, 104).

5. The size and nature of the kin groups involved varies from one wedding to another. Among some ethnic groups, and particularly in aristocratic weddings of the past, entire clans participated under the leadership of the titled clan head. Often the reality today is that a much smaller lineage or household concludes the negotiations.

6. For example, Lio informants routinely list as many as eleven separately named components of bridewealth. Some of these may involve payments to many different individuals, such as to each of the bride's maternal uncles. Others are made only in special cases, such as for adoptive parents or for an older sibling who is preceded in marriage by a younger sibling.

7. There are no elephants on Flores; see CHAPTER 11 regarding the history of the importation of ivory.

8. Cash is often used as a substitute for ivory or gold. In Manggarai, cash and livestock are the most important elements (Gordon 1980:57). In some areas, including Sikka and Rajong, pigs serve as part of the reciprocal gift from the bride's kin. In the Ende-Lio region, ivory was once used but has

now gone out of circulation. Its disappearance is often blamed on the Japanese Occupation. The few tusks that remain no longer circulate and have become clan heirlooms.

9. It is for this reason that the term "bridewealth" is preferred over the connotation-laden "brideprice."

10. In an ideal system, goods might flow through a closed circuit consisting of as few as three groups. More typically, as Robert Barnes observed regarding Kédang (1979:85), "...the system loses itself in a mass of particular arrangements."

11. Palm spirits are in some places a masculine good and in others a feminine one.

12. Regarding the history of Mbay, see CHAPTER 5. In Lamalera, clans trace their ancestry from Sulawesi through a series of intermediary locations before their final arrival on Lembata (Ruth Barnes 1989a:114). Vatter (1932:205) states that the Lamalera people brought weaving technology with them, but Barnes was unable to obtain confirmation of this (1989a:121).

13. Male weavers may occasionally be encountered in other villages, but not in such numbers. Men who weave are sometimes, though not always, characterized by their fellow villagers as homosexuals.

14. Many weavers who worked in a workshop established in Ende in the early 1980s left employment there because they considered the wages too low and they missed the freedom and flexibility of working at home.

15. Moreland (1924-25:243), cited in Gittinger (1982:155).

16. Indonesians were exhorted to grow cotton as "one of the tools to achieve final victory in the war for Greater East Asia" (Ishikawa 1943:25-26, author's translation). Although this policy was ostensibly promoted in the name of Indonesian self-reliance, elderly people on Flores recall that the crop was largely commandeered by the Japanese for their own purposes.

17. There have been various interpretations regarding the origins of some of these patterns and the degree of antiquity they represent in Southeast Asia. See CHAPTER 6 and Maxwell (1990).

CHAPTER 3

1. The genus *Gossypium* includes a number of species and varieties that have been carried around the globe by man and are not always distinguishable except by chromosomal analysis. The Dutch colonial government purposefully experimented with cotton varieties in Java and many of these may have made their way to Flores. The Japanese also introduced new varieties, particularly annual types sometimes referred to on Flores as "Japanese" cotton.

2. The appearance of this clump of seeds has led to the name "kidney cotton" among botanists, but on Flores it is referred to as "goat droppings." It is associated particularly with a cotton species of American origin, *Gossypium*

barbadense (Fryxell 1979:176).

3. Edited from translation by Lucian Heichler. Current informants in Sikka are unable to confirm the details of this account and suspect that it may have been embellished by the author.

4. Pers. com., Penelope Graham.

5. As with cotton, a large number of species and cultivated varieties occur in tropical regions.

6. According to Verheijen, *M. tomentosa* is also present on Flores and is identified with some of the local language names (such as *kembo* in Endenese) used for the red dye (1990:229).

7. This plant only grows high in the mountainous interior. Dyers as far away as Savu (an island with no high mountains) are dependent on *lobha* gathered in the mountains of Flores and exported by Endenese traders. The identity of the plant has not been established with certainty, but several sources suggest that it may be of the genus *Symplocos* (Burkill 1935:2112, Kajitani 1980:318, Warming & Gaworski 1981:68, Verheijen 1990:245).

8. For a description of different procedures used in Lamalera, see Ruth Barnes (1989a:29).

9. In Lamalera, a wood called *tenor* is the major alternative to morinda and in Larantuka *gemoli* is used (Ruth Barnes 1989a:31).

10. One plant used for this purpose is sappan. Another is *bakau*, the Indonesian term used on Flores for mangroves of the genera *Rhizophera* and *Bruguier* (Burkill 1935:2312). Dyers in the Ende-Lio region use a plant called *waé*, a term Verheijen equates with both *Pterospermum diversifolium* and *Peltophorum pterocarpum* (1990:58, 77). Dyers in Mbay use the inner bark of a tree called *rengit*, a sample of which has been identified as *Acacia glauca* by the Rijksherbarium, Leiden.

11. *Kayu kuning* is the Indonesian term, also known as *haju gulung* in Manggarai and *ga gulu* in Nagé. Verheijen (1982:109) identifies *haju gulung* as *Maclura cochinchinensis*.

12. The terminology used here in describing the various warping systems follows Yoshimoto (1991).

13. For a striped or ikat cloth, the warp actually consists of number of separate bands rather than a single filament.

14. Actually it takes on a pale ecru shade due to handling, mordanting, and some inevitable bleeding of the dyes. In the Ende-Lio region, the yarns are sometimes given a preliminary treatment with yellow dyes before the ikat work begins, producing bright yellow motifs. At least in some areas, this is a recent innovation related to the adoption of yellow chemical dyes.

CHAPTER 4

1. Some linguists have grouped Rembong and Rajong as dialects of Manggarai, while Verheijen (1977) maintains that they are distinct languages.

2. Pers. com., Maribeth Erb.

3. See Gittinger (1979:figs. 114, 115) for two typical Bimanese examples.

4. See Summerfield (1991:12) for an illustration of a cloth with a blue and red check pattern identical to some Todo *lipa curak* sarongs. However, the most characteristic types of Minangkabau textiles, decorated with supplementary-weft work in metallic yarn, are not produced in Todo.

5. Pers. com., Maribeth Erb.

6. The term *tarip* also became a measure of value for livestock; for example, *ela tarip* is a pig worth a loincloth in barter (Verheijen 1967:624).

7. This is according to the description given by villagers in Todo today. Verheijen (1967:720), however, defines *curuk* as "to embroider with silver thread." See FIGURE 1-7 for equivalent cloths made in the Lio area.

8. In everyday usage, the Indonesian term *kain* is often used rather than the Manggarai *lipa*. *Songké* is the Manggarai version of *songket,* the Indonesian word for supplementary-weft weaving.

9. An alternative name, particularly in Todo, is *bali bélo*.

10. *Naé* or *nai* is a term used in several languages on Flores to refer to a panel of woven cloth. *Sudi* refers to the decorating of cloth with weft stripes, according to Verheijen (1967:609). More specifically, it seems to designate the continuous supplementary-weft technique.

11. Pers. com., Maribeth Erb.

12. The similarity is evident in an illustration of a Bimanese *weri* that appears in Hitchcock (1983: fig. 36a). More generally, these cloths are the Lesser Sunda version of supplementary-weft cloth types that are widespread in western Indonesia. For example, both the design formats and the individual motifs found in Bima and Manggarai can be found in similar versions in Malay *songket* cloths. On the Malay Peninsula such cloths are called *kain Bugis* (Bugis cloth) and the pattern *corak Bugis* (Bugis pattern), referring to the role of Sulawesi people in making and trading these cloths.

13. *Ghun non*, nine pattern sticks; *ghun sepuluh zua*, twelve pattern sticks, etc.

14. One Rembong weaver married a Lio man and lived in the Lio region for many years. She has now returned to her natal area with her daughter and the two of them are making Lio styles of cloth in Rembong (pers. com., Maribeth Erb).

CHAPTER 5

1. *Ngadha* and *Ngada* are variant transliterations of the same term. Ngadha has come to be preferred in the anthropological literature as the name of the ethnic group, while Ngada is used in Indonesia as the name of the regency. These conventions are maintained here to avoid confusing the two meanings. On Flores itself, Ngada when used as an ethnic term refers collectively to all of the diverse groups in the regency. The group ethnographers designate as Ngadha is instead called Ata Bajawa (people of Bajawa).

2. Pers. com., Olaf Smedel and Andrea Molnar.

3. The language of Mbay differs sharply from Nagé and is more akin to Riung and Rembong. The affinities of other groups in this region are not clear. They include the Dhawé, originally from the hills above Mbay but now intermixed with the Mbay people; the Toto, in the eastern coastal section of Aesesa District; and the Rendu, in inland areas adjoining Boawae District.

4. Arndt based his description of Ngadha ikat on observations made in the hamlet of Utaseko, located near the south coast in Golewa District, suggesting that this area may once have been another center.

5. *Ragi mbiri bara* were white, while *ragi mbiri ngaju* were dyed with indigo.

6. According to one informant from Mangulewa, *wua wera* refers to "scattered fruit," an allusion to the fact that this sarong could be worn by people of all social classes.

7. Men's garments seem not to have had as many distinctions, although some informants claim the size of the horses on a man's *sapu lu'é* corresponded with his status.

8. In the Ngadha language, aristocrats are called *ga'é mézé*, "big men."

9. Bajawa informants contradict those in Lopijo, saying that *lawo kéto* properly applies to a sarong of relatively low status, but this term is little used in Bajawa. Arndt describes *lawo kéto* as figured festival garments, consistent with the Lopijo usage.

10. Pers. com., Olaf Smedel.

11. Author's translation. Recorded in Lopijo, 1991.

12. In Lopijo, the terms for *lawo butu* and *lawo ngaza* are *lawo ramba* and *lawo*

ngali, respectively.

13. *Niko nako* means, roughly, "higgledy-piggledy."

14. *Pojo* is the Boawae term for ikat. In Raja, the term is *peté*; thus *hoba peté.*

15. Sarongs made of two panels are called *nai zua.* Three-panel sarongs are *nai telu.*

16. These yarns, called *su subi,* are dyed with *Maclura sp.* (*ga gulu* or "yellow thorn" in Nagé).

17. Curiously, the finest pieces in museum collections usually have the fringe cut off and the edges neatly trimmed with stitching. Informants in Boawae recall that *sada géa* were fringed and speculate that the fringeless cloths may have been used as *sada bhago,* but this has not been confirmed. Maxwell states that the edged cloths were used as saddle blankets (1990:69), while similar cloths were described by Todo informants as wrap-around garments for horseback riders.

18. The Nagé call these garments *agi bai,* derived from *ragi Mbay.*

19. These are named according to the color of the fringe, *sada eko bha* (white fringed *sada*) or *sada eko to mité* (black and red fringed *sada*).

20. *Désé* in Boawae, *huwé* in Soa, *kekung* in Mbay and *keku* in Riung.

21. This plant was identified by comparison with specimens preserved in the herbarium of the Smithsonian Institution. In Nagé the plant is called *zama* (*rama* in Lopijo, *sama* in Manggarai). Verheijen (1982, 1990) has identified these names with *Pipturis argenteus,* a non-cultivated cousin of ramie, but perhaps the same term is applied to both plants.

22. Boxing is called *sagi* in Soa and *etu* around Boawae, but otherwise is identical. In fact, the leading boxers follow the entire circuit of sites through both regions.

23. In former times, this night was a time of sexual license, when many of the rules that ordinarily governed sexual behavior were suspended.

24. The Riung usage of the term *kaet,* meaning supplementary-weft decorations, appears to differ from usage in Rembong (see FIGURE 9-7).

25. For example, the motifs of the Mbay sarong in FIGURE 5-34 are nearly identical with those on a cloth from Kelantan, Malaysia (Selvanayagam 1990: fig. 166).

26. They call these *wo'i ma'u,* "beach motifs."

27. Tonggo sarongs with the less decorated side blank are called *zuka wo'i tembo,* while those with widely spaced motifs are zuka *wo'i uzu.*

CHAPTER 6

The research for this chapter was conducted in 1988 under the auspices of the Indonesian Institute of Sciences. Funding was provided by a Fulbright-Hayes Grant and sponsorship by Nusa Cendana University, Kupang.

1. According to a published account, this motif represents a holy bird (*péa ae*) flying over water (Kahn Majlis 1991b:183).

2. Occasionally it is said that sarongs with the elephant motif must be upside-down if worn at weddings or funerals, suggesting that these sarongs may once have been the subject of a special body of folklore.

3. In Ndona, weavers occasionally give an alternative name for the *zawo nggaja tendo,* calling it *lawo nggaja manu* (elephant and chicken sarong), even though there is today no chicken motif. It seems that the term remains in use regardless of the disappearance of the motif.

4. Very rarely one sees additional types of *zawo mangga* sarongs, including one with the elephant motif appearing in white on the blue-black bands.

5. The reason weavers have leftover yarns is rooted in the ikat tying procedure. Endenese weavers typically layer their ikat bundles in four when arranging the yarn on the tying frame. This means that they make at one time a minimum of four bands of each type. Yet a finished sarong requires only two *foko* bands (the widest ikat band in the end panels). The ikat bands in the center panels of most *zawo ngéra* sarongs are made of these left-over yarns, separated by minor ikat bands and plain black stripes. If she wishes, of course, a weaver can deliberately make extra yarns of any sort.

6. For other typical examples, see Gittinger (1979: fig. 127) and Maxwell (1990: fig. 327).

7. One old Endenese *sémba* illustrated in Bezemer (1931:43) has patola-like borders, a feature that appears today only in neighboring Ndona District. Another illustration (ten Kate 1894: pl. 9) shows the rebellious Endenese leader Bharanuri, dressed in a *sémba* that appears not only to have borders but also a banded structure throughout.

8. In practice, the proper Endenese term *sa nai* is indistinguishable from the Indonesianized term *senai,* which is used in many parts of Flores for single-panel cloths.

9. They have in the past two decades become quite popular among Sikkanese women and are sold in large numbers in the Maumere market.

10. In Nggela the term used for such sarongs is *lawo gamba,* from the Indonesian *gambar* (picture). In Tenda, a style of sarong called *lawo nggabha* has overall patterning. In Jopu informants used the term *lawo daki,* but this is not consistent with the usage of the same term in Wolojita, where it applies to a sarong identical to the Nggela *lawo redu.*

11. See CHAPTER 10 for a more complete accounting of men's shoulder cloths in Nggela.

12. More recently, Fox (1977:99) and Maxwell (1990:218) have also taken up this topic.

13. According to Fox (1977:99), it was the decline of the patola trade after the demise of the United East India Company that stimulated local production of patola-inspired designs. This suggests the possibility that morinda dyeing, and perhaps even the ikat technique itself, were not adopted in the Lesser Sundas until after 1800, although Fox and Maxwell (and obviously Bühler) believe that the ikat technique was in use well before that time, used for the making of banded patterns.

CHAPTER 7

1. *Ling* is the sound of coins jingling in a pocket; *wéling* means "cost" or "price"; in anthropological terms, *ling wéling* is bridewealth.

2. It is worth noting that the term *'iwang* derives from the root *'iwa,* which means "other" or "different."

3. In 1904, the Dutch created a second rajadom under the Raja of Sikka which included most of 'Iwang Geté. This political division, which was called Kangae, did not survive its first raja.

4. For a fuller ethnographic description of Tana Wai Brama, one of the seven *tana* of Tana 'Ai, see Lewis (1988a).

5. The footbeam of the Sikkanese loom has a hollow compartment into which a small piece of dense wood is inserted: each time the sword of the loom strikes the working head, the rattle at the foot barks hollowly.

6. Married women in Kabupaten Sikka wear ivory bracelets cut from the bases of elephant tusks. As the bases of the tusks have been whittled away to provide the bracelets, tusks have become shorter and shorter. Since the ceremonial value of a tusk presented as part of bridewealth prestations is calculated in terms of its length and circumference, as tusks have become smaller, more have come to be required in a given bridewealth prestation. Furthermore, in the past three decades, people throughout Sikka Regency have increasingly sold their tusks to Chinese traders in Maumere who cut

them up, carve trinkets from them and sell the broken tusks and trinkets off the island. The supply of gold coins, most of which are of nineteenth-century Dutch mintage, has also diminished as they have been converted into earrings, which have a ceremonial value throughout the district.

7. Today, *lipa* are produced mainly in Sikka Natar. In the past, larger numbers than those made today were produced in Krowé (especially in Nita). It is uncertain the extent to which *lipa* were made in 'Iwang Geté and they have never been produced in Tana 'Ai.

8. Ordinary cloths are called *'utang biasa*, lit. ordinary *'utang*, or *ngawung biasa*, ordinary things.

9. The people of Sikka Natar attach no special significance to the homonymy of the word *wungung*, which means: (1) the russet color which is produced by the over-dyeing of morinda and indigo and is the background color of *'utang* exchanged in bridewealth transactions; (2) clan or lineage; (3) in the phrase *du'a wungung*, "clan mother."

10. The young couple eloped and were married in a church ceremony elsewhere. Their children belong to the woman's house rather than to her husband's because to this day bridewealth has not been paid.

11. As it ages, the cloth might be worn to weekly mass in church and, later still, on more or less formal visits to kin and friends. Indeed, the wearing of such a cloth marks the formality of what might otherwise be taken as a casual occasion. Then as its colors fade, it is worn around the house, when fetching water and finally for working in the garden. In the end, a cloth becomes a rag used for cleaning up around babies and the house. Even then, a portion of a particularly valued cloth might be cut and saved to serve as a model for making a new cloth of the same design.

12. It is worth noting that the word *'utang* is related to the Indonesian word *hutang*, meaning "debt" or "obligation."

13. Further research should provide a typology of the motifs in the textiles of Sikka Natar. To date, I have identified some seventy major classes of *'utang* motifs in the village.

14. Individual warp threads are usually twined of two individual threads, with the exception of the monochrome threads which separate bands; these may be either single threads or twined of two threads. A single ikat may enclose more than one *siwang*, but rarely less than one. While individual threads carry meaning, weavers stress the elementary nature of *siwang* because this group of six threads is the unit of *beté* (ikat).

15. *Hura* is order, ordered sequence, the planned following of one thing after another, as successive events are interpreted as history or as the elements of narrative unfold in the telling of a myth. *Hura* pertains to the logic of sequentiality, and thus bears similarity to the linguist's idea of syntagm and syntagmatics. *Hura* subsists in relations of metonymy, whereas *kélang* are ordered as metaphor.

16. An important point about Sikkanese textiles is that while they might be considered inherently attractive to a museum collector or curator of "primitive" art, and while the historical influences on their design might be identifiable, their significance is not available to someone who lacks an understanding of the code governing their production.

17. This rule applies to the cloth in the asymmetrical form in which it is woven. When the cloth is cut and sewn into a sarong, an overall symmetry of the banding is produced.

18. Some *kélang* (motifs) must be ordered by particular *hura*. In other words, not every *hura* is appropriate for all the motifs that a woman might ikat. Hence the *hura* of a house must be sufficient in number to accommodate the sometimes large number of motifs to which its women have rights. Just how *hura* relate to *kélang* is a matter that requires further investigation in Sikka Natar.

CHAPTER 8

Fieldwork in the Lamaholot region was undertaken in 1979 and 1982, when a total of nine months were spent in the village of Lamalera. Preceding these visits, the author lived in Kédang for two years, from 1969 to 1971. The first research visit to the Lamaholot region was funded by the Department of Education for England and Wales, as part of a Major State Studentship. The return in 1982 was supported by the Social Science Research Council of Great Britain. All visits were carried out under the auspices of the Indonesian Institute of Sciences (LIPI).

1. For example, in the dialects of western Solor and the village of Lamalera, southern Lembata, words may end with a nasal /a/, which Keraf writes as /ã/. It occurs instead of the more common ending /-an/ or /-ang/, i.e. *mitã* (black) instead of *mitang*; *méã* instead of *méan*. Where possible, Keraf's spelling of Lamaholot is followed here.

2. Occasionally it can still come to skirmishes between villages that may result in the loss of human lives. This happened on Adonara as recently as 1982, and in the same year war nearly broke out between the villages of Wailolong and Léwotala in East Flores. The latter incident was sparked by a dispute over water supply, but ... "the real cause," it was said in Wailolong, "was that our two villages have always been at war."

3. Pronunciations of the word *kewatek* vary greatly: *kwatek, kewaték, kefatek, kewatak* are only a few of the local variations. As this chapter offers a survey, rather than a case study, I have chosen to use a version that although not always precisely correct should be recognizable by all Lamaholot speakers.

4. Therefore, despite the insistence on giving a locally made cloth, it is not appropriate to categorize the prestation given by the wife-givers in general as "indigenous" in contrast to that offered by the wife-takers, the origins of which are external.

5. This hypothesis is born out to some degree by the fact that in Kédang for the funeral of a man who has not converted to either Christianity or Islam, the corpse is dressed with a loin cloth made of bark. Another example of keeping a "new arrival" out of the ceremonial center, the old hamlet, is the prohibition on planting corn, which applies in some communities (R. H. Barnes 1974a:48).

6. The first serious discussion of Lamaholot textiles appeared in Vatter (1932: 217-226 and passim). Maxwell (1980, 1981) initiated a more extensive consideration of Lamaholot textiles in their cultural and historical context. Following up certain questions she raised, I have discussed the relationship between weaving and non-weaving areas (Ruth Barnes 1987). A more extensive survey of the region can be found in CHAPTERS 11 and 12 of Ruth Barnes (1989a).

7. Names may change from village to village. I use here the terms given to me in the village of Wailolong, located in the Baipito area that immediately surrounds Ili Mandiri. See Graham (1991:160) for a different and more complete list of cloth types (some of which are also illustrated in CHAPTER 11) from the neighboring Léwoléma area, located further west of the peak.

8. *Kenirék* is Lamaholot for "ikat pattern"; *bélén* means "large," but also "noble, respected."

9. According to weavers in Wailolong and other nearby villages in the Ili Mandiri region, all ikat for *kewatek méan* must be colored with both dyes. This is not necessarily the practice in all villages, however, as some *kewatek méan* in museum collections include narrow bands that are not over-dyed. In the Léwoléma area, *belapit* entails dyeing ikat skeins first with morinda and then with indigo, thus reversing the order of the dyes (see CHAPTER 11).

10. Actual practice is more mixed; *kewatek méan* with small spots of blue are sometimes made.

11. See Maxwell (1981:48) for a more detailed description of the differences in banding between the *kewatek makasar* and *kewatek kenumak*.

12. Patola cloths found their way into most parts of the Lamaholot region, but only in some areas are they implicated in bridewealth exchange. More generally, they became clan treasures, to be displayed on certain ceremonial occasions, including funerals (Graham 1991:244 & opp. 153).

13. The same situation apparently developed in East Flores in respect of the *kewatek ketipa*. In 1982 I was told that these textiles had become part of lineage treasures, and thus were inalienable wealth of the clan. Nevertheless, and to the great disapproval of my informants, they were eventually sold to "tourists."

14. *Biasa* is Indonesian and here means "common, ordinary." No translation for *temodol* was available.

15. No explanation for the term *makasar* was given in this context. It seems likely, though, that both textiles in some form refer to cloth from Makassar, possibly formerly imported into the area.

16. If textiles are exchanged for local products (rice or corn), rather than cash, an indication of relative local value can be established. This seems to remain stable over the years (Ruth Barnes 1989a:57). The red cloth is worth six times as much as the black cloth from Tanaléin.

17. Elsewhere I have discussed in detail the history and position of power assumed by Lamalera, in particular (Ruth Barnes 1989a:113-129). No extensive research has been carried out in Labala so far.

18. In Atadéi even five or seven panels may be combined in one cloth. I have not seen an example of these supposedly very long textiles, but I was told that the number of panels must be uneven.

19. Kalikur was not allied with the *lima pantai*, but seems to have been a trading port of some importance. When what remained of Magellan's expedition sailed past Lembata in January, 1522, the name Alicura was recorded in the ship's log. This can certainly be identified with Kalikur. See R. H. Barnes (1974a:5-13) for a summary of the complex political relationships between Kalikur and the *lima pantai*, especially the Raja of Adonara.

20. The relevant sources are Vatter (1932:223-224), Maxwell (1981:53,56-57), and my own informants from Lamalera (Ruth Barnes 1989a:74-76).

21. Maxwell, in her first contribution to the topic, put it in the following way: "Despite some general agreement about the exclusiveness of the major motifs, the actual lines of inheritance are extremely obscure today"(1981:53).

22. Khan Majlis (1984:86-87) takes Maxwell's cautiously phrased hypothesis as the likely explanation. Most recently, Maxwell (1990:90) quotes herself as evidence when she says: "In the Lamaholot areas of east Flores and the islands of Solor, Lembata and Adonara, the family affiliations of the maker or wearer are identified by certain motifs in the widest band or central panel of warp ikat (Maxwell 1980)." In the 1980 publication she does not make such a comprehensive claim, but is cautious about identifying specific locations where the link between designs and clan membership has been noted (1980:149). Actually, both authors are asserting something that has not been fully investigated. Maxwell's own information comes from mainland East Flores, and even if we add Vatter's and my own ethnographic reports, there is no mention of clan patterns for Adonara. My own report only regards Lamalera, and the evidence is not as firm as she implies (Ruth Barnes 1989a:74-76).

23. Not all lineages in Lamalera own a *patolu*, and some probably never did.

24. When making this value judgement, I am directly referring to comments made by women on Lembata.

25. Vatter collected several Lamalera textiles elsewhere on the island.

26. Of course it is possible that there are other, historical or symbolic reasons for the *belapit* process. I only refer here to how the ikat weavers themselves speak about their work.

CHAPTER 9

Research in northeastern Manggarai was conducted between 1983-1985 under the auspices of the Indonesia Institute of Sciences and the sponsorship of Nusa Cendana University in Kupang. The research was funded by a Social Science Research Council Fellowship and a National Science Foundation Grant. My gratitude is extended to all of these institutions. I also want to thank Father Stanislaus Mucek S.V.D., who was the missionary priest in Rembong at the time of my research, and provided me with much information about the changes that have taken place there. Thanks also to my "elder sister" Kristina Tia, who wove for me a traditional Rembong cloth and explained the process by which it was made; her husband Adol Anggur, who explained to me the analogies between weaving and harvesting; and Stanis Dasing, a Rembong school teacher who continues to help me gather information about Rembong beliefs and practices.

1. In central and western Manggarai *rona* is the word for male; thus *anak rona* is the term used there.

2. This mythology is also known in Riung, across the border in Ngada Regency (Arndt 1935). I do not know if the Riung people have ideas about weaving that are similar to those found on the Manggarai side.

3. Intercourse with the elder brother's wife while he lives is considered incestuous. In many cases there is no distinction made in Manggarai between incest and adultery, both being referred to as *jurak* (*zurak* in Rembong). Both are regarded as dangerous to the community and are finable offenses.

4. It is considered improper to partake of the meat of one's own sacrificial animal in sacrifices that are meant to enhance the prestige of the individual. This includes sacrifices performed at marriage rituals, which mark stages in the journey through life. Meat from such sacrifices should be given to one's affines.

5. During the period of my fieldwork, in Rembong an average family harvest was 50-100 bundles of maize, and about 30-50 *blek* of unhulled dry-field rice (a bundle is 20 or 30 ears of maize, depending on the village; a *blek* is about 15 kg. of rice). In southern Biting, a nearby non-weaving area, families often harvested as many as 200 bundles of maize and 50-100 *blek* of dry-field rice. In Rajong, where most rice is grown in irrigated terraces rather than dry fields, the harvest tends to be counted in tons. The Rajong eat only rice, saving their maize to trade with their Rembong neighbors. Most Rembong villages are located a long way from land that is suitable for wet-rice, perpetuating their cursed condition.

6. See Ruth Barnes (1989a:121) regarding Sumba and Lembata, and Ruth Barnes (1987:20-21) regarding eastern Flores.

7. However, the two types of exchange are not completely parallel in all respects. Although the Rajong receive raw foods from the Rembong at their new year's feast, they also accept "cooked" Rembong textiles in barter for their surplus food.

8. They may, of course, give away cloths they have received themselves in exchange with others.

9. For details on marriage rituals among the Rembong see Erb (1991).

10. In at least one Rembong village, however, weaving is prohibited in the fields for fear that rats and wild pigs will ravage the crops.

11. This is explicitly stated for rice and other food plants; see Erb (in press).

12. Clearly there are practical aspects to these prohibitions, as grease or acid from sour fruits would interfere with the absorption of the alkaline

solution needed for indigo dyeing, and soap would inhibit the fermentation (see CHAPTER 3).

13. Except for the thread used for supplementary-weft motifs, the weft thread is bought without color and dyed by the weavers.

14. Recent communication with friends in Rembong disclosed that my "elder sister," who wove the cloth in FIGURE 9-6, has given up spinning and dyeing her own thread. Apparently this has become a trend in the more modernized villages near the district administrative center in the past 2-3 years.

CHAPTER 10

Postdoctoral research in 1987-88 and 1990-91 was supported by the Canton of Zurich, conducted under the auspices of the Indonesian Institute of Sciences, and sponsored by University of Indonesia, Jakarta, and Nusa Cendana University, Kupang. Most data are based on the experience of Nggela's weavers, which they generously imparted to me. The historical data are mainly inferences from oral history. Genealogies of Nggela descent groups were kindly provided by the *adat* leaders laki Meba, laki Leroux, Village Headman Pius N. Sare, Laki Suki and Laki Nggomba. I am also indebted to Bapak Frans Dale for information on the history and culture of Nggela society.

1. Western scholars who have written about Lio textiles have relied mainly on cloths in museum collections or short visits to weaving villages. See Watters (1977), Maxwell (1980), and Warming and Gaworski (1981).

2. This contrasts with the more egalitarian *adat* community of Wolofeo in the eastern Lio region where, according to Prior (1988:90), clan membership is rather irrelevant.

3. According to Watters (1977:87), the Lio region was long ago divided among three sons of a king, with each area assuming a monopoly over the production of certain goods. I was able to confirm the monopoly of weaving (in Nggela, Wolojita and Mbuli) and of pottery (in Lisé), but the region specializing in the plaiting of mats and baskets could not be clearly identified. Nggela people get their mats from adjacent villages to the west and do some basket plaiting themselves. The story of the three sons of the king is probably a myth. The five autonomous Lio *adat* districts (Nggela, Wolojita, Mbuli, Lise, and Nduri) were united by the Dutch colonial administration only in 1914. However, inter-community agreements (*tura jaji*) may have been contracted between the leaders of the *adat* districts before 1914.

4. Although not all cloths are produced any more, the present tense will be used for this discussion.

5. *Luka* is a generic terms for men's cloths, covering a number of different types of shoulder cloths and sarongs.

6. The Nggela *luka mité* and *lesu* are identical to the *luka* and *lesu* discussed in CHAPTER 6 and illustrated in FIGURE 1-7. The *luka bara lombo* is the Nggela version of the tapestry-woven shoulder cloth illustrated in FIGURE 6-34.

7. The only cloths allegedly borrowed are *lawo népa ndu'a, lawo jinga runu, lawo ranka, lawo lima désa* and *lawo gamba*. The *lawo mangga lo'o, lawo wenda jara,* and *lawo barai* all have a plain black band in border panels, indicating that they originated in Ende.

8. *Songgé sindé,* for example, means "copy of a *sindé* cloth." *Sindé* is the Lio name for patola (Bühler 1959:2).

9. Today it is difficult to get information about the traditional ranking system, which was formally abolished with independence and remains a sensitive subject. Nevertheless it is still influential in certain ways, for example in connection with marriage practices (cf. Ndate 1988:14).

10. Other interesting cases of cloths securing rank systems, as in Melanesia and Polynesia, are described by Weiner (1989).

11. The writings of Petu and his former student Aloysius Ndate (now also a priest) from Nggela present a particularly interesting perspective. As native experts on Lio culture, they represent a partially emic (insiders') point of view. Both stress the magic and religious meaning of ikat weaving in addition to its sociocultural values.

12. Maxwell (1990:127-128) confirms that anthropomorphic motifs on Southeast Asian textiles may be highly schematic, so that their meaning is not obvious and may not be known to today's weavers.

13. Originally a pattern of *lawo népa nua* seems to have been taboo as well. With *lawo redu*, new types of motifs were introduced, e.g. *gha'i mité,* which is the broadest pattern in the borders. This motif appears in similar form on *lawo mogha*.

14. The horse motif is found on textiles throughout Southeast Asia (Maxwell 1990:107). It is not clear when horses first came to this region.

15. In 1987 for example there was a small weaving project in Nggela organized by the governmental women's group PKK. Weavers could get thread and dyestuff to produce two *luka sémba,* one for the PKK and one for themselves. Since the 1970s the regional government has provided subsidies for synthetic dyestuffs.

16. *Gamba* is a cognate of the Indonesian term *gambar,* (picture), referring to the pictorial nature of these sarongs with overall motifs. An interesting version is illustrated in FIGURE 2-24. The *lawo gamba* may be the only type of sarong with overall motifs, because in Nggela, unlike Ndona, such sarongs seem to have been produced only since the 1970s. With the strong preference for small, traditional geometric and stylized figurative motifs, and with several types of prestigious sarongs extant, there might have been hardly any need for the Nggela weavers to copy this type on a large scale.

17. This knowledge seems to have been lost a long time ago, as weavers have access to knowledge that reaches back to the last century through information passed on by the grandmothers of today's oldest women. In general, informants seldom give information on the symbolic aspects of their cloths (Gittinger 1979:43, Schneider 1987:414). In Indonesia this may be because religious knowledge is often the special domain of the male *adat* leaders.

18. The more cloths are produced, the more are absorbed by the gift-giving system and cannot be sold directly for income. This strategy is not easily understood from a Western point of view and may be overlooked in the praxis of governmental and non-governmental income generation projects.

15. In Rembong I was told that women in other Manggarai areas may then stitch their own flower designs on the indigo-dyed background. This statement is difficult to evaluate, since the supplementary-weft motifs that ordinarily decorate Manggarai cloth must be woven in place at the time the cloth is made. Once the cloth is completed, motifs could only be added by embroidery, a technique that is known to have been used in Manggarai for decorating men's jackets but has not been documented for sarongs.

CHAPTER 11

The research on which this paper is based was conducted under the auspices of the Indonesian Institute of Sciences (LIPI) in Jakarta and with the sponsorship of the University of Nusa Cendana (UNDANA) in Kupang. My fieldwork in Flores, 1986-88, was financed by the Australian National University. I am grateful to these institutions for their support. Here I also express my thanks to the women whose work I observed in Léwoléma, especially those gathered around Sabu Aran in Rian Kotek, Muda Sogen and Ubu Hokor in Léwotala.

CHAPTER 12

Research on Palu'é has been conducted since 1979 under the auspices of the Indonesian Institute of Sciences (LIPI) and with the co-sponsorship of Universitas Nusa Cendana, Kupang. The most recent fieldstay (February-March 1993) was sponsored by the Department of Anthropology, Research School of Pacific Studies, The Australian National University, and funded by the Wenner-Gren Foundation for Anthropological Research. I am grateful to all these institutions for their support.

1. Rain-water tanks increasingly provide water during the months of the rainy season.

2. In recent years some Lio domains on the Flores north coast are said to have lifted this ancestral prohibition by sacrificing water buffalo to their Supreme Being and apparently some women from Palu'é who are married to Lio men have taken to teaching the local women the art of textile production.

3. A similar situation is reported from the domain of Laboya on the eastern Indonesian island of Sumba (Geirnaert 1992). Even though other ethnographers do not specifically mention it, I suspect that it is quite common in eastern Indonesia for men rather than women to be the ones capable of talking about textile symbolism.

4. A shortage of cotton during the Japanese occupation (1943-45) prompted a brief revival of the production of the ancestral bark cloth. These cloths were painted with the same motivs featuring on Palu'é ikat cloths. Unfortunately no examples have survived to this day, bark being very vulnerable to decay in humid climates.

5. The integration of later-settling groups did not follow the same pattern established by the providers of technology. New settlers did not receive a position quasi equal to that of the first settling group nor were they immediately granted ceremonial offices.

6. Depending on the availiability of goods, the installments can be tightly spaced and payments can be completed within a matter of a few years. In some domains, however, bridewealth is often still paid by the offspring of an alliance well after the death of their mother.

7. In everyday life, reciprocity is often delayed, thereby causing a temporary inequality between the giver and the receiver, a situation which is reversed as soon as a counterprestation has been made. In ritual context, however, reciprocity is mostly immediate.

8. In fact it is believed that the life of the dead in many ways mirrors that of the living and that inside the volcano the ancestors practice ceremonial exchange and conduct the ceremonial cycles of the domains in the same way their descendants do in the realm of the living.

9. For example, the concept of the Palu'é Supreme Being is expressed in ritual speech by the couplet "Sun-Moon // Stone-Earth." Here the sun and the moon are classified as male because they are located above the stone and the earth which are classified as female. However, as separate classificatory pairs the sun is viewed as male and the moon as female and the stone is considered to be conceptually male in opposition to the earth which in this context is female.

10. Libations are applied to specific spots at the ceremonial center to cool down the heat generated by transgressions of ancestral law; women coming out of labor are washed with coconut juice to cool down the heat generated by giving birth, as are widows and widowers to cool down the heat caused by loosing a spouse.

11. Sounding boards on Palu'é backstrap looms are a relatively recent addition borrowed from the Flores mainland.

12. In some of the "domains of pig blood" production of traditional cloth has virtually come to a halt. Furthermore, whatever old cloths that were kept in storage to be used on ceremonial occasions have in recent years been bought up by Western dealers based in Bali. Often these dealers would come to the island during the annual period of seasonal famine (*wula raré*), a time when the men are still on seasonal migration and when all provis-ions have been consumed and the new harvest has not been brought in yet. In such a situation the need for cash to pay for medical costs or for schooling forced many women to sell cloths that had taken them up to a year to produce for a price of less than $10 U.S. (1986).

13. The *morinda* tree is not indigenous to Palu'é. Palu'é men purchase this dye on their women's behalf in neighboring Lio, on Flores.

14. The women of Palu'é claim that the type of indigo existing on the island provides a darker color than indigo found on Flores. Its leaves are considerably smaller than those of Flores indigo.

15. The terminology applied to these bands is very much the same as that found on the Sikkanese mainland. However, the meaning ascribed to the bands is very specific to Palu'é conceptions about marriage and alliance.

16. In a similar vein, a candlenut is usually placed inside a drum together with a small model bow before it is covered with skin. This is done, as it is put, in order for the voice of the drum to be clear (like a throat treated with candlenut) and to be heard across large distances (like the flight of an arrow).

Orthography

The languages of Flores are primarily oral traditions. In many cases written sources are limited to word lists or dictionaries compiled long ago by Europeans. These vary greatly in the orthography employed as well as in their general usefulness. On Flores today, in the rare cases when terms from local languages are written, they are usually rendered in the standard spelling of modern Indonesian. Anthropologists and linguists have found this approach inadequate and have devised various systems to account for glottal stops, differences in /e/ vowel sounds, unusual consonants such as the implosive bilabial /bh/, and other irregularities that do not exist in written Indonesian.

Because there is so much variation and so little consistent data, it has been impossible to develop for this book a single standardized system of orthography covering all of the languages and dialects involved. Each contributing author has developed the most appropriate system based on fieldnotes and on the available written sources, as follows:

MANGGARAI

Verheijen's Manggarai-Indonesian dictionary (1967) is the most complete and accurate work on any of Flores' languages, requiring only minor adjustments to comply with current Indonesian spelling. It was used as the source for standard (central) Manggarai and contains additional information useful for dialect terms used in Congkar. Todo dialect terms were taken primarily from Hamilton's fieldnotes.

REMBONG / RIUNG / MBAY

Verheijen (1977) is the standard reference used by Erb for Rembong. There are no specific sources at all for the closely related dialects of Riung and Mbay, so the terms used for these areas are based on Hamilton's fieldnotes, adapted to the general practices used by Verheijen (1967 and 1977).

NGADHA

The most complete reference for this language (Arndt 1961) is highly idiosyncratic and a more recent work by Djawanai (1983) provides a better, though incomplete, model. Terms in the Bajawa-area dialect were based on Hamilton's fieldnotes and cross-referenced with the literature and through consultation with other researchers. Lopijo/ Teni terms are based entirely on fieldnotes.

The three main sources for this group of languages all have substantial deficiencies. Suchtelen (1921) contains a list of Endenese and Lio terms with single-word glosses; Arndt's Lio-German dictionary (1933) is useful but the orthography is outmoded; Sawardo (1987) uses only Indonesian orthography. The spellings adopted are primarily those developed by Hamilton and de Jong based on fieldnotes and the literature. There are no extensive sources for Nagé, so these terms are drawn entirely on Hamilton's fieldnotes, based on the orthographic system established for Endenese and Lio.

SIKKANESE

There are no comprehensive published dictionaries of Sikkanese, although various manuscript versions have been compiled. The terms used in this chapter are drawn entirely from Lewis's own work, as he has worked extensively with both the language of Sikka Natar and the Tana 'Ai dialect. Some contrasting transliterations can be found in the works of Petu (1992a), a native speaker.

LAMAHOLOT

Barnes has employed standardized Lamaholot terms following Keraf (1978), fully recognizing that this does not account for the high degree dialectical variation found in this region, which remains incompletely studied. Where Graham's terms differ from Barnes', dialectical variation is the cause.

Place names present some special problems. On Flores they are normally written using standard Indonesian spelling. To add diacritical marks would offer guidance for English-speaking readers, but would render some names unrecognizable to Indonesians and unfindable on maps. The solution adopted here is to give place names as they would ordinarily appear in Indonesia. Exceptions have been made in a few cases (such as Léwoléma and Palu'é) for the sake of consistency where the author has already established alternative spellings in previous writings.

A similar problem occurs with personal names, which, when written at all, are not normally spelled with diacritical marks. This may lead to pronunciation difficulties (for example, the name of the women to whom this book is dedicated might more instructively be rendered Theresia Su'é), but in the end it was deemed best not to tamper with what would most likely be used on Flores.

Looms

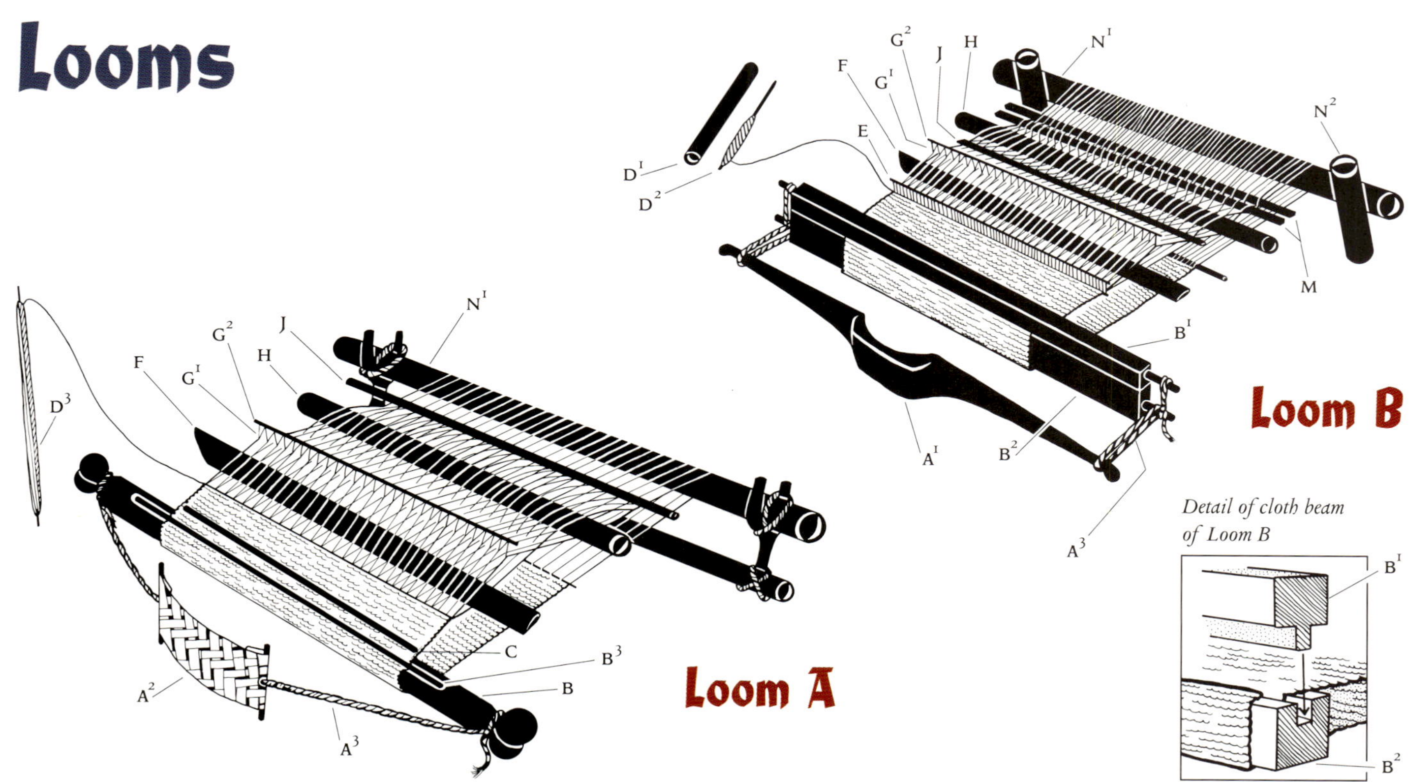

LOOM PARTS		COMMUNITIES:			
		CIBAL	RIUNG	MBAY	
A. BACK SUPPORT	A^1. YOKE	PARKINSU	LIHUR	PARA KINCU	
	A^2. PLAITED PANEL	X	X	X	
	A^3. TIE ROPE	WASEK TENTANG	WASÉ LIHUR	WASEK TENTANG	
B. CLOTH BEAM		PESA	PESA	PESA	
	B^1. "CHILD" OR "MALE" PART	X	X	X	
	B^2. "MOTHER" OR "FEMALE" PART	X	X	X	
	B^3. INSERT STICK	PA TEKOL	PETEKO	X	
C. TEMPLE		?	(TUKÉ)	(TUBHO)	
D. SHUTTLE	D^1. TUBE SHUTTLE	KEROPONG	KEROPONG	KEROPONG	
	D^2. BOBBIN	MONGKO KOSOR	KELIRIK	MUNGKU KÉLER	
	D^3. STICK SHUTTLE	X	X	X	
E. REED		ZANGKA	JANGKA	JANGKA	
F. BEATER (SWORD)		BAMPA	BAMPANG	LAMPENG	
G. HEDDLE	G^1. STRING HEDDLE	AKOT	HUM	GUGU	
	G^2. HEDDLE ROD	MONGKO AKOT	-	MONGKO GUGU	
H. SHED ROLL		BELANG	HELUNG	BHELANG	
J. SHED STICK		MONGKO REMPÉ	BILA	MUNGKU LEMPER	
K. SUPPLEMENTARY HEDDLES		MONGKO AKOT	HUM	GUGU DHOWIK	
M. LEASE STICKS		PASIKOK	LEKA	LEKA	
N. WARP BEAM	N^1. BEAM	X	X	X	
	N^2. POSTS	X	X	X	
	N^3. PLANK	PÉMALUK	TAMPANG	BHALUK	
	N^4. PLANK SUPPORTS	GHAZU PANGA	PASÉ	GHAJU PANGA	

LOOM C

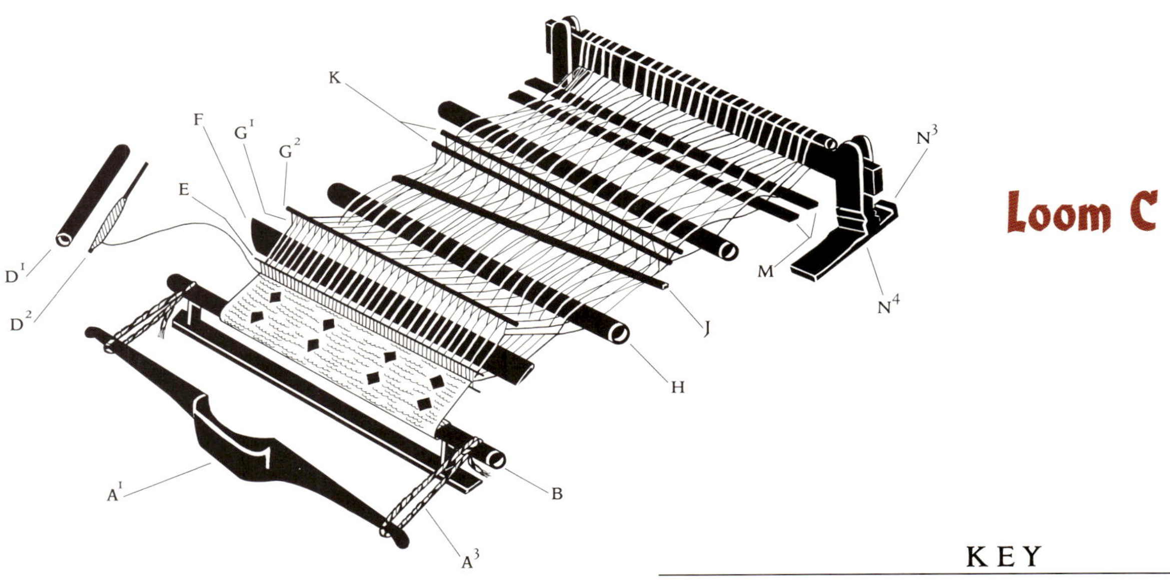

KEY

x	not usually present
( )	optional
-	no special term
?	uncertain

More than one type of loom may be used in a single community. Additional parts such as foot rests, beater rests, and pattern sticks not shown.

Drawing and terms for Loom A adapted from Barnes 1989:35; drawings of Loom B and Loom C adapted from Gittinger 1979:231.

BAJAWA	BOAWAE	ENDE	ONELAKO	WOLOJITA	LÉLA	LAMALERA
X	LOGO KUJU	KABHÉ	KABHÉ	KABHÉ	PINÉ	X
TAPI	LOGO ZÉ'A	X	X	X	X	SELIGU
AZÉ TAPI	TALI LOGO	TAZI KABHÉ	TALI KABHÉ	AJÉ KABHÉ	TALI LORUNG	SELIGU TALI
WEGA	ATI	KONGGO	KOGO	KOGO	A'I LORUNG	TENANÉ
?	ATI ANA	-	KOGO KAKI	KOGO HAKI	A'I LORUNG 'ANAK	X
?	ATI INÉ	-	KOGO FAI	KOGO FAI	A'I LORUNG 'INANG	X
?	X	X	X	X	X	NAPI
(WITU)	(TUBO)	(TUBHO)	(TIBHO)	(TUBO)	(TUBUNG)	(NUGI)
X	OKA NIKU	BHOKU	BHOKU	BHOKU SEDA	LEGU	X
X	ANA NIKU	NIKU	NIKU	NIKU	'OJANG	X
GHOA	X	X	X	X	X	FANI
X	X	(KÉKÉ)	(KÉKÉ)	(KÉKÉ)	(JANKA)	X
BHIRA	HAMÉ	FI'A	FI'A	NGEWI	PATI	HURI
GHUNA	GUGU	GURU	GURU	GURU	HAWÉNG	GURU
KUKU	KUKU	KUKU GURU	KUKU GURU	KUKU TÉKI	BOLENG 'ANAK	GURU KAJO
LONGA	LONGA	MBEZA	BELA	BELLA	BOLENG 'INANG	FULO BÉLA
WITU	HEPA	KUKU RETTÉ	KUKU RETÉ	KUKU RETÉ	POLET	TENIÉ
X	X	X	X	X	X	X
X	HEPA	SIPÉ	SIPÉ	PEPA	NALAR	X
BHODA	MADA	OZOZI	ELELI	LANI KOLO	A'I PLAPAR	POLA
REDHA	POSA	OZO SENDA	ÉLÉ SEDA	KUKU TOKA	-	-
X	X	X	X	X	X	X
X	X	X	X	X	X	X

References Cited

Alderwerelt, J. de Roo van
1906 "Historische Aanteekeningen over Soemba (Residentie Timor en Onderhoorigheden)." *Tijdschrift van het Bataviaasch Genootschap van Kunsten en Wetenschappen* 48:185-316.

Aoki, Eriko
1988 "The Case of the Purloined Statues: the Power of Words Among the Lionese." In *To Speak in Pairs: Essays on the Ritual Languages of Eastern Indonesia*, edited by James. J. Fox, pp. 202-227. Cambridge: Cambridge University Press.

Andaya, Leonard Y.
1981 *The Heritage of Arung Palakka: A History of South Sulawesi (Celebes) in the Seventeenth Century.* Verhandelingen van het Koninklijk Instituut voor Taal-, Land- en Volkenkunde, No. 91. The Hague: Martinus Nijhoff.

Aragon, Lorraine V.
1990 "Barkcloth Production in Central Sulawesi." *Expedition* 32,1:33-48.

Arndt, Paul
1929-31 "Die Religion der N̊ad,a."
   Anthropos 24:817-861; 26:353-405, 697-739.
1932 "Die Megalithenkultur der N̊ad,a (Flores)." *Anthropos* 27:11-63.
1933 *Li'onesisch-Deutsches Worterbuch.* Ende: Arnoldus.
1935 "Aus Mythologie und Religion der Riunger."
   Tijdschrift voor Indische Taal-, Land- en Volkenkunde 75:333-393.
1936-37 "Déva, das Höchste Wesen der Ngadha."
   Anthropos 31:894-909; 32:195-209, 347-377.
1938 "Demon und Padzi, Die Feindlichen Bruder des Solor-Archipels." *Anthropos* 33:1-38.
1944 "Der Kult der Lionesen (Mittel-Flores)."
   Annali Lateranensi 8:155-182.
1959 "Totenfeiern und Bräuche der Ngadha." *Anthropos* 54:68-98.
1961 *Wörterbuch der Ngadhasprache.*
   Studia Instituti Anthropos, Vol. 15. Fribourg: Posieux.
1963 "Die Wirtschaftlichen Verhältnisse der Ngadha."
   Annali del Pontificio Museo Missionario Etnologico 27:13-191.

Barbier, J. P., and D. Newton, editors
1988 *Islands and Ancestors: Indigenous Styles of Southeast Asia.* New York: Metropolitan Museum of Art.

Barnes, Robert H.
1974a *Kédang: a Study of the Collective Thought of an Eastern Indonesian People.* Oxford: Clarendon Press.
1974b "Lamalera: A Whaling Village in Eastern Indonesia." *Indonesia* 17:137-159.
1977 "Alliance and Categories in Wailolong, East Flores." *Sociologus* 27:133-157.
1979 "Concordance, Structure, and Variation: Considerations of Alliance in Kédang. In *The Flow of Life: Essays on Eastern Indonesia*, edited by James J. Fox, pp. 68-97. Cambridge: Harvard University Press.
1982 "The Majapahit Dependency of Galiyao." *Bijdragen tot de Taal-, Land- en Volkenkunde* 138:407-412.

Barnes, Robert H. and Ruth Barnes
1989 "Barter and Money in an Indonesian Village Econony." *Man* (New Series) 24:399-418.

Barnes, Ruth
1987 "Weaving and Non-weaving Among the Lamaholot." *Indonesia Circle* 42:16-32.
1989a *The Ikat Textiles of Lamalera: A Study of an Eastern Indonesian Weaving Tradition.* Leiden: E. J. Brill.
1989b "The Bridewealth Cloth of Lamalera, Lembata." In *To Speak With Cloth: Studies in Indonesian Textiles,* edited by Mattiebelle Gittinger, pp. 43-55. Los Angeles: UCLA Museum of Cultural History.
1991a "Patola in Southern Lembata." In *Indonesian Textiles: Symposium 1985*, edited by Gisela Völger and Karin v. Welck, pp. 11-17. Cologne: Ethnologica.
1991b "'Without Cloth We Cannot Marry:' The Textiles of the Lamaholot in Transition." *Journal of Museum Ethnography* 2:95-112.
1993 "Change and Tradition in Lamaholot Textiles: The Ernst-Vatter-Collection in Historical Perspective." In *Weaving Patterns of Life: Indonesian Textiles Symposium 1991*, edited by M.-L. Nabholz-Kartaschoff, R. Barnes, and D. Stuart-Fox. Basel: Museum of Ethnography.

Beker, G.
1913 "Het Oogst- en Offerfest bij den Nagestam te Boa Wai (Midden-Flores)." *Bijdragen tot de Taal-, Land- en Volkenkunde* 67:623-627.

Bellwood, Peter
1985 *The Pre-History of the Indo-Malaysian Archipelago.* Sydney: Academic Press.

Bekkum, W. van
1944 "Warloka - Todo - Pongkor: Een Brok Geschiedenis van Manggarai (West-Flores)." *Cultureel Indië* 6:144-152.
1946a "Geschiedenis van Manggarai (West-Flores)." *Cultureel Indië* 8:65-75.
1946b "De Machtsverschuivingen in Manggarai (West-Flores), Tengevolge van de Goaneesche en Bimaneesch Invloeden." *Cultureel Indië* 8:122-130.
1946c *Manggaraische Kunst.* Koninklijke Vereeniging Indisch Instituut te Amsterdam, Mededeeling No. 68. Leiden: E. J. Brill.

Bezemer, T. J.
1931 *Indonesische Kunstnijverheid.* 's-Gravenhage: Ten Hagen's Drukkerij en Uitgeversmaatschappij.

Biermann, P. B. M.
1924 "Die Alte Dominikanermission auf den Solorinseln [and] Nachwort." *Zeitschrift für Missionswissenschaft* 14:12-48, 269-273.

Bloch, Maurice, and Jonathan Parry, editors
1982 *Death and the Regeneration of Life.* Cambridge: Cambridge University Press.

Blust, Robert
1976   "Austronesian Cultural History: Some Linguistic Inferences and Their Relationship to the Archaeological Record." *World Archaeology* 8,1:19-43.

Boxer, C. R.
1947   *The Topasses of Timor.* Mededelingen van het Koninklijke Vereeniging Indisch Instituut te Amsterdam, vol. 73, no. 24.
1968   *Fidalgos in the Far East.* Hong Kong: Oxford University [reprint of 1948 second revised edition, The Hague: Martinus Nijhoff].

Brummend, J.F.G.
1853   "De Expedities van de Stoomboten Hekla en Semarang in 1851 Tegen de Zeerovers." *Indiana* 1: 67-156.

Bühler, Alfred
1941   "Turkey Red Dyeing in South and South East Asia." *Ciba Review* 39:1423-1426.
1942   "The Origin and Extent of the Ikat Technique." *Ciba Review* 44:1604-1611.
1959   "Patola Influences in Southeast Asia." *Journal of Indian Textile History* 4:1-43.

Bühler, Alfred and Eberhard Fischer
1979   *The Patola of Gujerat: Double Ikat in India,* 2 Vols. Basel: Krebs.

Bühler, Alfred, Urs Ramseyer, and Nicole Ramseyer-Gygi
1975   *Patola und Geringsing.* Basel: Museum für Völkerkunde.

Burkill, I. H.
1935   *A Dictionary of the Economic Products of the Malay Peninsula.* London: Crown Agents for the Colonies.

Coolhaas, W. P.
1942   "Bijdrage tot de Kennis van het Manggaraische Volk (West Flores)." *Tijdschrift van het Nederlandsch Aardrijkskundig Genootschap* 59:148-177, 328-360.

Coolhaas, W. P., editor
1976   *Generale Missiven van Gouverneurs-generaal en Raden aan Heren XVII der Verenigde Oostindische Compagnie.* Deel VI: 1698-1713. s'Gravenhage: Martinus Nijhoff.

Cornelissen, P. F. J. J.
1929   "Totemism op Flores en Timor." *Nederlandsch Indië Oud & Nieuw,* 13 (11):331-344.

Cortesão, Armando, editor
1944   *The Suma Oriental of Tomé Pires and the Book of Francisco Rodrigues.* London: The Hakluyt Society.

Departemen Pendidikan dan Kebudayaan
1984   *Upacara Tradisional Daerah Nusa Tenggara Timur.* Jakarta: Proyek Inventarisasi dan Dokumentasi Kebudayaan Daerah.

Dietrich, Stefan
1983   "Flores in the Nineteenth Century: Aspects of Dutch Colonialism on a Non-Profitable Island." *Indonesia Circle* 31:39-58.
1984   "A Note on Galiyao and the Early History of the Solor-Alor Islands." *Bijdragen tot de Taal-, Land- en Volkenkunde* 140:317-326.
1989   *Kolonialismus und Mission auf Flores (ca. 1900-1942).* Hohenschäftlarn: Renner.
ms   "Rajas and Kompeni: Dutch-Indonesian Relations in the Timor-Archipelago During the Nineteenth Century." Unpublished manuscript.

Djawanai, Stephanus
1983   *Ngadha Text Tradition: The Collective Mind of the Ngadha People, Flores.* Pacific Linguistics Series D, No. 55. Canberra: Australian national University.

Dooley, L. M.
1931   "Ria Rago." *The Christian Family and Our Missions,* vol. 26.

DuBois, Cora
1944   *The People of Alor.* Minneapolis: University of Minnesota.

Elbert, Johannes
1912   *Die Sunda-Expedition des Vereins für Geographie und Statistik zu Frankfurt am Main,* vol. 2. Frankfurt: Hermann Minjon.

Elmberg, John-Erik
1968   *Balance and Circulation: Aspects of Tradition and Change among the Mejprat of Irian Barat.* Stockholm: Etnografiska Museet.

Erb, Maribeth
1987   "When Rocks Were Young and Earth Was Soft: Ritual and Mythology in Northeastern Manggarai." Doctoral dissertation, State University of New York at Stony Brook.
1991   "Stealing Woman and Living in Sin: Adaptation and Conflict in Morals and Customary Law in Rembong, Northeastern Manggarai." *Anthropos* 86:59-73.
in press "Cuddling the Rice: Myth and Ritual in the Agricultural Year of the Rembong of Northeastern Manggarai, Indonesia." In *Contributions to Southeast Asian Ethnography,* Vol. 10.

Fatta, Muhamad
1982   "Beberapa Masalah Perkawinan Umat Islam Dalam Hubungan Pelaksanaan Undang-Undang Nomor 1 Tahun 1974 (Undang-Undang Perkawinan) di Kabupaten Daerah Tingkat II Ende." Thesis, Institut Ilmu Pemerintahan, Jakarta.

Fischer, H. W. and W. H. Rassers
1924   *Katalog des Ethnographischen Reichsmuseums. Bd. XVII, Die Oestlichen Kleinen Sunda-Inseln.* Leiden: E. J. Brill.

Fischer, Joseph
1979   *Threads of Tradition: Textiles of Indonesia and Sarawak.* Berkeley: University of California.

Forth, Gregory
  1989a "Witches, Animals, and Wind: Eastern Indonesian Variations on the 'Thunder Complex'." *Anthropos* 84:89-106.
  1989b "The Pa Sése Festival of the Nage of Bo'a Wae (Central Flores)." *Bijdragen tot de Taal-, Land- en Volkenkunde* 145:502-519.

Fox, James J.
  1977 "Roti, Ndao and Savu." In *Textile Traditions of Indonesia*, edited by Mary Hunt Kahlenberg, pp. 97-104. Los Angeles: Los Angeles County Museum of Art.
  1980a "Comments" (following the article "Early Austronesian Social Organization: the Evidence of Language," by Robert Blust). *Current Anthropology* 21,2:234.
  1980b "Figure Shark and Pattern Crocodile: The Foundations of the Textile Traditions of Roti and Ndao." In *Indonesian Textiles*, Irene Emery Roundtable on Museum Textiles 1979 Proceedings, edited by Mattiebelle Gittinger, pp. 39-55. Washington: The Textile Museum.

Fox, James J., editor
  1980c *The Flow of Life: Essays on Eastern Indonesia.* Cambridge: Harvard University Press.

Frassen, C. F. van
  1976 "Drie Plaatsnamen uit Oost-Indonesië in de Nagara-Kertagama: Galiyao, Muar en Wwanin en de Vroegere Handelsgeschiedenis van Ambonse Eilanden." *Bijdragen tot de Taal-, Land- en Volkenkunde* 132:293-305.

Fryxell, Paul A.
  1979 *The Natural History of the Cotton Tribe (Malvaceae, Tribe Gossypieae).* College Station: Texas A&M University Press.

Geirnaert-Martin, Danielle C.
  1991 "The Snake's Skin: Traditional Ikat in Kodi." In *Indonesian Textiles: Symposium 1985*, edited by Gisela Völger and Karin v. Welck, pp. 34-42. Cologne: Ethnologica.
  1992 *The Woven Land of Laboya: Socio-cosmic Ideas and Values in West-Sumba, Eastern Indonesia.* Leiden: CNWS.

Gittinger, Mattiebelle
  1979 *Splendid Symbols: Textiles and Tradition in Indonesia.* Washington: The Textile Museum.
  1982 *Master Dyers to the World: Technique and Trade in Early Indian Dyed Cotton Textiles.* Washington: The Textile Museum.

Gittinger, Mattiebelle, editor
  1980 *Indonesian Textiles.* Irene Emery Roundtable on Museum Textiles 1979 Proceedings. Washington: The Textile Museum.
  1989 *To Speak With Cloth: Studies in Indonesian Textile.* Los Angeles: UCLA Museum of Cultural History.

Gordon, John Lambert
  1975 "The Manggarai: Economic and Social Transformation in an Eastern Indonesian Society." Doctoral dissertation, Harvard University.

  1980 "The Marriage Nexus Among the Manggarai of West Flores." In *The Flow of Life: Essays on Eastern Indonesia*, edited by James J. Fox, pp. 48-67. Cambridge: Harvard University Press.

Graham, Penelope
  1991 "To Follow the Blood: The Path of Life in a Domain of Eastern Flores, Indonesia." Doctoral dissertation, Australian National University.

Hain, Robert Cameron
  1978 "Ende: The Structure of Endenese Society - A Handbook for Ethnographic Fieldwork." Bachelor's thesis, Oxford University.

Hamilton, Roy W.
  1989 "Textiles of the Ende-Lio Region of Flores Island, Indonesia." Master's thesis, University of Washington.
  1990 "Local Textile Trading Systems in Indonesia: An Example from Flores Island." In *Textiles in Trade*, Proceedings of the Textile Society of America Biennial Symposium.
  1993 "Textile Change in 20th Century Ndona, Flores." In *Weaving Patterns of Life: Indonesian Textiles Symposium 1991*, edited by Nabholz-Kartaschoff, Barnes, and Stuart-Fox. Basel: Museum of Ethnography.

Hauser-Schäublin, B., M.-L. Nabholz-Kartaschoff, and U. Ramseyer
  1991 *Textiles in Bali.* Berkeley: Periplus Editions.

Heerkens, P.
  1943 "Noengoenangé van Wonga Wéa." *Cultureel Indië* 5:1-24.
  1944 "Van Katoen tot Ikat-doek: Studie over het Ikatten onder de Sikaneezen op Flores." *Cultureel Indië* 6:1-19.

Heine-Geldern, Robert
  1937 "L'art Prébouddhique de la Chine et de l'Asie du Sud-est et Son Influence en Océanie." *Revue des Arts Asiatiques*, XI:177-206.
  1966 "Some Tribal Art Styles of Southeast Asia." In *The Many Faces of Primitive Art*, edited by Douglas Fraser, pp. 165-221. Englewood Cliffs: Prentice-Hall.

Hens, A. M.
  1916 "Memorie van Overgave van de Afdeeling Flores." Le Roux Collection, Algemeen Rijksarchief, The Hague.

Hitchcock, Michael John
  1983 "Technology and Society in Bima, Sumbawa, With Special Reference to House Building and Textile Manufacture." Doctoral dissertation, Oxford University.
  1985 *Indonesian Textile Techniques.* Aylesbury: Shire Publications.

Hoskins, Janet
  1989 "Why Do Ladies Sing the Blues? Indigo Dyeing, Cloth Production, and Gender Symbolism in Kodi." In *Cloth and Human Experience*, edited by Annette B. Weiner and Jane Schneider, pp. 141-173. Washington: Smithsonian Institution Press.

Howell, Signe
  1989 "Of Persons and Things; Exchange and Valuables Among
    the Lio of Eastern Indonesia." *Man* 24:419-438.

Ishikawa, Teijiro
  1943 *Bertanam Kapas di Djawa.* Djakarta: Balai Poestaka.

Kahlenberg, Mary Hunt, editor
  1977 *Textile Traditions of Indonesia.*
    Los Angeles: Los Angeles County Museum of Art.

Kahn Majlis, Brigitte
  1984 *Indonesische Textilien: Wege zu Göttern und Ahnen.*
    Krefeld: Deutsches Textilmuseum.
  1991a "Supplement: New Acquisitions in Krefeld and Cologne."
    In *Indonesian Textiles: Symposium 1985*, edited by Gisela Völger
    and Karin v. Welck, pp. 233-293. Cologne: Ethnologica.
  1991b *Gewebte Botschaften: Indonesische Traditionen im Wandel /
    Woven Messages: Indonesian Textile Tradition in Course of Time.*
    Hildesheim: Roemer-Museum.

Kartiwa, Suwati
  1986 *Kain Songket Indonesia / Songket Weaving in Indonesia.*
    Jakarta: Djambatan.

Kajitani, Nobuko
  1980 "Traditional Dyes in Indonesia." In *Indonesian Textiles,*
    Irene Emery Roundtable on Museum Textiles 1979
    Proceedings, edited by Mattiebelle Gittinger, pp. 305-325.
    Washington: The Textile Museum.

Kate, H. F. C. ten
  1894 *Verslag Eener Reis in de Timorgroep en Polynesie.* Tijdschrift
    van het Koninklijk Nederlandsch Aardrijkskungdig
    Genootschap, Vol. XI.

Kennedy, Raymond
  1955 *Field Notes on Indonesia: Flores 1949-1950.*
    New Haven: Human Relations Area Files.

Keraf, Gregorius
  1978 *Morfologi Dialek Lamalera.* Ende: Arnoldus.

Kluppel, J. M.
  1873 "De Solor-eilanden." *Tijdschrift voor Indische Taal-, Land- en
    Volkenkunde* 20:378-398.

Lévi-Strauss, C.
  1969 *The Elementary Structures of Kinship.* Boston: Beacon Press.
    Translation of 1949 edition, *Les Structures Élémentaires
    de la Paranté.*

Lewis, E. D.
  1988a *People of the Source: The Social and Ceremonial Order of Tana
    Wai Brama on Flores.* Verhandelingen van het Koninklijk
    Instituut voor Taal-, Land- en Volkenkunde, No. 135.
    Dordrecht: Foris Publications.
  1988b "A Quest for the Source: The Ontogenesis of a Creation
    Myth of the Ata Tana Ai." In *To Speak in Pairs: Essays on the
    Ritual Languages of Eastern Indonesia*, edited by James. J. Fox,
    pp. 246-281. Cambridge: Cambridge University Press.
  1989 "Word and Act in the Curing Rituals of the Ata Tana 'Ai
    of Flores." *Bijdragen tot de Taal-, Land- en Volkenkunde*
    145(4):490-501.

Ling Roth, Henry
  1977 [1950] *Studies in Primitive Looms.*
    Third edition, Halifax: Bankfield Museum.

Lynden, D. W. C. van
  1851 "Bijdrage tot de Kennis van Solor, Allor, Rotti, Savoe en
    Omliggende Eilanden." *Natuurkundig Tijdschrift voor
    Nederlandsch Indië* 2:317-336, 388-414.

Mauss, Marcel
  1923/24 "Essai sur le Don."
    L'Année Sociologique (Nouveau Série) 1:30-186.

Maxwell, Robyn
  1980 "Textile and Ethnic Configurations in Flores and the
    Solor Archipelago." In *Indonesian Textiles,* Irene Emery
    Roundtable on Museum Textiles 1979 Proceedings,
    edited by Mattiebelle Gittinger, pp. 141-156.
    Washington: The Textile Museum.
  1981 "Textiles and Tusks: Some Observations on the Social
    Dimensions of Weaving in East Flores." In *Five Essays on
    the Indonesian Arts*, edited by Margaret Kartomi, pp. 43-62.
    Melbourne: Monash University.
  1983 "Ceremonial Textiles of the Ngada of Eastern Indonesia."
    Connaisance des Arts Tribaux 18.
  1985 "De Rituele Weefsels a Oost-Indonesië."
    In *Indigo: Leven in een Kleur,* Loan Oei, editor. Amsterdam:
    Stichting Indigo, Uitgeverij Fibula-Van Dishoeck.
  1990 *Textiles of Southeast Asia: Tradition, Trade and Transformation.*
    Canberra: Australian National Gallery, and Melbourne:
    Oxford University Press.

Metzner, Joachim K.
  1982 *Agriculture and Population Pressure in Sikka, Isle of Flores.*
    Development Studies Center Monograph No. 28.
    Canberra: Australian National University.

Moreland, W. H.
  1924-25 "Indian Exports of Cotton Goods in the Seventeenth
    Century." *Indian Journal of Economics* 5(3):225-245.

Nabholz-Kartaschoff, M.-L., Ruth Barnes, and David Stuart-Fox, editors
  1993 *Weaving Patterns of Life: Indonesian Textiles Symposium 1991.*
    Basel: Museum of Ethnography.

Nakagawa, Satoshi
  1988 "The Journey of the Bridegroom: Idioms of Marriage
    Among the Endenese." In *To Speak in Pairs: Essays on the
    Ritual Languages of Eastern Indonesia*, edited by James. J. Fox,
    pp. 228-245. Cambridge: Cambridge University Press.

Nawawi, Norwani Mohd.
1989 *Malaysian Songket.*
Kuala Lumpur: Kementerian Pendidikan Malaysia.

Ndate, Aloysius
1981 "Tenun Ikat Tradisional Nggela di Kecamatan Wolowaru
Kabupaten Daerah Tingkat II Ende Ditinjau dari Proses
Kerja dan Nilai Sosial Budaya." Thesis, Universitas Nusa
Cendana, Ende.
1988 "Pentingnya Upacara Tarian Tradisional Mure Pada
Masyarakat Nggela." Thesis, Sekolah Tinggi Filsafat
Katolik, Ledalero.

Needham, Rodney
1983 *Sumba and the Slave Trade.* Center of Southeast Asian Studies
Working Paper, No. 31. Melbourne: Monash University.

Nooteboom, C.
1939 "Versieringen van het Manggaraische Huizen." *Tijdschrift
voor Indische Taal-, Land- en Volkenkunde* 79:221-238.

Nooy-Palm, Hetty
1980 "The Role of the Sacred Cloths in the Mythology and
Ritual of the Sa'dan-Toraja of Sulawesi, Indonesia." In
Indonesian Textiles, Irene Emery Roundtable on Museum
Textiles 1979 Proceedings, edited by Mattiebelle Gittinger,
pp. 81-95. Washington: The Textile Museum.
1989 "The Sacred Cloths of the Toraja: Unanswered Questions."
In *To Speak With Cloth: Studies in Indonesian Textiles,* edited by
Mattiebelle Gittinger, pp. 163-180. Los Angeles: UCLA
Museum of Cultural History.

Ormeling, F. J.
1956 *The Timor Problem: A Geographical Interpretation of an Under-
developed Island.* Jakarta: J. B. Wolters.

Petu, Piet (P. Sareng Orinbao)
1969 *Nusa Nipa: Nama Pribumi Nusa Flores.* Ende: Nusa Indah.
1976 "Pengaruh Dualisme Dalam Seni Tenun Ikat Flores."
Dian 1(4):5.
1977 "Kamus Dasar Motip-motip Tenunan Flores."
Dian 5(4):11-12.
1992a *Seni Tenun Suatu Segi Kebudayaan Orang Flores.*
Nita: Seminari Tinggi St. Paulus Ledalero.
1992b *Tata Berladang Tradisional dan Pertanian Rasional Suku-
Bangsa Lio.* Nita: Seminari Tinggi St. Paulus Ledalero.

Pigeaud, Theodore
1960-63 *Java in the Fourteenth Century: A Study in Cultural History,*
5 vols. The Hague: Martinus Nijhoff.

Prior, John Mansford
1988 *Church and Marriage in an Indonesian Village.*
Frankfurt am Main: Verlag Peter Lang.

Reid, Anthony
1988 *Southeast Asia in the Age of Commerce 1450-1680: Volume One,
Lands Below the Winds.* New Haven: Yale University.

Ricklefs, M. C.
1981 *A History of Modern Indonesia.* London: Macmillan.

Riedel, J. F. G.
1886 "The Island of Flores or Pulau Bunga: The Tribes Between
Sika and Manggarai." *Revue Coloniale Internationale* 1:66ff.

Riesenberg, Saul H. and A. H. Gayton
1952 "Caroline Island Belt Weaving."
Southwestern Journal of Anthropology 8:342-375.

Rockhill, W. W.
1915 "Notes on the Relations and Trade of China with the
Eastern Archipelago and the Coast of the Indian Ocean
During the Fourteenth Century," Part 2. *T'oung Pao*:
16:61-159, 236-271, 374-392, 435-467, 604-626.

Rodgers-Siregar, Susan
1980 "Blessing Shawls: The Social Meaning of Sipirok Batak
Ulos." In *Indonesian Textiles,* Irene Emery Roundtable on
Museum Textiles 1979 Proceedings, edited by Mattiebelle
Gittinger, pp. 96-114. Washington: The Textile Museum.

Roos, S.
1872 *Bijdrage tot de Kennis van Taal, Land en Volk op het Eiland Soemba.*
Verhandelingen van het Bataviaasch Genootschap voor
Kunsten en Wetenschappen 36. Batavia: Bruining & Wijt.

Rouffaer, G. P.
1923a "Naschrift over het Oud-Portugeesche Fort op Poeloe
Ende; en de Dominikaner Solor-Flores-Missie,
1561-1638." *Tijdschrift Nederlandsch-Indië, Oud en
Nieuw* 8:121-128, 141-148.
1923b "Chronologie der Dominikaner-Missie op Solor en Flores,
vooral Poeloe Ende, ca. 1556-1638; en Bibliographie over
het Ende-Fort." *Tijdschrift Nederlandsch-Indië, Oud en Nieuw*
8:204-222, 256-260.

Sawardo, P. et al.
1987 *Struktur Bahasa Lio.*
Jakarta: Departemen Pendidikan dan Kebudayaan.

Schneider, Jane
1987 "The Anthropology of Cloth."
Annual Review of Anthropology 16:409-448.

Selvanayagam, Grace Inpam
1990 *Songket: Malaysia's Woven Treasure.*
Singapore: Oxford University Press.

Summerfield, Anne and John
1991 *Fabled Cloths of Minangkabau.*
Santa Barbara: Santa Barbara Museum of Art.

Stapel, H. B.
  1914   "Het Manggeraische Volk (West-Flores)." *Tijdschrift voor Indische Taal-, Land- en Volkenkunde* 56:149-187.

Staveren, J. A. van
  1915   "De Rokka's van Midden-Flores." *Tijdschrift voor Indische Taal-, Land- en Volkenkunde* 57:117-175.

Suchtelen, B. C. C. M. M. van
  1921   *Endeh (Flores)*. Mededeelingen van het Bureau voor de Bestuurszaken der Buitengewesten, Bewerkt door het Encyclopaedisch Bureau, No. 26. Weltevreden: Papyrus.
  1923   "De Ruïne van het Oud-Portugeesche Fort op Poelau Endeh (Zuid-Flores)." *Tijdschrift Nederlandsch-Indië, Oud en Nieuw* 8:78-95.

Taylor, Paul Michael, editor
  1994   *Fragile Traditions: Indonesian Art in Jeopardy*. Honolulu: University of Hawaii Press.

Tietze, Käthe
  1941   "Sitten und Gebräuche beim Säen, Erten, Spinnen, Ikatten Färben und Weben der Baumwolle im Sikka-Gebiet (Östliches Mittel-Flores)." *Ethnologica* 5:1-64.

Vatter, Ernst
  1932   *Ata Kiwan: Unbekannte Bergvölker im Tropischen Holland*. Leipzig: Bibliographisches Institut.

Verheijen, Jilis A. J.
  1951   *Het Hoogste Wezen bij de Manggaraiers*. Vienna: Modling.
  1967   *Kamus Manggarai, Vol. 1: Manggarai-Indonesia*. 's-Gravenhage: Martinus Nijhoff.
  1977   *Bahasa Rembong*. Ruteng: Regio S.V.D.
  1982   *Dictionary of Manggarai Plant Names*. Pacific Linguistics Series D, No. 43. Canberra: Australian National University.
  1990   *Dictionary of Plant Names in the Lesser Sunda Islands*. Pacific Linguistics Series D, No. 83. Canberra: Australian National University.

Visser, B. J. J.
  1925   *Onder Portugeesch-Spanische Vlag: De Katholieke Missie van Indonesie 1511-1605*. Amsterdam: R. K. Boek-Centrale.

Völger, Gisela, and Karin v. Welck, editors
  1991   *Indonesian Textiles: Symposium 1985*. Cologne: Ethnologica.

Vogelsanger, Cornelia
  1980   "A Sight for the Gods: Notes on the Social and Religious Meaning of Iban Ritual Fabrics." In *Indonesian Textiles*, Irene Emery Roundtable on Museum Textiles 1979 Proceedings, edited by Mattiebelle Gittinger, pp. 115-126. Washington: The Textile Museum.

Vroklage, B. A. G.
  1939   "Beehdhouwwerk uit de Manggarai (West Flores)." *Cultureel Indië* 1:356-361.

  1940   "De Prauw in Culturen van Flores." *Cultureel Indië* 2:193-199, 230-234, 263-270.
  1941   "Eine alte Metallkunst in Lio auf Flores." *Internationales Archiv für Ethnographie* 40:9-40.

Warming, Wanda, and Michael Gaworski
  1981   *The World of Indonesian Textiles*. Tokyo: Kodansha.

Waterson, Roxana
  1987   "Mythical Cloths: Toraja Textiles in the National Museum of Singapore Collection." *Heritage (Singapore Museum Journal)* 9:3-24.

Watson, Andrew M.
  1977   "The Rise and Spread of Old World Cotton." In *Studies in Textile Hostory*, edited by Veronika Gervers. Toronto: Royal Ontario Museum.

Watters, Kent
  1977   "Flores." In *Textile Traditions of Indonesia*, edited by Mary Hunt Kahlenberg, pp. 87-93. Los Angeles: Los Angeles County Museum of Art.

Weiner, Annette B.
  1989   "Why Cloth? Wealth, Gender, and Power in Oceania." In *Cloth and Human Experience*, edited by Annette B. Weiner and Jane Schneider, pp. 33-72. Washington: Smithsonian Institution Press.

Woodward, Hiram
  1980   "Indonesian Textile Patterns From a Historical View." In *Indonesian Textiles*, Irene Emery Roundtable on Museum Textiles 1979 Proceedings, edited by Mattiebelle Gittinger, pp. 15-35. Washington: The Textile Museum.

Wouden, F. A. E. van
  1968   *Types of Social Structure in Eastern Indonesia*. Koninklijk Instituut voor Taal-, Land- en Volkenkunde, Translation Series No. 11, translated by Rodney Needham. The Hague: Martinus Nijhoff. Translation of 1935 edition, *Sociale Structuurtypen in de Groote Oost*, Leiden: Ginsberg.

Wurm, Stephen A. and Shirô Hattori
  1981   *Language Atlas of the Pacific Area*. Canberra: Australian Academy of the Humanities.

Yamaguchi, Masao
  1989   "Nai Kéu, a Ritual of the Lio in Central Flores." *Bijdragen tot de Taal-, Land- en Volkenkunde* 145:478-489.

Yoshimoto, Shinobu
  1991   "Typological Studies of Indonesian Handlooms." Paper presented to the Symposium on Textiles from Indonesia and Related Areas 1991, Museum of Ethnography, Basel.

FRONT COVER: Detail of FIGURE 6-25. Inset image: see FIGURE 3-5.

PAGES 2 & 3: The 2,245-meter peak Inerie is one of nearly a dozen major volcanoes that punctuate the length of Flores. Roy W. Hamilton.

PAGE 4: Detail of FIGURE 8-22.

PAGE 5: See FIGURE 3-5.

PAGE 7: Roy W. Hamilton.

PAGE 8: A colonial-era mailman in the Tangahdei region of East Flores delivers a letter, wearing a checked sarong. Koninklijk Instituut voor de Tropen, Amsterdam.

PAGE 10: Steam rises from the summit of the volcano Ebulobo, in Ngada Regency. Roy W. Hamilton.

PAGE 15: Women spin cotton at the weekly market in Boawae. Roy W. Hamilton.

PAGES 16 & 17: Sisilia Sii works at her ikat tying frame in Onelako, Ndona District, 1988. Roy W. Hamilton.

PAGES 78 & 79: Lio man's shoulder cloth displaying ship motifs, *sémba kapa.* 271 x 112 cm. Dallas Museum of Art 1983.102.

PAGES 192 & 193: Young women dance at the dedication ceremony for a reconstructed village temple (*koko*), wearing women's red cloths of the highest grade, *kewaték mé'an*, with patola cloths draped across their shoulders. Léwotala, 1987. Penelope Graham.

BACK COVER: see FIGURE 3-19. Roy W. Hamilton.

1-2. Roy W. Hamilton.
1-3. Roy W. Hamilton.
1-4. E. D. Lewis.
1-7. Roy W. Hamilton.
1-12. Roy W. Hamilton.
1-13. Roy W. Hamilton.
1-15. Penelope Graham.
1-16. Penelope Graham.
1-17. Roy W. Hamilton.
1-18. Roy W. Hamilton.
1-21. E. D. Lewis.
1-22. Denis J. Nervig, FMCH.
1-25. Roy W. Hamilton.

2-1. Roy W. Hamilton.
2-3. Maribeth Erb.
2-4. Maribeth Erb.
2-5. Maribeth Erb.
2-6. Roy W. Hamilton.
2-7. Roy W. Hamilton.
2-8. E. D. Lewis.
2-9. Roy W. Hamilton.
2-10. Andrea Molnar.
2-11. Andrea Molnar.
2-12. Roy W. Hamilton.
2-13. Roy W. Hamilton.
2-14. Roy W. Hamilton.
2-16. Roy W. Hamilton.
2-17. Penelope Graham.
2-18. Roy W. Hamilton.
2-19. Roy W. Hamilton.
2-20. Roy W. Hamilton.
2-23. Roy W. Hamilton.
2-25. Roy W. Hamilton.

3-1. Roy W. Hamilton.
3-2. Penelope Graham.
3-3. E. D. Lewis.
3-6. Christopher Pawlik.
3-7. Roy W. Hamilton.
3-8. Roy W. Hamilton.
3-10. Roy W. Hamilton.
3-11. Roy W. Hamilton.
3-12. Willemijn de Jong.
3-13. Roy W. Hamilton.
3-15 Roy W. Hamilton.
3-16. Roy W. Hamilton.
3-17. Willemijn de Jong.
3-18. Roy W. Hamilton.
3-19. Roy W. Hamilton.
3-20. Marie Colvill.
3-21. Penelope Graham.
3-22. Roy W. Hamilton.

3-23. Denis J. Nervig, FMCH.

4-2. Roy W. Hamilton.
4-4. Maribeth Erb.
4-11. Maribeth Erb.
4-13. Denis J. Nervig, FMCH.
4-14. Roy W. Hamilton.
4-19. Denis J. Nervig, FMCH.
4-20. Roy W. Hamilton.
4-21. Denis J. Nervig, FMCH.
4-22. Roy W. Hamilton.

5-5. Denis J. Nervig, FMCH.
5-6. Denis J. Nervig, FMCH.
5-8. Roy W. Hamilton.
5-12. Roy W. Hamilton.
5-13. Roy W. Hamilton.
5-17. Denis J. Nervig, FMCH.
5-18. Denis J. Nervig, FMCH.
5-20. Roy W. Hamilton.
5-22. Roy W. Hamilton.
5-23. Denis J. Nervig, FMCH.
5-24. Denis J. Nervig, FMCH.
5-25. Denis J. Nervig, FMCH.
5-26. Roy W. Hamilton.
5-27. Denis J. Nervig, FMCH.
5-28. Denis J. Nervig, FMCH.
5-29. Roy W. Hamilton.
5-30. Roy W. Hamilton.
5-31. Kletus Dhena.
5-32. Roy W. Hamilton.
5-33. Roy W. Hamilton.
5-34. Denis J. Nervig, FMCH.
5-35. Roy W. Hamilton.
5-36. Denis J. Nervig, FMCH.

6-4. Denis J. Nervig, FMCH.
6-5. Denis J. Nervig, FMCH.
6-8. Denis J. Nervig, FMCH.
6-9. Denis J. Nervig, FMCH.
6-10. Denis J. Nervig, FMCH.
6-14. Denis J. Nervig, FMCH.
6-17. Denis J. Nervig, FMCH.
6-18. Denis J. Nervig, FMCH.
6-19. Denis J. Nervig, FMCH.
6-21. Denis J. Nervig, FMCH.
6-22. Denis J. Nervig, FMCH.
6-24. Denis J. Nervig, FMCH.
6-25. Denis J. Nervig, FMCH.
6-26. Denis J. Nervig, FMCH.
6-27. Denis J. Nervig, FMCH.
6-29. Roy W. Hamilton.
6-34. Roy W. Hamilton.

6-35. Denis J. Nervig, FMCH.

7-1. Denis J. Nervig, FMCH.
7-7. Denis J. Nervig, FMCH.
7-8. Denis J. Nervig, FMCH.
7-9. Denis J. Nervig, FMCH.
7-10. Denis J. Nervig, FMCH.
7-12 Denis J. Nervig, FMCH.
7-13. Denis J. Nervig, FMCH.
7-14. Denis J. Nervig, FMCH.
7-15. Denis J. Nervig, FMCH.
7-16. Denis J. Nervig, FMCH.
7-17. Denis J. Nervig, FMCH.
7-19. Denis J. Nervig, FMCH.

8-2. Ruth Barnes.
8-3. Robyn Maxwell.
8-4. Denis J. Nervig, FMCH.
8-5. Ruth Barnes.
8-10. Ruth Barnes.
8-11. Ruth Barnes.
8-12. Ruth Barnes.
8-18. Ruth Barnes.
8-19. Ruth Barnes.
8-20. Ruth Barnes.
8-22. Denis J. Nervig, FMCH.
8-24. Courtesy of Frau Hanna Vatter.
8-26. Denis J. Nervig, FMCH.
8-28. Denis J. Nervig, FMCH.

9-1. Maribeth Erb.
9-4. Maribeth Erb.
9-5. Maribeth Erb.
9-6. Denis J. Nervig, FMCH.
9-7. Maribeth Erb.
9-8. Maribeth Erb.
9-9. Maribeth Erb.

10-1. Heini Schwob.
10-2. Willemijn de Jong.
10-3. Heini Schwob.
10-4. Willemijn de Jong.
10-5. Willemijn de Jong.
10-7. Willemijn de Jong.
10-8. Willemijn de Jong.
10-9. Denis J. Nervig, FMCH.
10-11. Willemijn de Jong.
10-12. Willemijn de Jong.
10-13. Denis J. Nervig, FMCH.
10-14. Heini Schwob.
10-15. Heini Schwob.
10-16. Heini Schwob.
10-17. Willemijn de Jong.

11-1. Penelope Graham.
11-2. Penelope Graham.
11-3. Penelope Graham.
11-4. Penelope Graham.
11-5. Penelope Graham.
11-6. Penelope Graham.
11-7. Penelope Graham.
11-8. Penelope Graham.
11-9A. Penelope Graham.
11-9B. Penelope Graham.
11-9C. Marie Colvill.
11-9D. Penelope Graham.
11-10. Penelope Graham.
11-11. Marie Colvill.
11-12. Penelope Graham.
11-13. Penelope Graham.

12-1. Michael P. Vischer.
12-2. Michael P. Vischer.
12-4. Michael P. Vischer.
12-5. Michael P. Vischer.
12-6. Michael P. Vischer.
12-7. Michael P. Vischer.
12-8. Michael P. Vischer.
12-9. Michael P. Vischer.
12-10. Michael P. Vischer.
12-11. Denis J. Nervig, FMCH.
12-12. Michael P. Vischer.
12-13. Michael P. Vischer.
12-15. Michael P. Vischer.
12-14. Denis J. Nervig, FMCH.
12-16. Michael P. Vischer.
12-17. Michael P. Vischer.
12-18. Roy W. Hamilton.
12-19. Michael P. Vischer.

DRAWINGS BY JILL BALL:

3-14A. Adapted from Barnes 1989.
3-14, B & C. Adapted from Gittinger 1979.
PAGE 77, GARMENT ASSEMBLY: A-D.
6-3, A-E.
6-12, A-C.
6-13, A-C.
6-37, A-C.

Contributors

RUTH BARNES is curator of Eastern Art at the Ashmolean Museum, Oxford. She received her D. Phil. from the University of Oxford, based on her research in Lamalera (Lembata) in 1979 and 1982. Her dissertation was published as *The Ikat Textiles of Lamalera. A Study of an Indonesian Weaving Tradition.* She has written numerous articles on Lamaholot weaving and related art forms, among them a contribution to the Fowler Museum's publication *To Speak With Cloth* (M. Gittinger, ed.). As part of her current research interest in pre-European Indian Ocean trade, she is preparing a catalogue of a large collection of Indian textiles traded to Egypt, now at the Ashmolean Museum.

MARIBETH ERB has contributed articles to several books and journals about Indonesia, including her chapter about Flores in *Islands and Ancestors: Indigenous Styles of Southeast Asia* (J. P. Barbier & D. Newton, eds., 1988). In the mid 1980s, she conducted two years of research among the Rembong and Rajong peoples of northwestern Manggarai. She completed her dissertation, *When Rocks Were Young and Earth Was Soft: Ritual and Mythology in Northeastern Manggarai,* in 1987, earning her doctoral degree from the State University of New York at Stony Brook. She is now Assistant Professor at the University of Singapore.

PENELOPE GRAHAM is a founding member of the Indonesian Arts Society in Melbourne, where she was involved in 1976 in developing the exhibition *Textiles of Indonesia* at the National Gallery of Victoria. She earned her D. Phil. degree at the Australian National University, based on field research conducted in eastern Flores from early 1986 through mid-1988. Her research interests are in the art and ritual life of various Southeast Asian peoples, primarily in Indonesia and Malaysia. She is currently an Australian Research Council Postdoctoral Fellow at the Department of Anthropology, Research School of Pacific Studies, Australian National University.

ROY W. HAMILTON, who specializes in the study of Indonesian material culture, has conducted textile research in Ndona and other parts of central and western Flores since 1987. He holds an M.A. in museum studies and anthropology from the University of Washington, Seattle. As Curator for Asian and Pacific Collections at the Fowler Museum of Cultural History, UCLA, he is currently involved in additional projects focusing on the use of betel and on the art of Kalimantan.

WILLEMIJN DE JONG was born in Holland but has lived since 1970 in Switzerland, where she is currently Lecturer at the University of Zurich. In 1983 she began her ongoing study of women's labor, weaving, and textiles in Indonesia. Her doctoral dissertation was published in 1986 by the University of Zurich. From 1987 to 1991 she conducted two years of postdoctoral research on textiles, work, marriage, and ritual in the Lio region.

E. D. LEWIS is author of *People of the Source* (1988a) and is recognized as the leading international authority on the culture of the Sikkanese, among whom he has conducted research for over fifteen years. He received his Ph.D. from the Institute of Advanced Studies at the Australian National University and is now Head of Anthropology at the University of Melbourne. He has recently presented lectures about Sikkanese textiles and produced an ethnographic film about ritual life in Tana 'Ai.

MICHAEL P. VISCHER holds a Ph.D. degree in anthropology from the Australian National University, Research School of Pacific Studies and has been conducting general ethnographic field research on the island of Palu'é at regular intervals since 1979. He is currently a Research Fellow of the International Institute for Asian Studies (IIAS), Leiden, The Netherlands.

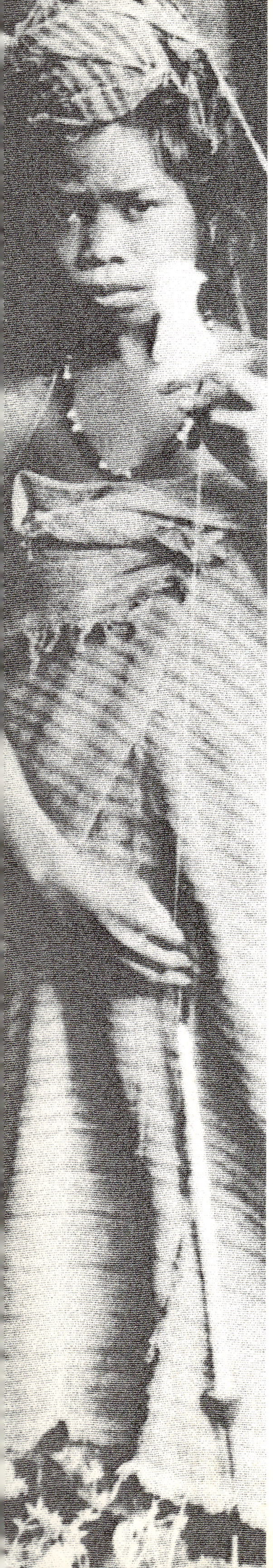

Fowler Museum of Cultural History

CHRISTOPHER B. DONNAN *Director*

DORAN H. ROSS *Deputy Director*

DONALD H. McCLELLAND *Assistant Director*

PATRICIA B. ALTMAN *Curator Emeritus of Folk Art and Textiles*

PATRICIA ANAWALT *Director, Center for the Study of Regional Dress*

DANIEL R. BRAUER *Director of Publications*

ROGER H. COLTEN *Curator of Archaeology*

CLARISSA M. COYOCA *Accountant*

KYRIN EALY *Director of Development*

CYNTHIA D. ECKHOLM *Associate Registrar*

BETSY R. ESCANDOR *Administrative Assistant*

ROY W. HAMILTON *Curator of Southeast Asian and Oceanic Collections*

JUDITH HERSCHMAN *Librarian*

JO A. HILL *Conservator*

SARAH JANE KENNINGTON *Registrar*

ANTHONY A. G. KLUCK *Assistant Director of Publications*

VICTOR LOZANO, JR. *Exhibition Production*

DAVID A. MAYO *Exhibition Designer*

OWEN F. MOORE *Collections Manager*

DENIS J. NERVIG *Senior Photographer*

DARCY NICOLE O'BRYAN *Receptionist*

DINA M. OGLE *Accounting Assistant*

RACHEL L. J. RAYNOR *Administrative Assistant*

BETSY D. QUICK *Director of Education*

CHRISTINE SELLIN *Director of Public Relations*

DON SIMMONS *Exhibition Production*

BARBARA SLOAN *Assistant Director, Center for the Study of Regional Dress*

DAVID SVENSON *Publications Processing Assistant*

POLLY SVENSON *Museum Store Manager*

FRAN TABBUSH *Assistant Collections Manager*

BOBBY WHITAKER *Director of Security*

PATRICK WHITE *Exhibition Production*

Publication Presentation:

ANTHONY A. G. KLUCK
Design

HENRIETTA COSENTINO
Editing

DENIS J. NERVIG
Photography

JILL BALL
Publications Assistant

DANIEL R. BRAUER
Director of Publications

*Editing and design were accomplished on Macintosh computers
using Aldus PageMaker 5.0, Adobe Illustrator 5.0 and
Monotype fonts Columbus, Matura, and Gill Sans.*